# Sleights of Mind:
# One and Multiples of One

# Sleights of Mind:
# One and Multiples of One

Harold N. Boris

**JASON ARONSON INC.**
*Northvale, New Jersey*
*London*

Production Editor: Judith D. Cohen

This book was set in 11 point Baskerville by Lind Graphics of Upper Saddle River, New Jersey, and printed and bound by Haddon Craftsmen of Scranton, Pennsylvania.

**Library of Congress Cataloging-in-Publication Data**

Boris, Harold N., 1932–
    Sleights of mind : one and multiples of one / by Harold N. Boris.
       p.  cm.
    Includes bibliographical references and index.
    ISBN 1-56821-082-5 (hard cover)
    1. Psychoanalysis—Philosophy.  I. Title.
    [DNLM: 1. Psychoanalytic Therapy—methods.  2. Psychoanalytic
    Interpretation.  WM 460.6 B734s  1994]
    RC509.B68  1994
    616.89'17—dc20
    DNLM/DLC
    for Library of Congress                                              93-3833

Manufactured in the United States of America. Jason Aronson Inc. offers books and cassettes. For information and catalog write to Jason Aronson Inc., 230 Livingston Street, Northvale, New Jersey 07647.

# Contents

# Prologue
# [Past as]

*"If it is any point requiring reflection,"* observed Dupin, as he forbore to
enkindle the wick, *"we shall examine it to better purpose in the dark."*
— Edgar Allan Poe

What one contributes to psychoanalysis, insofar as one does, is not so
much a basketful of new facts as juxtapositions of ideas previously
seen only in different connections, rearrangements born of further
twists of the kaleidoscope. These undo old conceptual prisons before
becoming themselves imprisoning. As such, the essays reposing con-
tentedly beneath the right thumb of the reader are variously postcards
sent out along the way and messages set out in bottles. They come out
of both the loneliness and loony, jubilant bluster that are in the
moment of every fresh idea. With luck, they are way-lights to where
the further darkness can be found.

Like other children, I was fascinated by the mote dance in sunbeams
and the spiral nebula in the galactic broth of the lightly pressured
cornea. What butterfly net (Abercrombie & Fitch? Whorf & Sapir?)
could capture these swirls without in the process reducing them to
rubble? In what way, against the background sounds of my own life
and the croons, growls, and struts of others, could I reach beyond the
now and the then to the almost was and the yet to be? "The

philosopher," writes Nietzsche, "seeks to hear within himself the echoes of the world symphony and to reproject these in the form of concepts."

The papers newly published or reprinted here are products of my continuing concern to discover what the necessities, the *sinews*, of psychoanalysis are, and are not. From "The Seelsorger in Rural Vermont" early in the volume to "The Pair and the Couple," which is its epilogue, my ongoing concern has been for what the therapy and the theories of psychoanalysis are or might be when stripped down to their essentials. Psychoanalysis is too good, and, as Freud came to feel, not (yet) good enough, to be confined to the consulting room.

The psychoanalytic encounter is an intensely personal encounter, wherever and in whatever fashion it is conceived and practiced; inevitably the thumbprint of the practitioner is all over it. The reader, accordingly, must in some sense be put in touch with the writer. For the reader needs to factor in and out, as needs be, who this is who has been a participant in, yet subtracted from, the observations and events the writer has recorded. But a word of warning: this writer is about to provide us with his personal creation myth. The usual grain of salt is recommended.

There is a variety of memory that arises upon the abrupt shift from looking at everything from the lidded interior of one's self to that of *seeing one's self in the picture*, the caul of unconsciousness of self peeled away. One moment a camera — I; the next an inextricable part of the scene, the way one is forever after destined to appear in his or her memories of childhood.

When I have riffled through to find where this purview began, there are months and months of shadow, and then, like a slide coming on the screen, an ochre and lavender afternoon. I am sitting on the sofa next to my father and he is telling me a story. It concerns Country Gardens. It features Percy Granger and his little niece Jeanne. This has been an ongoing story, but now, as if he also senses I am an object, no longer just the subject, of my own experience, he asks, "And what shall it be today?" As usual, the story will chronicle the small domestic adventures of the two protagonists, the tune I like so well, and of course a metaphorical sense of gardens (gardens I still look for in each visit to a different corner of England, even in East Grinstead). But now I am to contribute!

Higgledy-piggledy, I blurb my material, with its chunks of event and feeling — and in no more than the time it takes me to write this, it is transformed by some miraculous alchemy into the episode I might have written, if I could have. But, despite his urging, no matter how detailed the elements of plot, the swatches of dialogue I could provide ("And then have Jeanne say, 'Let's go to the fair.' And have Mr. Granger say, 'All right Jeanne, and perhaps we will meet the Burgesses there,' ") left to my own devices, I could not make such stories up.

I thought it odd that my father, teacher and novelist that he was, didn't seem to know what went into fashioning stories, even if one was "old enough," as presently he began to suggest I was. (It has taken some time before I felt old enough to compose the psychoanalytic stories I tell in this collection.) When he felt I was being too much of a pest for a story he might tease me with the ditty—

> I'll tell you a story about Jack and his dory
> and now my story's begun.
> Then I'll tell you another about Jack and his brother
> and now my story is done.

I did not want to understand what he meant by his stories being so quickly done; only later was I to understand the extent to which his hurry for me reflected his sense of his own mortality. Nor did I want to know about my mother's hurry either: about her having had her two children already in a previous marriage and having borne me not so much for herself as for a love-gift to her much beloved husband. Despite my disinclination to know about them, these circumstances fomented in me an ambition to outgrow my childish ways exceeded only by a fear of tarrying so long as to grow out of them.

The next slide to come upon the screen finds me on the living room rug, snuggled down beside my father's bookshelves. I am taking out one of the volumes of Arnold Gesell's writings on child development. I have been there before: I know this because there is already a feeling of expectation as I pick up the pellucid book and read about the five-year-olds and then the sixes. The amazing addition of my self to the family has given this onlooker a cusp, a parapet around the self, and it is nice to have the good professor a Virgil at my side.

I don't so much read, of course, as put myself into the book. I get back a series of portraits. These are portraits done by a man who knows children, inside out, backward and forward. I know this because Gesell says things the way five-year-olds are apt to start any and every conversation with the news that they are five. As I do, did in fact that very morning. And this makes what I take back out of the book so sweetly soothing.

For as I muse, I feel graced: there is such care there, such interest. Each age, it seems, as I read it, is a different creature all its own. Questions of maturity and betterment do not arise. Fives are. And then they are six, and different: they are six. I replace the book feeling sanguine.

Slides flash by, tick, tick, then stop. On this one I am twelve; my father has recently died; I am now away at school. In a highly varnished room, there is another set of bookshelves. The room is in the Manor House of the Cherry Lawn School in Darien, Connecticut. The new books are a six-volume set by a man called Sigmund Freud.

Freud's portrayals seem as exact as the Gesell and Ames descriptions, but there is no escaping the fact that he fathoms and illuminates things they don't, even if, annoyingly, the best stuff is in Latin. From these journeys through the looking glass, I have much the same experience. I put in chaos and angst and get back rhyme and reason. I put in confusion and archaisms, and get back system and purpose. Indeed I put in willfulness and belief and get back uncertainty and question. In short, alongside the usual titillation and methods for analyzing my classmates' dreams, I garner ways upon ways of experiencing experience.

In this way I was immensely fortunate in my consultants: Gesell and Ames and Freud (later Adler, Jung and others) returned me from my vicarious forays restored! invigorated! better than new! And, to my supernal relief, they asked nothing from me or for me. I was given to believe that people simply "were." It was enough to take note and mark what was happening, to consider how and when, in what order and why. So, for me, these texts were filled with the observations and discoveries of *natural historians*, men and women who loved their subject wisely, deeply, but not too well.

When after a while I was looking for what to become (probably one morning before history class, while going over my dreams with Freud—I don't have a slide on this), I thought to myself: "What about me becoming a child analyst?" Whether this meant a child who was an analyst or an analyst of children was unsettled (as sometimes it still is). Yet I could sense I had, with this, somehow arrived at a decision. And a remarkably apt one: it could be really quite pleasing to do the sort of work they did: to be the sort of person who could return people to themselves, still themselves, a little more fully themselves, perhaps, but otherwise unscathed. Writing was inevitably to be part of this. (I have always tried to write for whatever five- or twelve-year-old might chance upon what I have written.)

Moreover, the psychoanalysis I wanted to practice, modeled as it was on natural historians, had also to be an enterprise in which change was secondary, even optional, when compared with a search for what is true, what is so, or that mélange called "sooth."[1] Thus I needed to find out what in psychoanalysis was necessary and sufficient, what superfluous and peripheral. I didn't know then that to have my own analysis I would also need to work out formulations that the particular circumstances of my own life made necessary — and possible. But if I had known it, I wouldn't have been surprised.

Psychoanalysis is both a psychology and a format for consultation (a therapy, as some call it). It ventures in two directions. Its one aspect spirals outward, pinwheeling centrifugally, toward different people in different circumstances, involving differing applications and methods. Its other aspect winds inexorably inward in search of what needs inevitably, ultimately, and always to be analyzed. In this, it seeks the pivot and the pinion: the first cause, the core, the irreducible nugget.

Psychoanalysis, that is to say, is the person exponentialized: the person universalized: one and multiples of one.

In my life I was to work in day schools and boarding schools, in hospitals, clinics, and offices, on street corners and in meager church basements, in lush corporate headquarters and poor rural villages, with people of every age and description, individually and in groups, some of whom took themselves to be patients, many of whom decidedly did not. Of this work, part would involve assisting people to know what they knew, but didn't know they knew. The larger part was to involve helping people discover from themselves what they didn't know and didn't know they didn't know. And as I went along in each aspect of that work, I was to need to consider and sometimes reconsider the fundamentals of the theory.

Youth is blessed by a caul of sheer, pure ignorance. One cannot know then what one knows now. I knew nothing of where my new identity would and wouldn't take me. Once I knew I wanted to be a child analyst, all I knew was that I couldn't wait to get started.

I knew vaguely about college and even more vaguely about medical or graduate school, but these had the status of rumors. Wanting to get

---

[1]Bion quoting Tolstoi.

started meant serving a kind of apprenticeship, and, as I shall chronicle, this meant attaching myself to anyone willing to help.

In this, I found many more people who helped than hindered, though, like most people, I had my share of the latter. The former included Christina Stäel von Holstein Bogoslovsky, the director of The Cherry Lawn School and Institute; Janet S. Greene, the consulting psychologist to the school and the person who taught me how to use projective tests and later bartered me my first psychotherapy in return for pieces of my sculpture; Evelyn Omwake, the director of the school at Vassar College's Family and Child Study Institute; Marilyn Schwartz, my chief co-worker there; Frederick Courts, professor and chairman of the department of psychology at Reed College, and the man who, against all odds, succeeded in enabling me to learn psychology; Erik Erikson, Bruno Bettelheim, and David Rapaport, about whom more anon; Royce "Tim" Pitkin, who brought me to Vermont; Donald A. Bloch, who there encouraged and supervised my first psychoanalytic work with patients; Paul G. Myerson, who brought me to Tufts Medical School and traded me good Freud for middling Klein; Harry Rand and the others who helped me learn the therapy of psychoanalysis; Jerome Kavka, my first analyst; and my subsequent analysts, each of whom in his or her fascinating and distinctive ways, helped me with my ongoing analysis of myself; and, not least, Wilfred R. Bion, the last and most *schaden* of my *Gesellfreudes*.

That all those who permitted me to consult to them — from the executives of the Duluth Power and Light Company through the countless people who were in groups with me to my patients, child, adult, and in between — were the primary teachers of what I learned can almost go without saying. It is one of those sad ironies of psychoanalysis (and parenthood) that what one patient teaches the next benefits from.

Those who out of indolence or malice hindered me will not here be named: they are daily recorded on softer, more cylindrical rolls.

At Cherry Lawn there came to be a Summer Institute, modeled closely after the Family and Child Study Institute that Mary Langmuir Fisher and Evelyn Omwake had established at Vassar. Parents of children ages 2 through 12 would together come for a month-long stay; save for daily visiting intervals, they would live separate lives, the children cared for by teachers, the parents by courses and counseling concerning themselves and their children. By that time I had been retained by Dr. Stäel to show prospective parents and students around the school (in between times tending gardens and painting and making other repairs). Being a child who was an analyst, I naturally spent every free moment, and some perhaps not so free, around the Institute hoping, as it were, to trade up.

The first assignment I won was that of helping the younger children ride the horses; few of the staff liked tramping around the ring one hand on horse, the other on child. Having myself been helped by reading "Little Hans," and so knowing something of the fear and fascination exercised by horses, I took these trudges as opportunities to talk a little of the anxieties and fantasies involved. That summer (of my 14th year) was when I learned something that has since become a part of my technique, such as it is. Walking backward and talking up to the child in the saddle was beyond me, so I would lead ahead and talk aloud, sometimes to the horse, sometimes to the child, sometimes to the air. I cannot assess with any accuracy the effect of what I said upon the horses, but it seemed to me and those who knew the children that frightened children soon reached some of the excited fantasies within the fright and brave children soon relaxed.

It was as much as anything else that I was a youngster (as compared with the graduates of Bank Street College and other such programs, who staffed the school for the children) that in subsequent summers, when I joined the staff of the Institute, I was given my head as much as I was and, in John Dewey's phrase, much admired at the time, allowed to learn by doing. For one of my makeup, a child too highly taught, this was ideal. The approach these Institutes took was child-centered: one tried to see what the kids were getting at and then, as needed, offered a less tippy block, a piece of cloth, an idea, a lap, another child, or, requiring equal delicacy, nothing.[2]

What began with horses ended eight summers later with dinosaurs[3]. This was the summer following my first year of graduate school; newly married, I was again at the Family and Child Study Institute at Vassar

---

[2]To one little model daughter, in her Florence Eiseman sunsuit and lace-ruffed panties, watching with dismay as the other sixes turned a yard into a mud bowl, the item to offer seemed to be a family-sized box of Ivory Flakes.

[3]I spent the summer I turned 18 with the Quakers in order to reflect upon my inclination to become a conscientious objector to the draft. Later that year the New England Society of Friends sent me as their representative to the planning sessions of the Mid-century Conference on Children and Youth, where I was sucessfully to lead the fight for integrated housing for the conference participants.

College, at which I had begun to work upon my graduation from Cherry Lawn. I was working with the 8-year-olds, a big step in different terrain from the fives and sixes of prior years. The eights, being preoccupied as latency-age children are—inside-out adolescents, Bion called them—with ruminations on survival and death, strength and power, mating and rivalry, and fuss and muss, there seemed to them no better way to spend a month of summer than to build an immense Triceratops out of lumber, chicken wire, papiér maché, and dream stuff. As I worked along, I felt, not for the first time, deeply impressed by how much children welcome psychoanalytic interpretations made to them as a group.

During these summers, the material for such interpretations came, of course, from the children themselves, but the formulations were often provided by observers and consultants. I remember with particular pleasure Barbara Biber, Alexander Essex, Elizabeth Guilkeson, Ernst and Marianne Kris, L. Joseph Stone, and Charlotte Winsor, with whom I spent many hours observing and talking of the children with whom I was working as well as other children I tagged along to observe with them.

One summer Muriel Gardiner bade me assist her in her research with "The World Test." A child would choose finger-sized items from the vast array provided, and arrange and rearrange them on the sand table to create his picture of the whole world. As he did so, Gardiner would dictate her notes, enabling me to follow as best I could a gifted mind at work. When she felt a child was encountering pain, she would offer a bit of interpretive help, and I would note the response. Presently she invited my own observations, and, since the construction of the world was a time-consuming process, we had additional chances to see which of the hypotheses we formed along the way would bear fruit. Today when I do supervisions in public session, I follow this model and try to make predictions of what the yet unpresented material will be like.

As an example of the spirit of those times, I can give none better than one involving one of my own children.[4] This was later, of course, and elsewhere: 1962, at Cloverly, the summer place of L. K. Frank and his family. One afternoon there was an informal party and most

---

[4]The conversations in what follows are reconstructed from memory, and Mnemosyne is a notorious artificer; if perchance they malign or misrepresent my interlocuters, I apologize in advance.

of the others who also summered at White Oak Pond were there. My son Neil, to his great frustration, had not yet mastered walking; he could creep but this was a poor second to him. Noting his struggles, Erik Erikson and Lois Murphy made their way to him and missing nary a beat of their conversation walked him up and down, up and down, the great long porch of Cloverly. Before long they were discussing erections vis-à-vis standing erect; I say "they" because every so often one or the other would bend and ask Neil his 9 months's old opinion. I was standing with Margaret Mead; she had been telling me about the pleasures of a party game called "Conversation." On overhearing this new discussion, she interrupted her description and called over to them: "Don't forget climbing!" as she explained to me that many of the peoples she studied held their children on tree limbs or bent over trees before they could walk.

Of my encounters during those formative years, four were particularly influential. My experiences at the Institutes at Cherry Lawn and Vassar had shown me the power of the structural environment in what was brought out in children and indeed in those who worked with them. Louis Hay, a long time family friend, was using just this insight — but not to develop special schools for disturbed youngsters in the New York City public school system, as had been the case there and elsewhere. Hay had gone beyond this to restructure a school so that it could teach both troubled children and their cohorts without the use of special classrooms or even special classes and without the use of special teachers. His articulation of the dynamics of his methodology and his chronicles of the adventures of everyone from the school superintendent to the custodial help in allowing themselves to participate in so novel a deconstruction made a strong impression on me. I had for some time no way quite to make use of it, but I knew it was there to be explored some day.

The child-centered tradition, in which one sees what the child is getting at and then sidles along to offer a bit of help, was one in which I was so thoroughly baptized and which fitted so snugly with what was the best in my nature, that everything I have learned about doing therapy and analysis since has been grafted onto it. As, indeed, my essay on confrontation (Chapter 9) will indicate, while I have been prepared to lead out from the unconscious, I have been loath to confront people with so-called social realities; the words "appropriate" and "inappropriate" do not trip from my lips. And (or so it seemed to me), the late '40's and early 50's were banner years for books that extended this tradition: Reik's *Third Ear*, Sullivan's *Interpersonal Theory*, Bettelheim's *Love is Not Enough*, Fromm's *Escape From Freedom*, the accumulating papers of Hartmann, Kris, and Loewenstein, and Melanie Klein's *New Directions* and *Richard*. (In England, Bion was publishing the papers that were to make up *Experiences in Groups*, but I was not to know this for another decade.) These were books I read and reread along with Freud's and Anna Freud's.

But even from these, how was I to know what to say to my first individual "patients," youngsters Fred Courts had referred to me when, with his tireless inventive tutorial help I managed finally to pass my qualifying tests in psychology and enter my senior year at Reed? I had spent an academic year at the Dalton School learning how to sort through outbursts of high tension as they occurred in individual children in the classroom, but I had not yet seen children individually and alone.

Erikson's *Childhood and Society* was also fairly newly out, and, to my great good luck, he was in the habit of making periodic visits to his son Kai, who was a college-mate of mine. When Kai was otherwise occupied, Erikson and I spent time together, often as not sitting up late over the cognac stashed in the silver-headed stick he carried. Like others I had come to admire, he was a man ever to see method; he saw it, of course, not only in the psychology of the individual but, notably, in the very shape cultures intuitively and otherwise gave the developing personalities of their young.

We talked of his work; I loved hearing how his mind worked. But, when I acquired my new clients, we spoke also of them. The two 10-year-olds had been referred to me because of reading blocks. At the time it seemed to me that talking of the children was of the greater value, but, as it was to turn out, it was just the more immediately worthwhile. Later, when I was to work in the R & D entities of large companies and then in the rural villages of Vermont, Erikson's sublime sense of the intricately purposeful fabric of a society linked to a culture was to return to me with great force; it was to join up in my thinking with Hay's work.

"Jimmy has taken over and over to run a car off the top of the bookshelf or windowsill. He makes it roll end over end in the air and then brings it to the floor upside down."

"And what do you make of that? There is the over and over and the end over end."

"It seems suggestive somehow, a man in free fall turning into a woman. A castration motif. But I don't feel able to say that to him."

"Ah, as to that: it is a matter of 'How much do you know?' Before anything else can happen in a therapy, the two have to take care of one another. Only then can they do the other work. The patient wonders, 'Are you, the adult, ready for this yet?' Jimmy says: 'See this? Are you ready to know about it? Because I'm not ready until you are.' And you have to know whether you're ready, so you can say, 'Yes, I see a lot in your play, and I'm ready when you are.' "

"Do you think the car represents an erotic castration interest?" Like many apprentices, I was keen to get right down to the depths of the matter, even if I had shamelessly to find some way of getting Erikson's authority to do so.

"Do I think—or does he think, or do you think? *Some* one has to think about it. Partly that has been your friend Melanie Klein's job. (Erikson knew that I had found Klein's 1932 *Psychoanalysis of Children* a revelation.) But in answer to your question, sooner or later doesn't everyone have to know what he knows about sex and the possibilities for dangerous intercourse?"

"Should I interpret this to him? Somehow I feel he is getting ready to be more explicit?"

"So what he must be wondering is whether you are ready to be explicit."

"Have you a suggestion for me on how to go about it?"

"I suggest you consider the again and again and the over and over. And meanwhile may I suggest a drop of cognac? This was given to me by an old. . . ."

Few people had smooth sailing with Bruno Bettelheim (he did not with himself, one felt) and I was no exception. And it was not as if Erikson had not warned me. But Fritz Redl, with whom I also wanted to study, was at NIMH for the next several years, so despite my reservations about the department of psychology,[5] Bettelheim (and the University of Chicago) seemed the place to go for graduate school. I

---

[5]These reservations were soon put to rest. In the first departmental meeting the chairman asked which of us hoped to go on from our studies to be a psychotherapist— because, he added, we were in entirely the wrong place. With more speed than I knew I possessed I ran across campus and begged to be enrolled in the Committee on Human Development. After some hasty interviews, I was given the last remaining place.

duly wrote ahead to Bettelheim the good news that I was coming to work with him, and asked him to let me know if that might not be possible. When I did not receive the encouraging letter I expected, I called, and called again, and again, only finally to be told by his secretary: "Dr. Bettelheim has asked me to let you know he has received your letter."

When, after another several phone calls, he granted me an interview for work at the Sonia Shankman Orthogenic school, he had only one question for me:

"What is your name?"

It was a late November afternoon, and it had already gotten dark and chill. Scudding clouds foretold a storm. I had been shown into a room that ran the length of the house, and I sat down in the only chair that had a lighted lamp next to it. It was deep into the room. When eventually he arrived, something I sensed rather than saw, he sat in the dark at the long diagonal from me.

I told him my name, and of course he asked again. I told him again, a little more loudly.

"I am asking you: 'What is your name?' and you do not appear to wish to answer."

"I am answering!" I replied, stung, and repeated my name.

"Boris is not a surname. What is your real name?"

"Boris!" I replied in what must have been nearly a shout. "My name is Boris and that's the only name I have." I wondered briefly if there was somewhere I could get another one. But what should the new one be: "Bettelheim"?

"Look you, you wrote me a year ago asking if you could work here, then you wrote me in April, saying you had been accepted by the University, and since June you have been calling here ten times a week, and now you have your wish and I agree to meet you and ask you one single, simple question—and you don't want to answer it. So as far as I am concerned, this interview is over. I do not hire persons with fake names who refuse to answer questions." And with this he walked out.

He was expensive in what he required, but if one could stand this, even while resenting it, he gave what at the time and no less in retrospect I consider to be of great value. Soon after I began working at the school, there was the instance, later written up, of the little girl who was too afraid of being poisoned to do anything but cover her

mouth and nose with both her hands. Her counselor was tugging at the
child's hands, coaxing her into accepting a morsel of something. "No —
NO NO *NO NO!*" Bettelheim bellowed. He waved the counselor away,
and sat down next to the child in her place.

"I have sent that no-good away. What does she know? You and I are
not afraid of a little starvation. *We* know there's *worse, much* worse, to
be afraid of!"

Soon afterward, he sat next to her once again and showed her his
hands.

"These are big hands, no? How about, *I'll* cover up your mouth, and
you cover up your nose."[6]

I remembered this incident as years later I undertook analytic work
with anorexic patients. Could one stand quietly to give interpretations
to a person whose weight became dangerously low? Could one respect
defenses that were as urgent as they were dangerous? Could one hate
what was happening without having to change the person making it
happen? Could one wait and wait until one saw what the person was
about before asking simply: Might this help? Is this of any use to you?

Bettelheim's absolute mistrust of the intellect as facile, enslaved both
to the emotions and to vanity, was not palatable to many, not,
certainly, to myself. But that he "cared enough to do his very worst" to
demonstrate this viewpoint ultimately made one sit up and take notice.
In The *Informed Heart* (1960), part of which is devoted to his own
internment in the camps, he tells of a time when it was so cold that the
inmates, himself among them, searingly lost the flesh of their hands to
frostbite. But rather than queuing at the infirmary door to ask be
excused from further labor, as the others in his account did, he asked
only that his hands be treated and bandaged so that he could resume
his work. He then went back to his pick and shovel until his captors
stopped him. He was, in a sense, to teach the implications of this
incident over and over. His message was that it was incumbent on
people, in that instance even the Jews, to know who the other is and
what he is about: that to treat any person or group as if it were a mere
object, there for use in the transference, was an unending source of
trouble from and to whichever side of the relationship such indifference came. Believing knowledge that was empty of such discovery to

---

[6]This vignette is linked to the frostbite encounter in Dachau or Belsen, recounted in
Bettelheim's *The Informed Heart* (1960) about which more in a moment.

be, more than merely facile, utterly useless, worse, in fact, than worthless, a virtual menace to its possessor and others, he attacked it wherever he met it.

Even in his professorial capacity, a question on the nature of transference would lead to something like this:

"Who is your movie star idol?"

"Whoever."

"*Not* 'whoever'. Zat is the point!"

"All right, Marilyn Monroe."

"Marilyn Monroe! He likes them —" this to the class, preceded by the usual gesture — "busty. Your mother is busty?"

Momentarily I think of denying this, but I nod, reluctantly, souring up my mouth to express disdain for this obvious inference.

"I thought so! All right, you are in luck! Marilyn Monroe is in town. So what do you do?"

"O.K., I call her up."

"Not 'O.K., I call her up.' *Do* you call her up or don't you?"

This goes on for a bit, concluding finally in,

"So you invite her to dinner at the Pump Room, *ja*? And so now, what do you do?"

"I meet her there for dinner."

"Looking like that?" Incredulously.

"I change my clothes and meet here there."

"Ah, I am relieved you do not go there looking like this. The Pump Room is a fancy restaurant. So tell us, what do you wear?"

As I was rather impecunious during these years and the Orthogenic school paid me poorly, I answer (this was the 50s): "A white shirt, a black tie, grey slacks, and my tweed jacket."

"And, pray tell, why that particular getup?"

"Those happen to be my best clothes."

"Those do not 'happen to be' your best clothes; you bought them because you liked them! Would you wear them if you thought Miss Busty Monroe would hate them?"

"No."

"So you must think she will like the way you look."

"I suppose so."

"Exactly! You 'suppose so.' Since your mother likes you in that outfit, you suppose Marilyn Monroe will also. And that — since you ask — is the transference."

Glasses gleaming, he turns to the "dumb blond" in the class and grins triumphantly at her.

This is my third course with him and I know by now that the "since you ask" is to remind me that it was I who wanted to know: not he who wanted me to, something that is designed to give my transference to him a brushup. The wolfish grin at the blond woman (there is one in every course) is to increase the homoerotic element in the transference. All of which is to remind me that in Beckett's elegant phrase, "The quantum of wantum is not negotiable."

As it happened, my mother did not like the outfit; a painter, she thought it too preppy, too lacking in color, but out of a bemused admiration for his didactic skill, I ceded the point to him. From the first, I felt I could fight with him; even as the rage coursed through me in that dark living room of my initial interview, I felt there would be nothing worse to fear from him than what he was showing me. He was quite right, there *was* sham in me, and, as I knew, would be until I had an analysis. But his hatred of sham and cant helped make it possible for me to drop it with him, and at the first opportunity, I generously provided him an analysis of *his* sham.

The exam for the first course I took with him consisted of only one question: "What have you learned of the role of the leader in a group?" And I did learn what he wanted to demonstrate: namely that, if allowed, the leader can manipulate a preexisting group almost at will. But in analyzing what, as leader, he did and how he did it, I taxed him with the many gratuitous manipulations to which he had exposed the class, of which one was:

"How dare you masturbate in my classroom! How would you like it if I came into your living room and masturbated all through dinner?"

"I am *not* masturbating! I am knitting!"

"That's what *you* think! At least if you were open about it, something perhaps could be said for it. But you are a secret masturbator. And like your classmates and ostriches you think if you fool yourself, everyone else will be fooled. But we are not fooled"—this to the blond in *this* course—"and you will either stop masturbating, or I will stop this class."

"Dr. Bettelheim, you do this every year. You are famous for this trick. Get off my back!"

"You knew this before you started with your masturbating? So you hoped to get me, as you so engagingly put it, on your back. I see. You are here pretending you want an education, but what you really want — well, we all know what you really want. But this is a classroom, so you are in the wrong place. So out you go."

The three hours I spent chapter and versing his sins gave me the greatest of pleasure. I remember suggesting for example that if the woman had said "get out of my hair" he would have weaseled around until she said "get off my back" or something like it.

"What is this expression, 'get out of my hair'? Someone help me."

"It means 'leave me alone'."

"It cannot mean 'leave me alone' because she does not wish to be left alone! Does anyone here think she wishes to be left alone?"

"It means, 'get off my back.' "

"Ah! That gentleman says you mean get off my back. But I want to know from you, are you telling me to get off your back?"

He gave me an A + for my pains. But then what else could he have done?

Carl Rogers was also in residence at the university at that time and the source and transit point of inspiration and funds for intersecting studies of the outcome of psychotherapy. A certain cachet was thought to have been added by putting projective data in the outcome evaluation schema alongside of Q-sort ratings of self-descriptive statements and counselor ratings of success. Rogers was no enthusiast for this, since it was contrary to his philosophy. But other principals felt that inclusion of measures less subject to the witting management of client and counselor would be more persuasive to the larger psychotherapeutic community. The Thematic Apperception Test (or TAT), and several other measures, were given clients at the time they applied, the time they started, the time they concluded, and at various stages of follow-up.

Having demonstrated a certain facility with the TAT, I was asked to join the project as research and as teaching assistant. Given the new expenses of my analysis and how much more needed to earn than I was able to at the Orthogenic school, I agreed.

For a couple of years things went swimmingly. To enable me to give more and more of my time to the project, (by now the *Dreikurs* group of Adlerians were to come into the study and measures that reflected their orientation had to be devised and validated) I was given a bye in required courses, apportioned my own portion of the research to write up for my doctoral dissertation, and bountifully paid. In addition, instead of having to pause to take an M.A., I was awarded a Master's Equivalency degree.

As the work progressed, however, and the "Zebos" and "Zadres" began eventually to be unfurled, trouble unfurled with it; the TAT gave ratings of the outcome of the counseling in many cases opposite to those told about "Zebo" by "Zebo" himself, and by his counselor. To make matters worse, as if anybody needed worse, the TAT indices *did* show changes by group: "Zebo" and group showed change (at p = .08) in the direction thought to be positive, but between the time they applied for counseling and the time counseling began.

Needless to say, the atmosphere in my part of the project was soon mottled with uneasiness. Factor analyses were commissioned in the hope of squeezing out better conclusions, but while some of these replaced negative change with zero change—cold comfort—none produced reflections of systematic client progress under any of the therapy conditions. Indeed, the longer the counseling the worse the results.

It was about this time that David Rapaport came out from the Austin Riggs Foundation to The Veterans Administration hospital where I was doing my internship. He gave a talk on his classic formulations concerning the autonomy of the ego. The talk, the question and answer period that followed, and the long discussion I had with him after these, were an intellectual treat; until then I had had none but written exposure to psychoanalytic metapsychology.

At the party that evening we fell to telling jokes. Rapaport had a connoisseur's feeling for jokes, especially Yiddish ones, and we and others told jokes and limericks in a blizzard of delight. As the hour grew late and we ran out of new stories and people drifted home, he and I remained to exchange the different versions of each story we each knew just to savor the differences. The next week brought a letter from him with another story in it; when I heard a good joke, for which my brother was an ever fertile source, I sent it to him. Soon our correspondence expanded to include glosses on the jokes, then ideas about this or that, with or without jokes and stories.

I wasn't exactly in Coventry, but as things became strained in the Committee, I felt lonely and much looked forward to the correspondence I had with Rapaport. I told him of the tensions that were gathering around the TAT data, and of the pressure I was under to revise my indices to "make them consonant" with the other ratings.

"You mean, not only is the food you feed them no good, but the portions are too small?" Rapaport wrote by way of commiseration. He suggested I let him review my indices and their derivations; having done so, he pronounced them entirely adequate, adequately derived. All the same within a month, I had the sad chore of describing how I had been relieved of my duties, almost of my data records, and had been given a pledge to sign that, though I could use my data for my doctoral dissertation, allowing the department to choose my committee, I would never make my data public.[7] Outraged, Rapaport telephoned to urge me to pack up the university and come to Riggs.

I was sorely tempted. On the other hand I was in the depths of analysis by then, as was my wife, and for that reason neither of us felt like moving. Still I could not see what my future was at the university, the course work on which my prelims would be based had, like the wake of an ocean liner, drifted into the past, and except that my scholarship was in effect, and I could take whatever courses I liked, I felt disconnected from my program, the Committee, and the university. (In urging me to come to Riggs, Rapaport had warned me that people who treated one shabbily do not like to have to look in his face.) I was also at a low ebb financially: we had what my wife earned teaching in the college and what I earned from my internship at the V.A., and could pick up from testing, but there were two analysts to feed and clothe, and my daughter on the way. Hoping that by clawing away my defenses in my analysis I could wrest inner option where outer possibility had seemed to thin, I felt very misunderstood when Kavka suggested I sit up for a while.

Still feeling wobbly about the years I had put into the outcome study, I took an Independent Study on Rorschach theory with Samuel Beck. I wanted to think about validity — not overall validity, but the precise meaning of individual variable — in Rorschach terms, movement, texture, color, and so on. I asked him whether there had been studies done in which particular states of mind were known ahead of time and corollaries looked for on the test protocol. This led to considering whether what we called "bland" tests could be given, followed by "state of mind" tests. We discussed whether the induction

---

[7]I did not, of course, sign the pledge, but neither, until now, have I made my findings public. The other findings were published by C. Rogers and R. Dymond, eds. (1958). *Psychotherapy and Personality Change*. Chicago: University of Chicago Press.

of particular states of mind via hypnosis—fright, sorrow, rage, lust—
might show up in particular changes in that person's Rorschach. When
one or two senior people in the department of psychiatry, with whom
I was studying hypnosis, turned out to be willing to evaluate subjects
for their psychiatric suitability and to induce the trance states, idle
discussion bloomed into a research possibility. We could determine
what someone's protocol was under ordinary conditions, under hypnosis, and how these differed, if at all, from conditions in which the
same person was hypnotically induced into a state of sorrow, then
rage, next fright, then joy. All of a sudden I had a whole new line of
dissertation-grade research, and I could not wait to share the news with
Rapaport.

"Don't you know," Rapaport said, his voice on the telephone like
sharp cold stone "of Brenman's and Gill's work on hypnosis as
transferentially driven role-taking?" (I did not.) Well, then, I was to
read it immediately. If despite this I proposed to conduct the research,
the results of which, he said bitterly, would be published in a trice, he
would pursue it like the hound of heaven, castigating me in every
journal he could. He was, he added unnecessarily, not without
influence.

A few days later, suspecting that his jeremiad had put me into a blue
funk, he telephoned to suggest we meet in Stockbridge. There he
reiterated his stance against my proposed project, but went on to tell
me of his thinking on the psychology of the impostor, a subject about
which Brenman-Gibson's and Gill's work had led him to think. Why
was it that when in a normal ego state people had limitations or
inhibitions that, when they impersonated someone else (including,
perhaps, impersonating someone in a so-called hypnotic trance), they
no longer had? Now *that* was something worth researching! Soon after
I returned from my visit, he wrote me the joke about the inmate, the
guard, and the wheelbarrows full of hay.[8] This story was forming his

---

[8]In one of the camps there was a gate past which once each day an inmate came
wheeling a barrow filled with hay. And each day, while the inmate stood mute, head
bowed, the guard searched through the hay. But each day, he found nothing. So each
day, he waved the inmate through. But not before the inmate gave him a sideways
look. Finally, just to avoid this irritating look, the guard would elaborately turn his
back when he saw the inmate coming, contenting himself with unexpected searches.
And then the war was over and the guard quite by chance encountered the inmate in

hypotheses about the impostor. (I tried not to think it had anything to do with my research proposal.)

Reluctantly, I conceded that Rapaport was correct. But, as I had argued with him, couldn't the same interpretation—that it reflected transference assumptions—be put on any test-taking behavior? The fallout from these reflections heightened my interest in the intersubjective nature of the imaginative response. I began, for example, to wonder whether someone sees the same things in the ink-blots under different testing situations.

Morris Stein, another professor of mine, was taking that view in respect to scientific creativity. Creativity, he had discovered, flourished in certain institutional environments and not in others, depending not on the personnel so much as the climate of the company. People who made discoveries good enough to patent while with one company, often lost their fizz in another. Stein had developed a survey that, he felt, measured that so-called climate for creativity, and he offered it to Science Research Associates, then better known for its reading laboratories and standardized achievement tests. He wanted to commercialize his survey instrument at the same time as he collected additional data. This way of thinking about an interacting milieu in which learning and development could optimally take place took me back to the Cherry Lawn and Vassar Institutes and the Orthogenic School. And it took me back to Erikson and Hay. When he and SRA approached me about taking on the job of promoting and using the survey, I thought it might now take me forward.

I knew nothing of course of commerce and industry; even the stock tables in the newspapers were arcane. But it wasn't difficult to discover that productivity and creativity were not always compatible, and that those productive people who were promoted to management positions (in a variant of what was later to be called "the Peter Principle") were often quite unable to fathom the nature and needs of those who were creative, or potentially so. Moreover, I could see right away that the focus on the individual was slightly askew: that here were matters of the group, the system, and the culture. Quite soon, therefore, in places so otherwise unfamiliar to me as Dow Chemical, Jones and Laughlin Steel, Phillips Petroleum, and Sun Oil and government laboratories, like Sandia, I felt conceptually quite at home. Moreover, I found this

---

a bar where both were having a beer. "You remember who I am?" he asked. "Yes." "You can guess what I want to know?" "Yes." "So tell me." "Wheelbarrows."

new world of commerce fascinating. I would not for some years be able
to formulate the dynamics, but I could already think that in group
situations when bad things happened (or good things didn't) it wasn't
only likely to be a function of individual pathology or of a few
troublemakers, but of something which, in ways obscure to each,
served the purposes of all. I spent in all several instructive and pleasant
years working at SRA. But the work, however much I grew into it, did
not grow into me. This was not who I was, nor who I meant to be.

When my analysis drew to a close, therefore, I felt that the time had
also come when I must go back to where I left off, which was with an
internship in Children's Memorial Hospital, get back into a clinical
situation, and apply for analytic training.

I put this to George Pollock, then Director of Training for the
Chicago Psychoanalytic Institute. Pollock told me that it would take
20 to 25 years before psychologists would be trained without having
first to pledge their training would be used only for research purposes.
Knowing what I knew about institutions and organizations, I had no
difficulty believing him. (As it turned out, he was optimistic.) And
feeling as I did about research and signing oaths, I had no wish to
strike such a bargain. I also looked into resuming clinical work and
learned what my Master's level qualifications would buy me: a position
doing psychometric testing.

I still had Rapaport's invitation to come to Riggs, and had from
Harry Levenson and Will Menninger, for whom SRA was a publisher,
invitations to join the Menninger Foundation's industrial consultation
service. But somehow I had become what felt like being an adult.
Rapaport, I felt quite sure, wanted a protégé; and to repeat what I was
doing at SRA at Menninger's seemed like going sideways. Nor did I
feature what would amount to starting afresh at the university: There
was just too much else to do and learn. I felt as if in a labyrinth. I could
not find the thread. I could only hope there was one.

My wife and I put our wish lists together: Upon the birth of our
daughter, she had moved from classroom teaching to the preparation
and use of home study materials, and this move had turned out to be
a more satisfying mode of teaching than the classroom had been.
Moreover, she hadn't much taste for the upscale living that would be
our reward were I to continue working with industry and expand my
travel schedule. She thought a quiet life centered on the children
somewhere in New England, where she had roots, would do her just
fine (her work in teaching via home study could be conducted from

anywhere there was a mailbox). On my list there was having a consulting room, a chance to try out an epistolary novel concerning a young man's adventures in psychoanalysis that I had been on and off discussing with Phil Roth, and a place to do a little teaching. Given fortuitous circumstances, I could continue to improvise my training in much the same way I had been doing from the start of my apprenticeship.

As to what was to become of me, now 30, with neither a degree nor a career path, I had, rather alarmingly, no idea. This worry, however, had the virtue, if that's what it was, of obscuring from me a deeper, less manageable worry: my father had been 38 when his coronaries proved fatal.

Thanks to SRA's lovely new Xerox machine, I made 100 copies of a letter of self-introduction and mailed these to universities and colleges throughout the Northeast, from Tufts at the south and east to the University of Vermont in the north and west. Of these, one might somehow prove to be the thread to the labyrinth, though how, I couldn't have said. Yet that was the point of the endeavor. Though I could not see how, perhaps someone else would. As it was to turn out, the President of Goddard College in Plainfield, Vermont had an idea, and he was on the phone, calling from Chicago.

Goddard, I learned in my meeting with him, had received from NIMH funding for a project in which a psychologist or psychiatrist would consult with the members of both the town and gown communities on their respective efforts to improve, primarily through preventative means, the mental health of their constituencies. When Tim Pitkin, the president of the college and the moving force behind the project, heard my letter read to him over the phone by his assistant, he like she, perceived a potential dovetailing of a high order. For my part, I felt greatly intrigued.

How might one enable those people to do so, who, if they did not also feel the attempt was impermissible, unfeasible, or wrong, would want to understand what made them and theirs tick? Could one, in the out-of-doors of an entire community, create a climate for introspection, as one could for creativity in an R&D facility? Finally, was prevention possible?

The college, in its status as a truly successful experiment in education, had, I also learned that afternoon, many regular visitors. Most came to one or another of the conferences sponsored by the college; others just came up for the weekend. As director of the project, I would be expected in time to hold such a conference. Among those who visited regularly were Larry Kubie, Sam Kaplan, Genia Hanfman, Harry Rand, and Maury Green. If, true to Pitkin's prediction, each would be unstinting in the time they gave me to go over my analytic work with the individuals who would come to me from the precincts of the college and elsewhere in the region, I would have found the thread that was able to take me out of the maze and into a degree of psychoanalytical competence.

On the visit my wife, daughter, and I made to the college, a curious thing happened. Driving about in an interval between interviews and discussions, I found myself on a stretch of road on which I had paused some five years earlier to wonder what living and working in such a place might be like. Upon our return to Chicago, my wife and I decided that if this wasn't a materialization of our wish list, it was the next thing to it. Since the work is chronicled in Cultures in Conflict (Chapter 1) and Seelsorger (Chapter 3) and also in my book on the subject[9] I shall reserve any description of it till then, except to mention my introduction to the work of Wilfred Bion.

After a year or so, I had begun to establish the conditions under which people in the community felt able to come into groups with me. But they had the rather dismaying habit of coming once and not again. No one I talked with, not Bettelheim, not Roy Menninger, could help me to identify what was at issue. One day, while in the Goddard library, I came upon Bion's[10] little book on groups. Seldom can a book have brought surcease to more furrowed a brow. What Bion termed the tacit agreement on "basic assumptions" exploded a doorway in what had been a blank wall. As earlier I began to understand the culture of the region and the dynamics of the community, so with Bion's insights was I then able to understand that the individuals who were somehow recognizable from the last time had, as a group, undergone a metamorphosis, as puzzling to them as Kafka's protagonist's was to others and himself. When I became adept enough to interpret these transfigurations, matters turned around.

Two examples may suffice. I had been working in a local school with groups of teachers and such children as they needed seen. But there was nowhere to meet, except in folding chairs along the side of the gym that was outside the lavatories. When, with the help of Bion's

---

[9]Boris (1967). *The [Un] Examined Life*. Plainfield, VT: Goddard College Publications.
[10]W. Bion. (1961). *Experiences in Groups*. New York: Basic Books.

exegesis, I was able to understand this situation as a split off element in the "fight/flight" group, I was able to find the interpretations that followed from this. This changed things around for the teachers enough that the members of the school board brought tools and lumber to their next meeting and in a couple of hours built a room both warm and private. Much the same happened in regard to my request for a private line instead of the nine party line my house was on. Only after I could offer Bionesque "whole group" interpretations to the couples group of which the manager of the telephone company and his wife were a part did the countless reasons a private line could not be installed suddenly evaporate.

In the tradition of the college, my project sponsored a conference. I thought it might be informative if all the participants were to be in groups of the sort I was by then conducting. I arranged for groups of teachers, parents, and so forth with whom I had already worked to reconstitute themselves for demonstration sessions. Through Elvin Semrad I found Max Day and Norman E. Zinberg to conduct these groups. When the demonstration groups had done, the conferees, professionals in the area of mental health and other interested parties, assembled into groups, which were worked with by Day and Zinberg even as the people in the groups they had observed had been. Such conferences generate a good deal of intensity, and I was very happy that Lawrence K. Frank, that grand old man of the field, agreed to chair it.

The conference was to have two immediate effects for me personally. One was to introduce me and my work to Day and Zinberg, who took word of it back to Boston. The second was to introduce the project to Harold and Ruth Mayer, who went on to produce a television documentary about it for PBS. By these means Miles Shore and Paul Myerson of the Department of Psychiatry at Tufts and the New England Medical Center Hospitals came to hear of my project. Shore came to Vermont for several days to inspect the work first hand and on his return kindly invited me to do a grand rounds on the subject. Over the lunch following my presentation, Myerson consulted informally with his staff, and after lunch invited me to join the department when the project concluded.

As I flew back to Vermont that evening, I had an inkling I had emerged from the labyrinth that had seemed to fashion itself around me from the day "Zebo" made his particular confession.

I would teach and work at Tufts–NEMCH for the next eighteen years as well as, albeit to a lesser degree, at Harvard—at the

Massachusetts General, McLean, and Cambridge Hospitals — before, soon after Myerson's retirement, I would move over to Harvard altogether, where I teach now.

Norman Zinberg and I would collaborate on demonstration research projects that applied my methodology to drug use among children and adolescents and racial prejudice among school teachers[11] This work would take my wife into the field of child and later infant psychology, where, my wife no longer, she makes contributions of her own.

Thanks to our funding from the Ford and Field Foundations I could write up my developing theory concerning groups: see Chapter 5: People's Fantasies in Group Situations.

I would also, at age 39, survive the massive coronary I feared would be part of my heritage from my father, as he had thought his would be from his.

Without my quite noticing it, my theories had begun to grow askew from Bion's. As is so often the case for succeeding "generations," I was bedeviled by Bion's unreconciled "splits." Bion thought the group to be an expression of man as a political animal, in the Aristotelian sense. He felt that Homo politicus had characteristics and qualities dormant when man was Homo individualus but ready to come forth in group situations as unquestioned basic assumptions regarding the use and meaning of Others. These situations he thought to be powerfully stimulated as an emotional alternative to the mental holler and din of the couple in the primal scene. In short, he wrote as if there were something that could be called a group.

But how could that be? A group could only be an aggregate of individuals who somehow decided that they were not an aggregate but a group. And that disposition, if that's what it was, would have to reside in the individual — or *some* times in the individual, because on other occasions he would be acting on different assumptions. One would thus have to think of the individual *as someone in continual dialectical movement — from being part of a couple to being a part of a group and back again, depending which mental and interpersonal conditions are activated at the moment.* Since a twosome could contrive either to form a couple or a group, one should name the twosome who are not a couple, a pair.

---

[11]N. Zinberg, H. N. Boris, and M. Boris. (1976). *Teaching Social Change*. Baltimore: Johns Hopkins University Press.

Had Bion continued to think about it, I think he might have seen for himself how such a realization concerning the couple and the pair might give his own theories the link between the intra- and inter-personal aspects of them, now still uncertain. But his work was for the most part following other courses. And these were as thought provoking as his study of group psychology: see Chapter 15 (Bion Revisited). When I discussed with him my own work-in-progress on groups and on hope[12] he saw right off where the sticking points were; I found his help immensely clarifying. As in my discussions with Bettelheim, Erikson, Gardiner, and Rapaport, I was able to observe how his mind worked (and played) on data, more accurately, in creating data.[13] My visit with him enabled me to travel easily and at speed to where the next darkness lay.

The ideas that very occasionally, often only momentarily, alight such darkness arrive at unexpected moments. One glimmering day, while plying off Mt. Desert Island in Antic Foot, our 17-foot runabout, the children taking turns at steering line-of-sight legs, I sat rereading Piaget. I was trying to think further about the nature of hope. From time to time, I read aloud those questions of his, like how does the sun stay up in the sky, and presently the children and I fell into a conversation concerning why children of a certain age think clay rolled out into a cylinder is bigger somehow than the same amount massed into a ball.

"Did you say 'think it is bigger — or better?' " asked one of the kids.

"Better — I mean bigger." said another.

"Maybe to most kids bigger is better," remarked the third.

"Or better is bigger."

They began to play with this, but for me just then a penny was about to drop. "*Er*-ier!' " I cried, and in an instant the following story occurred to me.

Suppose someone wanted to go to someplace, but didn't know where or what that place was, only that he would somehow know it when he got there because it would be properly "er." Not knowing where this place was, he had no idea what direction to take, nor, being unable to describe it, could he ask directions. On the other hand, wanting to find it, he

---

[12]H. N. Boris. (1994). *Envy*. Northvale, NJ: Jason Aronson.

[13]For an intimate view of Bion's mind at work, see his notebooks published as *Cogitations*, edited by Francesca Bion. London: Karnac Books.

couldn't remain still. So what to do but strike off in some direction, any direction, hoping that he would find his destination when he arrived.

Bar Harbor!

Bar Harbor, then. But upon his arrival this traveler felt that Bar Harbor, excellent though it is, was yet not the place he wanted to reach. Although still unknown to him, that place existed nevertheless in his mind. He thought of it as "The *not*-Place," for though he did not know it in the affirmative, as for instance as Northeast Harbor, he believed he could be said to know it in the negative — Bar Harbor is a *not*-Northeast Harbor. He reasoned that if this were so, should he chance upon the place that *was* Northeast Harbor, he would know it in an instant — just as he knew instantly that Bar Harbor was a *not*-Northeast Harbor place.

Accordingly he continued to travel, feeling at each arrival that, though he had not yet come to his *not*-place, it was somewhere and that just as he knew the feeling "Oh-oh" when he failed to arrive at his objective, so he would know the feeling of "Ah-ha!!" when he chanced upon it. He contrived a theory that the "Oh-oh's" were the obverses of the "Ah-*ha!*'s" and that if he journeyed patiently enough, he would, like an ant on a large leaf, come to the end of the "Oh-oh's" and suddenly enter upon the plane of the "Ah-ha!'s." This vantage point on his life and travels inspirited him greatly, for every *not*-place seemed to bring him one step closer to his Yes-place.

Since his was a footloose life, at least in the smaller scale — in the larger, he was a man on a quest — he began to divert himself with wondering what precisely those qualities might be that would mark his true destination. What configuration and lineaments would his Yes-place have: what contours and features would appoint it?

As he wandered he gave consideration to all that he disliked of where he had thus far traveled; as each evening he rested, he tried to create an assembly of all that had thus far met his favor. Would the place he sought be larger or smaller, fancier or plainer, warmer or cooler, sunnier or shadier than one city or another? Would its curves be more concave or more convex, its holes, holer, wholer or holier? His contemplation of er-ier features presently began to exert a curious effect. As he arrived at each city or town, he no longer subjected it merely to the yes-no test, but began to study its features for hints toward the nature of "er."

In this occupation he spent some years. But one day he had quite a start, for he suddenly saw that "er" could possess none of these features; it would always be but "er-ier" than the one — and always "er-ier" than the other. He began to bethink himself that his was a journey not so much to a so far undisclosed place as to a state of "er." Yet without the landscape of "er" itself to compare "er" with, he now wondered if he would know it when he found it.

He began to look about him now with a squint, his neck held at an angle. Strangers beholding him wondered whether he was trying to see or not to see what he was looking at. And of course he was older now, and evenings found him, chin on chest, staring blankly into the fireplace, wondering if his quest was worth its candle. Bar Harbor seemed to him in retrospect a finer place than he remembered thinking. "Perhaps I will return there," he bethought himself, and for the first time in some years he felt impatient for morning to come that he might get started.

Though it was not altogether clear what, I thought this little story contained something not unnegligible regarding choice, selection, desire, and hope, which with the state of mind called envy, were to occupy the next twenty years of my work: see Chapters 18 and 19; also my (1993) *Passions of the Mind: Unheard Melodies — A Third Principle of Mental Functioning*; and (1994) *Envy*.[14]

That was the mid-70s, the summer the gas went up at the pumps. By the mid-80s, I too was older, and, being also slowed by the consequences of my earlier coronaries, to which fate had added the succubus of an active and chronic hepatitis, I was more easily drawn to reflection than adventure, to writing than practice. As I came to putting my work to paper, I had the inestimable assistance of Carol Lounsberry Boris, who gave me her hand not only in marriage, but in the work I would have been hard put indeed to do without her.

Upon hearing of Bettelheim's sad and angry death, I sent a letter of commiseration to Jerry Kavka, to whom ("Well, it's about time!") Bettelheim had referred me when I decided to take the plunge into analysis.

In an elegiac spirit I referred also to my own ever more apparent limitations. In the same elegiac spirit, Kavka wrote back: "Well, you have had a very good run of it."

And so I have.

---

[14](1993) New York University Press and (1994) Jason Aronson, respectively.

# I

# Conditions of the Other

# 1

# Cultures in Conflict: Mental Health and the Hard-to-reach

The idea of conflicting cultures was already with me when I worked as a consultant to corporations and government agencies — and particularly their R&D efforts. I soon began to know that when a director of research quoted Edison about the ratio of perspiration (99 percent) to inspiration, there was a high probability that he was going to have, if perhaps a productive unit, then one of no distinguishing creativity. And I already knew from my anthropologist friends how culture-bound one could be without noticing this — indeed, having no place to stand from which to notice this. Arriving in Vermont and sending myself out into those who dwelt there, I was able to begin to glimpse what my sort looked like — and how they felt their sort would look to my sort. Since they were naturally making manifest the kind of behavior that was apposite to my sort, and how my sort thought of their sort, I was eventually able, by adding, subtracting, and otherwise factoring, to get the drift. Giving the drift was of course another problem.

Available statistics indicate that although some 25 percent of all Americans have at one time or another experienced psychological difficulties of some magnitude (one in five having felt themselves to be on the verge of a "nervous breakdown"), fewer than 4 percent have seen fit to seek or accept care from mental health resources (Joint

Commission on Mental Illness and Health 1961). Our work in several rural Vermont communities, however, suggests that both these percentages may require the footnote "under ordinary conditions." For, although figures from Vermont agencies follow the national ratio of one in 25 accepting care, our program over the last several years has been, and is, producing ratios of a substantially different magnitude.

In this program the adult members of every family in which children under 18 are living at home are invited to request participation in groups that will meet once a week with me. The purpose of these groups, they are told, is to discuss anything and everything in which they feel a psychologist could be helpful. Because we approach families, our statistics on those who make use of this mental health resource are based on family units. The national figures given above when extrapolated to such units indicate that yearly 0.56 percent of families can be expected to have one or more members seeking or accepting assistance from a mental health professional. The response to our own program has been close to 40 percent of the number of families invited (on a random basis) each year.

Since the approach we employ (invitation) differs from the ordinary conditions of self-referral or referral by others, any comparison between our results and others can only be an uneasy one. But such a comparison does suggest, perhaps, two points worth noting: first, that the size and make-up of the so-called "hard-to-reach" group are responses to the mental health system itself; and, second, that by altering some components of that system it may be possible to diminish the size and alter the make-up of this group.

## THE MENTAL HEALTH SYSTEM AND THE POPULATION AT LARGE

I am suggesting, in other words, that the relationship between the mental health system and the response of the population to its services is a transactional one in which changes in the one can induce changes in the other. In some respects this transactional relationship has the characteristics of the free market place. Starting with the figure of 25 percent of the population expressing need (my own figures suggest that need is more prevalent even than that), we can define the market potential. Erik Erikson (1950) speaking of the cultural differences among peoples, provides, by analogy to the educational system, a model that appropriately adds the two other factors we require.

"Naturally," he writes, "the rewards of one educational system mean little to the members of another, while the costs are only too obvious to them." One can say, then, that our market operates with need, cost, and reward; thus we can describe a dynamic for decisions regarding the use of mental health services as a ratio of need to cost to reward.

The market place, however, is a curious one. At first glance we see that the available services are heavily oversubscribed. One statistic for the 1960 use of outpatient psychiatric care has it that three-quarters of a million people were seeking assistance from but 30,000 professionals (Rioch et al. 1965). In that sense it is a seller's market. But this is deceptive. Most professionals are only too eager to diminish the number of their prospective clients. They seek, therefore, ways of offsetting the degree and consequences of the need they observe all around them. Prevention and earlier intervention are key factors in this effort. And yet we are, or have been, confounded by the reluctance of those we might wish to help to accept our services. Thus, at the same time that it is a seller's market, it is also a buyer's market. Many groups, agencies, and centers are actively seeking ways to bring their services to the hard-to-reach or to make themselves more reachable.

It is difficult, therefore, to avoid the conclusion that buyer and seller aspects exist on both sides and that the mutual confounding that is taking place has to do with the terms of the transaction. My own view is that the resulting confusion is at once reasonable and unnecessary. It is reasonable when viewed as the natural, but not inevitable, discongruity between two cultures, that of the mental health system and that of the unreached or unreaching population. It is unnecessary insofar as many of the transactional terms are gratuitous in functional, though perhaps not in cultural, ways.

To make this plain, let me begin by suggesting that those who currently make use of mental health services do so under three conditions: first, when need is so great as to brook any cost and accept any reward; second, when, under lesser need, the costs are less in proportion to that need; and, third, when—whatever the extent of need and cost—the reward is highly valued.

In the first group are, of course, the desperately afflicted. Often these are people whose sense of inner need is augmented by the compulsion, direct or implicit, of a referring agency, a court, an employer, a parent, or some sort of social pressure.

To describe the second group, I must pause long enough to elaborate on the issue of cost.

Costs can be material and non-material, but seldom immaterial. The material costs of mental health services are clear: time, money, distance, waiting. Clear as they are, they are likely to exist in a context of less obvious non-material costs. These latter can be defined as a person's or, more broadly, a culture's values; but, in a real sense, they are more than that, because to treat them very long as values fragments what is a dynamic and organic experience of self.

Non-material costs, moreover, exist on several levels. As an example, we can take the matter of acknowledging need. For those whose culture considers illness a deviant status, to confess to mental illness means accepting that onus. Negative sanctions, the offshoots of unconscious envy, are leveled against the self-declared ill person; and any exemptions he should require from the usual or non-deviant status come dear. Only when he is clearly at the end of his rope is the envy of others appeased; short of that he must bear the sanctions and the stigma and the interpersonal consequences of his status. In a family that has had difficulties for some time, for one member suddenly to acknowledge that he needs "help" is a serious defeat, sometimes an unendurable loss of face. Few are likely to make such a concession unless there is an overweening superego in conspiracy with the spouse. The victory of the superego brings on a crushing sense of defeat, perhaps a suicide, perhaps the compulsive need for such punishment as the series of surgical procedures people often undergo before going into psychotherapy. But almost always one can expect a deep sense of failure, a depression, a sense of hopelessness, which all mean that therapy has to proceed very slowly before what therapy is all about can really begin.

With such punishments awaiting the members of this culture, either need must be very great and alternatives invisible or the reward we offer must be enormous. But what can mental health as a service or practice offer? Only one thing, really: assistance in a person's efforts to understand himself and to examine his life. To be sure, we offer an environment for this: courteousness, steadfastness, a benign optimism, and our professional promise not to act out with or exploit those good enough to consult us. But these are scant intermediate and ultimate rewards when weighed against the costs exacted. Yet we will not, as perhaps we should not, offer commensurate rewards.[1] If our

---

[1]This is not to say that the issue of rewards should remain closed. On the contrary, when in competition with such self-prescriptions as drugs, alcohol, and adolescent

job is to offer assisted self-scrutiny, we may not pay, feed, or marry our consultees, nor may we find them jobs (ordinarily), punish their enemies, or endure any more of their punishment of us than we have to.

Still, as I have suggested, there are those who do not experience the necessity of making such sacrifices as I have much too briefly described. The intellectual is sometimes exempt. When he is, it is often because he is already a member of a deviant group, and deviation permits him freedom from certain of the sanctions against which others have no immunity. The wealthy, the Park Avenue matron or the movie star, are examples of those for whom material costs, such as time and money, represent scant sacrifice, while their superordinate social status permits them prerogatives others do not enjoy. Those for whom reward is great include many mental health professionals, whose competence, ethic, or prestige is gratified by their own analysis or psychotherapy.

But when the three conditions are exhausted, we are left with 96 percent of the population whose need is insufficient in proportion to cost and reward. Some of these people are enviably situated; others are in grave trouble. If we are not to await an increase in their need to the point where they seek our help, we must find ways of reducing the cost of our services.

## A PROGRAM FOR THE HARD-TO-REACH

The program to which I have alluded was created to do just that. We began with two assumptions. The first I have already made plain. It was that the divergence between the two cultures implied a conflict. And, if we were not to await the initiative of the community, it was we who would have to take the initiative, for otherwise the conflict was not going to be resolved. The second assumption was that conflicts among need, cost, and reward were broader than their specific reference to mental health. They affected other recourses and alternatives as well,

---

sexual engagements, we may have to review our standards. Transference realization may not be enough. The solution will probably have to be sought out of a consideration of the differing significances rewards have for the two cultures. Synanon and other efforts for addicts that replace, actually or symbolically, the "turn-on" of the original drug or behavior may provide leads in this direction.

especially within a cultural group in transition. Thus, although people did not necessarily want help with conflicts that kept them from seeking mental health assistance, they might well want help with the same order of conflict that, more ubiquitous in nature, was also precisely what kept them from seeking or accepting assistance. It followed from these assumptions that we must proceed in two phases, a pre-resolution or amelioration phase, in which the conflict could be attenuated enough for help to be requested, and a second or actual phase, in which assistance could then be provided.

We have come to call that first phase the "overture phase," the second, the "group phase." Essentially, however, the process, from the first call upon a family member to the last group session, is continuous and organically unified. It consists of nothing more or less than assisted self-scrutiny. But the initiative varies from the beginning, in which we take the sole initiative, to the point where the individual takes the sole initiative. Preceding each development in this continuum of initiative is a developmental step toward the resolution of the need-cost–reward conflict. The goal we seek is to accompany people through independence, in which the costs of interdependence seem too high, into interdependence, during which period the conflicts are analyzed and alternative ways of being are tried and mastered, to autonomy, in which independence is restored free of the awful threats of interdependence.

To make the overture we have employed local indigenous persons — project associates — now three in number. It is through them that we take the initiative by seeking out our prospective clients where they are — at home — with either specific imagery of the prospect of working with the mental health professional or a basic image into which the dawning of the prospect is all too readily fitted. Whatever the image, the reaction to the prospect tends to be intense. In most respects it resembles the transference reaction; it is an amalgam of transference expectations and the imputation of what Erikson (1958) has called the "negative identity."

The project associates are equipped to deal with these first percep-tions and stances of the family members upon whom they are calling by having gone through a series of group sessions themselves. They have come to know in themselves some of the images imputed to the program; they also know it as a reality. Being of the same culture as those upon whom they call, and recognizable as such, they can identify with the householders, as the latter can with them. Continual work on their own remaining ambivalences prevents them from becoming proselytizers of the program, which, together with their own success as active and articulate people in the community, enables them to present themselves and the program openly. Through discussion and role-playing in weekly staff meetings, they have a chance to work on the problems and issues in their job. Still, theirs is not an easy task.

At any one time each associate is responsible for making and following through overtures to about seventy-five families in our nine communities. Traveling over back roads to remote farmhouses or going from one door to the next in villages, they call on six, eight, or ten families a day. Their task is twofold: to invite the householder to consider whether working with a psychological consultant might be useful — offering the family that option at *their* option — and to demonstrate just what it is that working with a psychologist involves.

The associate begins by calling unannounced, introducing himself (or herself), and telling the householder that he is working for a mental health project. When invited in, his next step is to find a way to engage the householder in a discussion of how life is going for him or her. He does this by picking up on what the householder, from a glance, seems to care most about, whether it be television, sewing, a car, children, or worries and problems themselves. At first, the associate must ask questions or otherwise direct the conversation. From his own group work, he is skilled at looking inward to measure the degree of caring expressed and at directing the householder toward a deepening expression of that caring. Such subject matter begins then to take on its own momentum, with the householder taking over the initiative. This shift in initiative allows the associate to listen, reflect, and, when the time is right, wonder with the person about the person's life and experience. The associate resists calls for advice, asking instead what the person himself does. From time to time, when necessary, he comments on the nature of the present interaction, largely as he did in a group. He does this primarily when he is being cast in a role (made a recipient of a resistance-engendering transference reaction) as critic, enemy, friend, or sympathizer. Aware of the presumptuousness of his conduct, he is aware, too, that resentments, doubts, and suspicions have to find as much expression, recognition, and acceptance as does the pleasure of his caring to call in the first place.

All of this takes more than one visit, so that when the first visit ends or becomes uncomfortable, the associate raises the question of whether he shall stay or leave, come back or not return. This is the second shift of initiative. Here the associate tries to find the narrow line between taking a "no" at face value and treating it as a preliminary statement that invites reflection and, perhaps, a final "yes." He then makes his own plan to return at an interval determined both by what the needs of the individual seem to warrant and by what the logistics of forming groups call for.

The invitation to consider extending the process initiated by the project associate to work with me is made when, after one or more visits, the conflict between need, cost, and reward has begun to weaken. Just how long this takes varies, of course, from person to person; a rough average is three one-hour visits. In coming to the point of accepting the invitation or not, the householder has by this time visualized it against the backdrop of the accomplishments and problems he or she has been discussing; he has inspected what has been taking place between the associate and himself, found it useful and meaningful without feeling that he has been found sick or unworthy, laughable or depraved, bad or ennobled; he has wondered about the prospect of replicating past relationships within this new context and found this prospect either subject to comment or deprived of mutual role-taking; he has, in all this, decided yes or no. This answer has, in turn, been inspected and wondered about by associate and householder together, with additional hopes, needs, and resistances brought out and viewed. If the answer remains affirmative, an appointment with me is duly made.

The appointment marks still another shift in initiative, for now the householder must come out of the home, be at an office at a certain time, and get there by his or her own means. But the change is not too drastic. My consulting room is in my home and has little of the clinical office about it; it does not appear to be a place where sick people are seen, diagnoses made, tests given, pathological conditions located, or even notes taken. I do not, in fact, give tests, take histories, or undertake any such interview activities. I try, rather, to conduct the session as if it were the fourth or fifth session of therapy, asking for self-observations and commenting on conditions that seem to obstruct the free presentation of the self.

The process started by the associates thus continues without interruption. My intent in these individual sessions is to locate the conflict in the troublesome situation, detach it somewhat from the circumscribed guise it has taken, interpret it to a degree, listen to the recognition that it is wider or broader or more ubiquitous than it seemed, wonder how it might affect the person's feelings about being here with me—and thereby assist the transition from the present meeting to the prospective group sessions. At the end, I ask whether the sort of work we have been doing seems useful enough to be continued, assuring the person meanwhile that his word is good enough for me. Unless I encounter someone simply too agitated for the group sessions, I abide by the person's own inclination—no matter what the absolute diagnosis. Enviably well-functioning and gravely disturbed people, and all in between, may make up the membership of any given group.

Throughout the overture, as we are attempting to demonstrate what we ask of people and what we don't, we are in other ways reducing costs as well. In general, much of what we do and how we do it adds up to a dispensation with the medical model, which is otherwise so much part and parcel of mental health as a cultural system. We go *to* people—to all the people and not identifiable problem groups; and our groups, group *people*, not symptoms or statuses in life. We *forswear* pressing our invitation or declaring that people "need" our services. We give over the initiative as fast as we can, yet not so quickly that people have to ask before they can bear to. We take sick and well alike. We are as indifferent as we can be to whether or not our invitations are accepted and thus do not imply that we want to change those we call upon. We hold our group meetings in group members' homes, not in a clinic or office. In all these ways we eliminate the usual costs as much as we do the literal cost by not charging for our services.

The group meetings themselves begin with a trial period of several sessions, after which the groups decide on the ultimate termination point. Since these are "consultative" groups, my alliance is made with the goals the individual members set. These may be couched in terms of situations or relationships they wish to understand, problems they wish to solve, or circumstances they wish to alter or improve. It is made clear that *my* understanding, at least, is that we are individually and collectively embarked on a collaborative working relationship. When, as it inevitably does, the group departs from that collaboration for another designed to afford it certain satisfactions other than those attendant on the working relationship, I must interpret or bring to cognizance the fact and significance of this abrogation of conscious intent.

The history of each group consists of alternations between collaborative pursuits in a working relationship and attempts to circumvent these pursuits for other sorts of realization. But because the nature of groups and the economy of the individual are such as to coalesce over central issues, one's observations can be directed to either developments in the psychodynamics of the group or the manifest contributions of the individual, with the result that the effects of one's comments touch both. Interpretations touching both contribute to the goals of the members of the group and, with luck, achieve the purposes of those who, many weeks back, responded (sometimes uneasily) to our first overtures.

## DISCUSSION

Although viewing the aspirations and orientations of the culture of the mental health professional and that of the unreached public as alien and, in some respects, even inimical to one another, I have suggested that it is possible for them to coalesce around the essentials of mental health practice as assisted self-observation and insight. Indeed, the approach and methods I use in my own work are largely psychoanalytic; and if I compromise these in any essentials, I am not aware of it.

It is equally clear, however, that we knowingly violate certain canons of the mental health cultural tradition. Foremost among these are our invasion of privacy (when we call unsolicited on people) and the seeming solicitation of "business" that we make. I am not unaware of how few of those who are likely to have read this would welcome such initiative with respect to themselves. The mores that a man's house is his castle and that it is improper to intervene, unsolicited, in the internal affairs of others go back at least to the Magna Carta. Moreover, it is the essence of the tradition of professionalism that the professional, as opposed to the businessman, does not solicit custom or even advertise for it. Then, too, there are certain ethical questions that, in traditional practice, are held at bay by the simple fact that the client seeks out the professional. The cultural system of mental health is not an empty conglomerate of historical derivations; it has much to recommend it.

Yet, though it is not difficult to understand why many would find themselves unwilling to violate tradition and feel ashamed or abashed unless they persuaded themselves to a double standard, our view is easily enough presented. Intentional or not, there is such a thing as cultural arrogance, in which the deeply held traditions of one's own culture supersede those of others. In effect, we cherish ourselves over and above others. This cannot make for an optimal therapeutic relationship with others; and we do not reflect this attitude when we are at work with others. But, if the effect of our "pre-working" relationship is such, must we not also consider potential as a part of the kinesis? In the fundamentals of the work itself, we shall want to be ourselves, only because, so far as I know, that is what is functionally necessary; in the preludes to that work we can allow others to be themselves. Have we another choice? The final outcome is the parity of courtesy as Moore (1965) describes it:

> Courtesy implied more than civility or good manners. It meant that while being completely yourself, you were all the time helping the other person to be himself, through your appreciation of his point of view, your respect for his individuality, your sensibility and quiet awareness of how he thought and felt and who he was.

Within this framework, it has become possible to enable many families to receive psychoanalytic group consultation even as they term the groups, "groups," "classes," "discussions," "group therapy sessions," or "mental hygiene parties."

## SUMMARY AND CONCLUSIONS

Mental health (viewed as a system of concepts, practices, and customs), no less than any other cultural system with a tradition, has been created and fostered in the image of the men and women who as professionals and as patients have participated in it. Their values, their needs, their identities are reflected in it. Although this is only reasonable and proper, mental health has, nevertheless, come to represent an alien cultural system and tradition to a broad swath of the American people. Only some 4 percent of all Americans, some 21 percent fewer than those with an acknowledged need for help, make use of mental health resources over a lifetime.

It is, we submit, the obligation to sacrifice precious values that keeps those who seek or are offered assistance from accepting it. These sacrifices are not intrinsic to the basic process of the mental health procedures of therapy, consultation, and education. If, as we suggest, the basic intent of mental health as a practice is to provide assistance to people in their efforts to understand themselves, no one wishing this service need be asked to accept the onus of illness, problem typology, failure in self-sufficiency, the threat of subordination to a seemingly powerful doctor, or, indeed, any of the "hidden" charges we now make.

Rather, as the program here described is intended to illustrate, the same work can be offered and performed in a different cultural framework, with far greater acceptability and less consultee "motivation." Indeed, it appears possible to hope that further changes along the lines of reducing the costs, broadly speaking, of program participation will serve even more to alter the size and make-up of the so-called "hard-to-reach" group than have those we are able to report at present.

## REFERENCES

Erikson, E. H. (1950). *Childhood and Society*. New York: W. W. Norton.
_____ (1958). *Young Man Luther*. New York: W. W. Norton.
Joint Commission on Mental Illness and Health (1961). *Action for Mental Health*. New York: Basic Books.
Moore, J. (1965). *Waters under the Earth*. Philadelphia: Lippincott.
Rioch, M., Elkes, C., and Flint, A. (1965). *Pilot Project in Training Mental Health Counselors*. Washington, DC: U.S. Public Health Service.

# 2

## Spreading Mental Health: The Pioneer Spirit Revisited

How much do we, as a society, do for others? "Save me from being saved!" as Oscar Wilde used to pray, or might have. But he did say that "every country's doormen are dressed like every other country's generals."

It is probably impossible for well-intentioned people not to want to do good. Strachey's famous paper on the moderating influences of psychoanalysis speaks of how the analytic perspective will come to replace that of the archaic introjects when the patient identifies himself with the analyst, as he was bound, it was hoped, to do. This beating of swords into ploughshares doesn't quite take account of the possibility of enabling the patient to live, not in the world of introjects, but of people, the one (free association) making possible the other.

Although people argue about what good is, they cannot argue whether good is good, which may be the interesting question. Don't ask the peacock about his tail. Time and tide have blessed him with the accursed thing.

---

The authors of *Mental Health Consultants*—who were the research director and the consulting psychiatrist of the project it describes—write in their preface:

[This] documents the development of a community mental health program in New Mexico. It is the log of a pioneering venture by lone mental health workers who developed coordinated, comprehensive, locally based mental health services in communities far removed from centers of professional practice. In four years of dedicated effort, a variety of new or substantially revised community-based mental health programs were enacted, reflecting in their variety the dynamic and responsive relationship each consultant was able to establish with his many and diverse communities. [Griffith and Libo 1968, p. iii]

And, indeed, the story is in its way a splendid one. The scene in New Mexico was specifically the rural areas of the long desert reaches surrounding the state's central core of cities. These rural communities are barren of mental health services and facilities, though not, of course, of the need for them. At the time the story opens, previous efforts to inaugurate and provide services had been tried and had failed: Travelers from the core of cities had come to the rural areas and gone without leaving their stamp. In the meantime local people, including physicians and, for example, one school guidance counselor, had established a kind of hegemony of service, but a service that was, at least in the authors' view, not quite so useful to the community recipients as to the profferers themselves. Then the project began — and in the end, after many vicissitudes, it succeeded in developing a strong foundation for, and in some areas even the structure of, mental health services. If the book reads like a story of the conquest and colonization of the West, it is not by accident. The people involved, the consultants, had to have a missionary zeal strong enough, first, to wish to move (from the urban areas that were their own natural habitat) into these distant parts; then, to offer themselves to an unasking and indeed often antagonistic public; and finally, to face and sustain the retaliation of those who feared and resented them. Progress was inevitably slow, and they had to pay out a good deal of trust and hope before they could see any return. At the end of the four years, however, these consultants — a nurse, a social worker, and two clinical psychologists — could claim substantial achievements.

Although written as if it were a final report to the National Institute of Mental Health, the book aspires to serve as a handbook for other projects. And it is as a model for future projects that I propose to consider it.

Along with the superabundance of facts and figures the book presents, feelings are also expressed. One of these would seem to account for the fact that this project, like others of its sort, did not enjoy greater success than it did. It occurs, significantly enough, in the first sentence of the first paragraph on page 1:

> Short of the nightmare we might envision as the aftermath of a nuclear holocaust, it is inconceivable for most of us to imagine a world without professional mental health facilities.

The anxiety inherent in this statement cannot help but have significance for the project. Although the authors themselves, in Chapter 3, closely examine the consultants' motivations, personalities, and value systems, the matter of anxiety also bears analysis. Anxiety of the sort expressed above, for instance, is often precisely what engenders the very sense of mission without which such a project may be impossible.

Put plainly, however, the quoted sentence says this: We feel unsafe when help is not available—for ourselves or for others, as the case may be—and must do what we can to persuade you to create such help. It must follow that those who do not comply with this condition for safety become intolerable in proportion to the anxiety they don't allay. Naturally, such an unallayed feeling is only partially evident in the report. And, of course, everyone has hang-ups that represent important motivations for the work he does. However, one seeks and gains distance from these unresolved needs or anxieties in order to avoid acting them out, for it is their acting out that may impede the success of one's work. Mental health professionals have by now been schooled in the theory of dynamics, derived primarily (though not exclusively) from psychoanalysis, that views behavior as a consequence of forces—drives, needs, feelings, or motives—in conflict with one another. In this framework behavior is seen as the best compromise formation that people can make out of their conflicts. When that compromise formation, however workable it may be for certain purposes, fails of other purposes—as in the case of a symptom like compulsive hand-washing, for example—the individual involved may come to see it as a poor compromise and thus seek help in discovering the elements of the conflict in order to effect a more workable solution. Psychotherapists have learned, however, that the conflicting motives usually are not wholly conscious, and that considerable time and skill are often required to enable them to become so. They have also learned that even more fundamental than time and skill is their willingness to keep a neutral attitude about the conflicting forces. The successful therapist is as interested in, and sympathetic to, the compulsive's urge toward filth and sadism as he is concerned with the countering motives for cleanliness and scrupulousness. And, indeed, only when he is do both motives reveal themselves to him and to his patient.

Somehow, this neutrality too often flees the mental health professional upon his entry into the community. Perhaps the very pressure of his own motives has increased to the point where, no longer content with the impassivity of office or clinic practice, he is seized by a righteousness or anger or anxiety or guilt that will not be stayed. And thus he forays, neutrality abandoned, to rescue the sufferers and do battle with the vanquishers.

We have, then, a situation in which, on the one hand, an intensity of concern seems to have provided the sense of apostolic mission without which the project's accomplishments might have remained unachieved, and, on the other hand, the indifference to outcome that is necessary for the indication and resolution of conflict seems by its absence to have impeded achievement. Is there a way out of this bind?

Suppose a project were undertaken in which the mental health consultant begins with a curious act of faith: He assumes that there is reason for the community he encounters to be as it is. If the situation seems catastrophic to him, he will take that as the measure of the reason. Having made such an act of faith, he can then express this to the people: "I can't help feeling frightened by the lack of mental health resources in your community, and yet you yourselves don't feel that way. Or maybe you do, but something else weighs even more heavily with you. I wonder what it's all about? Maybe I'm too alarmed, and what you can tell me would help. Or maybe I'm alarmed because I can't see that you too are alarmed, and I end up feeling that I have to do the worrying because no one else is. Can we discuss it?"

I don't insist on the set of words I've used, but however one phrases it, the alternative would, I think, have to include a clear profession of the consultant's own motive, a statement that he knows his own motive and has enough distance from it to realize that it is his own burden and needn't become the responsibility of those he is addressing. These ingredients express the neutrality necessary to enable the conflict response to emerge safely, after which consultant and townspeople can jointly consider whether the existing solution of no, or inadequate, or problematic mental health resources is the best compromise for the diverse motivations of the people, and then whether the solution represented by these questionable mental health resources is worth the maintenance of the conflict.

Let's see how this might work. Mental health resources, as Talcott Parsons among others has pointed out, are generally for those who, it is believed, cannot help themselves. Most people believe that those who can should, and when they themselves experience difficulty in doing as they should, they increase the "should" component proportionately. They do not want to be led into temptation — into passivity, dependency, and the like. Perhaps they envy those others who can let themselves be passive and dependent, and are as little interested in smoothing the path for such people as they are to have the path for backsliding, as they would see it, smoothed for them. Since basically they don't wish temptation to be available, they are pleased not to have too many resources around. Where resources are deemed necessary, they prefer them to be staffed by professionals who are not sympathetic to the patient — who won't "spoil" the patient. And quite naturally, when people who feel this way are in the majority, they create resources like the many existing state hospitals, resources that are hells on hills, and thus stigmatize or otherwise deter those who might wish to avail themselves of help.

Given the urgency of the need not to backslide, the solution of having few and bad resources makes sense. However, for the people holding it this formulation isn't likely to be conscious, no doubt because its explicit acknowledgment of self-need might border on being intolerable. Yet it can emerge, given the sympathetic neutrality of the consultant, and then be there for those of the community who have this attitude to inspect it also. Their inspection will pose to them the question: Are they in fact so temptable as all that? And if they are, is it really so bad to get themselves a little help?

It is unlikely, however, that their conflict will emerge without any attempt by the people to use projection. The wish for mental health resources and its implied interest in the people's passivity and dependency will be attributed to the consultant. Then, feeling filled with righteousness and good conscience, the people of the community will attack the consultant: "You, not we, are the bad wisher for these regressive temptations!"

If the consultant is in fact what the projection has him being, the conflict now takes place between community and consultant. Since, fortunately, the natives no longer eat the missionary, their perception of him as a powerful and dangerous person is not likely to result in direct harm to the consultant. But it advances nothing, at the least, and it may set things back simply by helping the people indigenous to the area to feel even less conflict about their solutions of no, few, or bad mental health resources than they felt before the consultant's arrival on the scene. On the other hand, neutrality on the part of the consultant would, precisely at this point, supply to the intractable conflict a leavening necessary to avert the hardening of attitudes. For in his neutrality he is not selling anything. He is asking. He is even offering. But he doesn't need anything. The people will have no cause to fear that the consultant's need to deal with his own anxieties will take precedence over his attention to their own. Instead, the consultant will appear as someone able to tolerate his own conflicts, and therefore he will inspire the hope that he can further tolerate theirs. This, in turn, will help the projected aspect of the conflict to be taken back inside. It is better to have a good consultant and a bad conflict than the reverse, and the neutral consultant has at least the promise of being a good one. He is not, at any rate, a person with a cure, trying hard to persuade people to develop the prerequisite illness.

Since, as *Mental Health Consultants* shows, much can be achieved through "gentle persuasion," there is clearly room for sensitive missionary efforts. Moreover, this is true throughout the indoor practice of mental health as represented in the clinic, hospital, and consulting office. However, just as the limitations of gentle persuasion in the one-to-one treatment situation argued for a dynamic psychotherapy (this as long ago as the nineteenth century, when Freud abandoned hypnosis and the laying on of hands), so what cannot be thus achieved in the community would seem to argue for dynamic consultation.

Dynamic consultation, however, like dynamic psychotherapy, is difficult — not methodologically, but personally. The neutrality it requires means that its practitioners have to renounce the luxury of getting people to change in ways that make them, the practitioners, feel better. Its objective is not This or That, but the freedom compounded of outer possibility and inner option to elect either. The consultant's client may make a choice other than that which the consultant needs, likes, or deems wise, leaving the consultant with what may feel like the poor satisfaction of having helped create an option only to see its potential frittered away. But the alternative may really prove to be worse. The spirit that pioneered the West, for all its achievements, was, after all, a bit hard on the Indians.

# REFERENCE

Griffith, C., and Libo, L. (1968). *Mental Health Consultants: Agents of Community Change.* San Francisco: Jossey-Bass.

# 3

# The *Seelsorger* in Rural Vermont

Akin to "Cultures in Conflict," this is a meditation on working with people in such a way that they, in turn, find the work usable and then useful. It can be read — as it was written — with a broader view: are we iatrogenically hindering people from finding the deep delight and special virtue of "the examined life" (Socrates thought the unexamined life not to be worth living). From that question one can quickly come to another: of that which the analyst thinks and does, what is form and what function: what necessary, what part of the cultural artifacts we have inherited?

One day I was sent a patient, not someone indigenous to the community, with the counsel: "She has a hole in her ego a mile wide and ten deep. What she needs is support. Help her figure out how to get meals on the table." After a half-hour this person, sobbing heartbrokenly, prepared to leave, saying, "I had hoped for better from you, I had hoped you could see that I am perfectly well capable of getting meals on the table when I am capable of it."

I think people of all sorts are perfectly well capable of having a nice analysis if one becomes capable of making it usable and useful, thereby assisting them to be capable of it. In the part of *The Question of Lay Analysis* (1926) in which Freud alluded to the *Seelsorger* function, he was in some despair about how good a therapeutic instrumentality psychoanalysis was going to become. I wonder if he was not about to notice that the analyst's "therapeutic" purposes can ruin the analysis

23

for the patient. And not alone because they bring countertransference into the matter — but because they introduce the analyst as a
member of a culture to which he attempts, through what he calls an
alliance, to acculturate the patient as part of a pair.

Lawrence S. Kubie used to say: "Each thing you do, everything
you say, must be designed to rescue the analysis from the repetition
compulsion, yours as much as your patient's. Now. . . ."

---

Our nation's foreign policy has been much in the news in recent years,
and as I have followed the debates, I have gained the conviction that
there is an analogy to be drawn between it and the foreign policy of the
mental health community. In the national sphere there is on the one
side the fervor of the Dulles–Rusk position, with its difficulties
concerning neutrality and its missionary attitude toward cultural
differences. This establishment, if it can be called that, appears to have
in mind certain goods — self-determination and autonomy — which it
wants for the world, so much so that it seems at times to such critics of
the establishment as Senator Fulbright that in the name of fulfilling
what it takes to be universal aspirations, it positively wishes to impose
these goods. The antiestablishmentarianists hold that to want these
goods for our sister nations really means wanting things *from* them,
thus constituting, in Fulbright's phrase, the exercise of an arrogance of
power. They observe that to enforce self-determination is a contradiction in terms, while to impose autonomy constitutes a usurpation of it.

Let me now assume (in order to pursue the analogy) that a
community, in the sense of the mental health community, can also
have a foreign policy. In its essence, the practice of mental health
undertakes with willing people a study of their motivations. Now, of
course, anyone can undertake this with anyone else — friend with
friend, spouse with spouse, bartender with customer, hairdresser with
client — but we have come to learn that the success of this undertaking
is intimately related to a particular stance on the part of the one who
would assist the other. The assistant, we have learned, is far and away
most useful, perhaps only useful, when he can manage not to take on
the subject of the self-study of motivations as an important object for
his libidinal-aggressive needs, when, that is, he wants next to nothing
for or from the subject, save, perhaps, some recompense for his time
and energy.

In this disposition, the assistant, as representative of the mental health community, has no foreign policy. His commitment extends only to the goals of the process in which he collaborates: the fullest revelation of motives and the management of their vicissitudes, past and present. This would be simple enough were the subject's commitment so uniform and enduring as the assistant's, but, of course, it is not. There will be times, and for very long periods indeed, when the subject will propose to change the contract in such a way that, rather than merely studying the subject's motivations, the assistant can be induced to collaborate in fulfilling them. But with tact, sensitivity, and very considerable skill, the assistant will help the subject use these times as a rich source of material for the investigation which prompted the formal alliance. His neutrality toward the subject, his capacity not to need anything for him or from him, and hence his ability to both forswear and withstand invitations to fulfillment, will prove to be the assistant's, and therefore the subject's, greatest asset.

This, it would seem, goes without saying. But let us take a second look. Let us look at the assistant in four of his professional aspects: as a psychotherapist, as a community mental health specialist, as a promulgator of findings, and as a social programmer.

As a psychotherapist, he is a functionary who wishes to regard himself as one whose purpose it is to cure and whose work, therefore, is with ill people called patients. His desire to cure he communicates by calling himself a therapist and by dealing in such terms as diagnosis, symptomatology, pathology, illness, cure, improvement, and change. People are thereby warned that this personage, this representative of the mental health community, does not merely wish to assist in the investigation of motivations but to bring or return ill people to something called normal, for illness, pathology, health, and cure all imply norms, statistical norms or inherent norms, or both. And it cannot but follow that a community, representatives of which intend to treat ill people, will seek to have them obtain or change to a norm. The purpose of the undertaking, then, is no longer self-study, or even self-study for purposes of autonomously established objectives, but self-study as a means of physician-induced change toward physician-held norms. The doctor wants something for his patient. The doctor has an objective. There are goods and values involved.

For the potential self-surveyor of his motives, this, of course, means that first he has to be sick and then he has to want to become better. "Better" is the accurate word, since it encompasses both a return to health and a return to social virtue. This is nowhere clearer than in the process the patient goes through when deliberating about seeking psychotherapeutic assistance, for a central feature of his considerations is the question of whether he is bad and can help himself or sick and cannot. Fortunate is he whose manner of compromise formation lends itself to symptoms that are ego-alien. For the characterological types and many of the so-called borderlines who lack clearly alien elements in their make-up, this debate can become agonizing and endless.

The logical inference for people, then, is that their motives will not come to be merely described, that is, identified and defined, but altered, with good ways of being or behaving implied or prescribed.

It has been but a step from this missionary zeal for health to the fuller blossoming of our foreign policy as exemplified by our other professional activities. For the representative of the community in his second professional aspect, as a community mental health specialist, we have the pattern whereby some people — clergy, police, physicians, parents, or teachers — are instructed in goods so that from them the mental health specialist may exact behaviors deemed good for third parties — parishioners, patients, children, and so on.

As promulgators of findings, it is clear that the profession has in mind ideals for the socialization of the presocial — the child, for example — and for the dis-social — those adults, such as the drug-taking student, whose behavior violates institutional or social canons. Our advice and consent on these matters we convey to the layman as we advise on the proper modes of child rearing, family management, and institutional organization.

But our prescriptive role is nowhere clearer than in our fourth professional aspect, our role in interventive programs. This can be illustrated by taking the "Head Start" program as an example. We begin, of course, with a group called culturally deprived or disadvantaged. It is not seen that this group has other ways of doing things, another culture and social organization, another form of personality patterning; rather, it is seen that this group, lacking our own folkways and mores, is considered deprived or, more sociocentrically still, disadvantaged; and so we want things for them. Sometimes it is clear — almost — that we want things from them: to get off the streets and stop making trouble, or off the relief rolls and stop costing us our hard-earned money, or to stop their profligate, impulse-serving behavior so that we can stop contending with our unconscious envy.

An article in *Psychiatry* argues for making our disadvantaged socially competent. The author, Thomas Gladwin (1967), a consultant to

NIMH, reporting on a conference held at the Institute, offers as one of the conferees' conclusions the following: "In order to become effective the psychologically inadequate person not only needs to relieve his anxieties and correct his maladaptive behaviors, but also to learn alternative success-oriented ways of behaving in society" (p. 37). Note the words: effective . . . inadequate . . . correct . . . maladaptive . . . success-oriented . . . society.

Shared countertransferences have a way of escaping notice. If, however, we apply the theories we have learned so well, we shall not miss the meaning of these gratuitous assumptions. Since we know that in psychoanalysis Freud designed a procedure in which the assisted, systematic self-study of what Hartmann has called "self-deception and its motivations" could and would result in the autonomy of the ego, why need we ask more or other by way of objectives? Why do we not simply offer self-determination of outcome or autonomy in undertaking? What is our need to cure or save, rescue, socialize, or acculturate? Our own theories tell us that such zealousness conceals an ambivalence about our own ideals. And since we know that in wanting things from others we seriously compromise the very process which would provide them, we are, moreover, acting out that ambivalence. Were it possible for social systems to be interpreted in the same fashion as psychic systems, we would recognize ourselves as unconsciously impeding precisely those ends we ostensibly seek. As Eissler (1963) puts it:

> The analyst must never become an evangelist: insight into psychological processes, to the analyst an end in itself, is usually aspired to by patients for purely therapeutic reasons. It is one of the many apparent paradoxes I have encountered . . . that just those patients who are less interested in their therapy, but become absorbed in the delight of increasing their knowledge of self have, in my experience, a better chance of recovering from their psychopathology than those who adhere to what psychoanalysis offers at the social level — a therapy. [pp. 461–462]

Bion makes the same point in a slightly different context. Speaking of the psychoanalytic investigation of the delinquent, he writes:

> I suggest that the lack of success will continue so long as the investigation is carried out with the predisposition to see the object of the investigation as a "delinquent," no matter what his life may have been, and to do so with the humorless attitude that seems to be inescapable

from having suffered a psychoanalytic training course. [Bion, 1966, p. 576]

Carrying out his discussion of such predispositions, Bion adds:

There may well be vertices which are not regarded by the group as respectable and therefore of which it needs to be unconscious. The group tendency would be to foster unconsciousness in other groups of these defects in itself while claiming their discovery elsewhere. [p. 576]

To my mind, the key term in Bion's observation is "to foster unconsciousness." I take it to suggest that in order to preserve certain hopes of our own — and to keep them immune from self-study — we must find people who share them (colleagues) and people who have reciprocals to them (patients). The agreement, tacit or otherwise, is to maintain a system within which our hopes will not be jeopardized. But to do so means that we cannot examine with those who consult us their motivation for undertaking their work with us because we cannot examine our own motivation in doing that work. In our domestic policy, then, a peculiar and not altogether helpful situation obtains.

But that is the least of it. The greater by far is that such a domestic policy obviously calls for a foreign policy which has the effect of excluding those who will not play things our way. In this context our enemies are those who, like the little boy in "The Emperor's New Clothes," can see through us by virtue of not sharing our predilections: the so-called hard-to-reach and the "disadvantaged." Our failure to foster unconsciousness in them causes us to need to "help" them toward a position of common investment in our ideals, for only their willingness to share our hopes and the unconsciousness which protects those hopes will preserve the nonphysical sanctions that a community can exert.

## A PARTICULAR COMMUNITY

These remarks have been in the nature of a prologue to the introduction of a particular rural Vermont community and an alternate mental health function, that of the *Seelsorger*.

In 1962, I moved to a village of some 400 people through which, five years earlier, I had passed at tourist speed on my way to a vacation in

New Hampshire and Maine. I remember wondering at the time what
it might be like to live in so tiny and isolated a village with its
paint-flaked houses, collapsed porches, and tumbledown barns. I
could almost smell the dank, musty air of the interiors, see the faded
floral wallpaper hanging from the cracked plaster of the walls and the
water-stained ceilings. Against the backdrop of the conversation in the
car, in which my wife and the friends who were traveling with us were
exchanging the sort of gossip members of English departments of
universities do, I briefly mused whether someone like myself could
ever live and work in so lost and ramshackle a community: I could just
see the farmers and their crusty wives lining up for their consultations!
And yet, I was struck by what their inner experiences of life must be
like, given the desolation, the isolation, and the decay of their
surroundings. With the once-cleared pastures gone over to bracken
and thorn and the hills more scrub than timber, there was nothing even
of the Eugene O'Neill neoclassical about it. It was as if everything had
collapsed downward upon itself, and no proud tragedies could be
played again.

Five years later I moved from a high-rise apartment building on
Chicago's lakefront into a house in that village.

The farmers, by then mostly ex-farmers, and their wives did not
line up for my services, nor did anyone else. In five years there I
received only two self-initiated requests for my services. Fortunately,
I was paid out of NIMH grant funds. The life I had envisioned for this
village was not materially different from the life I found. Granted that
I had painted the scene with a fairly broad brush, if I had exaggerated
at all, it was in overextending the uniformity of what I had assumed.
People in some instances were livelier than I had believed, in rather
more instances depressed in ways that beggared my earlier imaginings.

It did not take me long to learn that my presence in the area was not
to be greeted with impassivity. People were actively indignant. The
foreign policy of the mental health community both preceded and
accompanied me, and when I moved in, the clear implication of my
presence was that I was out to burrow from within, to take over and
change the villagers. It took no time at all, in this land of the nine-party
line, for people to identify me with a conspiracy, although opinions
varied as to whether the conspiracy was Communist (like in Moscow)
socialist (like in Washington), or hippie (like in the college with which
I was affiliated). In any case, not only was I alien, I was inimical.

At first, of course, I put all of this down to transference, an unconscious desire of the population to be taken charge of, entered, raided, freed, and raped, against which, naturally, were pitted part of the superego and most of the ego forces of resistance. And, indeed, there is no doubt in my mind that this was in fact the case; but what I only gradually—and I may say painfully—came to realize was that before this fantasy I was helpless because it was not, in truth, a fantasy. The mandate of my grant called for the inculcation of mental health principles and practices in the life and schools of this and neighboring communities. And being an emissary, a sort of CIA-diplomat with an embassy appointment in this foreign land, I was presumably supposed to see to the salvation of these lost tribes, this anachronistic culture.

That the people understood this better than I is natural. It is hard to see one's own values as values; to oneself they are truths. But since I had no alternative but to learn, I learned. I learned well enough, at any rate, to abandon my mandate.

Having abandoned my mandate, I lost, too, something of my role and function, which, of course, catapults one into a small identity crisis, ideology being an important element in identity. To resolve that crisis, I looked about for something to replace my clinical-psychotherapist-educator role and function and remembered Freud's notion of the *Seelsorger*.

Freud, you may recall, was ever reluctant to give up the idea that in psychoanalysis he had constructed a method of study of motives and their means which incidentally, as it were, also had effects that could be regarded as therapeutic. In *The Question of Lay Analysis* (1926), he wrote not only to argue the more familiar point but to reaffirm his conviction that the analytical process need not be restricted to the medical or therapeutic model. He conjured as an alternative the idea of the *Seelsorger,* a kind of secular, nonreligious, or lay pastorate in which the analyst simply assists his neighbors in the care and tending of their psychic life. No doubt Freud agreed with Socrates that the unexamined life is not worth living, no matter the precise state of one's intrapsychic organization.

The model is not a very good one, and Freud did not pursue it very far. But it does evoke a posture toward a function which I prefer to regard as the consulting function. The consultant, like the *Seelsorger*, is an assistant to those who are in business for themselves, are capable of doing the work, but who require or want the advantages of specialized

expertise. Just as the consulting physician does not undertake to cure
the consultee physician's patient, so the consultant *Seelsorger* does not
undertake the care of his neighbors but assists them to take care of
themselves. In any case, a function like that seemed a legitimate one to
me in my Vermont work, and I trusted that my neighbors would view
it in that light as well. Certainly I could not ask or expect them to
become patients for my benefit and go through all the prerequisites we
commonly require of those with whom we work; I could not, that is,
require that they conclude that something was amiss, require that they
assume their difficulties to be rectifiable, require that they must feel
their difficulties to be germane to what our profession concerns itself
with, require that they feel they were unable to change themselves,
require that they must be willing to change, must share our presumed
loathing for the way they were and our valuation of the way they wish
to be, and require that they must believe that we have the wherewithal
to convert their inability into willfulness and then into willingness.

The question then became a technical one: could one conduct
analytic consultation, arrange some forms of group procedure, on
behalf of people who were not motivated as we understand that term
today, given, that is, our foreign policy?

Theoretically I saw no problem. Freud's method provides, in the
transference, an intrinsic motivation, and in the splitting of the
transference into the so-called working alliance, a second source of
motivation. Too, resistances also split, following part of the transference into the alliance through introjections and identifications and
opposing the other aspect of the transference in the more usual sense
of the term "resistance." And, so far as I knew, the duality of motivation is the sole dynamic required for analytic consultation on motives
and their vicissitudes, whether conducted individually or in groups.

Empirically I saw that transference and resistance were already
present, if in negative form. This meant to me that the structure of the
situation was appropriate. The next question was how to bring the two,
structure and theory, into propinquity. Clearly, one major requirement toward that end would have to be my making plain that I had no
foreign policy. Since logical inference that I had was backed up by
transference, against which was pitted "resistance" of a very high and
socially organized sort, words would not do at all. I should have to
demonstrate my stand. Still, in the face of the threat and the costs
involved in interaction with me, this was manifestly impossible. One

cannot ask defenses to be relinquished unless there are alternatives for these defensive needs. I had, therefore, first to provide such alternatives if later I proposed to interpret the defenses.

Of course, what I am saying of this rural Vermont community is true in every psychotherapy. Something has first to make defenses dispensable. What we are accustomed to using to achieve this is amelioration; for example, in hindering mobility by asking the patient to lie on the couch, we ameliorate for him the threat that an upsurge of impulse may, among other things, cause him to harm us. In like ways, the milieu created in institutional care, in a hospital, for example, when well thought through, creates a powerful adjunct to interpretive work by creating alternatives for defensive operations or by diminishing the strength of the impulses.

I had, then, first to create, or at least to sketch in, the rudiments of the milieu in the out-of-doors of the community. Needless to say, it took me a good deal of time to figure out how to do this, and in the end I cannot say that I managed it as successfully as I might have. But as in all milieus, matters of time and timing, inclusion and exclusion, organization of activity, example and demonstration, had to be arranged and meshed. While attempting to do so, I remained aware that amelioration is worse than useless — it is destructive — when it creeps into the range that properly belongs to the consultative process.

Since generalities are confusing, let me take the problem of initiative as an example. Our profession is used to yielding the initiative to its patients or clients. But need can be very great indeed without there being corresponding motivation, and thus, I decided that, just as one may visit people on rounds in the hospital, the *Seelsorger* may visit people on rounds in the community. If one is rejected, one is rejected. One's narcissism need not be wounded. On the other hand, to maintain the initiative beyond the point at which one's consultee can gracefully assume it is an expression of countertransference or ignorance and no longer a useful amelioration. Thus, it was necessary to construct a program in which initiative would be gradually relinquished by the professional and passed over to others. Because of the very strong feelings toward me, I employed and trained several local people who made the rounds, calling on everyone. This ameliorated the fear of being singled out that characterizes small communities in which individual autonomy is reposed so largely in the social matrix, and, at the same time, this procedure demonstrated that I was not interested simply in certain sorts of people (patients, for example) but in everyone. We called to ask how life was going and whether we could be useful. In calling, our purpose was to demonstrate what the assisted self-study of motives is all about.

People know all about our values, all about our forms and formats, all about our ideology, but next to nothing about how we function. It was this that we showed them. And when we did it well, it made a very great deal of sense to people.

Space prohibits my outlining this overture phase and the rest of the ameliorative measures in any detail, and indeed I am sure the reader can imagine what these must entail as people, safe from having to ask for anything, struggle to tell us or, as often, show us, what they want but cannot accept and what they forever accept but no longer want, and of all the puzzling and frightful things in us and in themselves.

As we got better at this, we succeeded in enabling forty percent of the families in the area to "send" one or more of their members to consultation groups. (Dealing in terms of families is an amelioration, as is offering groups as a context for consultation.) These groups met with me weekly for an hour and a half at the members' homes with the object of discussing whatever the members felt a psychologist could be useful with. People might talk of themselves, their children, their spouses, or anything else; but what we studied was motives. The groups were made up by design of "everyone," of, that is, an absolutely faithful cross-section of the community, something I checked out with census indices. I worked with the poor and the better-off, the educated and the dropout, the farmer and the truckdriver, and the storekeeper and the mechanic, with the married and single, older and younger, clinically sick and enviably well.

I suspected that the very first session would prove to be the crucial one. In it I should have to accomplish three major tasks: I should have to pass the tests made of my intentions, and so enable resistances to be lowered; I should have to enable internal resistances to come into active conflict with wishes for some benefit; and, finally, I should have to be of use in interpreting the resulting inner conflict in ways that people found meaningful and interesting. As I pondered these inherent requirements, it seemed to me that I should have to work fairly actively, even deeply, with people I had either not yet met or was far from knowing well. But active, deep work can be very frightening unless a collection of people can first be helped to hold and strengthen their natural proclivity to identify with one another. Since my own theory (Boris 1968, 1970) was that the development of an alliance through means of orientation, contract, and other procedures designed to elicit some identification on the part of the members with the consultant would serve only to weaken the group members' allegiance to each other, I decided I should have to forgo any such efforts. Rather, I reasoned, I would have to adopt the exclusively interpretative stance Bion developed, but adapt his procedure of referring only to group phenomena in the situation I was working with, in which motivation would not be sufficient to offset "flight" reactions (Bion 1961). I suspected that the material brought in by the members would soon center on the transference preoccupations of the group and that I would have to touch on them in displaced form. Active work is experienced as assaultive, and though the experience of feeling assaulted can also be interpreted, so much interpretation induces passivity, with some chance of ego regression. I concluded, therefore, that it would be useful to proceed by exemplifying how analyses of experience can be made. So much, then, for methodology.

The next matter to consider was the content that would likely preoccupy the groups. I have already referred to the population as being of a depressive cast. If I were to succeed in passing the tests of my intentions, and thus decrease the need to take arms against the projections with which I had been filled, then the conflicts that result in depression would be activated. If a depressive posture became paramount, narcissistic issues and introjective solutions would become rife and make for an initial session that held relatively little personal meaning for the participants. I, therefore, had to find a way to alleviate depressive experiences through interpretations of oral issues.

It naturally took some time to translate these rather abstract schemata into passably sensitive work with groups, but I was benefited by having thought this much out ahead of time, for I then could concentrate more closely on the material and experiences I was exposed to in the sessions themselves. No two groups were alike, of course, but there was a pattern to them that was not out of range of my anticipations.

The eight or twelve people gathered in the living room or kitchen of one of the members' houses would, as I entered, have been idly chatting, each making himself known to the rest. Soon after I got seated, but not so soon as to suggest a lack of collective self-sufficiency, a silence would fall and the women present would look to me. The men would usually look out of a window or at a magazine. Regarding the women's gesture as an invitation to take over, I would decline, remarking, instead, that no one seemed to want to begin.

Since plainly the people present felt that in putting themselves at my disposal they had begun, my remark was treated with some surprise and annoyance. But in time someone would begin again, often by asking what they were supposed to do; were they supposed to ask questions or what? To this, I generally replied that I was getting the feeling that the group was taking charge of me in order to tell me to take charge, as if there were some trouble about doing what one wants to do.

After whatever small space of time it took for the group to agree to ignore that comment, someone would go ahead and ask a question: "What should you do about a four-year-old who. . . ." I often had the feeling that asking such a question was the last thing the group would do for me, that once it was answered, the questioner and the others would go home and never return. Beginning seemed to mean that the people present wanted something from me, just as if, had I begun, it would have signaled some wants of my own. Since wanting was, for them, a pretty bad business, it meant that something even more urgent had overcome their powerful reluctance. Perhaps it was an answer from me that would at last indicate the nature and extent of my ideology, show what I thought of them, how even I assessed their intelligence and experience, and so reveal what I really wanted of them.

Aware of these feelings and their intensity, I knew that, were I to fail to speak in order to increase their need of me, they would recoil violently from need altogether, turn briefly to one another, and soon angrily leave.[1] So, I would ask what the questioner did about a four-year-old who. . . . When she told me, whatever she told me, I would ask how it worked. She would say it worked fine, and I would say, great.

There would be a brief silence while the group considered my hands-off attitude. Then there would be a further spate of questions, with some cross-discussion. The feel of things at this juncture was quite different. In the earlier segment, my fantasy was that it was as if the group would rather make the breast bad and suffer persecution

---

[1]In Bion's terms, a (barely) dependent group would turn abruptly into a flight group (Bion 1966).

from it than feel it to be good and abjectly hunger for it. Now my fantasy would be that it had proved less dangerously bad, but elusive, even tantalizing, and that it brought out the impulse to bite at it with a barrage of questions. There was a livelier atmosphere, but one still cautious about whether I in my turn could be made to bite. Often the questions that the group would settle on would concern feeding situations with their children.[2]

In the situation portrayed in the questions and cross-discussions, the conflicts were experienced as a struggle between parent and child, sometimes between two parents and/or the child. Here is where I opted to accept the externalizations and displacements and deal first with the manifest form of the conflicts rather than directly relating them to the transference in the group to me. Thus, when (and only when) I was invited to give an opinion, I would explicate the two sides of the struggle, first in terms of the anxiety, then in terms of the impulses. I would remark that the struggle was about finding a compromise between the parties to the conflict, adding that it seemed that, even when compromises were not very satisfying, they were better than the conflict itself. In framing these analyses, I did much of my thinking out loud so that the group could see how I derived my formulations. I generally treated the anxieties very seriously, but in stating the thrust of the wishes, I dramatized the conflict, exaggerating the impulses slightly, as a way of offering a manic icing to the interpretation. People could then smile or laugh or argue provocatively at the same time as they seriously assimilated the interpretation. After some of this, usually by way of clarification of what I had said, I would often allude, as if in analogy, to the here-and-now group situation and speak of a reluctance to "taste" strange people, the inclination to clam up, mixed feelings about swallowing what I had to say, feelings of being fed up or, the reverse, feelings about what one can do to others.

Interpretations at this level, when they do not imply the need to change one's disposition or behavior, exert a fascination for people, though, at times, an unholy fascination. When the session ended (I would ask, not say, when it did) and I left the house, the people would

---

[2]One group of six couples were so incensed by my opening remark, which in that group was, "Who wants to begin?", that they ignored it and me, talking only in cliques to one another or leafing through magazines. When they finally did begin, they raised questions concerning kids who regularly held their breath until they turned blue. Four of the couples had such children.

remain behind. Then, together, they would organize a collective response to the experience, orienting one another to positions from which they could accept the next encounter without intolerable shame, anxiety, or guilt. Often they would close ranks for a frontal attack — a denial of what I had said or an elicitation of what they wished to require of me. That strength allowed me to continue the intensity of my work, until I sensed that the group could do a fair bit of its own work.

I worked somewhat differently from the way others in our field do because I worked not only with a culturally different population but also under different contractual terms. People in my groups did not think of themselves as patients, nor did they consider themselves in any other category, except as citizens of the towns they lived in and as members of a family. They sought not cure but proficiency in self-understanding, not relief but competence in understanding the life situations with which they were intimately concerned. Accordingly, I made efforts to enable that motivation to endure, for truth is anguishing until it is firmly enough established, until, that is, the blessing of coming close to the heartfeltness of things repays anguish. When that happened, I could become the passive consultant, the role to which we are all more accustomed.

It is a deeply meaningful experience when women, for example, talk about their kitchen floors and gradually come to see that this has to do with their bodies, and then talk of the issue in those terms — with a man, in a group — without first having to become sick nor, in the end, having to become well. It is a meaningful experience, and also in its way an astonishing one, as I think back on that initial ride through my village those years ago and consider in juxtaposition how these depressed and isolated people found it possible to come into groups with me and came to call these weekly events their "mental hygiene parties."

## REFERENCES

Bion, W. R. (1961). *Experiences in Groups*. New York: Basic Books.
———— (1966). Book review: Eissler's *Medical Orthodoxy and the Future of Psychoanalysis*. *International Journal of Psycho-Analysis*. 47:575–579.
Boris, H. N. (1968). Orientation and contract in group psychotherapy. Unpublished manuscript.

_____ . (1970). The medium, the message and the good group dream. International Journal of Group Psychotherapy 20:91-98.

Eissler, K. R. (1963). On the psychoanalytic concept of cure. *Psychoanalytic Study of the Child* 18:424-463. New York: International Universities Press.

Freud, S.(1926). The question of lay analysis. Postscript. *Standard Edition* 20:251-258.

Gladwin, T. (1967). Social competence and clinical practice. *Psychiatry* 30:30-38.

# 4

# The Medium, the Message, and the Good Group Dream

By now I was able to move in — slow zoom to medium shot — on the group. Two matters interested me equally. One was the question of what sort of work one could usefully do if, to make the event usable, one couldn't ask people to talk or work or otherwise cooperate. The second was what people might do with the space left for them. The reason, after all, for the analyst to be self-effacing is not to hide himself, but to create room for the devolution of the patient into the encounter. If one left people to their own devices, by restricting one's own, what would happen?

It is very peaceful not to have to lead groups (or psychotherapies) or otherwise conduct them. One doesn't have to begin the encounter by leaving the false impression that one knows how it could or should work, an illusion which itself might benefit from perusal. People who know each other — for example, staff or residents who work to-gether — need, they often feel, to be careful of what they let each other know. So much do they wish to be singled out in what they feel would be a good way that they are terrified to be singled out in a bad. Can they be left their anonymity and still discover what they are like when they are with others?

---

The medium, according to Marshall McLuhan, is at once the message and the massage. He was, of course, speaking of books and television.

But he might have been speaking of groups as well, for in groups, too, the medium is contrived, at one and the same time, to both express and exemplify, convey and elicit.

In groups the medium is behavior — more precisely, enaction. I do not have in mind here the verbal-nonverbal distinction. Rather, I am speaking of the whole of behavior, including verbal and nonverbal elements, as being the medium by which groups attempt to achieve what they are after. If, then, we focus less on what people in groups say than on what they do, we become the beneficiaries of a great deal of information concerning what groups are about.

Using this fund of information, I shall discuss the behavior of groups as representing a collective dream from which, as I shall show, it is possible to reconstruct the latent wishes of the group, or what I term the Good Group Dream.

Consider that we are now sitting with a group, quietly absorbed in the proceedings. Part of our attention is wide open to the group, the remainder to what, in response to the group, is occurring in ourselves. Someone is speaking; others are listening; still others are in various modes of abstraction or inattention. As the speaker concludes, someone enters a parallel experience or opinion. Someone else disagrees. A fourth becomes his ally. A fifth then comes in, perhaps to join the fray, perhaps to take a middle course. And so it goes. But sooner or later a silence falls and all eyes turn to us. Clearly something is now expected of us, but what? We pause, hesitate, summoning and collecting our thoughts.

My own experience, at moments like these, is in the form of a fantasy. I feel like the spectator at a play who is suddenly given to realize that, unbeknownst to himself — perhaps before he entered the theatre or during a momentary lapse in attention — a part in the play has been assigned to him. And now he has not only missed his cue line, he is holding up the play. It is as if no one can proceed until he has assumed his role.

But even while playing host to this fantasy, the group seems to have resumed its own activity. On our part, we feel some relief. Yet we cannot quite get resettled on our observing seat. We have been served notice that something is expected of us in this arena and very likely we shall be called upon again.

And indeed, as we tune into the proceedings once again, we find that the group is essentially repeating its previous activity, only — in the words of the song—"a little bit louder and a little bit worse." If we thereupon get the feeling that the group assumes that some lack of subtlety and perception on our part was responsible for our poor performance previously, we are not likely to be much mistaken. For not only is the activity a bit more strident and insistent, like the second ringing of an alarm clock, but, sure enough, it is soon followed by another requiring silence.

This time not all eyes turn to us. Some appear to be averted as if to spare us witnesses to our humiliation; others are turned away as if to discount expectation. But even so there is a signaling silence, more forceful than the first.

At this juncture we are likely to be able to see that the group is acting as if it had a theory—almost a conviction—that if they do such-and-such, as they have, and if they say thus-and-so, which they have, then we, in turn, will come forth with a contribution of our own.

Now, to be sure, the group is not reporting this at the moment, though if we hesitate any longer it may make itself more explicit. Rather, it is signaling it, as if in mime. Its expectation seems to be that we know the theory as well as they. And, of course, we do. We know it as well as we know that someone who finishes a spoken sentence without lowering the inflection of his voice proposes to continue speaking, but when he lowers his inflection and provides a caboose on the end of his train of speech by ducking his chin and lowering his head, he is done.

So, then, let us suppose that we do comply with the group's theory and venture some remarks. Suppose, for example, we say exactly that we have inferred, namely, that the group is acting as if it were host to a theory that when it does such-and-such and says so-and-so, interpolating here both mode of action and verbal theme, something of value will be forthcoming from its therapist. Since most people in therapy groups do, after all, come for our assistance in understanding their behavior, this seems a reasonably valuable contribution.

The people in the present group, however, do not seem to share this view. At best, they appear lukewarm toward our remarks. Some, indeed, seem quite stunned; it is as if what we said were irrelevant, incompetent, and immaterial. And that would be putting it politely. Others seem actively mistrustful, as if victims of a practical joke, and a bad one at that. One or two people seem inclined to regard our comment as a piece of grit in the clockwork, although perhaps one with a pearl concealed in it.

At the same time as they make their reception of our contribution evident to us, the members of the group are also taking stock of one another's reactions. This activity and its consequences will now begin to involve the group, for as they check one another out, each is likely to act on (or hope someone else will act on) what he finds. As we settle back to observe what ensues, we shall shortly see members acting as if the differences in reaction to our comment pose a threat. Efforts designed to change others in the direction of one's own or at least a common position will be made by various members of the group. It is quite as if the group shared the conviction that "united we stand, divided we fall."

Indeed, although there may be impassioned conflict, we shall soon gain the impression that the conflict is in the service of an attempt at union. As we listen, we may then come to the view that the group is acting as if it had two further aspects to its implicit theory: first, that there is great strength in numbers providing there is unanimity, but, second, that there is jeopardy in making a common cause which imperils one's own private theory about how things should be.

The basic problem for the members of the group at this point will therefore be that of finding a group common denominator which accounts for three factors: (1) what is wrong; (2) what will remedy the wrong; and (3) how to get from wrong to remedy.

Those who have felt tricked and abused will feel doubtful about looking to us for any further remedies and will advocate looking elsewhere, or developing self-sufficiency, or employing themselves in place of us as remedies. Those who felt us merely to be stupid and incompetent may either hold for giving us another chance at some other sort of problem or else advocate, usually through example, some other means of delivering both message and massage. Those who are convinced that a pearl lies within the grit may empearl our comment by deprecating their own ingratitude and their competence to receive it.

Each, and such other exemplified prescriptions that may emerge, will be in effect advocating their own characteristic (and characterological) means for realizing their dreams of group therapy.

Teachers of English call such sentences as "Do that" or "Come along," "you-understood" sentences, meaning that the subject of the sentence is so clearly the pronoun "you" that the speaker can omit it. As we listen to the interaction that takes place in the group at this juncture, the object is equally so obvious that it seldom receives mention. The object is "us," the group's leader. And if we do not surmise that at the moment, we shall, directly the group leaves the huddle and lines up for its next play.

The so-called topic of discussion might be anything, but the thrust and meaning of the discussion will reflect the compromise solution that the group has come up with as the result of its efforts to find a common denominator. Let us suppose the topic is parents, bearing in mind it could as well be doctors, political leaders, children, people, bosses, or men. Whatever the topic, the *way* it is discussed will, as we listen, convey to us a message, as if it were a parable or a morality play.

We will know that parents fail children. We will also hear why parents fail children. This last will ascribe a motive that is designed to massage us. It may be calculated to invoke our guilt or our gratitude for the group's generosity. It may be contrived to summon our anxiety — for example, through tales of children leaving home — or to awaken our sympathy. Even so, there may be a minority report or dissenting opinion also offered, a verbal stick added on to the prevailing carrot, conveying that in some quarters the theory is that talking to us is simply a waste of breath.

Then, once again, silence will fall. I say "silence," but perhaps this time the group is wary and will no longer expose its expectations. Still, the silence will be audible within the talk, for at the point where, in a more optimistic group, silence might have fallen, there will be behind the talk a hollow, echoing sound that expresses the vacuum that we are to fill.

We are now in a position to infer that the group has found a common answer not only for how to get from wrong to remedy but for what the remedy is. From these inferences, it is a fairly simple matter to infer the group's diagnosis of what is wrong with it.

Were we to interpret all of this, we might say: "The group has acted as if it has a theory that if their parents had not failed them, and I would not fail but rather help them, then it would have abandoned and now still could abandon being angry and helpless and instead achieve good successes."

Were we, in fact, to say something like that, we could expect a fairly mixed reaction. There is likely to be some relief that we at last, if at least, see what is expected of us. And we could expect some vexation at the fact that our good understanding has failed to get translated into the requisite action. These are likely to be the primary reactions. Secondarily, we can expect to see reactions to the renewed conflict which our interpretation has posed for the group. In respect to this last, it is as if a fractious union (or management) has finally and painfully agreed among itself on a bargaining position and strategy, only to find the other party unresponsive.

But let us leave our particular group there and reflect further on what we have discerned so far. Groups, we inferred, act as if they had an "if this, then that" theory which included a contribution from the therapist that would satisfy some deficiency or rectify some defect the group felt itself to have. Moreover, we inferred that groups took certain means by which they hoped at once to convey a message and deliver a massage, both of which were calculated to elicit the requisite remedy from the therapist. The remedy wanted, furthermore, was something that would alleviate internally conflictful experiences.

On the other hand, people in groups are generally realistic enough to know — if not to appreciate — that hopes for such wishes are more dreams than certainties. In deference to that realization, I have found myself thinking of the unconscious wishes of the group as a Good Group Dream.

That Good Group Dream is for the membership of the group plus its leader to together constitute a utopian universe in which only perfect experiences take place. These perfect experiences are of two sorts, and in the basic version of the dream, the fulfillment of one sort is assigned to the group and the other to the leader or therapist.

As regards the first, each member dreams that the others will join him in a unanimity of viewpoint and a community of intention. This will, in turn, give him several fine experiences. It will prevent any apprehensiveness lest the other members, individually or collectively, gang up against or in rivalry with him. On the contrary, in that unity of purpose, they will, he hopes, lend him the strength of their numbers and the diversity of their special skills. Thus, given such a consanguinity, he need neither fear nor envy but can feel augmented by, and grateful for, such strengths as are represented in the group.

That divine unanimity also means that he will feel Right (in terms of conscience), True (in terms of consensual validity), and Good (in terms of ideals)—a state of self abrim with the value to which self-estimation can freely and unhesitantly flow. In this aspect of the dream each member is but part of an enlarged self, a kind of super-self, rich with quality and competence, untroubled by internal doubts. And in the dream members believe that such mutual identifications can occur through a process of condensation and distillation reminiscent of what Freud called the "dream work."

If the motto in that first portion of the dream is *e pluribus unum*, that for the portion of the dream involving of the therapist is *vive la différence*, for to the therapist is assigned the countervailing function of being the differentiated person present. The therapist, in the dream, is he who has the equipment, supplies, and willingness to fulfill the group's various libidinal needs. When they feel little and afraid, he is to be big and brave; when they are empty, he must be rich and full with succor; when they are combative, he must be yielding; and when they are excitedly defiant, it is for him to be excitedly (but not too excitedly) exacting. In short, he is cast as the perfect reciprocal to their each and every wish and sense of defect.

Each portion of the group's dream is designed to make possible the other. The group could not dream of such basic and manifold fulfillments from its relationship with the therapist were it not for the antidote to guilt, shame, and anxiety its perfect mutual identifications afforded it. On the other hand, it could not sacrifice the possibility of reciprocally differentiated relationships within the group—which must be sacrificed if identifications of such completeness are to be made— were it not for its good dreams of the therapist. Thus, only when the parts are together and in harmony can the whole Good Group Dream be realized.

Utopias, however, escape capture. The latent content of the dream must succumb to the intermixture of factors that compromise it. One man's meat turns out to be another's poison. Some members turn out to need to renounce pleasures to avoid pain, while others arrange compensatory alternations, and others still meld wish and guilt into what may seem unappealingly tepid compromises. The group must, therefore, evolve a manifest dream that accounts for the members' various primary urges, their special defensive preferences, their particular anxieties, their preferred cognitive and expressive styles, and their unique transference anlages.

At the same time, because the group's enactment of the dream so successfully discharges impulses, its nature and meaning and its

function as the source for the behavior that attempts to achieve it may
fail to become conscious. As therapists, therefore, we will choose not to
comply with, but rather bring to light, the function assigned us in the
dream. If, thereby, we too contribute to the dream's frustration, such
is the determination of the dreamers that in the face of each frustration
they will but elaborate a modified edition designed to prevail where the
previous ones have failed.

Let us now return to the group we left to pursue these thoughts.

We noted that the activity of the group proceeded in cycles. At one
point in the cycle of action, the group was preoccupied with assembling
and welding the components of what was to be a collective position.
This was to fulfill the group portion of the dream that calls for
unanimity. At the same time, each member had to advocate his own
view or combat another's in order to assure that his own individual
elements would be part of the collective dream. Much, if not most, of
this activity was implicit. People told of experiences, feelings, or
events. But each of these anecdotes had a moral. They were illustrative
of a thesis. The way they were told, moreover, was designed to have an
impact.

What was being worked out were such issues as whether parenting
was needed (the group could as well, we noted, have framed matters
in terms of men, doctors, bosses, etc.), and, if so, what kind. Then,
too, the group confronted the risk of disappointment or loss of
self-esteem. They determined the means by which the precisely
favorable response could be achieved: should it be earned, won, or
demanded, and by what measures? At length, these matters were
compromised and a collective edition of the dream drafted. It was as
though a repertory company had written or revised a script, and now,
secure in its common understanding of the purposes and thrust of a
scene, could turn from one another and, with each in his assigned
role, turn to play upon us. Then, when the scene ended, silence fell,
and we were expected to supply the response the scene was designed to
elicit.

Our response was, however, to locate the dream and its components — wish, anxiety, and defense — that lay within the action. As
interpretations do, this facilitates the group's capacity to narrate,
rather than dramatically enact, its dream, and in doing so, gain
distance from and conscious perspective on that dream. To be sure,
this narrative and analytic activity will only exist partially; even it will

soon find a place in the medium by which the group attempts to activate its dream. But in time the accumulative effect of interpretations by the therapist and responsive narrative by the group will enable the stuff of the group's dreams to be more evident to it and thus more susceptible to its will for conscious management.

# 5

# People's Fantasies in Group Situations

This was originally published as a chapter in a previous book, *Teaching Social Change* (Boris, Zinberg, and Boris 1976a). Though in a book previous even to that one, *The (Un)Examined Life* (Boris 1967) I had begun to try to formulate a theory about what happens in groups, I had not yet plucked myself free from thinking of the group as an entity instead of as a reification, indeed a fantasy. Even Bion, to whose work I was much indebted, had failed either to see or to note that the basic-most of the "Basic Assumptions" would have to be that there is such a thing as a group, out of (or in) which, only if assumed, could what he called the Basic Assumptions become activated.

(I sent Bion a version of this paper when it was almost incomprehensibly mired with one on "Hope" [1976b], and even when we met to go over things, neither of us referred to what almost immediately thereafter became obvious. But I wouldn't be surprised if that is how he worked.)

Once I was able to do away with the actuality of the group incarnate, it was possible to look into some of the functions the fantasy that there is such a thing as a group serves. It would — such is the "numbing sense of reality" of the group of which Bion wrote — be years later before it would dawn on me to wonder where the "genotype" for group formation might be held, a question that eventually took me to the notion of the PAIR.

This paper is also an attempt to understand the movement between the uses of the so-called inner and outer worlds of object relations relative to one another. I have not really followed up this idea of a field theory to the extent I think it deserves, though there is further elaboration of it in my *Passions of the Mind: Unheard Melodies* (1993).

---

In 1921 Freud presented his major essay on group psychology. Since he had not studied groups from the vantage point of the group psychotherapist, it was inevitable that his theory could only surmise the unconscious fantasies that are at the heart of psychoanalytic formulations. But, by the same token, it is all the more remarkable that Freud was able to replace the then current thinking concerning the group mind with dynamic and even genetic concepts and thereby lay the groundwork for a systematic psychoanalytic model. (For a detailed consideration of Freud's contributions, see Yalom's review, Yalom 1974.) Freud, moreover, never confined his treatment of any subject to one work. If taken together with formulations available, notably in his works, *Totem and Taboo* (1913), "On Narcissism" (1914), "Mourning and Melancholia" (1917), *The Future of an Illusion* (1927), *Civilization and Its Discontents* (1930) and *Moses and Monotheism* (1939), his basic work on groups gains in dimension and richness.

In the approximately fifty years following Freud's essay, major additions have been made to group theory. Perhaps chief among these are Kurt Lewin's, whose work opened the way for further insight into the phenomenology of groups, and H. S. Sullivan, whose treatment of the subject detailed the vital function of the group as introject in the establishment of the personality both phenomenologically and developmentally (Lewin 1948, Sullivan 1953).

Nor has there been a shortage of contributions from within the psychoanalytic group therapy movement itself. Redl (1945) and Buxbaum (1945) both presented important papers, and the work of Ezriel (1950), Slavson (1954–1972), Wolf and Schwartz (1962), Foulkes and Anthony (1965) and Scheidlinger (1968) has been helpful both to group theory and group therapy.[1] But among these it has been

---

[1]We are by no means referring to the entire works of any of these authors, as we are equally failing to mention other writers of value to the field. Yalom's (1970) work

Bion who made the most searching study of groups; his 1961 work attempts a thoroughgoing formulation both of group dynamics and, ultimately, of the meaning and function of those dynamics, particularly in terms of Kleinian theories of early object relations and their vicissitudes — a formulation to which he has continued to add, as in his 1970 work.

Perhaps paradoxically, the very scope and wealth of these contributions inexorably puts each of them into question. Theory is derived from data and then goes on to elucidate the data from which it arose. But in the very act of elucidation, the data change, invalidating theory. If theory is not to consist of rumor — of theory quoting theory as if the latter were fact — then theory must periodically return afresh, even naively, to the data.

Although this is necessary for any theory, it is particularly necessary for psychoanalytic theories. For in psychoanalysis the data are largely not in evidence. They must be inferred — reconstructed from behavior that is as much calculated to conceal as reveal. The hypotheses which attend to the labyrinthine transformations that people use to make their unbearable experiences more tolerable are psychoanalysis' major clinical tool. Solecisms in inference, as Glover in particular showed, merely add to the patient's repertoire of available transfigurations (Glover 1955).

Accordingly when, with thanks to support from the Ford Foundation, we found ourselves with the opportunity for studying more than twenty groups formally, at the same time bringing to bear our own previous and concurrent work with a variety of other groups, we elected to go back to the essentials. The question we posed ourselves was: When in what they take to be a group situation, what possibilities do people generally imagine there to be?

The nature of this question accounts for the approach we have taken in writing up the answers. Rather than offering modifications of or additional accretions to the theoretical formulations of the last half century, we make our formulations in a way that seeks to be all of a piece. As much as possible we have sought to make plain the inferential relationship our formulation bears to the data from which it is drawn. This process of thinking out loud, as it were, is designed to allow the

provides the interested reader with a far more just compendium of the range of contributors and contributions. See also the survey by Semrad and Day (1966).

reader to check our inferential derivations where need be. Some readers, for example, will find us seemingly neglectful of member–member relationships, transferential or otherwise. They will want to examine closely why we have come to regard this as secondary or even tertiary among the possibilities people seem to see in group situations.

For much the same reason we have attempted not to transpose terms from previous theoretical treatments to our own inferences. Instead we attempt to describe what we see. If the reader then says, "That is 'identification' of which they are speaking," we prefer this to having spoken of "identification," only to have the reader wonder whether we are here echoing Freud's or some other use of the term.

People in the groups we have studied speak of "making a group." By that they seem to mean finding or making manifest a good deal in common, each with the others. *Their* theory seems to be that there is such a thing as a group, and that a group may be contrived if people make evident much in common. The energy and persistence they show in making a group suggests, moreover, that a group is a very valuable thing to have.

At first blush there seems nothing very remarkable in that theory, held by the people we have studied. But if we venture to examine it more closely, it begins to appear rather more remarkable.

The first matter one notices is the extent to which the beliefs are shared. No one seems to challenge either the belief that there is such a thing as a group or the belief that the manifestation of things in common can possibly out-measure the differences of every sort and variety that, in actuality, exist among the people present.

That no one challenges these beliefs certainly bespeaks the fact that these beliefs are held in common. But that it takes more than these commonly held beliefs, as suggested by the efforts to make or find things in common, indicates that the degree to which things in common out-measure differences occupies their attention as well.

It seems, therefore, that a group exists as a potential state, which can be realized when the people comprising it find more in common than the differences that separate them.

This again seems commonplace — until we reckon more closely with the differences. These are of age, sex, marital status, occupation, background, temperament, physique, cast of mind — the list threatens to become endless.

What similarities, therefore, could possibly out-measure the differences? It is plain that actual similarities cannot out-measure the actual differences unless a collusive blind eye is turned to them. Similarity, we have to conclude, like beauty, is in the eye of the beholders: only insofar as all present elect to regard the fact that they are fellow somethings — e.g., human beings — as more important than their limitless differences, can a group, as the participants conceive of it, be said to exist.

If that is the case, the belief cannot be faulted: all present *are* human beings. Yet one senses that such a common denominator is not really what the people present have in mind. "Human being," one senses, is too broad a category; it fails to distinguish them from all those who are also human beings but who are not to be regarded as "in" the group. Nor does such a category spare those present from laboring to make manifest additional things in common. We must conclude, therefore, that not only must a "group" have more in common than in difference but they must be more different from than similar to others not to be "included" in the "group." For this latter dimension, "human beings" does not serve; yet the differentiations that must also be made manifest in order to distinguish who is to be regarded as "in" from those considered to be "outside" the group, threaten to encroach on the common denominator among those to be included. Once again, as artifice was required to take as evidence similarities and to overlook differences, so in establishing distinctions, those who wish to regard themselves as composing a group must contrive to take as evidence their differences from those outside the group, while ignoring the host of similarities which, by the same token, they share (e.g., all are human beings) with those to be excluded.

If this is so, we are obliged to regard the "group" as a number of people who are prepared to accept or contrive similarities, disregard differences, and accept the resulting perception as the truth. We, therefore, are obliged to regard the resulting "group" as an invention in both senses of that word.

To do so, however, leaves us, as would-be theorists of groups, with precious little to theorize about! As the theologian depends on the actuality of his God for the basis of the theology he writes, so the group theorist requires his group. And all we have left in the way of a group is aggregates of people collectively attempting to give substance to a fantasy each of them shares.

But suppose we take that phenomenon itself as our starting point, and attempt to understand what it is about the fantasy that so appeals to those who hold it. For surely what happens in groups is that people labor to actualize that fancy, through this means and that, in order, in the end, to claim benefit from its accomplishment. Why, what benefit, and how they labor may, after all, be worth knowing, especially considering the ubiquity of people's beliefs in groups.

To begin, it seems that we must begin with fantasy itself. Fantasy, it is fairly plain, functions to enthrone a version of something in preference to the absence of that something or to its factual version. The very function of the imagination is inviting, in that the active and personal mind of the imaginer is necessary, whereas only his senses are required to know of things as they are or are not. And the product of the fantasy delights insofar as it replaces drear fact with versions more palatable. In both its manner and its matter, fantasy is king—indeed creator.

The group, people seem to believe, is something other than an aggregate of people, something that can be created of an aggregate, with a whole something more than the sum of its parts. And this belief, we have concluded, can only be established and supported through the exercise of fantasy.

That this very exercise of fantasy can be delightful is easy to see. Order comes from chaos, with but a flick of the mind's eye. A hundred different girls can be made a single "unit" by common costumes and lock-step dances. Life is simplified when numbers of discrete individuals, all different, can be subsumed into categories—black, white; middle-class, lower-class; normal, psychotic, whatever. But the first example differs from the second insofar as the girls must dress and dance alike, while to classify individuals into categories requires only the inventive art of the categorizer. What we need to focus on is not solipsistic fancy, but the collective actualization of shared fancy.

What beyond the self-emolument pleasure of fantasy induces people collectively to deceive themselves into believing in groups? The leading idea concerning "groups" is that the people comprising them are more similar than otherwise. Must it not be that groups are invented as an antidote to the fact[2] of differences?

But though this inference seems logical, it seems, at the same time,

---

[2]Though we say "fact" here, we mean to regard differences much as we do similarities; differences are as much a function of comparisons as similarities. It is the issue of the selective perception or use of both difference and similarity with which we are engaged here.

unreasonable. *Vive la différence,* say the French, and indeed differences seems quite the nicest thing in the world: the frightened, hungry child::the comforting, providing mother; the ardent male::the attractive, eager woman; the bold contestant::his brave opponent. But when we notice that the pairings we have mentioned are all reciprocal, all complementary, we see that we are dealing only with "good" differences. What about other differences: the clinging child::the harassed and busy mother; the ardent male::the otherwise committed woman; the bold contestant::the overwhelming opponent? These differences are anything but complementary and reciprocal. Until and unless they are resolved, they will lead to a fight, a separation, or an otherwise painful relationship. The child may get spanked, sent to his room or scolded; the male may become intolerably rapacious: the girl he covets may leave; the contestants may hurt each other too badly and one may be destroyed. Each member of the pair would no doubt wish first for a reciprocal relationship with the other; but failing this, each will wish to avoid the painful eventuality for which they may be heading. It is here, it seems, that "making a group" provides the alternative.

If that is indeed the case, one can see that Dick, the ardent lover, will consent to be just friends, that is, form a "group," with Jane, only as a second resort. Jane, however, is far from willing because she has Tom, her differences from whom she finds complementary and, therefore, cherishes. If for Dick "grouping" with Jane helps avoid complete separation, a painful struggle or great jealousy, what does grouping with Dick do for Jane?

The most apparent answer is that Jane rather likes Dick, enjoys the interests and viewpoints they have in common, and even enjoys the affection he still maintains, if in modulated form for her. In fact, being a good friend, Dick encourages her in her love affair with Tom; sometimes, after talking with Dick, she feels blessedly free of the doubts that occasionally plague her about her relationship with Tom. Though she is sure her parents would like Tom, something in her wonders; then, too, she is sometimes frustrated by Tom's difference in their lovemaking.

If we schematize these feelings of Jane's, we see the following. Jane talks of "something in her" which she does not regard as identical with her self—that aspect of her which she experiences and describes as I, Jane. This "something in her" is "in" her, but not of her *self*. It is associated in some way with Jane's parents. Yet neither is it identical with her parents. Nevertheless, this "something" causes that which Jane talks of as "I" and as her "self" to feel doubts. At the same time she—Jane's I, self—feels very enthusiastic. Dick's support somehow helps this; after their talks she feels only enthusiastic.

Let us call that something in Jane her conscience. Then there is her self. Jane's conscience, though not identical with her parents, is sometimes identified with them; likewise, though not identical with Jane's self, her conscience can invade Jane's self with doubts and discouragement. Dick, however, can influence these psychic "events."

In like manner, Jane's sexuality wants more satisfaction than Tom will afford "it." Jane is undecided, at times, whether to identify her self with her sexuality against Tom or to take Tom's side, as it were, against her sexuality. Here too Dick is of some help, reinforcing her—self's I's—determination to put her sexuality—it—away from her, and to accept Tom's attitudes as hers—Jane's self's own—without feeling too unhappy.

So schematized, in deference to Jane's fantasy of being somehow in three parts—conscience, sexuality, and self—we see that Jane feels that she has things to contend with "within herself." Dick helps her contend with these "things" by getting them "out" of her "self," though they remain in her somewhere. It is that Dick comes into her self and helps her repel the impingement of sexuality and conscience?

Clearly that is impossible in the realm of fact, but fantasy, as we have noted, reigns supreme. If Jane already has fantasies concerning a tripartite going on of things in her self, to reject the inference that she also has fantasies that she can take Dick inside her self would seem to swallow the camel while straining at the gnat. Let us, therefore, go the whole hog (as Jane does) and assume that in her imagination Dick's support and reinforcement are tantamout to having Dick enter the room of self and there, repel other figures. If we make this assumption, what comes clear is the great value of an external relationship of grouping for the I's—self's—internal relationships, much as a good alliance between one country and another could help both with not only their struggles with yet other countries, but with problematic factions within each.

But one can also see that Jane can be rather afraid of Dick as well. Suppose that rather than grouping with her I-self, Dick allies himself—takes a position in common—with Jane's conscience or her sexuality. The odds, which were so helpful to Jane's self, will certainly have changed. If Jane felt bad to begin with, Dick, were he to enter allegiance with Jane's conscience, "could" make Jane feel very bad indeed. Likewise, Jane, by coming around, with Dick's "help," to feeling "at one" with Tom against her sexual wishes could, should Dick support the cause of her sexuality, feel quite at one with "it" and at odds with Tom.

Dick cannot, of course, effect these changes; any more than he could offer support to Jane as self, without the active collaboration of Jane's fantasies. But Jane, we are inferring, treats psychic "events," internal reality interactions, as if they were somehow like physical events, external interactions between real, live people. Since this is the case, we can guess that when Jane, with help from an inner Dick, repudiates the voice of conscience, she herself will feel less bad; she will also feel more lonely. That is, she will respond to conscience as if it were a person, her mother, and her "estrangement" from this figure will make her feel lonely—quite as if she lost an actual person. No doubt this is why Jane often imagines that she has "something in her" and why she continues to imagine this, despite the unpleasantness of the doubts this fantasy imposes. Dick's affection is required to keep her from feeling too lonely for her conscience at those times when she has lost touch with it.

But in following Jane's experience, we have lost sight of Dick and his experiences with and of Jane.

Dick didn't altogether want to "group" with Jane: He preferred to celebrate their differences than to establish so much in common. On the other hand, neither did he want to quarrel with or to lose her. But her repudiation of him both frustrated Dick sexually and opened him to doubts about himself. Dick was thus in much the same boat as Jane, so that Jane's offer of friendship is helpful to Dick in the same way his is to her: Dick employs Jane to augment his self against fault-finding from his conscience and from unmannerly uprisings on the part of his sexuality. His "grouping" with Jane is brandished by Dick to offset pressures from both directions. In the same way, Dick will, as Jane was, be afraid of Jane's becoming identified with either his sexuality or his conscience. Indeed, were Jane to be a little too seductive, Dick's self will feel quite angry at her, nor will he take criticism from Jane, unless he him*self* agrees with it, at all gladly. Jane and he are to have much in common; differences between Jane and himself will not be welcome.

If, however, the alternative of "grouping" is invented to counteract problems of "internal" and "external" differences, it seems in one respect at least to be a solution to a nonproblem. The internal situation, as we have noted in passing, can only be regarded as a fantasy. Thus, it is all very well to infer that the imaginary merger of self and other in a "group" provides good augmentation to the self's struggle with conscience, but to infer that fails to account for why conscience is imagined in the first place.

But this we can do fairly easily by examining the reverse of the procedure by which conscience and self become fused as self by dint of an internal grouping. Under those circumstances, the fantasy seems to be: conscience and myself are one and the same. But though that fantasy seems to evoke a feeling of great well-being, sometimes indeed euphoria and elation, unless the self's relationship with conscience, which previously was based on difference, is replaced with a relationship based on difference with some other figure, a feeling of loneliness ensues. Conscience and self when differentiated give the illusion of an actual relationship.

That actual relationship, we can surmise, is modeled on one the person once had with some real external figure. But when it was real and external, it was, we must assume, also problematic in one of the ways we have been discussing. The choices were the usual (schematized) choices: endure, separate, fight, succumb, or group. Of these, grouping was the method of choice, and the individual then imagined himself to be at one with that other person. This, however, though it solved the problem posed by the distasteful nature of the other alternatives, proves not to be a good antidote for loneliness. As a result, another choice is forced: resume the external relationship and conduct it in one of the other modalities—endurance, fighting, and so on—or disgorge the other person from the "self" and conduct the relationship, as if real, in imagination. Since, at a given time, the first of the two choices means jumping back from the frying pan into the fire, the other option has more appeal. The relationship is conducted as a differentiated one, but in fantasy. If a differentiated relationship can be termed an I–Other relationship—an I–Other relationship in reality is replaced by an I–Other relationship in fantasy.

Yet it is not quite an I–Other relationship either. For not all of the actual I–Other relationship need be represented internally, nor need all the I–plus Other–equals Me, which was the midstage of the devolution, be allocated to conscience.

The person who is to be imaginatively reconstructed and represented in a fantasied interior need not be assimilated wholesale. Just as Dick and Jane and Tom and Jane continue to conduct actual relationships in spaces all regard as external and yet at the same time each maintains figurative, inner relationships with the other inside,[3] so only aspects of the Other and only elements of the relationship need be taken in and moved about there.

The same appears to be the case for movements through internal boundaries. Jane may retain some of Dick for her "self" and assign some of him elsewhere. Similarly, she may take Tom's point of view regarding sex and experience it as her own self's view or conscience's.

But it may well strike us that conscience is a word inadequate to describe these creations of fantasy. One objection to these terms is that they imply forbidding or critical functions, and this is neither accurate nor true. But the more serious issue is that they suggest something far too limited and unitary. In fact, people act as if they have a variety of Others represented internally and conduct many and varied relationships with them. Our own imaginations cannot be limited if we are to envision the fantasies other people have of the nature of their internal relationships. We are likely to be more accurate if we envision a state of affairs akin to a populous dream, indeed a series of dreams. The cast, if not quite "a cast of thousands," is, neither, a single voice of conscience.

The separation of I from these internal Others is neither absolute nor resolute. Internal groupings take place much as external relationships flex and flux — and, indeed, in fashions complementary each (internal and external) to one another. For in creating an internal representation of an Other, a person creates something akin to the Sorcerer's Apprentice, who, enlisted to solve one problem, lives on to create others. Thus, if the creation of a fantasy relationship makes up for the loss of an actual one, that fantasied relationship may go on to prove a problematic one, necessitating external "grouping" to cope with *it*. This we may imagine was the case for Jane, who created "something (someone) in her" who she imagined could love her under certain circumstances, but which also, it turned out, could make her feel quite bad under others. Dick helped with this, by augmenting her self in support of her relationship with Tom. But what if Dick should leave? Jane might continue to "retain" Dick in memory and self to continue as an antidote to that someone in her. But what if, in the end, Jane should change her mind (self) about Tom? Now she will have inner-Dick to contend with as a new source of doubt. Will she be able to part with

---

[3]Discussion of the devolution of "inner" and "outer" spaces and boundaries follows.

Dick altogether, sacrificing the good Dick whose approval of Tom makes him now a bad Dick, or in hoping to hold on to the good Dick, will she have to offset the bad Dick with a new grouping with someone else?

Parsed out this way, it can be readily seen that Jane's original inability to tolerate and endure one of her actual relationships led first to her replacement of that relationship, or aspects of it, with a fantasied grouping in and with her self, and then to a fantasied relationship based on greater differentiation placed within her conscience. These steps, in turn, led to others — each taken out of the same motivation: to dilute suffering. With each maneuver, Jane hopes to preserve the hope that her hopes of the original relationship can come true, so that with each maneuver Jane replaces a bit of the facts of the original relationship with an additional bit of fiction.

Much as one "group" may, while opposing another, challenge everything that other group stands for or contains, but never doubt that the other is a group, so Dick, for his own purpose, may come to oppose Jane in every way but that of challenging the processes of fantasy she uses. His use of them requires that Jane remain unselfconscious of using them herself; together, therefore, they collude to remain unaware of their substitution of a process of fantasy for processes by which facts are maintained.

Such a collusive endeavor is evident in the very phenomenon with which we began this essay into theory. All those present in the groups we studied believed in grouping: none challenged that belief. The people, indeed, used the classical hiding place for their belief; they put the belief in that most casual of places: the belief went without saying. Thereafter, the only matters that preoccupied the participants were tactical in nature. The problem was how to assure that others become one with the self and not with any of the internal others to which each participant plays host.

The hope attached to this, we have already analyzed: augment the self vis-à-vis internal representations of differentiated others. This means that others deemed similar are to be assimilated into the self. But in the groups we have studied, there is a "leader" present, and with this we come upon a new dimension. Not only does each participant's self want augmentation vis-à-vis internal figures, each wants augmentation in respect to the external figure of the differentiated leader. Since the leader is external, it is as if assimilating others into the self is not the useful thing; each person's self must be attributed to some external locus.

The participants, accordingly, reinvent and then invoke the concept of "the group." And they reinvent and invoke a trend that is the reverse of the ones Dick and Jane employed, of taking in; instead, they project their selves out and into the group. The colloquial word they use for this is being "open." Open, in this connection, means not open *to* ideas or suggestions or anything else external, but open so that what is within can issue *forth*. The fantasy is that the psychic, mental, or personal domain behaves analogically with the physical self, and as such contains ingresses and egresses through which, when "open," substances capable of "making" a group can pass. It is irrelevant to our present purposes, though not to the analysis of the fantasies of specific people who feel they comprise groups, to consider which of these apertures they have in mind. It is important only to note the fantasy itself, that the self, or parts of what it contains, can exit from within boundaries attributed to the person and fill up a space around which a boundary separating "our" from other groups is drawn.

Once there, commingled with the issuances of other "members" it creates an entity called the group. This entity is in one sense an objective correlative of the self: but it is, in another respect, taken to be the whole that is greater than the sum of its parts, as an army is more than the soldiers, a country more than its people, or a team more than its players.

Once this entity is formed, it rather than its elements can (people seem to believe) be reassimilated into the self, where far more than Dick could to Jane or Jane to Dick it can augment the self. Part of this increment or effect appears to have to do with numbers. "One for all and all for one" is better the more there are to the "all." But numbers are probably no more than one expression of magnitude, another one of which is size. The functional aspect of numbers is that, as for the Lilliputians, numerical strength can measure well in respect to physical size. If the inner or outer other is deemed to be sizable, numbers appear to have as much symbolic value as, in some circumstances, they have literal value — one more instance of metaphorical fantasy.

But the now-created group is also believed to have great force in respect to the external object of the group's interests — the "leader," or whatever other Other. Jane was not only able to deal better with that "something in her" thanks to her grouping with Dick, but, we should not be surprised to hear, she might have hoped to deal better with Tom. This, partly out of the increased confidence she gained within but partly too because Tom might have been more impressed by Dick and Jane together—two against one—than by Jane alone.

The "group" then hopes and trusts that its hope for a differentiated and reciprocal relationship with the Other they have selected will be the more realizable thanks to their having become a group. The fantasy is that they are now collectively worthy—but, failing that, they are now substantial enough to avoid having to endure, succumb, or separate—and if it comes to a struggle, they are strong enough to compel the Other into a reciprocal relationship. Their worthiness, of course, comes from the group's ability to induce respect and good treatment from the inner others.

So cherished and believed is this fantasy, and all the subsidiary fancies that go into its making, that should it prove to be fallacious, the whole edifice of fantasy threatens to collapse, leaving behind, like so much rubble, only absolute hopelessness. The only remaining fantasy is that the external other, the leader, has so much more substance than the group that he is awesome indeed. A contagious—or shared—panic results, and separation or flight or a frozen succumbing seems finally the only alternative remaining.

But if that response is one measure of the hope vested in the group, another measure is the degree to which, short of such an emergency, the hope remains undaunted; for, failing an adequate response from the object of the group's hopes—the Other—the group can find other objects. It can, for example, divide into two "subgroups," each of which can work out an Other relationship with one another. Such subgrouping is believed to preserve the grouping from "disintegrating" into a series of Other relationships, with the affiliate loss of self-augmentation as a source of effect on inner or external others. And it provides a temporary measure against losing the relationship the participants hope still to find with the original Other. That all participants share in the belief in and contriving of this strategy indicates that the grouping, effected by holding things in common, remains intact, despite appearances of subgrouping.

Other tactics are similar in nature and, as such, are important more in respect to the fantasy they attempt to realize than in the precise devices employed, for which ingenuity is the only limitation. That fantasy, as we have seen, is in two parts, the first of which relates to the object or objective of the group's interests, the other of which to the hopes of the individuals comprising the grouping. The first seeks satisfactions based on reciprocal differences and related to persons deemed to be different and hence outside the perimeter of the group. The second seeks self- or group-augmentation to come from within the group.

The two sources of gratification are, people hope, susceptible of working complementarily, but it turns out that there is a conflict between them. The conflict is in one sense that which Jane faced with Tom. If she were to feel at one with Tom, she had to side with him against her sexuality, striking a compromise between satisfactions requiring difference and those requiring commonality. The hope of people in respect to the group is that this will not be necessary. The belief is that by splitting the two kinds of satisfactions all the way apart and assigning the fulfillment of one sort to the group and the other to the person who is deemed different, both sorts of satisfaction can be received without the need to diminish either by compromising. Were this hope to work out, there would be no need for choice and hence no conflict (Boris 1971).

But hopes can remain hopes only insofar as they remain unfulfilled, whereas satisfactions cannot be realized unless desires are fulfilled. Much as the group might wish it to be otherwise, there is an irreconcilable conflict between hopes and satisfactions. Satisfactions suborn and weaken hope by virtue of the immediate pleasures they afford, tempting people to be satisfied with feeling satisfied. Hopes require that the potential be better than the actual: to feel "Stay, moment, thou art so fair" is to settle for the actual.

Faced with satisfactions, the group escalates its hopes; in the face of frustrations, the group can preserve its hopes. When the self is so augmented, as by grouping it is imagined to be, hopes once abandoned appear to be reassumed, and hope becomes boundless. The hatred of succumbing is experienced with great force, unimpeded by the effective "presence" of inner or external others. When grouped, people feel themselves to be able to begin as if for the first time — to begin again with all the mourning and reconciliations they have gone through, all the enduring and suffering, set aside. This hope — that one may triumph over those who challenged one's proposals to treat one's hopes as convictions and so made cowardly one's courage — is a function of people's belief in the power of the group to still others.

The concept of satisfaction based on differences is more familiar to us, partly because psychoanalytic thinking has focused more on it. But some consideration might, nevertheless, prove useful.

We have seen that from time to time people feel it is both necessary and possible to rid themselves of certain sorts of experience. One of these experiences is that of desire. When experienced, desire can become transformed into satisfaction and fulfillment, but it can also shade into tension, frustration, and deprivation, all of which may prove exceedingly frightening and painful. Since the painful consequences of desire are thought to hinge upon desire itself, people may be tempted to rid themselves of desire.

Desire, however, is extraordinarily difficult to be got rid of, rooted as it is in the appetitive and sensual nature of the organism. But the experiencing of desire is something else again; people feel that they can get rid of the experiencing of desire or, failing that, their knowledge of their experiencing of desire, providing only that a place be found for it.

Only imagination limits the number, variety, or activity of the places created or found. Equally, only imagination limits the fashion by which people feel the disgorging of desire or the experiencing of desire can be accomplished.

A desire to bite the breast, for example, may be dealt with in the following ways. For placing the desire, the baby, let us say a boy, may divide himself into two: a self that does not experience a desire to bite and a not-self that does. The self will be organized to remain in ignorance of this not-self. The not-self may be located in a part of his body, for example, his penis. Since location of the desire takes place not only in space but can change in time, later the penis, when it becomes a more important space to the growing child, may no longer serve as a useful vessel for urges to bite. The urge to bite may then be reassigned elsewhere — to the breast itself, to someone else's mouth, e.g., a dog's, to someone else's penis, e.g., a snake, or to the vagina. Once a place has been found, the urge to bite may be desired to continue unabated or to be tamed by its new host in ways one could not oneself tame it. The new host may be assumed to have the desire in reverse, now desiring one, as if one had now become the breast. Or the new host may be assumed to want to free himself of the desire attributed to him or her by insinuating it back into one. Under these circumstances, one may well feel that prudence dictates either the conversion of the desire into its opposite or avoidance of the host currently containing the desire. Thus when the new repository of the desire is someone, or part of someone, other than a part of one's person, that someone is transformed by the addition of the desire. The Other one dealt with previously, for example, now has a breast that wants to bite one. The previous relationship that obtained will be dramatically changed, and this will prove fateful for the conversion of an actual I–Other relationship into an "interior" one. The Other with which one conducts either the actual relationship or the relationship in fancy will no longer be the actual Other but an Other transformed by the attribution or substraction of characteristics of desire.

These fancies, concerning where and how desire can be reallocated, are often made before the culture has been able to make its recommendations — as, for example, when the baby is quite young. Nevertheless, the mother who believes the worst concerning the dangers inherent in the breast (or bottle) may be capable of stimulating or reinforcing an infant's disposition to use the breast as a vessel for wishes whose authorship he wishes to disclaim. One mother nurses baby, offering the breast. Baby roots for the nipple in a series of head-ducking movements. Upon connecting, he sucks vigorously. Mother sees baby's nose is pressed close against her breast. She retracts the breast which, as it happens, withdraws the nipple. Baby, rooting, seeks the nipple. The same series of events ensues. Finally, upon the latest loss of the nipple, baby refuses to suckle. As mother, leaning toward baby, brings the nipple to him, he turns away crying. The desire has passed, as it were, from baby to breast.

But the nature of these fancies may prove to be idiosyncratic with respect to the prevailing culture. The reprocessing of experience any one individual makes may be unconsonant with the processing or revisions others prefer. Insofar as the success of the operations on experience require secrecy, so that one may not find what one has got rid of, the existence of several versions of experience threatens the security of each one's version. Pluralism or relativism are in these circumstances endangering. People are offered alternative beliefs instead, in order that all may reach consensus, absolutism, and universals. Individuals may find it convenient to replace an idiosyncratic allocation of desire — from one's own mouth to mother's breast — with a culturally "validated" assignment — from our mouths to the enemies' mouths. Even if an individual does not redesign experience to obtain greater consonance with the culture (though if the culture is a breast that bites, he may feel it wiser to do so than not), he will at

minimum feel tempted to borrow from the culture the fictions with
which he replaces those experiential facts which he has found too
painful.

That is, under simple sorts of exchanges, as between breast and
mouth, the only change is in who desires. But this way of coping with
desire may not work very well. Desire may not be so easily got rid of;
indeed desire is quite difficult to get rid of. Easier to be got rid of is the
knowledge about one's desire. Therefore, knowledge rather than desire
is the first casualty in the struggle to revise experience. Knowledge can
be denied, forgotten, banished. But in that case it leaves a space where
it once was. That negative ("not this") space, from which experience or
fact has been subtracted, functions better if filled with a fiction ("not
this but that"). Since the fact may be remembered, triggered to
recollection by some associational shard, or relearned from subsequent
experience, the substitution of fiction for fact helps more than the
simple absence of knowledge can. It further helps if the fact that a fact
has been got rid of is also forgotten, and it helps even more if to fill the
space left by that now forgotten item the fiction that what is "so" — the
case — instead was always "so." That "so-ness" is even more invulner-
able to the testimony of fact if other people can be induced to attest to
it — at least in words, preferably in actions. Thus if many agree that
breasts desire mouths and mothers devour babies, the "fact" that the
mouth contains no desire seems truer as a result. If, further, the
mother/breast can be induced to devour/desire the mouth/child,
the desire may be located without question. Mothers do desire their
children as breasts do "desire" being suckled: these facts, however, are
employed untruthfully to sustain a fiction. Mothers with extraordinary
desire for their children may thereby assist their children in the latters'
efforts to deny their own desires for their mothers; the *quid pro quo* in
which the mothers' desires are linked to the children's rather than to
others' (the mothers' own mothers, for example) suggests the complicity possible between one person's need not to know and another's.
The management of desire and the acknowledgment of desire is a vital
activity both in the formation of "groups" and the use of group
"membership."

The concept of hope may also require further exposition.[4] As we
contemplate people's fantasies concerning grouping, we gain the

---

[4]For an extended theoretical treatment of hope, see Boris (1976).

impression that people are Platonists: they act and react as if there were an ideal to which all that is real only approximates. It is difficult to account for this conviction. Some people experience the ideal as if it were something to return to—a Paradise Lost—and some theories have it that such a conviction implies a wish to return to such early times of fulfillment as infancy or the womb. This might be a tenable explanation were there certain evidence that the womb is remembered or that infancy was ideal, but there is no certainty about the first and some certainty that infancy is something less than ideal. Other people experience the hope as one toward which to go forward—Paradise gained. Were there certainty about a heavenly afterlife, this too might be explicable, but once again the ideal is located forward of present by people who do not believe in an afterlife of any sort.

Some theories have it that since the real is so disappointing, people comfort themselves with an ideal, as if to say: "There must be something better than this!" But this leaves over the question of what the disappointing reality is *compared with*. An answer for this has, however, been offered—one's own experience is compared with what *others enjoy*. Yet those "others" may neither enjoy nor feel they enjoy more than those who compare themselves with them enjoy. If one supposes a misperception, uncorrected, nevertheless supplies the comparative standard, such a reply does not account for why the overestimation takes place.

Once arguments based on experience fail, it becomes tempting to replace the Nurture thesis with a Nature thesis: there is something inborn or inherited, something in a racial unconscious, perhaps. Ethologists have added to our understanding of in-built readinesses or reflexes—showing that much as a newborn duckling will freeze at an overhead shadow, so does the newborn infant turn his mouth to a pressure on his cheek—and it is conceivable that there is an inborn expectation of good things and bad.

This thesis, which requires a mental representation, a thought, or picture of that ideal good and bad thing, to be conjured or congenitally "remembered" if it is to be a psychological theory, competes for credibility with theories that rest on creativity. Such a theory might argue that people invent an ideal much as they invent anything else by making an inductive leap from the experienced to the possible. A theory such as this is akin to structural theories in anthropology and linguistics, and parallels *gestalt* theories in psychology, in imputing, as it does, an inborn readiness to depart from experience and construct something new or different, which at the same time is universal in the sense that the readiness itself is both universal and limited.

Whatever the explanation, it does appear that people imagine ideal versions of experience and that these versions hold claim on their activities by virtue of the hopes invested in these ideals. And whatever the origins of this idealizing process, it also seems that experiences are ransacked in order both to provide evidence for the ideals and to buttress or insulate the hopes invested in the ideals against erosion by the continuing presence of perceptual–sensory reality. Thus people may choose one instance here and another there, overlooking contrary or modifying examples, in order to fuel their hopes and reinforce their ideals.

Is the belief in groups a reincarnation of such an ideal? Our own inference is: Yes. People appear to contrast the group with the differentiated object of their desires, assigning to the object the function of providing to them what they want and lack, while to the group they assign their hopes of having (rather than needing) and being (rather than becoming). The group, we have remarked, is an empty potential which people imagine they can fill. Once imagined, hence, presumably, filled, the group is experienced as if it were an entity, present, palpable, sufficient, as if so many fractions have made an integer. The group then appears to be a manifestation of completeness. People feel capable of being both contained by the group, as within something like a circling embrace, and yet having — containing — within the group a sense of fullness and plenty. It is as if, in the group, people at once contain bounty and are contained by it: they have, they are. Or, at least, this is the ideal and the hope.

But the presence of the group's object, the Other, appears to stimulate longings and, in stimulating longings, puts into question the fantasy of being complete and replete; such a presence jeopardizes hope. Thus, no matter how fulfilling the object (indeed the more fulfilling the more so), the more the object becomes a source of envy: he or she, containing what the group hopes to contain and be contained by, appears better to approximate the group's hope of being replete and complete than does the group itself.

We must conclude, therefore, that the group's ideal is to refuse the differentiated object in both meanings of the word. It wishes to re-fuse with that object ("fuse once more") — to contain it and to be contained by it — and thereby to refuse benefits the group might receive were the person seen as different and separate from the group. This ideal bespeaks a hope that a grouping can supply the wherewithal necessary to realize the hope that individual frailty cannot itself fulfill.

If in the psychology of individuals investments of hope and pleasure in the self take over when receipts from others fall short, in the psychology of people's theories about grouping, transactions with "others" only take over when investments in the self prove insufficiently fulfilling. Grouping represents an attempt to supersede needing others and to make those others superfluous.

If our inferences concerning people's fantasies about groups are approximately correct, we should expect to find that their behavior in situations — which they take to be group situations — follows identifiable patterns expressive of these fantasies.

Chief among these patterns should be those expressive of the fundamental duality of hope versus desire. That is, we should expect to see behavior primarily motivated by hope and behavior primarily motivated by desire, with oscillations between these two.

Behavior governed by hope will find fantasies that the group is replete and complete being expressed through self-fulfilling activity and an indifference to or scorn of what the group's object has to offer. If we term that object the Other and for convenience's sake place that Other vis-à-vis the group as its eucharistic leader, we will expect to find the group going on about its business as if that Other, the leader, had nothing of value to offer. Instead, the group will find sufficiency and value preferable in simply *being*, or failing that, in engendering experiences for itself.

If the fantasy of people who take themselves to be members of groups is that collectively they embody the be-all-and-end-all of things, they act as if their ability to enjoy and sustain that fantasy is subject to two sources of jeopardy. One consists in the emergence of desire in the members; desire, since it forces an acknowledgement of the desirability of someone or something outside the group, routs the hope that the group contains all that is necessary. The second blow to that hopeful fantasy comes about insofar as the "group" is not desired by others; for if the group embodies all that is desirable, how is it that others do not desire the group?

Although the threats are from different sources, they bear a relationship to one another. If, in the first instance, the members wish to "rid" themselves of the stirrings of desire, they can the more easily remain oblivious of their desires by attending to whatever desire may be evinced by others, especially by that other who might otherwise be the object of their desires. Similarly, to be desired can satisfy hope sufficiently so that desire can be the better resisted. The corollary to these is that when the potential object of the "group's" desires fails to desire the "group," the members experience that other as containing more and better of what they hoped to embody, which then stimulates intense desire, while shattering hope.

A good deal of activity, accordingly, will be directed to preventing any member from looking to an Other, especially that Other who is most easily available and, as such, represents the greatest temptation to abandon a "We–Us" position for a "We–Other," namely, the leader. If the group cannot prevent this looking-to-an-Other, it will try to substitute itself for that Other. One or more members will be stimulated to try to provide the supplies or services the straying member or members seek. Subgrouping is thus one alternative by which to maintain hope within the group.

Failing that, the group will attempt to influence the doubting Thomas to look beyond the leader to some other Other. God may serve this purpose; historically, the belief in God has made people relatively immune to the demands or delights of Caesar. But whatever the incarnation of the Other, it will be offered as a palliative, a promise, not a remedy with any actuality or substance. Its offer will be designed to hold the members' hopes in the group by placating them with hopes sufficient to temper their desires.

If this measure also fails to enshrine hope above desire, the object of the errant members' desires will be denigrated and denuded of value and the implication will be plain that this fate, akin to wearing the scarlet letter, awaits the member who strays toward that Other.

At the same time the value of what the group contains and is contained by will be escalated. Great value will be found in people's silent thoughts and fantasies, other activities or engagements, relationships with other Others.

Failing all of this, the group will feel depressed, as if hated and persecuted by the inner Others over which they now imagine they have also failed to triumph. This state of affairs will reveal itself in apathetic, dispirited behavior.

At this point, desire is likely to threaten to outweigh hope, for all of the group is feeling quite hopeless. Where previously it was preoccupied with the leader, now it becomes occupied with him. But what it wants from the leader is a restoration of hope, not gratification of its desires. The group wishes the leader will take in what it is and has been, and then offer to the group, as might an adept portrait artist to his subject, a talented conductor to a composer, a version of itself that restores its flagging hopes. It wants to be made good and nice and sufficient. The leader is thus to be employed as a Mosaic or instrumental leader; the group is not ready to concede to him possibilities of being a eucharistic leader.

Under the pressure of these wishes and the now rampant criticism from the inner Others, the group is prepared to begin weeding out its less than ideal members. This eugenic preoccupation may begin with efforts to convert members to the ideal, but can end with attempts to "purify" the species. Inquisitions, witch hunts, and exactions of good faith will precede, accompany, and follow the effort to have the new Mosaic leader restore the group to its former glory.

The group will, however, feel frightened of the leader: it has tried to repudiate him in the past and still wishes to do so. And it now wishes to have the leader come "into" the group, away from his Other position into a prime-ministerial position. This is not an intent of outright destruction, but it is an attempt to deprive the leader of his actual position by making him into an inner Other whom the group can use at its pleasure or group with.

None of these efforts are ever wholly renounced, but if they do not succeed, they become latent to, yet modifying of, the preeminence of desire. For now desire becomes paramount, and the group becomes frankly occupied with the task of winning gratification from its Other.

The experience of desire brings with it either envy or jealousy — in either case, rivalry. The group wants gratification, wants the leader to provide it, but continues to want to have, possess, and control the Other they now acknowledge to contain or be contained by the gratification they want. As such, they view themselves at odds either with the leader's autonomy over those parts of him (or her) they covet or in competition with whomever they imagine the leader prefers to provide these to. Since these realizations go hand-in-hand with the acknowledgment of desire, hatred and longing go hand-in-hand as well. The accompanying hatred arouses guilt, fears of retaliation, fears for the Other's safety and well-being, and beyond that fears for what the group desires from the Other. Insofar as these fears prove to be unfounded, the group will feel much relieved, but the sense of relief will be set against the group's realization of its impotence and helplessness. This latter realization will further erode the group's hopes of itself, and the group may need once more attempt to buoy up its hopes even at the expense of its desires.

To avoid this contingency, the group goes about attempting to influence its object into requiting its desires in so ample a measure that gratitude will supplant envy and satiety will outmatch jealousy. But the specific desires of each individual will be as different as each individual is from the others. In mobilizing to collectively address the leader–Other in respect to desire, the members of the group must compose their desires into commonality. This process becomes their first priority.

Next they must compose the means by which their ends are to be fulfilled. This involves, among other things, reconciling each of the others, and weighing the outcome of these deliberations in terms of each person's theory concerning what will influence the leader–Other. So formidable is this task that the absolute consensus for which the group strives is not easily, if ever, achieved. If it is not achieved, the united front the group has hoped to present to the leader–Other and their inner Others is weakened. And this, in turn, may require a scaling down of the most ardent desires and boldest means. Scaled down, the original intentions are frustrated, and the frustration gives rise to efforts on the part of the members to convert each other from a status too like either the leader of the inner Others to one identical with the group "self." These efforts also need to precede, if not the first attempt at gaining satisfactions, then the second, third, and fourth.

But even if the participants can gain consensus on ends and means, and even if they can achieve the satisfaction of their more urgent desires, this satisfaction will be less than they hoped because their hopes of grouping are so extravagant. So once more the group will feel torn between hope and desires, and once more it may return to a quest after hope in preference to desire.

Assuming such a return to behavior governed by hope — indeed assuming a series of such oscillations — the group may, in time, return to desire. With that return, the group will have to make a choice between certain of its hopes, for example, its hopes for omnipotence vis-à-vis the Other or the hope for longing unaccompanied by hatred, fear, or guilt. Yet even if it manages these renunciations, it will be confronted with the probability that the very pleasures for which it abandoned its hopes and ideals will prove themselves to be less engaging than they wished and, in their wishes, believed.

That realization can be met either by modifying the belief or by an increase of envy, jealousy, and hatred. When the group adopts the former stance, it will suffer the very jeopardy of hope out of which it came to believe in the group. But, perhaps, by now the capacity to suffer both the abandonment of hope and the pain of absent pleasures will have increased the group's willingness to take pleasure in those desires that are gratifiable and gratified. If so, there will be fewer oscillations of shorter duration and lessened pendularity. When this develops, there is less of a wish to replace actual Others with inner representations, and consequently a diminished need to use grouping as an antidote to problems with inner Others.

With the need for grouping vis-à-vis inner Others reduced, grouping in respect to actual, external Others can proceed in ways more appropriate to the actual requirements of the situation. Greater differentiations can now "take place" — differences can be acknowledged — between members of the same group, and divisions of labor based on those differences can be employed. These divisions, accompanied by greater autonomy for each of the participants relative to others, serve factually to enhance the ability of the several to pursue their related (probably no longer identical) objectives. For examples of how these conflicts between hope and desire and envy and satisfaction are made manifest by a group, we turn to the rendition of a group with which one of us worked. The people comprising the group are psychologists, psychiatrists, and social workers, all in training at a major hospital. A "group experience" has been deemed by the training faculty to be a useful part of their training.

## SESSION ONE

People assemble, greet each other, and make small talk until what they seem to feel are enough people to begin with have arrived. At this point, they fall silent and look toward the "leader," who is the only stranger present.

Since the leader also remains silent, the participants exchange looks. One, Dr. D., wears a look expressing something like amusement, skepticism, and annoyance. He looks at the others with particular intensity and frequency. In time most look mostly at him. He then speaks.

Dr. D. (to the leader): You didn't introduce yourself. Am I correct in assuming you are _____ , our leader?

Leader: I am _____ .

Dr. D.: May we ask what the purpose of this seminar or group, or whatever it is, is?

Leader: I don't know.

Dr. D. (to the others): I give up. Is he kidding?

The question, "Is he kidding?", becomes a source of discussion. Various theories are put fourth until most people seem to agree that the "leader" conducts groups this way, which is good, since this way enables people to make of the experience what they want.

However, though this conclusion would seem to open the way to making the experience whatever they want, everyone now becomes silent, looking, at the same time, rather gloomy. After a while, Dr. D. once more searches faces and, when people look at him, speaks.

Dr. D.: What sort of group do we want? Speaking for myself, I want a group where I can be open. I want to get to know you all and I want you to get to know me.

Everyone lists reasons for wanting exactly such a group. The discussion is fairly animated. But then someone asks: What about him (referring to the leader)?

Dr. D.: I don't know. He can join us if he wants, or not. It's up to him.

Everyone seems to approve of this view of matters, yet no one speaks. After some minutes of silence, the "leader" says: It seems that no one can take me — or leave me alone.

This remark appears to have the effect of renewing the discussion concerning the leader's role in the open group everyone has said he wants. The discussion is inconclusive.

## SESSION TWO

The people present for Session One assemble, but a newcomer is present. Dr. D. attempts to "fill in" the newcomer, orienting him to the open group idea. The newcomer resists the implication that he is to cooperate with the "decisions" taken last session. The rest of the session is spent in alternations between furious attacks on the newcomer and efforts to ignore him, which efforts, however, fail to find the group going on with their wish to be open with each other.

The leader remarks that the newcomer represents himself.

## SESSION THREE

Session Three is a close relative of Session Two.

## SESSION FOUR

Several people are late. When they arrive, the others take up the issue of lateness. After much discussion, all agree to be on time since that will facilitate openness. This settled, the group falls silent. The leader observes that the group still cannot fulfill its hopes of having a fine, open group despite the issue of lateness being settled. He suggests that the group is still preoccupied with himself. This suggestion is actively denied by Dr. D. and others, but not by all others. Dr. D., noticing this, polls those who have remained silent. One or two "admit" to feeling that the leader's place in the scheme of things still remains a source of irresolution. Silence ensues. Then Dr. B. says that the rule concerning promptness bothers her. Rules don't enhance her own willingness to be open. She proposes the group be a place where everyone does his or her own thing. Everyone agrees this will make an ideal group.

## SESSION FIVE

Dr. L. asks the leader if this is his last meeting before vacation. The leader wonders why Dr. L., who knows it is, asks. Dr. L. replies he doesn't know why he asks, just curious. Then he asks where the leader is going. The leader suggests it is the belief of Dr. L. and others that friendliness would assist the group in some way and that people present feel now that the leader is going away they can afford to be interested in him.

These remarks infuriate several of the participants who say that the leader is making too much of himself. After several comments of this sort are made to the leader (who remarks that it appears he must not enjoy any ideas that he might be of some importance to those present), someone suggests that the group continue to meet in the leader's absence. All agree, though some express the reservation that the leader will not know what happened. Dr. L. replies that if the leader wants to know, he doesn't have to go on holiday.

## SESSIONS SIX TO TEN

Most members of the group continue to meet during this time.

## SESSION ELEVEN

As the leader enters, he is told by those present that the group continued to meet in his absence. Dr. L. asks if the leader had a good vacation. The leader wonders why Dr. L. asks, wondering too if the idea that the group has met in his absence is regarded by Dr. L. as a fact which should alter the leader's behavior. Dr. L. denies this. Dr. D. then enters. He tells the leader that the group has met in his absence. He then asks the leader if he has had a good vacation. He then quickly warns the leader that he should not be asked why he asks, that he is only trying to be friendly. Dr. L. then tells Dr. D. about his interchange with the leader. Dr. D. laughs extravagantly at the leader's idea.

The group then falls silent. Dr. J. finally observes that the presence of the leader is ruining things. The leader comments that the group's meetings in his absence were designed to ruin his good vacation, but the group, feeling this has failed, also fears that it has backfired.

The group discusses the idea, professing not to understand it. Dr. D. assures the leader that, contrary to what the leader thinks, the previous sessions were excellent.

## SESSION TWELVE

Dr. F. breaks a silence by speaking of how uncomfortable he feels. In turn, everyone draws him out until he is speaking of himself and his background. The leader's impression is that no one is listening very hard, but only enough to be ready to draw him out further once he halts.

Dr. I. eventually remarks that he does not feel what Dr. F. is saying is interesting — or that Dr. F. is really being open. He goes on to say that while he is perhaps jealous of the attention accorded Dr. F., he still doesn't believe Dr. F. is living up to the reputation for openness the others are giving him.

Dr. D. quarrels with this, expressing great interest in what Dr. F. is saying and admiration for him that he says it.

Dr. I. remains unconvinced.

Dr. D. accuses Dr. I. of only being interested in what the leader has to say; he says that Dr. I. was critical of the meetings held without the leader. Dr. D. is quite angry.

An argument ensues between Dr. D. and Dr. I., with most others joining in to help them to "get things out in the open."

The leader comments, in time, that Dr. I. represents himself.

## SESSION THIRTEEN

Various people discuss their reluctance to speak — no one feels he has anything worth saying. Everyone reassures the others as to their interest in whatever they might wish to say. Some venture to speak of themselves and are drawn out as was Dr. F., but it is not the same. Eventually some accuse others of being insufficiently open or insufficiently responsive.

## SESSION FOURTEEN

Once more people profess the wish to be open but confess their inability. The session proceeds much like the previous one.

The leader comments that no one feels their breasts to have the value of his; when they wish to be open and give, they fear that only shit will emerge. They fear this because they regard everyone else's contributions as so much shit in comparison with what the leader has to offer. But they do not recognize this because they envy the leader and do not wish him to be able to be valuable.

People divide, some taking this as a judgment, others as a description. After some discussion, all agree it is an accurate description. Those who took it as a judgment are reassured that, this being incorrect, the group itself is really valuable, only it's hard to feel that way, as the leader said. Everyone now feels quite hopeful: the group itself is of great value, the problem was they could not see it.

Thus even in Session Fourteen, the hope reposed in the group as an entity and experience complete and replete survives the actuality of the participants' experience. Only in time do those present allow the leader to have some value, but not until they get over wanting him first to have none and then to have all.

Though obviously a good deal of what transpired was left out of the natural history of this group, even the condensation reveals the two sorts of leadership functions people visualize. Dr. D. exemplifies one: the nominal leader, the other. Dr. D., as was Moses, is an instrumental leader, applying his abilities to help achieve the group's purposes. In this case those purposes were to remain self-sufficiently independent of the nominal leader, and Dr. D. acted consonantly with them. The nominal leader is assigned the function of eucharistically embodying and providing all that the group wants but neither contains nor is contained by. In the present illustration, since the group hoped to contain everything and so to want nothing, no role was to be given the nominal leader. In later sessions when the group tolerated the discovering of its wanting things from the nominal leader, Dr. D. would be replaced as instrumental or Mosaic leader, with that role given to a member of the "group" whom the rest felt best capable of influencing the nominal or eucharistic leader. Dr. D. would be permitted to reassert leadership when self-sufficiency or devaluation of the leader was considered useful once again. (In the session that directly followed Session Twelve, Dr. L. absented himself, therewith standing in the wings as a potential leader for a position even more determined than Dr. D.'s.)

In the final analysis, the belief in groups as an antidote to the envy and helplessness that are aroused when the fantasy that two people are as one and that one—oneself—gives way. The belief also functions as an antidote to the feeling that, although distinct, the other and self are less than fully and mutually reciprocal. The function of a grouping vis-à-vis actual differentiated people is regarded as having an equivalent functional counterpart with respect to "inner people" who behave "within" as also distinct, separate, autonomous, and less than fully and mutually reciprocal to one's desires and who, when such, also arouse envy and helplessness instead of gratitude and satiety.

What happens in groups is the story of the vicissitudes of these twin antidotes when applied to the actuality of the public situation.


## REFERENCES

Bion, W. R. (1961). *Experiences in Groups*. New York: Basic Books.
_____ (1962). *Learning from Experience*. New York: Basic Books.
_____ (1963). *Elements of Psychoanalysis*. New York: Basic Books.
_____ (1965). *Transformations*. New York: Basic Books.
_____ (1970). *Attention and Interpretation*. New York: Basic Books.
Boris, H. N. (1967). *The (Un)Examined Life*. Plainfield, VT: Goddard College Publications.
_____ (1971). The *Seelsorger* in rural Vermont. *International Journal of Group Psychotherapy* 21 (2): 159–173.
_____ (1976). On hope: its nature and psychotherapy. *International Review of Psycho-Analysis*. 3: 139–150.
_____ (1993). *Passions of the Mind: Unheard Melodies*. New York: New York University Press.
Boris, H. N., Zinberg, N., and Boris, M. (1976). *Teaching Social Change: A Group Approach*. Baltimore: Johns Hopkins University Press.
Buxbaum, E. (1945). Transference and group formation in children and adolescents. *Psychoanalytic Study of the Child*. 2:351–366. New York: International Universities Press.
Ezriel, H. (1950). A psychoanalytic approach to group treatment. *British Journal of Medical Psychology* 23:59–74.
Foulkes, S. H., and Anthony, E. J. (1965). *Group Psychotherapy*. New York: Penguin.

Freud, S. (1905). Three essays on sexuality. *Standard Edition* 7:
_____ (1913). Totem and taboo. *Standard Edition* 3:1–162.
_____ (1914). On narcissism: an introduction. *Standard Edition* 14:67–102.
_____ (1917). Mourning and melancholia. *Standard Edition*, 14:237–258.
_____ (1921). Group psychology and the analysis of the ego. *Standard Edition*, 18:67–143.
_____ (1927). The future of an illusion. *Standard Edition* 21:5–56.
_____ (1930). Civilization and its discontents. *Standard Edition* 21:64–145.
_____ (1939). Moses and monotheism. *Standard Edition* 23:7–137.
Glover, E. (1955). *The Technique of Psychoanalysis*. New York: New York University Press.
Klein, M. (1932). *The Psycho-analysis of Children*. London: Hogarth.
_____ (1948). *Contributions to Psycho-analysis*. London: Hogarth.
_____ (1952). *Developments in Psycho-analysis*. Ed. J. Riviere. London: Hogarth.
_____ (1956). Heimann, P., Money-Kyrle, R., et al. *New Directions in Psychoanalysis*. New York: Basic Books.
_____ (1957). *Envy and Gratitude*. London: Tavistock.
_____ (1961). *Narrative of a Child Analysis*. New York: Basic Books.
_____ (1963). *Our Adult World, and Other Essays*. New York: Basic Books.
Lewin, K. (1948). *Resolving Social Conflicts, Selected Papers on Group Dynamics*. Ed. G. Lewin. New York: Harper.
Redl, F. (1945). The psychology of gang formation and the treatment of juvenile delinquents. *Psychoanalytic Study of the Child* 1:367–378. New York: International Universities Press.
Scheidlinger, S. (1968). The concept of regression in group psychotherapy. *International Journal of Group Psychotherapy* 18:3–20.
Semrad, E. V., and Day, M. (1966). Book review: group psychotherapy. *Journal of the American Psychoanalytic Association* 14:591–618.
Slavson, S. R. (1954–1972). A systematic theory of group psychotherapy. A series of 10 papers in the *International Journal of Group Psychotherapy*. (1954) 4:3–29; (1955) 5:3–30; (1956) 6:3–27; (1959) 9:3–30; (1960) 10:3–21; (1961) 11:3–32; (1962) 12:411–420; (1966) 16:395–404; (1969) 19:3–16; (1972) 22:433–443.
Sullivan, H. S. (1953). *The Interpersonal Theory of Psychiatry*. New York: W. W. Norton.
Wolf, A., and Schwartz, E. A. (1962). *Psycho-analysis in Groups*. New York: Grune & Stratton.
Yalom, I. D. (1970). *The Theory and Practice of Group Psychotherapy*. New York: Basic Books.
_____ (1974). Book review: *Group Psychology and the Analysis of the Ego*, by S. Freud. *International Journal of Group Psychotherapy* 24:67.

# 6

# Groupgroup

That I would not give a name to this series of encounters and that the patients and staff—in calling it Groupgroup—would is perhaps the signifying matter. This series of meetings lasted for several years and proved a marvelous training field for many of the staff, especially when, as in later years, it was followed by a seminar given by myself and Dr. Schindelheim. One day an anorectic patient left the meeting for a visit to her "individual doctor." After some interpretation of the sort described in this paper, first one, then several, and finally all of the people there went upstairs to fetch the patient back. They asked that her individual doctor come with her, but he declined. Still, they somehow managed not to allow him to "lead" the remainder of the group. The young woman in question professed herself to be "fed up" with having fifty people troop after her, but that was as may be.

The great issue in work with chronic patients (and people in training) is how to shape the work to fit an hour and how to work with a floating population. One conducts each session as if it were the first and the last.

---

A group composed of medical students on their psychiatry rotation and psychiatric in- and day-hospital patients has been in session for almost 5 years now. To it have gradually been added the therapists of the treatment groups for the patients and other residents and staff interested in group therapy. The group numbers upwards of forty, with about fifteen being medical students. It meets once weekly for 50 minutes.

The idea arose while we (the training staff) were considering the problems of giving medical students a feel for psychiatry. (The medical students, in their third year, spend 6 weeks in their rotation through psychiatry.) Some medical students manage their rotation by keeping—passionately—a pencil's length away from patients. They docket, ticket, note, record, interrogate and prescribe, much as if they were observing laboratory creatures in a maze.

Others surrender to an acute case of medical students' disease. Everything they discover, everything about which they hear seems all too true of them. Of course not all students position themselves so that (as in the first posture) they cannot see the trees for the forest or (as in the second) the forest for their frightened preoccupation with the trees. But of most it can fairly be said that the tension involved makes very nearly impossible a warm but accurate perspective, a cool but compassionate regard, both to patients and to themselves in relation to patients.

Ruminating on that condition, we rapidly realized that much the same could be said of patients with respect to such other "nonpatient" people as doctors. Patients either fail to discern differences or they deny similarities—often both, simultaneously. This realization took us away from such familiar teaching methods as having medical students observe or "record" patient groups. There, only the students get educated (if such observations made under the influence of overwhelming internal commotion or, equally difficult, *no* internal commotion, could be called education).

The other alternative, of having patients observe or record a medical student group, also seemed in many ways difficult. We imagined medical students would find the arrangement rather overwhelming. Too few patients could observe, and the same issues of commotion applied. No one cared to take on the problem of keeping the patient-observers from actively participating. And so on.

In the end we saw that the matter of commotion in both groups *was* the issue they had in common. That was the element that deflected and distorted discovery.

Presently, therefore, an item appeared on the weekly schedules for both patients and students: "Mondays 1:40 P.M. Day Room—Group."

The day room is a large ungainly chamber in which chairs sprawl, tables stand about where left by previous arts and craft users, and air conditioners occlude audition. In short, it is a sort of multipurpose room so many hospitals have and hope soon to replace, and have had and have hoped to replace for years. An arrangement of people sitting in a circle and speaking so that they can easily be heard is not to be found. Rather, people sit in concentric circles on plastic pillowed couches and "easy" chairs that in one corner surround a coffee table littered with ashtrays. Everyone looks nervous. Everyone looks as if he or she were trying to look at ease. Were it not for the shining nameplates adorning the medical students and their slimmer-fitting clothing and the funnels of cigarette smoke spuming from the patients, expressions would go far to suggest there is a human condition in common.

Following are excerpts from three sessions.

## SESSION ONE

P:        . . . so you have to come to the hospital and there's nothing to do, so you ask for like a pool table or something . . . and nothing, etc.

P 2:    They don't care.

[Silence]

P:        I asked, what's her name, you know? And she gives me some crap. You know? About how [inaudible].

P 2:    What's it to them? It's always the same old shit, etc.

Ψ:       It is good to have someone to blame.

P:        Who's he?

P 2:    I don't know. He didn't say.

P 3:    What'd he say?

P 2:    I don't know. Something about blame.

P:        What's he say? I ain't blaming nobody. I'm just saying they don't do nothing.

P 3:    Ignore him. Anyway, he won't say who he is.

Ψ:       I am being blamed for thinking I am being blamed. [Silence] I get the idea that when people feel in danger of feeling at fault, it is good to find someone else to blame.

P 2:    You must feel bad because you are blaming us!

P 3:    Don't let's get into that. I didn't come here to discuss blame. I came here to meet them [looking at the medical students]. They have succeeded in life, and we haven't: so I thought we could learn from them. But they haven't said a damn thing.

Ψ:        When people feel helpless, it is good to find someone to blame.

P 3:      Shut up. I'm talking to them.

M.S.:     It's hard for us too — I don't know what to say. Could you — you
          know — sort of say what we . . . I . . .

Ψ:        When people don't know what to do and feel bad, it is a relief to find
          someone to blame.

M.S. 2:   I don't know if you know this, but all we got was a schedule saying
          Group 1:40–2:30. We don't know what this is for. We don't know
          what we are supposed to do. Any more, I guess, than you do.

Ψ:        Although people appear to believe they don't know what to do, what
          they do do is behave as if blame were a very useful thing to do in this
          group.

P:        Him and his blame!

P 2:      It's the exact same with us! The sheet — you know? Says like Art or
          Group Therapy, says just Group!

[Here everyone looks very cheerful and alert. Many laugh.]

Ψ:        What a good atmosphere! What a good feeling! Do you notice how
          everyone's spirits rise when it is clear that not only is there someone
          to blame but everyone agrees there is the *same* someone to blame?

[Silence]

M.S.:     That's true, that's really true. I've noticed when I can't do something
          or feel I can't — afraid — I look around for some excuse, something to
          blame it on — until I realize that if it's going to get done, *I* just have
          to do it anyway.

[Silence]

Ψ:        So, now we have the questions: Does helplessness make us want to
          blame, or does blaming make us helpless? Is it that I am helpless
          because you are letting me down, or, *because* I want to feel you are
          letting me down, I feel helpless?


## SESSION TWO

(Seven weeks later; hence, a new set of medical students. Some new patients,
some patients previously present.)

[Silence]

P:        This is worse than Community Meeting. At least there, there is
          something to talk about.

P 2:      That doesn't make talking about anything worth it. Community
          Meeting sucks.

P 3:      What's the purpose of this meeting, anyway?

P 4:      You think you're going to get an answer? They never answer, like
          (P 2) said about Community Meeting. It's this way in every group.

P:        So why did you come?

| | |
|---|---|
| *P 3:* | To see if they [*gesturing toward the medical students*] had something to contribute. Evidently they don't. |
| *M.S.:* | There are lots of groups? |
| *P:* | Oh, yes. Community Meeting. Therapy Group, Art Group, etc. |
| *M.S.:* | And they're *all* like this? |
| *P 2:* | Yes. Either they don't talk or they twist what you say. |
| *M.S.:* | Why do you suppose that is? |
| *P 2:* | How are we supposed to know? |
| *[Silence]* | |
| *M.S. 2:* | But no one talks in any of the meetings? |
| *Ψ:* | Insofar as people believe the needed information is elsewhere than in themselves, the interview technique would appear to make great good sense. |
| *P:* | Where do you believe the answers lie? |
| *Ψ:* | Since you believe good answers are in me, you interview me. |
| *[Silence]* | |
| *P:* | Well, what am I supposed to do? |
| *Ψ:* | Since you believe good answers are in me, you interview me. |
| *P 2:* | You see, that's the way all the groups are. |
| *M.S. 3:* | How many groups do you attend? |
| *Ψ:* | It seems a very nice idea that the really valuable information is outside one's own grasp and in someone else's possession. |
| *P:* | I agree. We never act as if we have the answers to our own problems. |
| *P 2:* | Well, if we did, would we be stuck in this dump? Do you think you have all the answers? |
| *P:* | Not all. No one does. |
| *P 2:* | Well, he thinks he does. Do you think you do? |
| *M.S. 3:* | No. |
| *P 2:* | No one thinks we have all the answers except you. Who are you, anyway? |
| *Ψ:* | I am being interviewed in the belief that I have valuable answers. But I am supposed to be the only one who thinks so. People who think they may have useful information get in trouble here today. |
| *P:* | See, he won't even tell you who he is. He wouldn't even answer your question. |
| *P 2:* | Why won't you tell me who you are? Why won't you answer my question? |
| *Ψ:* | People are getting the goods on me. I am being revealed as a person who has what it takes, but won't give it. |
| *P:* | I think he's right. What does it matter who he is? We have answers. It's just that we won't use them. |
| *P 2:* | Well, if you have all those terrific answers, what are they? |
| *Ψ:* | One can't believe one has usable information and be very popular. |

The only good idea is that the useful information is elsewhere and has yet to be discovered. That way we can feel better about feeling so stuck.

*P:*       Last time you were here . . .

*P 2:*    I don't remember; he was here before?

*P:*       I remember him.

*P 2:*    When?

*Ψ:*      Interviewing!

*P 2:*    Fuck off!

*Ψ:*      Take that for thinking you have an answer.

*P:*       Last time he was here he said that blaming others made us feel helpless because we were expecting them to do what we were afraid to.

*P 3:*    Oh yes, I remember!

*M.S.:*   It sounds like he is saying more or less the same thing.

*Ψ:*      No interviewing this time around.

*P:*       Do you think he's right?

*M.S. 2:* Do you?

*Ψ:*      It would be sad to think that ordinary answers inside of oneself were the best one could get.

*P:*       I agree.

*P 3:*    Right on!

*Ψ:*      So if we all agreed there were better answers elsewhere, we could feel better, even if not getting them kept us stuck. But watch out if you think your inside information, bad as it is, is good enough to go on.

*P:*       See, he even says himself that his inside answers stink!

*M.S.:*   No, I think I see what he means . . .

          [*Silence*]


## SESSION THREE

Most people present appear to have been present several times before. Fifty or sixty people are alertly silent.)

*Ψ:*      The door is the Breast. It is left open in the hope that there is more and better to come. My own Breast, like those of the others' here, is deemed insufficient — on this everyone agrees. This agreement is expressed in the silence. The motto of this group might be: "Only suckers take what they can get!"

*P:*       How are you getting along after your operation, Millie?

*M.S.:*   What sort of procedure did you have?

[*Further discussion falters; silence*]

*Ψ:*      The silence has become the Breast. It is left open in hopes that something more and better can come from it than what we have had so far.

*P:*        You and your fucking "breast."

**Ψ**:       My Breast has been discovered to be capable of sexual intercourse;
           perhaps the thought of it having had sexual intercourse makes the
           grounds for its refusal or for it being bitten to shreds.

*P:*        (This is Millie) If my husband knew I would have to listen to this
           kind of talk, he would take me out of here.

*M.S.:*     She has a point there.

*Millie:*   My husband doesn't approve of talking dirty.
           [*Nods all around*]

**Ψ**:       It is a relief, perhaps, to think of a couple where there are not filthy
           doings going on, instead of myself and someone where there might
           be.

*1st M.S.:* Don't you and Dr. S. meet after this meeting to discuss it?

*Dr. S.:*   Caught in the act!

[*Much laughter*]

**Ψ**:       The feeling of being left out of a sexual couple is painful: Why am
           I left out? What will it take for me to be included? Where will I get
           what it takes? The door becomes a breast that might be there. The
           silence might be the cupboard where what it takes is stored. But if
           we use up the silence, if we close the door, what will be left to hope
           for?

*M.S.:*     Oh, if you want the door closed . . . [*Closes it*]

*P:*        I don't think that is what he meant. I think he was saying that we are
           afraid we'll never get enough of what it takes to be loved and that we
           are scared to use up what we have.
               (This now becomes a matter of wide discussion; those present
           appear to need to sort out their positions on this and reach a
           consensus.)

*P:*        This is a good hospital; they take very good care of you here.

*P:*        What is it like for you people — the doctors, I mean?

*M.S.:*     [*Consults others with eye searches*] Very good. The training is excellent.
           But this group is, well, weird. We heard of it from other guys in our
           class. The say you go in feeling like a med student and uh . . .
           um. . . .

*P:*        It's the sex — all the time. Too much. I want to forget about it, see,
           but they won't let it drop. I mean, I can't think with it always going
           on! Who can think? Makes you crazy, sex all the time.

*5th M.S.:* I agree. He doesn't have to continually use sexual metaphors. I find
           it offensive. Why is the door a breast?

*M.S.:*     The knob!

[*Much laughter and foot stamping*]

*M.S.:*     No, but I mean seriously. . . .

**Ψ**:       [*to Dr. S.*] I think it is so difficult for children when they feel that
           something in the air that tells them that either or both the parents

are up to something, that they want to get together at least among
themselves. . . .

*Dr. S.:*  Yes, I felt lonely when they [*nodding to M.S. 5 and P 5*] were having
it off together. I found myself looking around for someone for
myself—

*P:*  —Dr. S. is lonely!

*P:*  Dr. S. is frustrated!! [*Much laughter, "Poor Dr. S.," etc. —nervously on the
part of the medical students, with whom Dr. S. works in a group of their own.*]

*P:*  It's a good thing you are in this group. He will give you a nice big
bosom so you can find some nice girl for yourself.

*M.S.:*  With a knob on it!

*M.S.:*  On her!

[*More laughter*]

Ψ:  By talking directly to you I appear to have stimulated thoughts of us
as a homosexual couple and thought that homosexual love might be
the way out of feeling left out. There are now two problems. One is
to find you a nice person so that you will stop having intercourse
with me. The other is which person in the couple keeps the knob and
which gives it up.

*P:*  Snob? Did you say snob?

Ψ:  When Dr. S. or I don't have intercourse except in words with the
other members of this group, we are naturally felt to be snobs.


## DISCUSSION


As group sessions are, these are rich with meaning. Perhaps more,
certainly other, than what we chose to pick up on might have been
selected by other workers. A few words concerning the reasons for the
choices we made might therefore be in order.

Already likely to be evident is why we chose not to focus upon
individuals. Our purpose, of course, was to discover (so as to uncover)
the bonds that people form when as fellow beings they confront the
difficulties that are here in a group. By displaying the similarities that
were revealed, we hoped to give flex to the distance between patient
and student, leaving each free to assert whatever qualities he or she felt
widened or closed that distance.

In the early years, before it had become clear how very much most
people could make use of, we stayed closer to interpretations that made
conscious sense: I would talk of the door without adverting to its
symbolic representation of, say, the Breast. This was a concession to

the staff, who attended these meetings and who were guided by their own hopes of maintaining a social alliance between themselves and their patients. As time went on, however, I was more and more persuaded that people sometimes need precisely those interpretations that don't make "sense"; and, moreover, that giving these in a group gave to them a resonant "sense" that devolved from the experience of hearing such ideas with people who were also working with and against them much as one is oneself. (The "knob" in the latter session is an example; already its meaning as both penis and as breast when cognate with penis is becoming evident.)

The reader will judge whether such interpretations can be said to have variously reached the people present — whether, for example, the reposition of hope by the patients in their hospitalization and by the students in their training and by both in leaving the (a) door open was properly inferred and communicated.

My own impression is that it was a matter of subsets, and that by the end of the group experience both of these subsets felt a curious and compelling fellow-feeling, each with the other. But each saw something, too, about their differences. Each, I think, came in touch with the private aspects of themselves that all felt when, inevitably, deeply alone in public.

# 7

# On the Systematic Study of Self-Deception

What *is* the psychoactive ingredient in psychotherapy? What *did* Freud mean when he said, "Where id was, let ego be." Did he mean an undoing of all that knowledge repressed to enhance one's reputation in the eyes of the self? All those insights from which one had previously turned into outsights (in the manner of outtakes of a film)? Does psychoanalysis have something to do with learning the truth about one's self? About others? About reality, whatever that is, when it's at home?

If so, what might the truth be—and better yet, who's truth might it be?

This little essay does not attempt to deal with what is indubitably the life's blood of the psychoanalytic endeavor—that esoteric relationship that makes encounters or re-encounters with "truth" finally bearable; that special kind of care—well, love—in which one person can stand to stand another without having to do anything about him—which might itself turn out to be the psychoactive ingredient! I take this question up in the next essay, on "Treat or Treatment." In this one I'm after smaller game.

---

In defining psychoanalysis as "the systematic study of self-deceptions and their motivations," Heinz Hartmann set forth a criterion that encompasses certain psychoanalysts more surely and less irrelevantly

91

than any theoretical or technical differences keep them apart. W. R. Bion (1966), who is one of those encompassed, speaks precisely to this point:

> I do not and never have been able to believe that what separates scientists are their differences in theory. I have not always felt "separated" from someone who differs from me in the theories he holds; that does not seem to afford a standard of measurement by which the gap can be assessed. Similarly, I have felt very far separated from some who, apparently, hold the same theories. Therefore, if the "gap" is to "be measured," it will have to be in some domain other than that of theory. [p. 578]

That domain, I suggest, is represented by the degree to which the analysts in question occupy themselves only with the truth. On the face of it, Hartmann and Bion look rather different. Hartmann is, first of all, a "Freudian," Bion a "Kleinian." As a Freudian, Hartmann has concerned himself largely with the degree to which ego functioning remains exempt from pressures of the impulses, while Bion has examined how pressures from the impulses influence ego functioning. But when Bion (1966) observes that "My suspicion of applied psycho-analysis, even if 'applied' to curing people, is that it is a method of bringing psycho-analysis under control and rendering it harmless to the Establishment" and that "as a rule, no analyst should permit himself to harbour desires; even the desire to cure is inimical to psycho-analytical development or the development of psycho-analysis, (pp. 575–576)" he joins Hartmann in viewing psychoanalysis as no more or less than the study of self-deceptions and their motivations. Bion (1970) writes:

> The psychoanalyst's view is expressed by Doctor Johnson's letter to Bennet Laughton: "Whether to see life as it is will give us much consolation, I know not; but the consolation which is drawn from truth, if any there be, is solid and durable; that which may be derived from errour must be, like its original, fallacious and fugitive." [p. 7]

Ronald Laing too is encompassed within this domain, sharing with Bion and Hartmann and other such psychoanalytic theorists as Erik Erikson a preoccupation with the truth and truth's vicissitudes. Though this is evident in his previous works ("There is little conjunction of truth and social 'reality'" — *Politics of Experience* [1967]) the first knot in his *Knots* (1970) makes it unmistakable:

> They are playing a game. They are playing at not
> playing a game. If I show them I see they are, I
> shall break the rules and they will punish me.
> I must play their game, of not seeing I see the game. [p. 1]

It is interesting to speculate what, in addition to the training analysis, enables these men to focus so clearly on truth, to see "the game." About Erikson one can guess that his experience in studying other cultures, other historical times, and even, to a degree, animal ethology, augmented whatever grasp of relativity preceded these studies. Bion, it seems clear, learned enormously from the groups with which he worked. For groups, when one does not set out to acculturate them, set out to acculturate *one*. No doubt Laing's work with families served a similar function for him. Something then in the way of a cultural analysis seems a necessary adjunct to the personal analysis, because the personal analysis is a cultural artifact. This is perhaps especially true of the training analysis, which is to a degree done by and for the institutes which are, of course, social institutions responsible to the larger social order of its members. But one also has to take account of the work done by Bion and Laing with psychotic personalities.

Work with psychotics who, as Bion notes, count on engendering resistance in the analyst and who therefore unequivocally require of the analyst a painful struggle with the need for his own self-deceptions, seems also to have prepared Bion and Laing to do without the comfort of conventional wisdom. Envy, and envy's wish to denude and drain another of his most valued attributes, is a prepotent feature of all schizophrenics. If the analyst has deceptions to defend, envy will grind the analytic relationship into what Freud called analysis interminable and Bion calls chronic murder.

Whatever the side-effects, however, the end result is plain. These men have developed that special feeling for the relativity of truth, a feeling not possible for those who fail to see an alternative. Only when there are alternatives does skepticism ignite the depth-giving, binocular view of experience. Since everyone's self-deceptions are jeopardized by the knowledge that there are alternative possibilities, it behooves everyone to find others of like self-deceptive predispositions, so they can together constitute a uni-verse. It is inevitable that men like Bion and Laing not only have to become social psychologists but also encounter difficulties with their nominal groups.

Not unexpectedly, this matter of truth engages Bion's and Laing's attentions. I have already quoted Laing's first knot. Bion discusses this issue in the chapter "The Mystic and The Group." He says that growth requires truth, but growth involves upheaval and psychological pain. The mystic is he who has access to new truths. Thus, the mystic is the source for both growth and pain. The group — or establishment — values the first and loathes the second, and wishes to use the mystic for the good in him, but annihilate the jeopardizing elements. The antiestablishment parts of the group proceed in an identical fashion.

That Laing has been embraced as a cult figure by the antiestablishment is a key to where he and Bion differ in how they use the truth. Much of what Laing has written is clearly inspired by D. W. Winnicott's formulations on the "false self." The "false self," according to Winnicott, is an entire organization of as-if's, would-be's and ersatzes which cumulate into a masquerade that lives a lie in order to live. The measure of the falsity, however, is not relative to the "true" coinage of consensual "reality"; to the contrary, the similarity the false self has to the facsimile of the well-adjusted being is all too exact. The falsity is discernible only by penetrating to the vestigial truth of the deeply held inner experience, the psychic reality — what Laing, borrowing, calls Om, and Bion calls is-ness and at-one-ment and grid-classifies as "O."

Laing goes beyond Winnicott in his meticulous attention to the transpersonal aspects of truth and falsity. His special talent for observing the minutiae of the transactions and his great patience in pellucidly parsing out what transpires make him a superior guide.

But Laing, in contrast to Bion, is attracted more powerfully to revelation than to discovery; accordingly he looks where the light is brightest. This is a common flaw in the evangelist, and in Laing's case his writings relate to the dominant psychiatric culture as the Black Mass relates to the Sacred Mass. But the Lord's Prayer said backwards is still the Lord's Prayer; contrariety still celebrates what it does not wish to consecrate. Nevertheless, inverting the order of things is a start, for that too is a way to see "the more that is there than meets the eye." And if Laing's revelations are approximations that are not quite yet truth, they are still helpful.

*Knots*, consisting only of observations, is free of the apocalyptic polemicizing found in Laing's previous books. Here his pleasure in startling us is confined to his intricate observations and a style curiously reminiscent of Eliot in "Ash Wednesday." The examples that *Knots* offers to the points in his previous books make it a useful adjunct to them, but the book also stands on its own.

In contrast, it might be said that Bion looks where it is least lighted and attempts a most difficult task. Disclaiming theorizing, Bion sets out to chart and codify what in this third book he calls the Elements of Psychoanalysis. His thesis is that psychoanalytic theory is a series of accretions which must be refitted to the observations from which the theory was derived. To do this, he uses a grid that has a classification of the development of psychologic activity on one axis, and a categorization of the activity on the other. This forges onto the grid everything from hallucinations to mathematical calculus. Once the elements are placed, the problem is understanding their meaning and function, and their transformations (the title of his fourth book) from grid category to grid category. "The grid is intended to remind the psycho-analyst . . . that what matters is both the communication and the use to which it is being put." If this sounds vexingly intricate, it is, especially as Bion constructs a language, sometimes to be free of associational distractions and sometimes to invoke other associations. Moreover his style, which begrudges every illustrative example that might deflect from the terse precision he is after, is as condensed as the mathematical formulas in which he yearns to convey his thinking.

Nevertheless, the result is elegant. Bion takes the familiar constituents of psychoanalytic theory and spins them as if in a kaleidoscope into forms and relationships that were seldom before evident. For example, the Oedipus complex, when searched for the meaning of the Sphinx and Tiresias, is seen to constitute a variation on a theme, other forms of which are manifest in the Eden and Babel myths; the common denominator is the problem of man's knowing God the (his) father. Clinically, the implications of this concordance range from thought disorders (one of Bion's particular interests), through stammering, to the function of telling lies.

Whereas Laing's fascination is with relationships, Bion's is with relationship. In his first book, *Experiences in Groups* (1961), Bion observes the behavior of groups, asking continually, as it were, what the members are trying to do. His sensitivity to relationship takes him well beyond the previously identified analogue, in which the group leader stands for the parent. Not merely by noting the interchange of objects (of leader into parent) but by noting the nature of the activity, the verb, he is able to discern what happens in groups to a degree so extensive and illuminating that, had he written nothing more, he should have to be counted among the generative minds of this century.

In his series of books from *Learning from Experience* (1962) to *Transformations* (1965) Bion concerns himself with fantasy, and the disinclination to achieve reverie. Here too the verb is the guide to his inferences about people's use of objects. In *Transformations*, for example, he delineates ways of relating facts extrapolated not only from the clinically familiar alimentary and reproductive modes of experiencing, but also those ways which can be described in sensory, spatial, and finally nonsensory terms. His examination of projective identification and the transference—the two prime sorts of relationship—takes careful account of how these two conjunctions modify or are modified by the various experiential modalities.

The potential for failure and the methodology necessary for developing the alternative are what Bion turns to in his most recent book, *Attention and Interpretation* (1970). How, he asks, can the analyst perceive the patient's essential experience from within its particular formations and transformations, and then formulate this experience for the patient—and how can the nature of this activity be conceptualized? But before turning to these matters, it is necessary to set the stage. If for Bion and Laing psychoanalysis as science and as "therapy" is to see the truth, the whole truth, and to do nothing more nor less—neither cure nor treat, reform nor educate—with what should truth contend?

My own set of words for the main lines of both men's thought is that the great enemy of truth is hope. Hope engenders the fantasies that overwhelm truth and establish in its place self-deceptions. One's own self-deceptions depend, at least in part, on fostering self-deceptions in others. One does this by tempting their hopes. While man is not an island, he is by these requirements in fact a group creature.

In *Knots* (1970) Laing documents how entangled we become by failing to abandon the primal hope, which is expressed as follows:

One is inside
then outside what one has been inside
One feels empty
because there is nothing inside oneself
One tries to get inside oneself
    that inside of the outside
    that one was once inside

once one tries to get oneself inside what
one is outside:
to eat or to be eaten
to have the outside inside and to be
inside the outside

But this is not enough. One is trying to get
the inside of what one is outside inside, and to
get inside the outside. But one does not get
inside the outside by getting the outside inside
for;
although one is full inside of the inside of the outside
one is on the outside of one's own inside
and by getting inside the outside
one remains empty because
while one is on the inside
even the inside of the outside is outside
and inside oneself there is still nothing
There has never been anything else
and there never will be [p. 83]

If the unsolvable paradox of the primal conflict lies in the simultaneously hoping to at once be contained by the "breast" (here as a
symbol for the womb) and contain it, one must be reconciled to
abandoning at least one of these hopes. Failure to find reconciliation
leads one on a prolonged, perhaps lifelong quest, which eventually
leads one no further than around another hapless circle, the symbol for
which is the knot. Each journey around may seem to prescribe a
different course over a cat's-cradle terrain marked by alternate desires.
But no matter. Regardless of the path's configuration, "one goes round
in a circle, in a whirl, going everywhere and getting nowhere" (Laing).

At the entrance to the Inferno, Dante puts the sign, "Who enter
here, leave all hope behind." Indeed, there is no torment quite like
hopelessness. But hopelessness marks the presence of thwarted hope,
not hope's absence. Laing, in the epigraph of *Self and Others* (1971),
quotes Confucius: "The way out is the door, why is it that no one will
use this method?" Man is so reluctant to renounce hope and so eager
to preserve it that he spurns its fulfillment lest he lose his hope.

Hope is for more and better; less than that induces despair. Despair
induces suffering, and man's willingness to suffer — to experience and
tolerate psychological pain, in Bion's phrase, and ontologic anxiety, in

Laing's — is limited. The psychotic individual, more than the rest of us, takes the precaution of preserving his hopes by losing his desires and by depriving the object of his desires of their desirability. "Some people exist," Bion writes, "who are so intolerant of pain and frustration (or in whom pain or frustration is so intolerable) that they feel the pain but will not suffer it and so cannot be said to discover it. . . . The patient who will not suffer pain fails to 'suffer' pleasure, and this denies the patient the encouragement he might otherwise receive from accidental or intrinsic relief" (1970, p. 9 ).

The temptations of pleasure, indeed of relief, lie beyond the door of which Laing speaks, and it is important to understand that they are kept there so they do not jeopardize hopes. Hopes, needing to be insulated, are best served when they are mediated by the group whose shared convictions protect hopes against erosion by pain or pleasure. Self-deceptions are susceptible to reinforcement or destruction by the examples of others. Groups barricade the members within from those "others" without. Man, unlike other animals, wars within the species to preserve the intactness of the boundary-preserving hopes. Truth is the first casualty of war, and war is therefore fought to preserve groups' deceptions.

Psychoanalysis takes place between people. The implications of Laing's thinking for the practice of psychoanalysis begin with his basic assertion that a man can only experience his experience of another man. The fidelity of that experience then has to be a function of the analyst's capacity to suffer the absence of hope. Collusion of hopes is the antithesis of psychoanalytic possibility:

Jill is a distorting mirror to herself.
Jill has to distort herself to appear undistorted
to herself.

To undistort herself, she finds Jack to distort her
distorted image in his distorting mirror
She hopes that his distortion of her distortion may
undistort her image without her having to distort herself.
[Laing 1970, p. 31]

Bion follows this line of thought in both subtle and far-reaching ways. He feels that the analyst cannot experience sensuous pleasures during the course of the hour or he fails to apprehend the ineffable presensuous pain analysands are preoccupied with. The analyst must school himself to be a kind of *tabula rasa*, a blank photographic plate, a medium upon which the analysand may leave his imprint. This includes and even goes beyond the absence of personal and cultural countertransference. It means (Bion quoting Keats) a "negative capability, that is, when a man is capable of being in uncertainties, mysteries, doubts, without any irritable reaching after fact and reason." And, in Bion's phrase, without permitting oneself "the opacity of memory and desire." And in Freud's, "blinding oneself artificially."

To attain to the state of mind essential for the practice of psycho-analysis I avoid any exercise of memory; I make no notes. When I am tempted to remember the events of any particular session I resist the temptation. If I find myself wandering mentally into the domain of memory I desist. In this my practice is at variance with the view that notes should be kept or that psycho-analysts should find some method by which they can record their sessions mechanically or should train themselves to have a good memory. If I find that I am without any clue to what the patient is doing and am tempted to feel that the secret lies hidden in something I have forgotten, I resist any impulse to remember what happened or how I interpreted what happened on some previous occasion. If I find that some half-memory is beginning to obtrude I resist its recall no matter how pressing or desirable its recall may seem to be. [Bion 1970, pp. 55–56]

Such a course, as Bion notes, is not possible for those who will not suffer and thus seek and serve that truth, our only consolation for the abnegation of hope. Is there consolation, then, in "mere white truth in simple nakedness" (Tennyson)? Perhaps none save that in Shakespeare's words, "Truth hath a quiet breast."

## REFERENCES

Bion, W. R. (1961). *Experiences in Groups*. New York: Basic Books.
_____ (1962). *Learning from Experience*. New York: Basic Books.
_____ (1965). *Transformations*. New York: Basic Books.
_____ (1966). Review of *Medical Orthodoxy and the Future of Psychoanalysis*. *International Journal of Psycho-Analysis* 47:575–579.
_____ (1970). *Attention and Interpretation*. New York: Basic Books.

Hartmann, H. (1959). Psychoanalysis as a scientific theory. In *Psychoanalysis, Scientific Method and Philosophy: A Symposium*, ed. S. Hook. New York: New York University Press.

Laing, R. D. (1967). *Politics of Experience*. New York: Pantheon.

_____ (1970). *Knots*. New York: Pantheon.

_____ (1971). *Self and Others*. New York: Pelican.

# II

## Aspects of
## Technique

# 8

# Treat or Treatment

If I have seen a person in therapy or analysis who did not actively wish to uncover a trauma of some determining sort, I do not remember who. There is something deeply satisfying about the "aha!" of "So that is it!" Freud's theories would not, I think, have gained the acceptance they did had they not initially been rooted in the idea of a forgotten childhood trauma. Even now people like Jeffrey Masson reinstate the view that it isn't that there wasn't a trauma, it's that the bad people stole it away.

But there is another basis: It is Why may I seek therapy but others not? Have I actually been chosen, or am I thrusting myself upon the world in a disorderly and unmannerly fashion? This is the survivor guilt for attempting to be among those who flourish.

If this question is not taken up, people have a difficult time feeling it is all right to be sick or get well. They will, accordingly, require of the therapist again and again to reassure them: "It is all right, no one else might know it, but we know how tough times have been — even if there isn't a traumatic incident by which to prove it."

This reassurance becomes a source of gratitude (where otherwise envy may have reigned), and there is no doubt that people do better for therapists who inspire such gratitude. Feeling better is not to be despised.

But feeling better has an ambiguous relationship to "getting better," which for a while involves feeling if anything rather worse.

The question is whether or not the patient can be assisted toward suffering instead of merely guiltily, angrily, or masochistically feeling pain. This, in turn, has a good deal to do with the therapist's capacity to suffer — to endure and allow pain without romanticizing it as something inflicted.

There might be something to be said for finessing the issue altogether, by making a close and systematic study of the inner person a routine part of life.

Seelsorgers: Take note.

---

The series of encounters of which psychotherapy is comprised constitute an intricate transaction. At the same time, the "success" of the transaction is neither so commonplace nor so absolute that students of the subject have been willing to stop trying somehow to isolate factors in psychotherapy, hoping first to distinguish the active from the inert ingredients and then to refine those they believe will bring about success.

Various practitioners, theorists, empiricists, and methodologists have come to favor one or another of the ingredients above the others. Eysenck, for example, has supported the candidacy of Time itself. His studies, matching groups of therapy patients with controls, have persuaded him that Time does make a difference in people's lives, though not always; and if psychotherapy also makes a difference, although not always, then the time spent in it, he argues, may be the prepotent ingredient.

This conclusion, not unnaturally, has failed to commend itself to psychotherapists, who propose nominees of a somewhat different character. Chief among their candidates are Insight, Social Learning, the Corrective Emotional Experience, and Frustration. To take the last first, supporters of the Frustration hypothesis argue that since so many of the people who enter psychotherapy do so as a last resort, having given preference to such environmental alterations as changes in job, spouse, life-style, or geographic location, their discovery that therapy too provides scant compliance with their wish to remain as they are at last evokes a shift in motivations that occasions personal change.

The Corrective Emotional Experience advocates represent a more complex hypothesis. Part of their thesis rests on the assumption that people who become patients have suffered deprivations in the course of their lives. Hence, the course of treatment is organized around judicious doses of the missing experiences. But only some of what is prescribed falls into the TLC genre, for example, Carl Rogers's "Unconditional Positive Regard." There is also a disciplinary side to the supplements; this is leveled against what are viewed as overdoses of previous indulgences. The Behaviorist school of treatment has simplified the Corrective Emotional Experience position to that of providing rather concrete rewards and punishments in order to tempt or coerce patients toward or away from particular configurations of behavior.

The Social Learning hypothesis has found its current zenith in the Sensitivity Training and Encounter group experiences. In these, the participants' behavior at the outset is exposed to increasingly candid responses, while at the same time each is encouraged to experiment with new ways of experiencing himself and of conducting relationships. Individual psychotherapy is also viewed, by those who nominate Social Learning as the active ingredient, as resting largely on the role model of the therapist and in a series of feedbacks from him concerning the socially functional adequacy of the patient's behavior.

Then there are those who hold for the Insight candidacy. Their thesis is that the patient is benefited primarily by coming to know and understand the reasons for his reactions and behavior. The assumptions here are that people act as if things are true that are not, that these beliefs — for all they motivate behavior — are unconscious, and that their revelation enables motivations to be modified.

The Insight hypothesis comes from, and remains the cornerstone of, classical psychoanalysis. But quite typically in the psychoanalytic situation, though interpretation is the primary occupation of the analyst, Time, Frustration, Social Learning, and the Corrective Emotional Experience all have a part to play. The two participants both require time, and timing is an important contribution of the analyst. Frustration brings conflicts to the fore, particularly over resistances. The therapeutic alliance, whereby the therapist often quite actively attempts to interest the patient in reflecting upon and considering what is taking place, is developed quite as much by what the analyst exemplifies as by what he occasionally counsels or cautions the patient about. So Social Learning has its part as well. Finally the analyst's reliability, consistency, and the fact that he can be trusted to serve no other cause than the elucidation of the patient's conflicting motivations, comprise essential contributions toward a corrective emotional experience. Stauncher proponents of the Insight thesis, however, argue that Insight via interpretations is the active ingredient and the others are either relatively inert — designed mainly to hold interpretation in suspension (I use the term in the pharmaceutical sense)—or essentially catalytic.

If therapists have their beliefs about what the therapeutic situation must consist of, so do patients. Not one of the nominees I have discussed so far is a candidate of the therapist alone. Each of the hypotheses mentioned has been put forward with some urgency and in varying degrees of explicitness by every patient I have encountered or whose therapy I have supervised. However, when studied one by one, and especially when taken as something to understand in some depth, the preferences of individual patients are not easily susceptible to generalization. And it is very much to this problem that Strupp, Fox, and Lessler (1969) have addressed themselves in their book *Patients View Their Psychotherapy*.

The authors report on two studies they conducted of ex-patients' retrospective experience of the encounter and current appraisal of benefits received. The first study involves people who underwent long-term, privately conducted psychotherapy with relatively more experienced therapists; the second, people who had clinical care of shorter duration with psychotherapists in training.

The research itself has a number of shortcomings, some of which the authors are the first to acknowledge. It is, first of all, a questionnaire study, and such studies, asking for verbal professions of attitude, rarely present an accurate—and never a balanced—picture. Second, the questionnaires make extensive use of rating categories of the "extremely much" to "nothing at all" variety, and the responses to such formats may more accurately reflect the way people *use* categories— some having a penchant for the extreme, others for middling statements—than the viewpoint held on the item as such. Third, the items by their nature make the meaning of the response equivocal, as for example: "I often had the feeling [my therapist] talked too much." Too much for what—for what he had to say? For my ability to listen? For my own sense of what I deserved? For my relative opportunity to talk? Clearly, the "fact" could be affirmed or denied for such a multitude of reasons that we cannot really know what in fact the situation was. Finally, and most to the issue of the favored ingredient, there is the shortcoming inherent in the research itself. The authors, as they have every right to do, focus almost exclusively on the ex-patients' retrospective view of the *therapist*, and not, as the title implies, of the therapy. In so doing they get the results they ask for—for example, that the therapist is the key factor in the process and outcome of the therapy. He may be; but, equally, he may not be: the fact is that we cannot know, and in this the data presented and much of the discussion offered by the authors could substantially, if unintentionally, mislead. The artifactual nature of research findings in studies of psychotherapy are, of course, far from exclusive to Strupp, Fox, and Lessler. But it does not help, I think, when they follow up what I read (and shall presently quote) as the key finding of their researches with: "Clearly in this instance, as in certain others, the patients' reports cannot be taken at face value" (p. 117). This is too much like the old conundrum about the man who says he is a Cretan but that all Cretans are liars for a research report on a serious study. May the authors really have it both ways?

The central finding of both studies, and the one to which the authors take exception, is this:

A positive attitude toward the therapist proved to be closely related to success in therapy, irrespective of how that success was measured. Patients who rated their own therapy as successful described their therapists as warm, attentive, interested, understanding and respectful. Furthermore they perceived the therapist as experienced and active in the therapeutic situation. Patients rated highly successful by their therapists have a similar description by the therapist. These patients were less likely to report intense anger toward their therapists than were their less successful counterparts, who also tended to report uncertainty about the therapist's attitude toward them. (p. 116)

That the authors wince at this ("We do not subscribe to the view of psychotherapy as the 'purchase of friendship,' although this is what the patients obviously wanted, and, if their reports are taken at face value, to some extent received" [p. 117]) is understandable, but in another sense. They too have their nominees for active ingredient: "The therapist teaches and the patient learns. . . . As teacher (or substitute parent), he dispenses rewards and punishments and employs a variety of psychological techniques for helping the patient achieve greater autonomy and self-direction. Once he — the patient — has deeply experienced and recognized the error or foolishness of his ways ('insight'), he may gradually modify his behavior" (pp. 2–3).

But even if we discount the possibility that a central finding may be a methodological artifact and fly in face of the authors' wish to disown it, we are left with yet another problem. Ex-patients, we learn, seem to favor the "good therapist" — that is, the warm, attentive, active, kindly therapist — as their candidate for the ingredient that makes the difference. But do they deem or dub him so because he has proved helpful, or has help indeed burgeoned from his kindly behavior? Or is it that both a sense of being helped and a friendly view of the therapist has followed from yet a third or fourth factor? This, as well, we cannot know.

Confronted by the presence of so little of the known, we might well be tempted to drop the subject and harvest vineyards of greater certainty. On the other hand, since we have been dealing in candidacies all along, it can do no harm to add one more.

Let us take it, then, that the person of the therapist is regarded by these ex-patients as a factor of signal importance — that he *was* the therapeutically active ingredient. And, further, that when he is "good," patients feel and act benefited. Can a hypothesis be drawn to account for this?

The Corrective Emotional Experience advocates will have little trouble adducing theirs, and it may be that the "finding" does support their theory. But there is at least one other hypothesis that suggests itself. It is that a therapist is imbued with goodness at least partly to the extent that he meets his patient's more particular requirements of him — *whatever* these may be.

Consider, for example, a young woman who was briefly a patient of mine. She held a profound and most urgent conviction that nothing could benefit her but some kind of massive assault of nearly annihilating proportions. Though she was partially prepared to allow me to help her explore and come to understand this conviction, she could not feel at all satisfied that this process would be of any use. When after two or three weeks she chanced to learn of the phenomenon of electrical shock treatments, she decided that these and only these would do. As it happens, electrical shocks are not among my own favored candidates as therapeutic agent, so I instead renewed my attempts to enlist her help in the mutual exploration of her convictions I had in mind. Far from regarding this effort of mine as kindly, she clearly began to view me as cruel, cold, misguided, and even brutal, a category she had previously reserved for her father, who, no doubt relieved by her removal of this painful view from him, thereupon arranged for a practitioner of the science to administer a course of thirty-six treatments.

It is not the extremity of the example that I wish to emphasize, but its particularity. Not all people are so particular about what benefit must consist in as was that young woman. But all people have their convictions if they are not to be gripped by a Kafkaesque experience. I do not mean by conviction at all what has been called "faith," though for people in whom faith is expectant, faith reposed will work wonders. Faith, then, is but one such expectation, as the need for assault is another, and fancies about the contents of a pill or the color of a pill others still. A conviction about the properties of rewards and punishments or about the value of a psychoanalysis is also an expectation in search of reciprocation. So it is that there is no ingredient proposed by empiricist, methodologist, theorist, or therapist that has not been put forward, albeit on a more näive basis, by one or another of the patients I have come to know.

Those practitioners who attune themselves to a close consideration of the views of their individual patients recognize such convictions as part and parcel of the transference. For when examined with care, these convictions reveal the patient's deepest preconceptions of what went wrong in his life, what needs to be set right, and what it will take from the therapist for the patient to get from talk to sufficiency and defect to wholeness.

It cannot be surprising, therefore, that even when simply in the presence of an experience that complements their expectations, people feel benefited. Thus one can quite agree that, as Strupp, Fox, and Lessler note, it was more the who and the what, than the how and the why, that the ex-patients in their studies drew from their therapies. But to regard this as something questionable—as if instead of seeking enlightenment, as they were supposed to, the patients merely basked in the sun and came away with a good tan—is to carp. For, as they also point out, the majority of ex-patients studied entered therapy after suffering from such complaints as "dissatisfaction," "lack of purpose," and the like—complaints which the authors sum up as a "generalized unhappiness and estrangement" (p. 57). Such people, not unnaturally, want above all to *feel* better. And they quite typically hope to accomplish this either through a restoration of a once better experience, or by having the therapist offset the internal sources of their unhappiness. This is thus *their* candidate for psychoactive ingredient. If these wishes are fulfilled, they can and do feel benefited. Feeling benefited, moreover, they will often act with the increased vigor and temerity which in turn elicits reciprocal conferents from life. This expansive cycle exponentially increases the sense of benefit.

To be sure, such cycles can all too readily unwind again once the patient has left the source of therapeutic beneficence. This may be particularly true if the patient's response to the divergences that inevitably accompany the basic concordance are not treated with in some depth. One might assume just such a failure to make the tensions a focus of the therapy in those ex-patients in the study who were angry in therapy and remain so since. There is much to be said, then, for offering a treatment instead of a treat.

And yet it is hard to think why the simple benefits of a largely concordant encounter should be despised. But despised they are. Though therapists traditionally speak of "termination," not completion, and remind their unready-feeling patients that they will still be there if needed, the culture of psychotherapy shares with the culture-at-large a belief that therapy should be a once-in-a lifetime proposition. Special circumstances withstanding are indeed the exceptions that prove the rule. But why *should* "cure" be a forever-more attainment? Why *do* therapists of the persuasion represented by the authors struggle and strain to press on their uninterested patients an education that isn't wanted? Especially when this impingement may well interfere with the benefits concordance can offer? I suggest that much less can often do more than quite a lot—when the circumstances propitious for more enduring goals are wanting.

These circumstances derive from a concatenation of factors neither widely found nor easily catalyzed. Patients, for example, who want quite simply to feel better, by virtue of what they receive in the way of kindliness from their therapist, may need to return for refresher course after refresher course before they feel ready to tackle the question of why their psychic metabolism is such that good experiences fail to stick to their ribs. Surely one way *not* to catalyze this ready disposition is for the therapist to press on the patient a treatment more oriented to the pursuit of the ideals in his ideology than to the capacities and objectives of his patient. Psychotherapy, with us as we now recognize it for at least a century, is likely to last a while longer. Its usefulness to people will doubtless increase. But there can be no less doubt that the degree to which its contributions increase will closely follow the extent to which ideologies are expunged from its practice—and study.

## REFERENCE

Strupp, H. H., Fox, R., and Lessler, K. (1969). *Patients View Their Psychotherapy.* Baltimore: Johns Hopkins University Press.

# 9

# Confrontation

Of course there is no reason to confront a patient, short of desperation. But desperation is an important event, not generally experienced unless push has come to shove. Why should the analyst preempt it? Paradoxically it is usually only after he feels himself afflicted by such desperation that analyst wants to shove it back — but why did he take it on in the first place?

And yet I do not think, outside of naked curiosity, that I would like to meet the therapist who is invariant in respect to patients. I have listened to arrant nonsense over the years from therapists who explain why they are being "flexible" or using this or that "parameter," but as often as not the nonsense was in the conceptualization and not in the intuition. Therapists camp on a fault. As with the San Andreas fault there are powerful upheavals in store as the earth develops and rearranges itself. The therapist must develop a lightness of being, if he is not to become a Canute raging at waves.

Joining in on a slow shift to chronicity, however, does no one a favor. Nor does an entitling of entitlements. The course of a therapy engages both parties in an ongoing act of mourning: both are frustrated and sad that there cannot be more to their relationship; yet it is exactly that limit which fuels the analysis. Indeed, the therapist is distinguishable from the patient only with respect to his ability to tolerate those limits without reprisal. Without that, no amount of clever talk helps.

That patients must employ confrontation with their therapists may
be more understandable. The Wolf Man, burdened with an analyst
more occupied with wolfishly proving the importance of the Primal
Scene to his beloved detractors than with his patient, felt he had to
freeze Freud in his tracks. And while it may look as if Franz Alexander
(whose classic paper was much cited at the conference at which this
paper was first presented) was the one who confronted his smelly,
entitled young patient, it is likelier that shambles of a young man was
pushing Alexander (who was at that time, probably for all manner of
reasons, anyway thinking how to shorten the analytic process) toward
an edge of resentful despair. So too was the patient I discuss in this
paper obliged to give me an emphatic nudge when I could not take
account of my hatred and see that it did have to do with her and not
the concurrent events in the family onto which I had fobbed it.[1]

I heard from this patient a decade after her termination because
the pharmacologic agent she had been given did not keep her from
yearning for the good old days of psychotherapy which, she asserted,
she could no longer afford.

"Is it the old therapy you miss or a new one you don't have?"

"Oh, Mr. Boris, that is exactly it. I always want what you showed
me I want: I want everything to be new and exciting and better."

"So you have probably stopped mining the therapy we did have."

"Going over it and over it again you mean? Yes, I suppose I have.
Probably you would say I am undermining it! Oh, Mr. Boris, it is so
good to talk to you. You never change. Even after all these years you
are there, sturdy as a rock in a sculpture garden. I will call you again
in a year or two. You can hang up on me if you don't want to talk to
me. That's it! I can trust you to hang up on me if you don't want to
talk to me. Do you have any idea—I'm sure you do—how terrific it
is to be able to count on that?"

She seemed pleased that I continued to have hold of the hatred she
had to confront me with.

In this chapter I am groping toward an idea of what the
psychoanalytic datum might be. But I am too busy with technique to
get very far. I couldn't at the time of the therapy understand this
patient's feelings of being wrongfully alive, except as split-off
hostility. But that it was both that and something else was immediately clear to me later, in even so brief an encounter. I might do
better by her now. Still, there is more for her in the first therapy, if
she feels so inclined.

---

[1] I was lucky also in my first adult patient, a man who was having rather a time of
it with some voices when I introduced myself to him as his therapist. "I am out of
contact, hallucinating, incontinent," he told me, "and you ask if I mind if you smoke!"

My sturdiness—she might have wanted to say "stubbornness"—in defense of the work we did together is an important "confrontation." It can be seen that she began directly to reconstitute the work she had been tempted to undermine. Yet I have found that colleagues often routinely take on anyone's ex-patient without so much as a phone call, as if there is no harm in endorsing a devaluation of the prior experience. The analyst I consulted when I came to Boston would not agree to see me further until I talked to the analyst I had worked with in Chicago, and even then the question of why I did not remove to Chicago if I wanted further analysis was ever on her lips. It was very aggravating—Who the hell was he, who the hell was she—until I could use it. Good questions, who indeed?

---

The practice of psychoanalytically oriented psychotherapy has by now accumulated a wealth of very useful technical precepts. Among these, one is to work from the surface downward. Another is to analyze defense before impulse. A third is to fashion a working or therapeutic alliance before going on to interpret certain material, particularly aspects of the transference. And there are, of course, others.

The value of these principles lies in their capacity to achieve certain ends. But in the course of time a kind of displacement has occurred in which these means to those ends have become valued almost more than the ends that they were originated to serve. The result of this displacement is that the principles such as I have mentioned have been given a weight unbecoming to a bit of technology, with the further consequence that alternative precepts that serve the same ends have become controversial. Such is the case, I think, for the technical device of confrontation.

At the same time, it is equally true that of the variety of measures the psychotherapist can employ, not every one of them will prove interchangeable with others; not all roads lead to Rome. Nor is a hodgepodge of eclecticism likely to serve the ends in view. Technical approaches work their effects in close complementation to one another. An integrated approach will accomplish more than a simple assembly of mediations. It is such an approach, with confrontation as its centerpiece, that I shall present here.

Departures from "standard" practice become most attractive when, of course, standard practice is least able to induce its effects. One such circumstance obtains when the patient is experiencing little or no inner conflict. This circumstance has two aspects. One is in effect when the patient, is mourning or in love, experiences matters as if all that is good and important is outside of him. The other, in essence the opposite side of the same coin, is the one that shall interest us primarily. This is when the patient feels that all that is bad is outside of himself. People who have failed to internalize one side of a potential conflict such that superego lacunae are notable and people who have all too well contrived to re-externalize conflicting factors come within this category. When either aspect of this circumstance exists, the people so arranged do not ordinarily present themselves for treatment. Instead, they direct their energies in attempts to do business with the environment. Those for whom the badness lies without will generally be busy either with psychopathic carryings on or with attempts to effect massive changes in and of their environments respectively.

But from time to time, "externalizers" do find their way into treatment, sometimes under a misapprehension, sometimes out of moral or legal requirement, but sometimes too, out of an experience of inner conflict, if one that is expended by the very application for assistance. Once there, however, such patients are by no means a breed apart, but stand in a matter of degree from probably all patients. Ignoring for the moment the countertransference implications of the phrase, the problem they pose for the therapist is that the patient so arranged cannot fathom the business of looking at and into himself. As such, the patient and therapist will both feel a distressing absence of something to meet about, indeed a degree of potential conflict over what there is for them to do. The therapist may feel the patient a threat to his therapeutic intents and procedures, and the patient almost certainly will experience the therapist as a most frightful (if potential) threat to his particular arrangements. If the therapist does not get rid of the patient on grounds of a lack of motivation or a deficit in psychology-mindedness, then what to do?

Clearly the therapist will attempt to induce the patient into undertaking that subdivision whereby part (the observing ego) of the patient joins with the observing therapist in a scrutiny of the remainder, or alien part, of the patient. But this, we must by definition assume, is not proceeding well enough to give the therapist reason to hope; and the itch to tell the patient, "Look, you're the one who is crazy, sick, impossible, wrong," is getting stronger.

If the therapist does finally convey something of this sort to the patient, he will be employing, to use Eissler's term (Eissler 1953, 1958), a parameter additional to and different from his usual clarifications and interpretations. He will be using one form of confrontation, the form that I think of as social confrontation.

Unlike interpretation, the function of which is to *resolve* internal conflicts by bringing unconscious fantasies or feelings to the patient's attention, social confrontation is designed to *induce* internal conflict.

The ego, as Freud observed, is Janus-shaped. One face looks outward to the external, real, or social world. The other, if only to avert its gaze, looks inward to feelings and fantasies, acting upon these as if they too had the hard, incontrovertible substance of fact. If interpretation presents to the inner face what it has failed to see of what is within and behind, social confrontation exposes to the outer face what it has failed to see of what has been externalized or left external. Both attempt to convey to the attending ego information that it has failed to acknowledge, assimilate, and take account of. In that sense, the undoing of a projection and a piece of a repression or the undoing of a denial and a reaction formation have much in common, the only difference consisting of the face, inner or outer, to which the information is conveyed.

And yet there is an important, even fateful, difference between an interpretation and a social confrontation. It is the difference between saying, "This is the third session you have wasted this week," and "You are once more reacting as if only bad can come from our work together." Although both statements deal with how the patient is using the sessions, the first derives from the judge's bench, the second from the translator's booth. The first unmistakably proscribes, the second describes something of which the therapist tries to make sense. To assent to the first, the patient must accept both the fact and the therapist, since the statement inextricably contains both. To assent to the second, the patient need only acknowledge the fact.

Social confrontation, then, is intended to oblige an internalization of the therapist. The patient is to identify his ego with the therapist's or, perhaps, to introject the therapist into his superego. Now it is true that patients sometimes receive an interpretation in the same way. But when the patient does regard an interpretation as conveying some design or intent of the therapist, it will be out of some motive of the patient's own; and, as such, the confusion can be clarified and the motive analyzed at any propitious time. A social confrontation, however, far from being a fantasy on the patient's part, is on the therapist's part an entirely deliberate fusion of content and intent, specifically contrived to convey particular force. As such, even supposing the therapist might subsequently wish to analyze its effects, it will prove far less susceptible to analysis. For though the patient may, in time, come to feel the confrontation to be far less assaultive than he initially felt it to be, will he have equal luck in understanding the meaning and function of his internalizing–externalizing propensities? It is with these propensities, after all, that the therapist felt himself to be confronted. Yet it was precisely these vehicles on which the therapist counted. Faced with the patient's use of externalization as a vehicle to keep truths out and away, the therapist turned the vehicle around and sent it right back, with himself now in the driver's seat.

Will it come clear to the patient, assuming it to be true of the therapist, that the therapist was not endorsing the patient's internalization–externalization dynamic? Or will the patient believe that the therapist was hoping only to reverse the flow of traffic and perhaps the choice of what the patient takes in and sends out?

Much of the undoubted effectiveness of social confrontation will be of value only to the extent that one also prefers or is prepared to risk its rather special sequel. Putting aside the more obvious possibilities — among which is that the patient may redouble his need first to externalize, then keep his distance from the external badness, and so leave therapy — one outcome may be that not only the alliance but the subsequent "cure" is effected via introjection. If the tough but good therapist is used internally to overshadow previously established internalizations, the patient may go on to conduct so ardent a relationship with the internal therapist as to manically triumph over his previous introjects. Under these circumstances, it is clear that therapy of the ordinary sort may subsequently prove impossible. Like the transference "cure," cures by introjection, even identification, are coin-flips of the original neurosis. In the latter two, the cast of characters in the internal drama may change, changing the effect *upon* the ego; but the helplessness of the ego *in regard to* the scenario will not have changed at all.

These special sequels to confrontation may or may not be acceptable to the therapist, depending, one supposes, on the degree to which the patient's symptomatology and previous inertness in therapy pose a technical or personal problem for the therapist. To the personal issue, there is little to say beyond asking why the problem a patient poses to the therapist becomes the therapist's problem; but to the technical issue posed by the relative absence of internal conflict, there is an alternative beyond social confrontation. This is confrontation of a different sort, the usages of which I propose to consider first where it is least necessary and then where, in my view, it may prove quite necessary indeed.

Let us suppose that we accept for treatment a twenty-year-old girl who comes complaining of a general depression, growing difficulty with her school work, and an uneasy relationship with her roommates. Let us further suppose that in taking the history the evidence becomes clear that her roommates stand for her sister who, in turn, stands for her mother and that the uneasiness in those relationships is of a fairly typical oedipal nature, with the problem in school work participating, at least to some extent, in the form of a success neurosis in which to succeed means to outdo mother and thus constitutes a strong source for guilt.

The precepts I alluded to earlier would translate into a course of treatment something like this. We would begin with the derivatives, on which the girl's affect is most strongly centered and out of which would flow the initial motivation for her willingness to work. Initially she would express her feelings about her roommates and convey her complaints. Encouraged by our respectful attention, those feelings would tend to heighten and broaden, taking on at times a mildly paranoid flavor. Transference feelings toward us would begin to emerge, casting us as the father, who must spurn these bad, jealous, and envious women. As this happens, her demands on us would increase to the point that listening and mildly commenting would not be enough. The situation now would increase in intensity, bring more painful affects to the surface. We would then begin to engage her further in an alliance, the thrust of which would be to have her look with us at the meaning and function for her of what she is and has been going through — to turn inward. As tactfully as we could, we would help her focus attention on the work of those attributes in herself that she found most alien. Fairly soon self-understanding, still vis-à-vis the roommates as derivatives, would begin to ease some aspects of her overinvolvement. As a result, she would begin not only to experience some relief but also to come further toward accepting the alliance for self-study that we are the while fashioning and exercising with her. In time, we would begin to demonstrate the displacements, on the one hand, and the derivatives of the conscious feelings, on the other. We would point out connections between perceptions of and feelings about the roommates and her sister and help her to move, thereby, toward a consideration of father's role in those latter feelings. As she became more immersed in this undertaking, we would show her the gaps in her feelings toward her sister that have been left by repression, splitting, or denial. The recovery of these lost feelings would bring the initial object, mother, more into view. And so it would go on until, depending on our assessment of her needs and vulnerabilities, we either took some of these issues further with her or began to taper the process off before further regressions could take place as the heirs and preludes to earlier experiences.

In the procedure I have just outlined, confrontation has found no place. But it is worth considering whether it could have a place. On the face of it, the answer would seem to be no. If, for example, we directly confronted this patient with the fact that it is her mother who is really at issue, we would likely be met either with massive disbelief, which would be a credit to her defenses, or with profound outrage. Outrage would, among other sources, come from her narcissistically well-wrought conviction that she has outgrown mother and all those old, dreary preoccupations with father; and we would be flying head-on into an already fragile self-esteem. Indeed, if we pressed the interpretation, it is not unlikely that the patient would abruptly terminate treatment. We are thus well cautioned against wild interpretations.

But if we go back over these consequences, we see the depressive and persecutory anxieties to which the patient would be subject were we to in fact make interpretations from, as it were, the id. Let us focus on these anxieties for a few moments. It is plain enough that we could have aroused these anxieties by wild interpretations, interpretations from the id. But are they not there in potential anyway? So what if, rather than beginning with where the patient is in terms of the real-life situation, we began with where the patient is in terms of her apprehensions about therapy — the very apprehensions we have been so carefully allaying or treating with so delicately in the use of our usual principles?

Now we can be sure that we are not the only ones who are trying to find ways around the encounter with these anxieties: the patient is, too. She will be doing so in the material she presents, the way she presents it, the means she uses to offset the potential threat we could present — in short, by the actions she takes.

If we race headlong into making wild interpretations, we would mobilize these anxieties and see them all too clearly for the brief moment before her emergency countering action would take place. But we do not need to see these anxieties directly. They are easily inferred from the precautionary actions the patient is taking in, round, and about the manifest content of the therapy. And though they occur instantly in the first session — really because they occur so immediately — only to recede in the face of the reality of our presence, they are transference anxieties. Their capacity to give way as our presence becomes felt and the alliance becomes wrought argues generally for the good reality functioning of the ego. But before the ego does its work, the anxieties and the fantasies that accompany them are very nearly delusional even in so basically neurotic a patient as is the young lady we have been considering. Her capacity to act appropriately obscures this for us, as the success of her active responses to her anxieties enables her to barely feel them and even less to become aware of the fantasies about herself in relation to us, and vice versa.

Now in time, were it a searching psychoanalysis we were assisting her in, these would reemerge at the depths of the transference neurosis. But there are patients, borderline and frankly psychotic, in whom these anxieties are foremost and are not susceptible either to delay or to therapeutically appropriate countering actions. I shall deal with these instances later. The point I wish to make here is that such anxieties are immediately present and in good evidence with any patient and that they can be dealt with immediately, should one wish to confront the patient with them.

Now the device of confrontation too has its principles, because the use of confrontation in therapy, however unfamiliar it is to therapists generally, is by no means unique. Winnicott (1962) subsumes the process as one that "leads from the Unconscious" (p. 297). Others of a more rigorously Kleinian bent suggest interpreting the psychotic anxieties first (cf. Klein 1957). But notice that when we are going to deal with psychotic anxieties or unconscious material we have to talk the language of the unconscious and of psychosis. This, as most of us know, is a very concrete language, and one with very active verbs in it. Its syntax is never elliptical, conditional, nor does it contain any negatives. It is causal and effective, in which the subject does something active to the predicate because. Action is the essence of the experience; real or fantasied countering actions are the defense.

Now as to the anxieties themselves. They will be of two basic sorts: (1) the talion anxiety, out of which the fearful, underlying wish is projected and the threat experienced as originating externally and (2) the depressive anxiety, in which the source of the fear is experienced as internal and originating from an internalized object. I would call this, with Anna Freud (1965), a superego anxiety, were it not for the archaic nature of some of these anxieties, which are more reasonably termed superego precursor anxieties. These two anxieties, though phenomenologically different, are, at root, really one. But projections and introjections do relocate the object that is experienced as the source of persecution and hence, the felt experience. It is of considerable importance to determine who the persecutor is, or at least where he, she, or it is located, and hence, the kind of anxiety — depressive or talion — that is being experienced or warded off.

If the principle of confrontation involves interpreting the patient's anxieties in terms that describe the unconscious fantasies that engender the anxieties, let me now go on to say why.

In confrontation, as I am using the term, one does without the usual therapeutic alliance. Insofar as one does fashion an alliance, it is not, as in the more familiar procedure, with a part of the patient's conscious, observing ego. It is rather with the repressed unconscious, that pathway to the id.

The ego, after all, is at least partly the agency that offers resistance to the repressed aspects of the impulse life, which transfigures them with its defensive maneuvers and which, in its narcissistic preoccupations and love-hate affairs with the internal objects, diverts them from realization and discharge. Rather than attempting to allay its vigilance with an alliance built up of the patient's identification with us and our therapeutic procedures, confrontation interferes with the defenses and bypasses that aspect of the ego. In using confrontation, the therapist reaches across to what lies beneath the ego. This is, of course, the restless stirring of the impulses, which, as much as they are held siege by the ego, hold it, in the symptomatic or characterological impasse, no less captive. That state of affairs reduces the autonomy of the ego, the restoration of which constitutes our therapeutic goal.

The autonomy of the ego, as Rapaport (1957) among others has shown, is comprised in two directions. As it tries to gather strength against the upward, outward push of the impulses, it throws itself into the arms of social reality for proscriptions, limits, indeed frustration. But once there, its autonomy threatens to be compromised from that direction also, for to be a "good" person all too often means excessive renunciations of the impulse gratifications that enrich and enliven the ego and give it a base of strength of its own. Thus, it must retreat and defend against the strictures of reality too, usually via denials and introjections, ultimately the formation of the superego. This increase of distance and hence autonomy from the social world can preclude impulse gratification, thus raising inner pressures again.

In effecting the usual therapeutic alliance, we offer a professional and sometimes a more explicitly real self together with a set of ego procedures to a patient whose own self and ego have been too well compromised in its mediative attempts to adapt impulses to reality. The benefits of this are obvious.

Not so obvious are the costs, for in fashioning the alliance we palliate the pressures the patient experiences and hence deprive him of the need to bring forth essential material. The balance between amelioration and cure is too much in favor of salving. But more questionable even than that is whether the identification with the therapist, the therapy, or the social values of the therapeutic system, so adaptive to us and our needs, is not at the same time a symptom for the patient that fails to get analyzed. In asking the patient to take a given attitude or in demanding he renounce one, in being real for the patient or even therapeutic, do we *unnecessarily* compromise his autonomy? Social confrontation seems to me to contain more of this risk than the inculcation of the alliance in usual ways. But, on the other hand, it is so pronounced a measure that it stands out and calls both therapist's and patient's attention to it. As Bion (1966) has observed, it rather is the countertransferences that the profession shares that escape recognition and analysis; surely the widespread, unquestioning belief in the therapeutic alliance is one of these.

Thus, if it is not necessary to inculcate identifications, we may do more for the patient by not doing so. The question is, then, can we avoid the traditional alliance?

With confrontation one can and does. As I noted with the patient we were considering, the effect of bypassing the ego is an immediate rise in anxiety. But there is also another effect. The transference-rooted longings immediately gravitate to the therapist, so much so that they directly occupy center stage; and it is his sense of this propensity that all the anxiety is warning the patient against. But the transference longings themselves can form a bond stronger and more adhesive than the usual therapeutic alliance. Thus, while the patient may consciously resist, he unconsciously cooperates with treatment. The easiest example of unconscious cooperation is the slip of the tongue, which, in indecent haste, infiltrates the ego's machinery of wary vigilance. But that kind of infiltration is not the only pathway; the ego is filled with interstices. Nonverbal behavior, silences, transitions, gaps in secondary process communication all reveal in their absences the presence of unconscious cooperation.

By attending to this, despite the disinclined ego, one cements the allegiance from the patient's unconscious. The resulting anxiety, however, must continually be interpreted. Its interpretation marks the difference between the "wild analysis" of the unabashed beginner and the careful crafting of confrontation.

The conscious aspect — the observing ego — listens in on these interpretations. Nothing more is asked of it in the way of participation. In this sense, its autonomy is respected. Though it will find some measure of relief from anxiety and guilt from understanding what it experiences, the object of the procedure is to enable it to assimilate the wishes it has warded off.

When it does assimilate and integrate the impulses, its captivity by social reality, internalized and external, is reduced. It can act more autonomously, with greater true distance and perspective. One need not, then, concern oneself with matters and experiences external to the analysis of the transference. One need only — and that just in the first stages of treatment — actively interpret the anxieties that constitute the resistance to the transference neurosis or psychosis. After that, the transference becomes the sole preoccupation of the patient.

It is, however, important, even vital, not to provoke, induce, or elicit the transference actively. One does not replace one alliance with another, but remains impartial. So however active one may be in clearing the way for the development of the transference by the interpretation of the meaning and function of the anxieties that comprise the resistance, the interpretation of the transference wishes themselves must closely follow the patient's own material. Wild interpretations, as I noted, are out.

In confrontation, then, one bypasses defense analysis, goes to the analysis of those anxieties that resist the full flowering of transference, and then goes on to interpret the transference (and only the transference) in the ordinary way. Thus it brings one to where one is going on behalf of the patient via allegiance from the unconscious, achieving the same ends by almost inverse means.

With these alternative precepts in prospect, let me now return to the young lady we were considering earlier. But this time we will eschew the procedure I earlier supposed — and with it, taking the history and making an evaluation. Instead, we shall get, as it were, right down to work.

The first thing one will notice is that she is experiencing some anxiety, and so one quite gently calls this to her attention. She gives a half laugh, allowing some of the tension to discharge and acknowledging that she feels a little nervous. Something frightening could happen here? One half says, half asks. This, however, she denies and then instead offers her story. But now one interrupts: "Talking about being frightened is frightening?" one asks.

Her response to this is a fugitive move of impatience, a hesitation, during which one may well imagine she is deciding how best to deal with one's intrusion; and then, having decided another denial would put her in a bad light, she says merely, "I guess so," and prepares to go on with what she came to do.

She goes on, then, with her story; and this time one does not interrupt, at least for a while. Interrupting directly would be experienced as so assaultive as to make the transference and the reality too difficult for her to distinguish.

As one then briefly retires to listen to her story, one listens less to the facts and figures (for we would hear all this again, and anyway, it is likely to be quite distorted in its present rendition) than for what effects her narrative is designed to have on one. Her narrative is a countering action to what she imagines one to be up to and about. It has its defensive components, designed to forestall or allay, and it has its courtship components, calculated to allure and entice. From these we can fairly readily infer what her anxieties are, especially if one, on his part, fails to comply with the intentions she has of her narrative. The restraint one places on his own inclinations to respond with um-hums, questions, nods, or the taking of notes, will bring his own impulses more clearly to mind. And, adding these data to what one has inferred from what the patient is attempting will make matters reasonably plain.

As the patient proceeds and as one makes no compliance, one will soon see the eruption of anxiety once again; and this will serve as a cue. The eruption will be experienced by the patient as ego-alien, as if an undesirable symptom; and so one's intervention at this point will be experienced as less intrusive than if one had not waited.

One might say, "You are disappointed." If she tentatively acknowledges this, one would add, "You had hoped for better?" If she denies that she is disappointed, one deals with the anxiety that prompts the denial: "It is better not to care—one could get hurt." Or, "It is better not to care, because one can hate oneself for not succeeding."

She is likely to give either of these a mixed response, as if to say, "Yes, I care but don't want to." And one says, "For fear of disappointment." If she acknowledges this, one will say, "From whom?" She will say, "From myself." One then will say, "It is not right to hope for better from me?"

With this the anxiety that was temporarily allayed by our empathic clarification of her disappointment will rise again with the guilt over what will seem to her our permission to let loose her transference wishes. And so, with this the issue is joined. The anxiety is high, the defensive maneuver curtailed, and the only thing in the circumstance that will offer some relief is the further emergence of the unconscious transference wishes.

From this point on, with one reaching backward, not into her history, but back to the beginning of this first session, there will be a counterpoint between the expression and interpretation of anxieties and then the expression and interpretation of wishes. The first will open the way to the second, and the second will engender the first. One can feel that the alliance has been really joined when she tells of the fantasies about this first session that she had before even the initiating phone call.

If I am correct that in cases like that which I have described, the choice between approaches amounts to six of one and half dozen of the other, such may not be the case in procedures open to us in working with borderline and psychotic patients. For there we have, on the one hand, approaches that attempt to buttress the besieged ego through doses of reality, supportive relationships, and facilitative interjections of counsel or limits — all of these intermixed with the painstaking elicitation of affects; and then, on the other, we have a confrontative procedure that reaches beyond the strenuated ego to the fantasies and feelings it so valiantly, though quixotically, is attempting to ward off. Both may be said to strengthen the ego: the first, by support, as it were, from the outside and above; the second, by facing the averted ego inward, from within and below. But beyond this shared strategy, through implementation, a difference may exist. Supportive approaches tend, generally speaking, to reinforce defenses against the return of the repressed, and intervene primarily with such troubling defenses as denial and projection. But confrontation here too tends, by and large, to facilitate the emergence of the unconscious by attending to the anxieties that induce not only the denials, regressions, and projections but the repressions as well. This can only have an outcome different from traditional ego-supportive measures. If, therefore, there is controversy over means here, it is likely to be a displacement from convictions about either their comfort or the possibility of the achievability of the ends.

However, since the prime medium of all therapeutic work is the therapist himself, his position in respect to the patient will be the governing factor in the workability of this, as of any procedure. The method I am discussing must be rooted in the absence of a very particular sort of countertransference. It requires that to the largest extent one can, one wants nothing for or from one's patient. Only under these circumstances can confrontation escape being a preemption in which "one strolls about the other's mind as if it were one's own flat."

On the other hand, such austere neutrality conveys in great potential the possibility of exciting the patient to a very considerable envy of the self-contained therapist. Once aroused, envy's urgent need to be quenched and its no less imperative need to bite the hand that feeds it can foil or despoil any therapeutic attempt until the entire therapy is frozen in an unending stalemate.

One can forestall envy sufficiently to appease it by becoming partisan—by caring, feeling thwarted, getting angry, and, in the end, socially confronting the patient's confrontation of oneself. Or one can analyze envy in the measure to which it arises and, by so doing, maintain the neutrality upon which confrontation of the transference resistance so utterly depends.

This point is illustrated in the example of confrontation I shall shortly describe. The case is one where the choices among approaches might each have led to different ends—a foreclosure of fuller effects in the more usual approach and what continues to look like an opening to a reasonably thorough therapeutic analysis through confrontation. But note, too, the effect of my countertransference reaction in the fourth session.

Since I am interested in conveying what I can of the feeling of the encounters that comprise the vignette, I shall not present background or historical material except as it was presented to me.

Miss Gallet phoned one evening to tell me that she was about to commit herself to a state hospital because she was very fearful of hurting herself but wanted, before doing so, to see me and thereby arrange for treatment that she could return to on her release some ten days later. I agreed to see her between appointments the following day, and she duly presented herself for the twenty minutes I could arrange.

I was at once struck by her eyes, which were almost flamboyantly made up. The next of her features to catch my attention were her teeth. For the rest, she was a somewhat statuesque young woman in her middle or late twenties who, though dressed with some style, had outgained her clothes.

Since the meeting was to be simply one in which to make arrangements, I simply sat back to hear what she had to propose.

She told me that she had just broken up with her boyfriend, on whom she had been very dependent; and she was afraid that unless she did something else, she would do what she did the last time she had broken up with a boyfriend and withdraw into a corner, as she put it, in a very masochistic way, for four years; and she just couldn't do that again.

But having said that, she interrupted herself to ask me what I thought of "Thyrozine," as she called Thorazine.

I said: "You have some thoughts about it."

She said: "What do you think of Preludin?"

I said: "Preludin and Thorazine."

She said: "That's just it!" And laughed.

It then developed that Preludin, which is an appetite suppressant, and Thorazine were felt by the patient to be at odds. Her medicine was Preludin, but the doctors (five psychiatrists, it turned out, had been involved in the last several weeks) gave her Thorazine, which she felt to undermine Preludin.

I said: "What kind of doctor am I? One who puts into you the wish to grow fat and sleepy and fill yourself up with mother and food, or one who will help you become independent?"

She sent her high arcing peal of laughter up again and then said simply, "Yes."

The second session was held two days later. The patient said that she had gone to the state hospital, but without an admission slip, and was therefore not admitted. She had then returned to her second psychiatrist, who filled out the paper; but now, handing me the paper, she came to ask me what I thought.

I said: "What kind of doctor I am?"

She said: "Yes."

I said: "You are asking because you are afraid."

She said: "Yes."

I said: "Of?"

She said: "That you think I should go into the hospital."

I said: "Like who?"

She said: "Them."

I said: "Them?"

She said: "The people."

These, it developed, were a considerable assembly who were testing her, giving her messages, and otherwise controlling her life.

I said: "You are worried about testing me with your questions, about giving me messages about taking me over. Doctors have Thorazine and hospitals and other things to put into people, and you are worried that you don't. So that you are worried that I can hurt you with my things worse than, in self-protection, you can influence me with yours."

She responded to this with another question: Could I do two things for her? One, go to Children's Hospital and get the records of when she was a patient at age four or five; two, find out if her birth certificate is authentic.

I said: "What do you wish?"

She said: "I just want you to see if they did something to my head. And I want you to see who my parents really are."

I said again: "What do you wish? What do you hope I would find?"

She responded to this then saying that her parents wouldn't be her real ones and that something had been taken out of her head.

I said: "That is the other side of what you said before. Sometimes you feel that you are missing something and want people to put it back into you, and sometimes you feel you have ideas that you wish were taken out of you. And these feelings have to do with your parents; sometimes you want to put ideas into them and sometimes to take them out, and always you are afraid of what you believe they can do back to you."

The patient then went on to elaborate on the meaning of the wishes concerning her head and her parents, something that was to occupy her for some weeks. Later, while she was in the hospital over the severe depression the abandonment of the splitting and projection introduced, she reconstructed the experiences of incest that had taken place between herself and her father, and the delusional material stopped abruptly.

But before this could happen one other episode had to be confronted. This took place before and then during what was to be our fifth session. The fourth had been in my office at home at six o'clock meeting time. There was an aura of reticence throughout, which I could not properly identify, partly because during that week I was preoccupied with certain occurrences in my own family. These were much with me, and I kept nodding to them and telling them I would hold an audience for them later. I didn't manage to see that their presence had also to do with this patient.

On the Friday of the fifth session the patient's mother called to say that the patient had barricaded herself in her room and taken "a whole lot" of sleeping pills and tranquilizers, had gone to sleep, but had wakened to tell her to call me to say that she wasn't coming.

But I insisted that she come and, when the mother said she didn't feel her daughter was in a condition to drive, told the mother to put her into a cab.

And so the patient came, looking bloated and pasty and altogether hag-ridden. Her mouth was dry and she had difficulty working it. She sat slumped in silence, but I noticed that she looked at the clock from time to time in an intent sort of way.

I had the fantasy that she had swallowed my clock, so I said: "You have feelings about the clock—it worries you."

She nodded.

I asked her what worried her, but she seemed confused and shook her head.

I said: "You hate the idea you had about the clock and have attacked the idea and so confused yourself."

She sat up straighter and said, "Something about six o'clock."

"Six o'clock," I repeated, "and about swallowing."

"It's suppertime," she said.

"Whose?" I asked.

"Yours?" she asked.

"So you are keeping me from my supper?" I asked. "That worries you?"

She nodded.

"Tell me," I said.

She tried to work her mouth, but gave up and sort of shook her head.

"You are worried that I might eat you," I asked, "instead of my supper?"

Now came the sudden peal of laughter. She sat forward now.

"I suppose you think that that's because I want to eat you," she said. "Is that why I took the pills?"

"Is it?" I asked.

It then developed that she was valiantly trying to diet, had been feeling starved, had envied my ability to eat, had wanted to deprive me of my supper, had felt some compunction, had felt hungry for me in an endless sort of way—being afraid of the long-seeming weekend—was afraid of these feelings, had put them into me, was afraid to come for fear that she would experience them again, and so had eaten her doctor-pills and spared me.

Further working through of this material opened the way for an emergence of more genital wishes and the intense depressive anxieties she experienced in relation to them. The regressive maternal transference shifted somewhat and new material came to the fore. But of particular note is that though the patient's life situation had been very difficult—including a 2½ month hiatus in treatment—she had managed to maintain the depressive position and keep her paranoid proclivities at bay.

Now, in conclusion, I thought I would like to say what brought me to try to learn the confrontational approach to begin with. It was not the task of working with neurotic patients where it is a six-of-one-half-dozen-of-the-other option, nor even that of working with borderline or psychotic patients, where it is often the approach of choice. Nor was it to work with groups, where I myself use it quite extensively, even exclusively. It was, of all things, to meet the task of trying to begin work with what statistically speaking is the normal person: the people of the community with whom, if anything is to be done, one must take the initiative and painstakingly develop a working relationship. For in such work, the consultant himself often becomes the epiproblem for the consultee. If one is not, therefore, to settle for working with the self-referred, the self-selected, and the coercively referred, one must, or so I feel I have learned, develop a method very like that which I have been discussing; for analysis of transference anxieties, which would otherwise induce in the consultee massive sorts of resistance and be managed, most usually, by avoiding the relationship altogether, proved to open the way to reaching and engaging with the very hardest of the so-called hard to reach (Boris 1971).

## REFERENCES

Bion, W. R. (1966). Book review: Eissler's *Medical Orthodoxy and the Future of Psychoanalysis*. *International Journal of Psychoanalysis* 47:575–581.

Boris, H. N. (1971). The Seelsorger in rural Vermont. *International Journal of Group Psychotherapy* 21:159–173.

Eissler, K. R. (1953). The effect of the structure of the ego on psychoanalytic technique. *Journal of the American Psychoanalytic Association* 1:104–143.

_____ (1958). Notes on problems of technique in the psychoanalytic treatment of adolescents: with some remarks on perversions. *Psychoanalytic Study of the Child* 13:223–254. New York: International Universities Press.

Freud, A. (1965). *Normality and Pathology in Childhood*. New York: International Universities Press.

Klein, M. (1957). *Envy and Gratitude*. London: Tavistock.

Rapaport, D. (1957). The theory of ego autonomy: a generalization. In *Collected Papers*, ed. M. M. Gill, pp. 722–744. New York: Basic Books, 1967.

Winnicott, D. W. (1962). The aims of psychoanalytic treatment. In *The Maturational Processes and the Facilitating Environment*, pp. 166–170. New York: International Universities Press, 1965.

# 10

# Interpretation

At the time I wrote this, on commission for a book on the various sorts of psychotherapeutic interventions described by Edward Bibring (or, Eissler, "parameters"), my grasp of the context for what one can and cannot usefully do had evolved from where it was at the time of "Confrontation" to the point where I could begin to write of it. But in preparing it for republication (the book gasped once and died) I was taken aback by my cordial view that there is a reality from which various distortions depart and, accordingly, to which interpretations return a "Really" (Really!). It is curious how difficult it is to see beyond the boundaries of constraint—how comforting intellectual prisons are; how often one, meaning I, may escape from newfound freedoms by the simple—even a child can do it!—expedient of not noticing there is a there there. Or isn't.

Apart from this sanguine solipsism, the essay says what I want it to say, so I have not revised it. Instead I wrote "Interpretation of Dreams, Interpretation of Facts." That essay (in Part Three) should be read along side the present one.

I don't have, at the moment, a philosophical position on what or where reality is, except that it doesn't return phone calls. I am, however, enduringly fascinated with other people's views—with how they shape, place, define, and nab reality. I attach the view that there is an is and, indeed, an isier, to the pressures of the selection principle, about which more in "Beyond the Reality Principle." (in

131

Part Three.) If people have to make choices, as they do, they seem to prefer to have choicer choices to choose. Real in the sense of absolute, true, so, ideal has great appeal in this regard. Even better are those reals that modestly do not appear unveiled but wreathe themselves as shadows on the cave wall or in phenomena which merely hint at the noumenon.

To interpret other people's experiences it is enough to know the cryptogram by which they have transfigured what was the case. That it needn't ever have been the case doesn't apply. People live histories that never occurred as ardently as they lived those that did, often more so. Freud's constructions, as any good archaeologist's should, searched for what once was but no longer is, for truths among the ruins. But people's inner life has only a peripheral relation to what might be called their actual life, so that as often as reconstructing what happened, one is busied with constructing what almost happened but didn't — what stayed real but never became quite actual and matter-of-factual. The paths not taken are much traveled.

The patient mentioned in this paper diligently continued her work with me, but I cannot say she consolidated it until after her father died. His death seemed to inspire her with a dual sense — of something ended and something completed. She seemed, upon his death, to relinquish her stalwart homoerotic attachment to him, which had only increased with his final illness. She stopped when she felt that my own death was not also necessary, and so grew bored with our meetings. At around that time she found her "own" life surprisingly interesting although it hadn't — actually — changed much.

---

When, in prehistory, something-in-itself was represented by a thought, a sound, a scratching on a cave wall, humankind realized its capacity to form symbols. When that same process of transformation was reversed, and the actual thing or event reconstructed from its symbol, interpretation was born. Thereafter, anyone who wished either to study humankind or extend our humanity — philosophers, poets, mathematicians, linguists, mystics — had to study or enhance the transformational processes.

Still it was for Freud to take up and solve a particular aspect of the matter. Symbols that were contrived to reveal — as these words are — can also be used to conceal. Experience can be as readily encoded to repress meaning as to express it. Experiences too painful to be endured can be transformed, also by rules systematic and lawful, into versions of the actual that at once represent and misrepresent the actual. Such transformations, moreover, must resist interpretation in a way transformations meant to convey the truth of the experience represented in them must not.

By 1895 in *Studies in Hysteria*, Freud (with Breuer) had found a way of intuiting from the bizarre symptoms of his patients the actual experiences that were transfigured in them. The interpretation of the symbolic meaning of symptomatology and the (re)construction of the historical events that were contained and ciphered in them were established.

By 1900 a further development had been made. Ego psychology, or the means by which these special transformations occurred, was in place. In the famous Chapter 7 of *The Interpretation of Dreams*, Freud (1900) wrote out the transformational rules by which we come no longer to experience what we experience but to experience some version of the actual experience instead. From a therapeutic standpoint, it was now possible not only to draw patients' attention to the presence of absences (the gaps in their knowledge of their experience) but also to the means (the so-called mechanisms of defense) by which the counterfeit versions of their experience were substituted for the actual ones.

So remarkable was this advance that only two major additions to the transformational/interpretive processes were left to make. Both were arrived at by seeing that there were other transformations needing interpretation.

The first of these has to do with people's propensity for transforming one experience (e.g., that having to do with a patient and a psychotherapist) into another (e.g., one having to do with a child and its parent) and then acting as if the second were as true as, or more true than, the first. This transformation, of course, is what we call the transference; and it, in turn, represents a kind of field of forces that influences the transformations embedded within it. Not only are different things experienced (e.g., remembered) within the sway of the transference, but things are remembered differently. Unless the transference is interpreted, the experiences that also are represented within it cannot be construed accurately.

Interpretations made within the field of forces that is the transference are also affected. At various times the same intervention — even one so otherwise simple as "What did you feel?" — can be experienced as anything from an accusatory attack through an examination question to a benign benediction. Insofar as the therapist hopes to be understood as simply conveying information, the view the patient takes of the interpretation also has to be subject to interpretation.

The second development follows from the increasing understanding of the force of the transference. This is the prodigious power of the person to whom the transference is made — in psychotherapy, the therapist. Earlier in psychodynamic thinking, the transfer of attributes to and from the therapist could be encapsulated by such placid nouns as identification, projection, and displacement. But thanks largely to Melanie Klein (1952), attention shifted from the result of these transformative activities (for example, "he has come to think of his therapist as a father figure") to the activities themselves.

We can now see that to the process of transformation the patient attaches quite specific fantasies. The so-called projection by which the patient imbues the therapist with certain characteristics is thought of by the patient as perhaps an act of evacuation or of gifting, of impregnation or of soiling. Reciprocally in the therapist's seeming reply to this act — that is, in the silence, movement, or speech that follows the patient's activity — the patient will see acts of menace or seduction. To quote Bion (1970, p. iv) on this subject, we must now "attend not only to the meaning of the patient's communication but the use to which it is being put." The topological and structural expositions of Freud's psychodynamics thus have been enriched by a lively sense of the relation of the "objects." This relationship — who is doing what and with which and to whom — accordingly must occupy the participants. For though the amnesias and paramnesias and the host of defensive maneuvers by which these are achieved are but sleights of mind — experiences contrived simply out of selective attention and inattention — they are imagined to be more than that.

Moreover, they are imagined to transform subject and object alike. Once a little girl and I watched some other children go for a boat ride after supper. "My name," said the little girl who was deemed too young to join the boat party, "is Galen." When the boat turned and headed back to shore, the little girl confided: "My name isn't really Galen. Her name is. But don't tell her I said I was Galen." One person's transformations are supposed by that person to transform others. My young friend might have imagined that the Galen from whom she borrowed her Galen qualities without permission might react as did the gods to Prometheus. Galen too was transformed by the little girl's act. Sullivan (1953) was alert to these matters, as well. He saw that when we cannot bear to know what we experience, we cannot bear to know the truth about others: they too are transfigured and continue to be until we can come once again to know ourselves. Interpretation alters not only our experience of ourselves, but also how we experience others and how we experience others' experiences of us. Let us see this process at work in the course of psychotherapy. I shall begin with the essential *structure* of therapy, for on it depends the experience of interpretation.

## THE PSYCHODYNAMICS OF INTERPRETATION: BACKDROP

Psychodynamic psychotherapy introduces a person to himself or herself. More precisely, it introduces the person at his or her present age to himself or herself at previous ages, and "previous" here can mean a few moments or years and years ago.

At age 5 one cannot know the 15-year-old one will become. A 5-year-old can extrapolate from 5 to 15 in imagination, but it is only a small child's vision of 15. Likewise, an adolescent can only know 5 from an adolescent's point of view. The adolescent cannot know 30 and so cannot know that 30 will know 5 differently. If only 5, 15, and 30 could meet and talk things over themselves! But surely an interpreter would be needed.

People think that pain can be reduced and pleasure gained by not knowing certain things about themselves and others. Of course, they have to know what they do not want to know, and this plainly presents certain difficulties. They are rather in the position of one of Kipling's characters who was guaranteed access to a great treasure, provided only that, upon encountering it, he did not think of a white rhinoceros.

Freud likened this dilemma to paragraphs excised from a newspaper by censors. The spaces give away the censor's activities. But what if the spaces were filled with false or innocuous typescript? Repression, not knowing, is not sufficient. One must have something else to know instead: a screen, a cover, a myth, a cipher, a code, a symbol, a dream, or a symptom. Perhaps if Kipling's character thought: Purple elephant, purple elephant, purple . . .

Interpretation is a two-stage process. It has first to identify the instead of. It has then to identify the instead-of-what.

Fortunately there is a pattern to transfigurations of the actual into the fictive. We say: "In acting (thinking, feeling, perceiving, or remembering) as he or she does, this person is behaving *as if* X were true or had once been true." Binstock (1986) writes of this as he imagines: This person is acting as if what we are doing together is not a psychotherapy in which she is a grown woman and a lawyer and I am a grown man and a psychotherapist. Instead she is acting as if this were a toileting experience and she is my mother. He further imagines: For this transfiguration to have taken place, the little girl to whom I must introduce my grown patient must have had the experiences (which he describes), found them unbearable, is afraid that they will still be unbearable, and has changed them by attending to them in a very constricted or selective way. Later still he confides his surmise to his patient—drawing her attention not only to the experiences, but to the system by which she transformed the experiences.

Freud first thought psychotherapy was a matter of making the unconscious conscious: "Where id is, ego shall be." Later he saw that putting his patients in the picture concerning their systems of trans-figuration—analysis of the ego—was also important. Since selective inattention (not knowing) combined with selective overattention (creating the instead-of) is so transparent a device, people need not only—as Laing (1969) puts it—to deny, but to deny that they are denying, and to deny that they are denying that they are denying, and so on. This they can do only by creating an "instead-of" for the fact that they actually are merely using selective attention. Thus if, as the Bible has it, one looks to the mote in the other's eye so not to see the beam in one's own, the whole "projection" collapses if one knows one is doing what one is doing. A projection cannot be known to be a projection if it is to survive. What if a projection is instead experienced as if it were a penetrating missile, and not selective attention? Now we have a version of the evil eye. Much better.

But that is what leaves us with the task of identifying not only the substitution of the substantive fiction for the actual one, but also the substitution of the methodological process for the actual one. This is hard work—so much so that therapist and patient often wish there were another avenue to salvation.

This wish, this hope, is at the core of what we term resistance. Normally both therapist and patient experience this, although for understandably self-serving reasons resistance is normally attributed only to the patient. But what therapist does not shrink at the prospect of bringing a patient's attention to aspects of an experience the patient feels unable to bear knowing?

The patient's resistance is better understood perhaps than the therapist's. The patient has predicated his or her life on fictions, such as that time is coextensive with possibility and that neither ebbs, and is not gratified to discover that efforts to realize this illusion are doomed. But the therapist too has wishes for or from the patient. These are evident when the therapist moves beyond displaying to the patient the instead-ofs and the instead-of-whats and starts trying to cure the patient. Any attempt to induce a patient to change reflects the therapist's resistance to interpretation and is, as such, an expression either of countertransference or of an identification that goes beyond empathy.

Interpretations grow out of sympathetic imagination of the sort captured in the phrase, "Nothing human is foreign to me." (Fortunately, as Harry Stack Sullivan remarked, "People are more human than otherwise.") This sympathetic imagination is at its most capacious when its owners (therapist *or* patients) feel receptive to the experience they are having. We can conceive, gestate, nourish, be fruitful and multiply, to the degree we can tolerate without loathing knowing what we and others experience. Insofar as we cannot, we will naturally try to change the experience or, failing that, to know as little as possible about it. At these times the therapist will want to speak to the patient in order to change the patient and get some relief for the intolerable (or about to be intolerable) experience the patient is visiting upon the therapist. Therapists are often unaware of this as a motivating factor in their interventions, interpretive or otherwise. Their own experiences as patients in psychotherapy will often have laid bare the heretofore unconscious elements in their transferences and countertransferences. But as Bion (1966) remarked, the conscious elements are often not subject to analysis for the simple reason that membership in the group — the school or orientation — of therapist makes these intentions appear unexceptional and unremarkable, when often they are anything but. As an example one might consider that psychodynamic psychotherapy deals precisely with that: the dynamics of the patient's psyche. Yet often therapists' ideas about patients' lives may stimulate them to make interventions calculated to affect what their patients do, and how, where, or with whom. To some who read this, the thought that such activities are in any sense a blurring of the line between counseling and interpretive psychotherapy will seem to be of no consequence. In their group that is how psychotherapy is done, and they would protest any implication that they were acting out counter-transferences or identifications. To my group, however, that is exactly what it looks like. To return to Bion's point, here it is not what we feel for (or against) any given patient—the unconscious element in the countertransference—but that some of us consciously feel that influ-encing a patient is within, and others feel it is outside of, the precinct of psychodynamic psychotherapy.

There is a sketch in a Monty Python Show in which a Some-thing-English dictionary is mischievously translated: the poor for-eigner laboriously thumbing through it to make a purchase at a tobacconist ends up asking for a kiss and getting belted for his pains. We take it as an article of faith that the interpreter interjects nothing of his or her own into the process, but with the greatest fidelity makes the meaning of one person's communication known to the other. The therapist's job is to be translucent.

This is not a happy point of view to those who wish to be psychoactive. Even capsules and pills are permitted more potency than therapist as translator, therapist as fiberoptic conductor! Indeed, it is not to be wondered at that so many psychotherapists find the work unendurable and wish to go back to being proper physicians, counse-lors, nurses, and social workers.

All the same, the efficacy of interpretation, as Freud himself counseled, depends more on the position of the therapist vis-à-vis the patient than on the brilliance, or even accuracy, of the interpretation itself. Accordingly, I shall now develop my thinking on this matter.

The patient ordinarily does not make use of interpretations until three conditions are satisfied. First, he or she must be disillusioned about salvation through means other than "systematically under-standing his self-deceptions and their motivations" (Hartmann 1953). Second, he or she has to feel convinced by the data. Third, he or she has to detach the giving of interpretations by the therapist from the belief that the therapist is engaging is lascivious acts in the guise of giving interpretation.

Fulfilling these conditions is at once a matter of technique (to which I will come presently) and a matter having to do with the therapist as a person.

If the therapist does not value interpretive psychotherapy, why should the patient? If the therapist cannot wait for (as Bion [1961] put it) interpretations to become obvious, and remarkable only in that the patient has not reached them on his or her own, how can the patient feel convinced? If the therapist is engaged in changing the patient, how can the patient distinguish the communication of bits of knowledge from expressions of love and hate, lust and yearning? Freud speaks of "sticking coolly to the rules."

Perhaps the single greatest distinction between the psychotherapeutic encounter and other human encounters is the capacity of the therapist to limit (through an act of continuous mourning preceding and during each therapy) what he or she needs from the transaction. As so often happens, this delimitation opens up other possibilities that might otherwise be latent — but of that, more later. People receive information from others all of their lives. Something, after all, has to make the giving of interpretations distinguishable from the welter of other information people are given about themselves. As I have been trying to demonstrate, much of this distinction lies in the patient's experience of the therapist's motives.

Parents, not unnaturally, give information to their children in order to make themselves or the children more lovable. The more urgent this need, the fewer chances the parent (later, perhaps, the lover) can take with a considered, empirical approach; "Because I say so!" is the unspoken, or sometimes spoken, attribution of authority for the information.

The therapist needs to eschew these claims to omniscience, the more so since many who become our patients have in their helplessness turned to omnipotent thinking as a comfort. Instead, the therapist must allow experience to cumulate and evolve until its interpretation can be assessed by the patient. Patients who complain of being treated as a case out of a book often have a good point. It is understandable that a patient will resist giving out precious or painful material if he or she feels it to be unnecessary to the interpretation. And insofar as the interpretation is based on material the therapist has about the patient (such as the life-history or some rumor, contrived perhaps by the referring agent or a supervisor or a recently read paper), the patient will feel irrelevant and supernumerary. Interpretations have to provide meaning and dimension to what the experience consists *of*. If they do not, the patient can only become more and more like himself or herself; he or she cannot become more and more himself or herself. As a patient of mine once put what I am trying to say, "I have a way of thinking of myself as if I were myself, which is like thinking of today not as Thursday but as if it were Thursday."

How intolerably boring it is when patients go and on about something we have heard a dozen times if we heard it once! But we may not have heard it once, which is why we are hearing it a dozen times. We may have heard it and interpreted it and in doing so closed it off from further consideration. Yet for the patient it needs to evolve. And if it cannot evolve in the patient's mind, the patient needs it to evolve in the therapist's. Consider a patient who might wish to find out how to go to Bar Harbor, Maine, but since he cannot bear to know that is where he wishes to go, asks the directions to Providence, Rhode Island. Given these, he will know they are wrong without quite knowing what to ask instead, except directions to Providence, again. Anyone who has hung around with 4-year-olds who keep asking "But why?" will know what I mean. Both the patient and the child may have to be asked whether they are asking what they really want to know.

Much of the information concerning what the patient is being comes from the impulses being with the patient generates in the therapist. Acting on those impulses relieves the tension but loses the information. The therapists who ask themselves *why* they want to nod or speak or yawn or look at the clock or remember that the patient lost his or her mother a year ago have a chance of knowing more of what the patient is experiencing then if they yield to these impulses.[1]

Between the instant that dice leave the roller's hand and the time they show their dots on the green baize of the gambling table lies either the mysterious workings of chance — or a series of activities that, if closely observed and repeatedly studied, make the outcome understandable, predictable, and controllable. Patients eavesdrop upon themselves; and the more details they provide the therapist, the more they learn directly from themselves. What seems mad, random, meaningless, purposeless can be seen by them to have pattern, design, coherence, intent. The therapist's patience is the patient's best friend. Provided therapists do not have too often to give themselves relief from waiting, patients become more and more obvious to *them*selves.

Now, of course, few if any of us can interpret so well that only

---

[1]This is true particularly in work with patients who devote great energy and skill to stimulating reactive impulses in the therapist — patients such as anorectics. (See, in this regard, Boris 1984a, 1984b.)

interpretation need serve. Nor does every patient who enters psychotherapy intend to accept a strictly interpretive approach. Preliminary
caution on both sides should be exercised: grandiosity afflicts all who
have once felt impotent to affect their fates. And, as I indicated earlier,
there is bound to be turbulence and upheaval in the course of a
psychotherapy that will be difficult for both parties to stand—and still
stick "coolly to the rules." "Parameters," in Eissler's (1958) phrase, are
useful, but, as Eissler indicates, when these are no longer used as a
means to make interpretation possible, they become the means to
make interpretation impossible. Since the object of the psychotherapy
is to enable patients to feel and understand the full reality of their
experiences so that they can recover what they have taken pains no
longer to experience, the task of the therapist is to become self-
effacing. Time and energy are limited and limiting; if the patient's
attention is to be drawn to himself or herself, past and present, it is not
helpful for the therapist to draw attention to himself or herself. And
yet insofar as the therapist wants something for or from the patient
(fees perhaps expected), the patient understandably will become even
more preoccupied with influencing his or her therapist than he or she
ordinarily would be—and "ordinarily" is. Thus interpretations often
are spoiled by the teaching or preaching that surrounds them.
Winnicott observed that he could tell when he left off making
interpretations: it was when he started saying "moreover." (For his
fuller treatment of this, see Winnicott 1958.)

The introduction of the (at once) deceived and deceiving self to what
it experiences requires that experiences evolve. This evolution must
take place in both patient and therapist. Neither should "head it off" by
analyzing it. Only in so far as the patient and therapist have an
experience in common to advert to can either feel convinced. Recog-
nizing the "truth" of an interpretation is only partially mutative. At this
stage it is, if shocking, akin to a confrontation, or if intellectually
assimilated, akin to a clarification. Only when the "truth" takes on an
air of inevitability does an interpretation do its work.

Repression is hard work. It is easier to know what one knows but to
detach significance from it. Patients ordinarily know far more about
themselves than they ever use. Sometimes they seem to know everything there is to know—except how the proliferation of knowledge
mitigates any single insight.

Therapists must, therefore, husband their additions charily. They
will need to be careful lest their contributions only add to patients'

profligacy of understandings. Only the fullness and intensity of experiencing can truly inform a patient, can help him or her rescue conviction from mere insight.

The dynamic tension in psychotherapy takes place between the patient's need to reveal and need to conceal. Much of this has to do with a wish to influence the therapist's disposition toward the patient in a direction the patient imagines would be favorable. But part of it reflects the fear of certainty. If the patient is the only one who knows what he or she experiences, that knowledge can be forever doubted or be denuded of significance. The same is true so long as the therapist is the only one who knows something. The danger lies in the exponential leap to certainty when something is known to both of them. In this conjunction also lies the immense power of an interpretation.

After some years of work, a patient confided the following:

> She wished she could be dressed in a gray pinafore and a white turtleneck and that the therapist would take her onto his lap, put his hand under her skirt, discover she was not wearing anything, and touch and fondle her to orgasm.
>
> She remembered, as a child of 6, standing with her back to a mirror and bending forward peering between her legs to see what she looked like. If her father should chance to pass on the way to his dinner with her mother, he would laugh.
>
> Once, before her menarche, she tried an experiment with her rowdy pal. He tried to put his you-know-what into her. His sister was present and they were all laughing. Some months later she felt very bad and isolated. She feared she was pregnant but couldn't tell anyone, not even her own dear sister. That winter she had her first menstrual period. She felt awful and didn't tell any of her friends. Two years later her rowdy pal's good friend and her own good friend asked her to show him how she put a tampon in. She showed him with pleasure. The good feelings associated with the experiment and previous times briefly returned. Her pal liked to look at and touch her breasts, but she hated that. She hated her breasts.
>
> With the exception of the fantasy concerning the therapist, the patient had mentioned all of these experiences over a span of months. The incidents were scattered over time as wreckage might be strewn over a landscape. Except for the solace of confiding personal and private pleasures and agonies, the patient, a woman now in her thirties, saw no special reason for telling her therapist of the incidents. They were things that happened.
>
> From time to time the patient allowed herself to have intercourse. She liked the men's excitement, but hated the act itself, though she felt that to be fair she must submit. In response to a question, she said that she did not

have orgasms except to her own masturbation. Later she added that as she touched herself she frequently imagined a man and woman discussing her: "How can we make her come? Is there anything we can do? Nothing. There is nothing we can do. Nothing at all."

She did not look at men she found attractive, except when they could not notice she was looking. Ordinarily she fastened her gaze at a point to one or another side of the therapist. She talked falteringly with many stops: "I-uh-uh-so-um. . . ." Someone in her therapy group called that manner of talking hostile. Later it was understood to be an enactment of the "nothing" fantasy: "There is nothing we (you) can do to make me go/come. When you have no-thing I will come/go, which will be something!" When she was 6, her parents, who always vacationed with the three girls on Cape Cod, went to Europe, leaving them with the measles and a nurse. Constipation, which may have started as adjunctive to the illness, became, in response to hounding by the nurse, a lifelong misery. Whether she was defying the nurse or holding on to her parents, or both, of course, matters, as does the question of earlier struggles with ownership and loss. But of no less moment is the series of symbolic transformations: breast = feces = penis = go = stay = come. Quite an achievement, the more so, perhaps, in that her own misery draws her attention from the pain inflicted upon others, on which the member of her therapy group commented (no doubt feelingfully). As do artists with "found" objects, we, all of us, seize upon the adventitious in life to craft and shape our transformations.

This material—both in the way it was communicated, implying at once strewn wreckage and a hostile attack on the therapist's deductive powers, and in itself a content in a life—tells a story of yearning, defect, fury, and a love in danger of being obliterated by envy. The material may be thought to say: Once I discovered I did not have a penis, I soothed my anguish first by believing the condition was temporary, then by forgetting the fact. Finally I had almost to rediscover it. Now all I want is to return to the days when there were no differences, and to feel alive and all of a piece and one of the guys.

An interpretation along those lines might (in fact did) produce a flock of additional memories, further elaboration of the patient's current experience, a sense of the absolute rightness of the construction of the child's experience to the grown-up patient. But what changes for the patient? The little pink "moosh" of the 6-year-old's genital is still the mushy, smushy "crotch" of the 36-year-old. Both are unconsoled. The 6-year-old is still heartbroken because her 36-year-old self has done no better for her than she herself could. What is the use of being 36? The 36-year-old weeps profusely at her current and her earlier plight. She thinks 6 might do better than she can at 36—6 has her whole life in front of her. Six had her mother, which 36 lost. Six could watch her daddy in the bath; 36 doesn't even get a phone call.

What is happening here? If anything, it has been in whatever 36 had to endure to make the interpretation possible. The interpretation reflects the experience back to the experiences. This augments, intensifies, and amplifies the experience, which, when communicated, makes the interpretation more exact, more vivid, more detailed, more inclusive. Akin to a laser, the interpretation can now further amplify the experience, which then further infuses the interpretation, and so on.

There is more to be learned for both parties, having perhaps to do with earlier disparagements of the mother and the horror of becoming a mother disparaged. But that too will have to be experienced to be communicated; and it is in the dawning realization that the experience need not be so cataclysmic now as it was then that the development takes place. Interpretation is retrospective; before it is mutative, the patient must have already changed. The adult must be able to stand being 36 and the 6-year-old must also stand it. If they cannot stand being in the same room together, there is no way of effecting an introduction. The interpretation makes them fathomable and comprehensible to one another, but that is only important if they have already decided to coexist — and to coexist in the presence of the therapist.

Much, perhaps most, of the work of the therapy lies in providing the conditions that make such a conjoining seem endurable. The child in people does not want to know of grown-up limitations. Its helplessness demands omnipotence of its elders. The elder does not want to know of its helplessness either, especially in conjunction with the passions of youth.

Bibring saw this, of course, and knew that while interpretation could put everyone on speaking terms, much else had to pave the way: abreaction, confrontation, clarification, and the like. But perhaps more than anything, it is the capacity of the therapist to stand his or her own helplessness, and the patient's, to make do with a good deal less than omnipotence, and to know a lot about passions, that keeps psychotherapy from being a refined sadomasochistic exercise and interpretation a tutorial.


## THE PSYCHOACTIVE INGREDIENT AND THE NATURE OF DEVELOPMENT

Well-being depends on outer options and inner possibilities. To some extent each conditions the other; and to some extent each has a life of its own. Psychotherapy allows people to experience what they experience, bear it, learn from it, and apply what they have learned to their sojourn in the personal and material world. But, as Freud himself knew, "neurotic misery" is all too often replaced by nothing better than "common unhappiness." Outer options do not surrender their constraints to the well-analyzed person.

Still there is something to be said for expanding inner possibility: for understanding that one's experience of past, present, and future are extrapolations from inaccurate appraisals of what is so. These inaccuracies are, of course, not products of faulty cognition. They are the result of wishful thinking. The future is often feared because it is unknown. But there is no special reason the unknown should be feared, or not feared. In fact, when the future is feared (or not), it is because it represents an extrapolation from the past or present. The only unknown thing in this is that it *is* an extrapolation.

Such extrapolations are at once necessary and unreasonable. It is (for most of us) necessary to act as if the sun will rise tomorrow. Some of us can see, however, that the fact that it has risen faithfully in the past holds no inevitable power over the future. Transference is compounded of the same wish-propelled, hopeful extrapolations. The transference, after all, requires a rather optimistic indifference to certain otherwise compelling facts: that time passes, that people differ, that things change. It is a testament to hope that such a thing as the transference exists (Boris 1976).

Development occurs insofar as one can stand the disillusionment of such wishes and hopes. Why some people can stand disillusionment — can grieve, mourn, and relinquish — and others cannot is not well understood, at least by me. Often we think that as people test reality in the course of psychotherapy, they get on more cordial terms with what is so. But is there any technique or approach in the world that can induce people to take a step that they are convinced will lead to calamity?

Many patients, for example, tell their psychotherapists that they simply cannot "say" something. ("Say" may at other times or in other therapies be "think," "feel," "try," "do," etc.) Their therapists can understand this as a situation needing interpretation ("You are acting as if to say this to me is tantamount to saying *x* to so and so"), confrontation ("Say it anyway!"), manipulation ("A bright person like you?"), clarification ("Is saying the same as doing?"), catharsis ("What does the thought of saying it *feel* like?"), and so on. Experienced therapists have shown the power of these interventions for nudging patients beyond the impasse and for taking the next step.

But what if the patient does not? What if the helpful nudges contained in the various interventions only frighten the patient more and stiffen resistance? Now there really is an impasse! Experienced therapists have a repertoire; there is more than one arrow in their quivers. They try, as they should, to see what will help when first one interpretation and then another does not.

But as important as trying is the capacity of the therapist to *stop* trying. It is the patient who has to take the plunge—who has to summon the courage to risk calamity—or what is perhaps the greater courage to give up the wish-driven extrapolation that conjured up calamity. For any intervention to be useful, the patient has to use it.

Take the widely known example of Freud and his patient, the Wolf Man (Freud 1918). For reasons not clear to Freud, at a given point in treatment, the Wolf Man froze progress. Nothing was happening. Interpretation after interpretation failed. The ever-pragmatic Freud finally imposed an ultimatum: six months more of treatment, and termination—no matter what.

The treatment unfroze enough to reveal that the causes of the freezing lay in the patient's observations of and reactions to the primal scene, and the extrapolations of these to the transference. For us there is this question: Was it the ultimatum, or Freud's relinquishment of hope, that freed the patient? Was it the active intervention, or Freud's mourning for his own therapeutic potency, that constituted the psychoactive ingredient?

The answer is probably both. But surely the patient simply had finally to take the next step, had to give up the thrall of past and future and attend to the present Freud, the Freud who was primarily Freud. It is the patient who conduces the treatment.

Viewed in this light, the psychoactive ingredient is not the intervention. It is rather the therapist's capacity to be in the treatment in the same way the patient is. Both parties have to develop. Each has to suffer disillusionment. Each has to mourn. Each has to learn from their common experience. When this happens each is as fundamentally necessary to the other as the other is. There is an equality, a jointness, a commensalism. Psychotherapy inevitably imposes a process of mourning upon both therapist and patient. This is not a matter of weaning, with which it is sometimes confused. It means that both therapist and patient must come to stand the limits in their relationship—that they cannot use each other in every kind of way, but must use each other up in the way of work. When, however, longings for different and additional pleasure are renounced and the therapist becomes resigned to the patient as a source of only *some* good experiences, those now delimited experiences become invigorated. For instance, when the therapist is resigned to learning what the patient has to teach, the sessions become less tedious; often the therapist feels bored when listening for things, such as those that make much of him or her, which are all too slow in coming. If the therapist is senior enough to do supervision, the therapists in training may be obliged to hear tales of wonder and woe, as the more senior therapist palliates the wounds to his or her narcissism delivered by his patients.

Insofar as such wishes are taken out of the therapy (even into the supervision), the therapist can treasure what in fact is abundant: One learns a great deal from one's patients—about them individually, about humankind generally, about (by comparison and contrast) oneself, about what helps and what does not, about how things get the way they are and how they change. If one does not have to make the patient help one be good at doing therapy, all this learning feels enriching and unfrightening. People who, as I do, have left over from childhood a certain dread about being inaccurately perceived or wrongly attributed, can have that experience happen again and again, and yet, with time, have it become progressively undone until one is able to feel freely and fully one's self. A lovely instance of this appears in Winnicott's (1977) *The Piggle*, an account of his analysis of a little girl with that nickname. At one point, some years after the analysis began, Winnicott greeted her at his doorstep by her real name, Gabrielle. Somehow, he intuited that he had grown from being Greedy Baby and Bad Mummy into being Dr. Winnicott, who of course greets a young woman by her own grown-up name! (Interpretations do not need to smell of antiseptic!) Szasz (1956) and Winnicott (1977) make helpful additions to the bounty of benefits a therapist may uncoercively draw from a patient.

There is at once much and little to be said for training. Anna Freud was an experienced psychoanalyst of children, a teacher and supervisor to others, when she learned that the person many took to be her rival was proceeding with children in a way Miss Freud had not thought possible. Melanie Klein was not troubling to educate the child's parents, or even the child. Indeed she thought this alliance-making tended to obscure the very transformations she wished to interpret.

More to the point, she found a line of interpretation that made the entire prologue unnecessary. Anna Freud (1954) altered her technique.

Such a person, one can imagine, can learn equally well from her patients. In this case she had not. So she learned instead from Klein. But what of those who learn mainly from books, from teachers and supervisors, from tradition? Here is the analogue to the extrapolations from the past that earlier we had identified as the impediment to patients' development.

Freud, fortunately, had no such impediment. Once he broke with his tradition, there were few but his patients to teach him. He knew his luck. What he wanted to send on down through time were a spare few discoveries: infantile sexuality, the unconscious, the transference — two more. "*Je ne suis pas un Freudian*," he said.

We are not quite so fortunate. There are even texts like this to teach us! But, of course, as in the instance of Melanie Klein and Anna Freud, tradition, comprised as it is of the experience of others, can be of great value. But only, I think, if we learn the spirit as well as the letter of it.

The letter is in each word of this and other books. The spirit is what made the letter possible. The letter has to do with finding, the spirit with seeking; the letter with the known, the spirit with the undiscovered; the letter with conveying, the spirit with inquiry; the letter with technique, the spirit with risk.

Above all, the spirit of psychodynamic psychotherapy requires us to remember whose treatment it is. And, in difference to that, to doing only what the patient cannot yet do for himself or herself when he or she is ready to do it. We put the patient back in possession of himself or herself by showing him or her how he or she lost it. We introduce the selves, but do not shape or direct them. Throughout, we efface ourselves so that the patient can do what he or she has to do about *him*self or *her*self. When the time comes that we can be entirely self-effacing, we politely withdraw from the process. We will not have completed our development with this patient as he or she will not with us, but there is something in the nature of development that requires the catalysis of the new.

## MAKING INTERPRETATIONS

There are several rather useful rules of thumb for offering interpretations to a patient, when (and this is the first) it turns out that the patient's efforts to know what he or she is experiencing absolutely requires offering them.

These are as follows:

Interpret
— patterns before specifics
— anxieties before defenses
— defenses before wishes
— derivatives before deeper material
— there before here
— now before then
and how the patient is interpreting each of the psychotherapist's interpretations.

The "grammar" of transformation is intricate but not really complicated. It is economical in the extreme. It has to be simple and economical because babies and young children need to be able to use it. Thus generalization ("I'm mad at everybody") and specification ("I've only my self to blame") are both "defenses." One, generalization, loses the true target in the crowd. Like Ali Baba, whose hideout was marked with an ineradicable X, and who therefore painted X's on every other door, generalization obscures what is so. But so can simple substitution, as self for other.

Since people come to psychotherapy with most of their transformations intact, their "chief complaint" is often a transformation of their actual complaint. If the complaint is overly specific, the therapist may have to expand it; if overly general, to contract it. The essence of the work here is the effort to display to the patient the role in the countless situations that cause the patient pain of a constant, repetitive factor that originates with him or her. The patient has to a degree to become alienated from himself or herself. In that measure the patient becomes allied with the psychotherapist. If the world causes the pain (which it well might), there is no cure in psychotherapy. Only insofar as by actual or transformational action the patient contributes to his or her own fate can therapy help. A survey of each situation is necessary so that the patient can see among the variables the constant factor brought by himself or herself. Patterns, then, before specifics.

This display generates anxiety. Transformations are initially effected to avert intolerable frustration and helplessness. The impact of the actual on the fictive threatens to reinvoke that original pain. It is, therefore, frightening and greatly to be resisted. The patient has to know from the therapist that the therapist knows of the anxiety. The patient who does not discover this may believe that the therapist is unaware of the anxiety, and this is as frightening as being with a dentist who does not know that drilling can hurt. Still, no matter how bad the patient feels now, once it was worse.

Reasonable people do not stand around being frightened; they take countermeasures. These are the defenses by which experience is transformed. Perhaps the simplest of these is evasion. As the patient's patterns are being identified, the anxiety that is generated will, in turn, stimulate countermeasures. The patient may feel reluctant to talk, may come late, may forget an appointment. He or she is trying to transform the experience itself. If this cannot be done, the patient will have to resort to transforming what he or she experiences of the experience. As a last resort, the patient will have to direct his or her efforts to transforming the very experiencing apparatus itself—destroying ego to save the self.[2]

These maneuvers happen so quickly (the patient, after all, has had years of practice) that the psychotherapist needs to link the brief experience of anxiety to the defensive responses that almost instantaneously follow upon it—relieving it, or obscuring it. Since the patient believes the security gained in using his or her defenses is reinforced by severing the connections between experience and transformation (e.g., anxiety and defense), he or she will generally not "know" of the link between, for example, his or her fright in one session and late arrival to the next. A patient who did might remember the anxiety, reexperience the pain of it, and be in danger of experiencing more of the particular experience of which the anxiety was only a foretaste. So, prudently, the patient will not only come late to shorten the session, altering the perturbing experience itself, but will also attribute the lateness to some other cause, some instead-of reason, thus altering the patient's experience of the experience.

"I am sorry I'm late, but the traffic . . ."

---

[2]Increasingly, current research into infants' cognitive, perceptual and memory functions, and skills shows that what Freud called ego functions are well established at an early age (cf. Gardner 1983, Miller 1983 for reviews and speculations on these matters). Perhaps Melanie Klein was correct in ascribing to infants and young children the mental sophistication she did. In any case, it is now clear that psychosis involves a systematic and ordered destruction of ego function rather than a developmental failure.

"Perhaps there was something in our last meeting."
Oh-oh!

Insofar as the patient discovers that anxiety evaporates when he or she dares to know of what he or she experiences, the patient will less "automatically" use the defensive transfigurations he or she can identify as such. Consequently, more and more of the constituents of the experiencings will become available, though still in the form they took as a result of transformations effected by earlier versions of himself or herself. These constituent elements are, in this sense, derivatives. We may know that the experience the patient is now describing or remembering was not ever thus, but the patient does not. To the patient it is so. And, if the patient's same-self forebears have done their job well, what the patient knows and remembers will have such verisimilitude that the counterfeiting can hardly be spotted — and certainly not by the patient who has so much reason to maintain his or her revisionisms.

Perhaps the most fundamental of the original transformations is this "*She would if she could*" into "*She could if she would.*" With it sorrow transforms into anger; resignation converts to hopefulness, and despair and helplessness blossom into a thousand possibilities concerning what *I* can do to induce her to do what she *can* (now!) do — if *she wants to*. The possibility that she does not do it because/therefore she is bad, leads to one whole branching of the tree (as the twig is bent). Alternatively there is the possibility that she does not do it because/ therefore I am bad, leads to another. "Bad" may be in terms of wicked ("I must reform"), size ("I must act big"), gender ("I must change"), and so on: each is fateful. A third transformation is "*She could if she would but will not because (or therefore) someone else is bad and coercive.*" This leads toward a "manic" view, as the previous ("I am bad") leads toward a "depressive" view and the first ("She is bad") to a "paranoid" view.

Perceived and remembered experience will be derivatives of this fundamental transformation and the various ones that followed upon it. From them one can infer what the patient cannot and could not bear to experience. These form the basis of working from the derivatives, here and now, to the deeper experiences, then and there. The rules of thumb follow the order in which the transformations were established: the last is first.

In the spirit of dynamic psychotherapy, however, rules are made to be broken. Early in the history of psychoanalysis, people experimented with saying such things as: "You wish to kill your father and lie with your mother, no?" The patient, visualizing the plump, dowdy, middle-aged woman who was his fairly irritating mother, thought it was perhaps his newfound therapist who could do with help of a rather urgent kind. If he confided this thought, it would be "interpreted" as hostile and castrating. "I am the father of whom you are afraid because of your wish to get rid of me and take the mother for yourself, *hein?*" If, at this, the patient got really angry, the therapist might be heard to give a little grunt of satisfaction. All the same, wild interpretations of this sort did not seem to help much, and the rules of thumb were given respectful development.

Wild "interpretations" of the sort I have parodied did not work, not because they leapfrogged where the patient was in his or her transformations, but because they drew from the books and not from the patient. The assumption behind wild interpretations was that experience is layered, with fictions overlaying the actual experience, but not really replacing them. The recognition that people have to remember what to forget if they are to repress the right bit of knowledge is part of this. We more or less express this when we speak of "at some level . . ." or "somewhere he must have known . . ." or "part of me. . . ." The transformed and the original experience are both present, simultaneously.

Actually, however, experience is not layered vertically or horizontally, but continually, being at once experienced and transformed, with the former in fleeting glimpses of the actual. It can be reached for and found by interpretations that do not follow the rules of thumb.

The breaking of these rules involves interpretations of a rather different sort. The experience to which they allude is what patients are continually doing to, with, and about their therapists: the transformation that is the transference. Everything the patients do has this element in it—what they say, how they say it, what they do not say, why they do not say it. Patients are continually acting upon their therapists—whom they do not know—as if therapists were people or some thing they know and must deal with in ways designed to avert a catastrophic experience and foment a good one. Accordingly, in Bion's (1970) phrase, the therapist listens not only for the meaning in what the patient is communicating, but for the use to which those communications are being put. No patient simply communicates information regarding his or her experiences—and certainly not for a long time. Patients speak for effect.

Let us say that a patient speaks in such a way as to seek to draw from his or her therapist a kind word. If we are lucky as therapists, we can sense this, intuit it. But even if we cannot intuit it from our responses to what the patient is doing, it will presently become possible to infer it from what the patient is telling us. If we still cannot tell, some patients will lose patience with us and overtly demand "feedback" or "some response." Some patients will even stipulate that warmth and caring are wanted.

In this, as in the figure in the carpet, the therapist may imagine he or she discerns the configurations of the patient's relationship to the therapist as mother or, equally likely, as breast, from whom the milk of human kindness is being drawn. What sort of breast is it that the patient conjures when he or she proceeds in this way? Where does goodness lie; where is catastrophic frustration? If the therapist can bear to experience himself or herself as breast being dealt with in a number of quite particular ways, why does not the patient tolerate the experience in such graphically precise terms? What factors has the patient to contend with that the therapist is spared? In whom, breast or mouth, are these factors located by the patient, that he or she proceeds in such a fashion? What early experiences can have accounted for this patient's particular re-creation?

All the information necessary to answer these questions is available to the therapist whose intuitive, inferential, and imaginative faculties are unimpaired. That information is in both what the patient communicates and in the effects he or she seeks. "Why am I being told this?" joins "What am I being told?" as coequal in the therapist's own interpretive meditations. When the therapist finds something to say, he or she will, of course, be aware that what is said is being experienced as emanating from the breast (or the space where the breast is supposed to be but is not, or the mouth, if the patient imagines that he or she possesses the breast and has been giving the therapist food for thought) and that his or her interpretations are at once being experienced as further information about the breast, feedings, and incitements to envy.

"Do you see what I mean?"

"Yes, I think so. Your wife didn't understand that . . ." (of the rules-of-thumb procedure becomes perhaps): "The breast needs to be primed, as if one can't be sure it knows it's needed."

All the good rules of thumb are violated, as they should be when the spirit of the enterprise takes precedence over the letter of it. We need the rules because we need to do something while we learn from the patient what his or her plight is and how, with our interpretations, we can help the patient retrace any transformations and be able to experience at 30 what the patient could not endure at 3 months of age.

In a lovely paper, Guntrip (1975) speaks of his first analytic session with Winnicott. Guntrip lies on the couch, and Winnicott sits in a wooden chair behind him, sipping tea. Guntrip has done all the talking and now the session is at its end. The analyst, Winnicott, has nothing helpful to say as yet. All he knows is that he is Guntrip's Mummy and that Guntrip, who is also an analyst, is likely to experience Winnicott's continued silence as if it were a nonfeeding from a bad mother with no-thing to offer him. Since that is the most and the least Winnicott can say, he says: "I have nothing particular to say yet, but if I don't say something, you may begin to feel I'm not here."

In that, one can see references to anxiety, defense, and so forth. The rules of thumb are not wholly absent. But there is the leapfrogging to the heart of the matter—the use to which Guntrip was putting his communication and so the meaning that silence would have. The original and actual are directly culled from the transfigured and fictive. Dr. Guntrip is introduced to himself at an early age. They meet and can stand each other, which is really rather nice, as things go.

## SUMMARY

The line "Lady, three white leopards sat under a juniper tree," from Eliot's "Ash Wednesday" can be read as is or as a line intended at once to evoke sensuous images and to convey the beginnings of a prayer to the Virgin concerning the mysteries of death and the intimations of hope and resurrection. Eliot, I believe, intends for the reader to interpret the line in the direction I have suggested; the image contains these meanings; they are not meant to be concealed.

The little boy lying still as can be in his bedroom for fear of disturbing the leopard in the night-shrouded corner has also created an imagaic fragment. Unlike the poet, however, who can interpret his own symbols, the little boy no longer knows what the leopard is meant to represent. The leopard contains meanings that are meant to conceal, not reveal, an aspect of experience. Bad as his fear of disturbing the beast is, worse, we can surmise, would be the opening out of the contained experience: a powerful, lithe leopard, ravenous with desire, unsuspectedly springing, throwing its weight upon a dear soft creature, turning it upon its back and plunging its fangs into the soft underbelly, while other, equally hungry, leopards stalk and skulk, jealous and furious, amid the sweet sickly smell of blood and heat.

Meanings meant to be revealed through interpretation and those meant to be concealed from interpretation require rather different treatment. Accordingly, much of this chapter is devoted to the conditions under which interpretive insights can be transmitted to a patient, who, like the little boy of my example, might rightly believe that his or her cure, the phobia, is better than the therapist's, psychodynamic psychotherapy.

Alone in his room, the little boy has only the configuration of his clothes heaped on the chair to sculpt his leopard from and himself to enact the other role in the couple—the victim. In a two-person psychotherapy, there are two people, and if the adult in one's consulting room is to realize what his then 4-year-old forebear was like, he or she has to realize that the leopard in the shadows was to the child the patient once was as his therapist is to the current self—that the dynamics of the transfigurations are the same and that these dynamics are similarly motivated. The decrease in the self-deceptions of the adult have to be accompanied by a counterpart decrease in the self-deceptions of the child. Memories from childhood can then give way to memories of childhood.

Interpretation is, as such, an activity within a process. Since interpretations given by leopards differ in intent, and so (one hopes) in effect, from those offered by psychotherapists, the patient's natural wish and lifelong habit of confusing the two needs continual attention. The utterly essential condition is that the psychotherapist not be predatory, at least toward his or her patients. Given that essential, the ways by which the patient transforms the therapist, the purposes these transformations continue to serve, and the dangers averted by containment and concealment can all become subject to interpretation.

The means by which the data are displayed to the patient for affirmation or refutation are considered in the last portion of the chapter. The main thing here, of course, is that two minds are hard at work with equal access to the raw material of experience, with the entire research project done with great consideration.

## REFERENCES

Binstock, W. A. (1986). Clarification: clinical application. In *Basic Techniques of Psychodynamic Psychotherapy*, ed. M. Nichols and T. J. Paolino, pp. 265–286. New York: Gardner.

Bion, W. R. (1961). *Experiences in Groups*. New York: Basic Books.

——— (1966). Book review: Eissler's *Medical Orthodoxy and the future of Psychoanalysis*. *International Journal of Psycho-Analysis* 43:575–581.

——— (1970). *Attention and Interpretation*. New York: Basic Books.

Boris, H. N. (1976). On hope: its nature and psychotherapy. *International Review of Psycho-Analysis* 3:139–150.

——— (1984a). The problem of anorexia nervosa. *International Journal of Psycho-Analysis* 65:315–322.

——— (1984b). The treatment of anorexia nervosa. *International Journal of Psycho-Analysis* 65:435–442.

Breuer, J., and Freud, S. (1895). Studies on hysteria. *Standard Edition* 2:1–305.

Eissler, K. R. (1958). Notes on problems of technique in the psychoanalytic treatment of adolescents. *Psychoanalytic Study of the Child* 13:223–254. New York: International Universities Press.

Freud, A. (1954). Problems of technique in adult analysis. *Bulletin of the Philadelphia Association for Psychoanalysis* 4:44–46.

Freud, S. (1900). The interpretation of dreams. *Standard Edition* 4, 5.

——— (1918). From the history of an infantile neurosis. *Standard Edition* 17:7–122.

Gardner, H. (1983). *Frames of Mind*. New York: Basic Books.

Guntrip, H. (1975). My experience of analysis with Fairbairn and Winnicott. *International Review of Psycho-Analysis* 2:145–156.

Hartmann, H. (1959). Psychoanalysis as a scientific theory. In *Psychoanalysis, Scientific Method and Philosophy*, pp. 3–27. New York: International Universities Press.

Klein, M. (1952). The origins of the transference. *International Journal of Psycho-Analysis* 33:433–438.

Laing, R. D. (1969). *Self and Others*. New York: Pantheon.

Miller, J. (1983). *States of Mind*. New York: Basic Books.

Sullivan, H. S. (1953). *The Interpersonal Theory of Psychiatry*. New York: W. W. Norton.

Szasz, T. (1956). On the experience of the analyst in the psychoanalytic situation. *Journal of the American Psychoanalytic Association* 4:197–223.

Winnicott, D. W. (1958). Hate in the counter-transference. In *Collected Papers*, pp. 194–203. New York: Basic Books.

——— (1977). *The Piggle: An Account of the Psychoanalytic Treatment of a Little Girl*, ed. I. Ramzy. New York: International Universities Press.

# 11

# The Problem of Anorexia

Though in this paper I deal with anorexia as it is best known, namely as an eating disorder, anorexia is more accurately a metaphor. I have never encountered a patient who was not in some degree enthralled with his or her capacity to do without. To say this is to say that anorexia, or anhedonia, is at once a kind of mastery and a special way of coping with envy.

Envy, of course, is what the have-nots feel in respect to the haves. When we are envious, it is of the other's wherewithal. The anorectic does not envy food or drink; she envies the capacity of the Other to manufacture and supply it. This is what incites the anorectic to a kind of hostile takeover. The anorectic's refusals become for the Other a kind of bad and empty breast, a no-thing from which only pain and frustration flow. The mother of the anorectic wants her daughter to "Take a little chicken, try a little . . ." not only because she wishes her daughter well, but because her skinny daughter represents a breast that excites her longings, frustration, hatred, and envy. The tables have been turned. The daughter can now imagine it is she who owns and controls the wherewithal.

The capacity to do without shows up in the therapy situation in many forms, among which wanting fewer sessions, coming late and leaving early, being indifferent to or forgetting what the analyst may have to say are commonplace. Because these behaviors are also manifestations of the patient's need to regulate the "volume" of the

157

therapeutic encounter, the analyst needs to distinguish regulatory
activity from the enactment of devaluative role reversals. When he or
she begins to feel resentful of the patient and begins, for example, to
make interpretations that start with the sentiment, "It is easier for
you to . . .", envy has likely come into it.

The truly envious do not, despite their need, seek therapy. They
do not like the would-be therapist to have something to offer. One of
the reasons for the success of self-help groups like AA and its derivatives is because there is no one to envy. Alcoholics, after all, have
substituted the booze for the supplier often precisely out of unbearable
envy, and cannot be expected to seek a cure that throws them headlong
into what with such effort and pain they have barely evaded.

But the pain of envy is everywhere, even in people who do submit
to becoming patients. The "anorexia" of the patient who hasn't an
eating disorder is also over the issue of supply: Who develops and
supplies the material? Who develops and works up the insights?
Many people long to have given birth and life to themselves.
However flawed they feel, they are at least their own work of art and
science. In the "Treatment" paper to follow this one, I note that the
therapy will be tolerated only insofar as the patient can feel essential
to the treatment. This may seem an odd thing to say; nevertheless it
is true that there are times in even the best of work when one finds
oneself telling rather than discovering with the patient what the
interpretation is. Or explaining without demonstrating.

---

About what anorexia nervosa consists as a disease entity there is little
disagreement. Since Morton—in 1689, and Gill—in 1874 (Piazza et
al. 1980), the description is much the same: self-starvation to a loss of
20–30 percent of the body weight previous to the onset of the illness;
cessation of the menses (sometimes before the weight loss or, in
bulimia, not always explicably attached to nutrition or weight); and an
indifference, approximating the "la belle," to the fatal consequences of
the programme of weight loss. Traditionally, too, the sufferer has been
(85:15 percent) female in gender, and more often than not identified
with upper-middle-class backgrounds (Bruch 1973; cf, Piazza et al.
1980; Thoma 1967). Alarmingly, the incidence of the illness appears to
be on the increase: up to 200 percent in the last decade (cf. *Life
Magazine* 1982).

I say "alarmingly" both because the illness is serious (a 10–15 percent
estimate of fatality) and because the long-term prognosis is not

satisfactory. People make symptomatic recoveries, but it is not clear that many go on to flourish (Hsu 1980).

If there is agreement about the nature of the symptoms, however, there is by no means a consensus about what the symptoms mean. What is it, exactly, that is being compromised in the compromise-formation that Freud regarded symptoms as embodying?

Part of this uncertainty may arise from the assumption that anorexia nervosa is the same manifestation in all sufferers. As I shall attempt to demonstrate, there is a grave anorexia and a more transitory — even faddish — one. They are related to the same conflicts, but one is temporary, phase specific, later in arriving, and often as spontaneously surrendered as it was adopted. At its worst it does not reach the proportions of the more serious illness and indeed may be present in the form of a fastidiousness about food intake in people whom one would not at first blush see as belonging to the same nosology: some — not all — vegetarians or health food devotees, people with concerns about exercise and training, and so on. (Men may show up in these areas escaping notice as anorectics.) Here one may note one of the other paradoxes that confound this problem: anorexia nervosa is a misnomer; anorexia means loss of appetite. Only in certain cases or at certain times is this true. Usually the anorectic feels ravenous. In bulimia, a variant of anorexia, this leads to "binge" eating.

The other cause of the uncertainty as to the nature of the illness is its relatively refractory quality when psychoanalysis as a psycho-therapy is applied. A major reason is this: the analyst, in so far as he maintains his neutrality, is considered by his anorectic patient a superior sort of anorectic! I shall elaborate this point presently; for now I will simply register it as one reason for the entry into the treatment field of family therapists, behavior modification engineers and psychotherapists of less classical dispositions. Bruch, to whose careful amassing of data I am otherwise indebted, puts it this way:

> It seems that many therapists in approaching an anorectic patient are tied to outmoded psychoanalytic treatment, even those who otherwise work with contemporary concepts. Many stress the symbolic meaning of the noneating and the unconscious problems, fantasies and dreams and interpret their meaning to the patient. . . . It does not matter whether or not an interpretation is correct; what is harmful is that it confirms a patient's fear of being defective and incompetent and doomed to dependence. [Bruch 1978]

Bad psychoanalysis is not "good" for anyone. And it is true that, as I indicated, anorectics, because what we call their symptoms they call their salvation (the religious connotation is deliberate), make for tough patients. But since an interest of mine is distinguishing the baby and the bathwater, anorectics, precisely because they are often so difficult to treat, repay my effort by helping me to see what helps, methodologically speaking, and what doesn't and why. Then, too, I was a finicky eater as a child, only partly consequent to celiac syndrome, and my own analytic work had perforce to attend to those areas of experience. Since it is necessary to ask especially little of anorectic patients, food for thought for these two areas of my interest sustain me when the going is particularly difficult or chaotic.

At some point, usually at the onset of puberty or, thereafter, at a time of separation like going off to school, camp, or college, some people develop a desperate need to control their intake of food. This may start off as an attempt to diet in the usual way, but it presently becomes tantamount to an obsession with amounts eaten, amounts lost, amounts gained. Holding aside the "choice" of obsession for a moment, the obsessiveness itself, like other obsessions, lends a certain density (as novas called black holes have density) to the world of experience. Everything that has dimensionality and depth is condensed into a peculiarly flat, unsensuous singlemindedness concerning intake and weight, calories and pounds.

This is the achievement of envy. The object whose value is heightened by the imminence of separation — whether that of pubescence or that of distance — is denuded of value. It does not seem to exist. When one might otherwise expect yearning or loneliness or the fright of aloneness, one sees instead a world narrowed to a pin-prick of light: the obsession with looks and weight. The object — mother, father, breast, penis, feces — is "gone."

What happened, then, to appetite and greed, to longing and object love? They are there, of course, in such measure, indeed, that the anorectic feels imperiled by them. Hence the attempt at repression. But such longings made all the more powerful by suppression of satisfaction and repression of the knowledge of what it is that is satisfying, cannot be ignored. It is imperative that as the repression fails, projections take its place. As the anorectic will in the analysis resist the transference by stimulating the countertransference, so in the family her refusal to eat "sensibly" excites (or reexcites) longings, tantamount in their intensity to transferences, from the parents. By concentrating her attention to her parents' wants the anorectic can become relatively oblivious of her own.

We think of a projection as a sleight of mind, of a fantasy in which intentions or attributes previously associated by a person with himself, as his own, are assigned new authorship. And, indeed, when necessary, people do imagine such a deportation. But what if the other to whom the reassignments are made fails to act consonantly with them? Either the projection fails or the projector must put such distance between him and the unaltered reality as to fail to observe it as unaltered, or he must interfere with his powers of observation — the observing ego. The last is the road to psychosis. The anorectic generally manages by her refusals to project her wishes for food and all it symbolizes (I shall come to that) "successfully." That is, parents and doctors do want her to eat in the precise measure she seems not to want to eat. At times these others will feed her through nasogastric tubes or I.V.s, or compel her submission with powerful antidepressant or antipsychotic medications. The others, in accepting the anorectic's projections, convert the projections into projective indentifications.

Such family therapists as Minuchin understand something of this. That is, they seem to understand that such "collusion" is necessary and that once in place, it is expedient to work with the family "system" that holds it in place (Minuchin et al. 1978).

Minuchin, for example, attempts to redefine the anorexia as adolescent rebellion. He stages a confrontation of which the centerpiece is a luncheon meeting with several of the rest of the family and what he calls the "designated" patient. The task he sets is for the parents, first together then individually, to make the anorectic eat. Generally speaking, they cannot. There is tension between the two parents, which they resolve by appealing to their daughter. He calls this "triangulation." For my present purposes, it is enough that they want more from her than for her. When each parent separately has failed (more or less) to "make" their child eat, Minuchin displays to them and herself the tyranny of the patient, and in balance, at the same time the parents' contribution to foiling "rebelliousness" in respects other than in matters of food intake.

In this he agreed with Bruch (1978), who also places great emphasis on the remarkable co-operativeness of the anorectic in her "pre-morbid state": she is what is generally thought of as "a good child," submissive to what ambitious parents in the bourgeois Western World often ask of their children.

My own experiences construe these data differently. The preanorectic history reveals the same dynamic as the post. Throughout, the anorectic does not wish to want: she wishes to be the object of others' wants. What earlier she achieved by docile cooperativeness, later she will achieve by stimulating people to want her to eat. Her repressions (so strong are her longings) will continue to need buttressing by projections.

These longings and their strength must now occupy us. They consist of a greed akin to gluttony. The very ruthlessness of this gluttony, its imperiousness in mentally disassociating the mother from the breast, is what makes first the model child disposition and later the anorexia such an achievement. By the simple expedient of declaring *Less is More*, greed for the breast is metamorphosed into a gluttony for punishment, yearning into abstinence, retention into elimination (in bulimia) via each and every alimentary orifice, indeed, by exercise and sweating, through the very pores themselves.

In structural terms, the nascent ego is so helpless against the strength of the (first oral, later other) drives that it can but infuse the superego with the drive energy, projecting what is left over into the parents and reinternalizing the parents, now transformed with predatory characteristics, into a precocious superego. At puberty or thereafter the only alternative to enslavement by either the internal objects or the parents is adherence to an ego-ideal which maintains the asceticism in look and deed in its core of autonomy.

Here is an example from one of Bruch's patients:

> "Sometimes I hear voices or feel things in my head and sometimes I get frightening mental images." The voices seemed to be in the conflict, some telling her to "eat, eat, eat" and others, "don't, don't, don't." These food thoughts filled her mind so completely that they drowned out her former interests. . . . At times she felt full of her mother—"I feel she is in me—even if she isn't there." [Bruch 1978, p.53]

(1) *I* do not want. (2) She, He, It wants. And (3) They shall not have what they want. The first asseveration leads to martyrdom, even sainthood. The world is safe from the subject's depredations. It is a statement of renunciation. The second also has a religious air; in earlier days, it might have been Satan who wants, working through others or through "It" the body, loathsome and corrupt. The third is more overtly spiteful.

The "Breast" is *so* desirable that its power cannot be forgiven. There is a detonation in the simultaneity of desire and envy. Somehow people who become anorectic (though it is not limited to anorectics) cannot get resigned to receiving. They want to possess. The very act of reception "reminds" them that they do not possess, and that is intolerable. The solution is obvious. Do not receive, do not take. Do not let them know they have what you want. Spoil it for them so they cannot revel in their possession of what is so infinitely desirable. The hope to possess gives over to envy, spite and revenge (for a further discussion of hope, see Boris 1976).

The hatred inspired by such envy is offset by the religious activity of renunciation and submissiveness. These latter, as I have indicated, serve also the purposes of first projecting and then experiencing desire as if one were the object, not the subject, of desire. Hence the seeming tractability of the premorbid anorectic.

But to be the object of desire, in the parsing of the anorectic, means also to be the object of admiration. Hence the strong achievement motif that predates the anorexia and finds its surreal outcome finally in the achievement of starvation and a thinness non pareil. Ordinarily, "a well lived life is the best revenge," to quote the proverb. The anorectic's envy of the breast is such that she cannot acknowledge its particular characteristics (to do so would also risk a resurgence of desire). She cannot therefore have a puberty and thereafter a breast-body the equal of or superior to her (early) mother's, as other envious children strive to have. Her breast-body-appetite is not of the positive, or actual breast, but of, as it were, a negative afterimage of it – the breast that is left after envy has negated what is desirable about it. In this respect the anorectic can episodically believe she is beautiful and not a bag of bones.

There is, of course, an alternative to enviously acquiring the breast ruined and deformed by spite. This is to spurn femininity altogether and acquire masculine characteristics. Much, indeed, has been made of the loss of the menses, the protuberance of the pubic region after all body fat has been lost, the hirsute look that accompanies these, and the undoubted admiration of masculine attributes (cf. Bruch 1978). But this, in my experience, is only partly true.

To see why, we have to begin with the anorectic's *bete noir* – desire. As desire becomes retracted from the person and possessions of the mother, due to frustration and envy, and equally ravenous, equally ruthless greed is directed to the father and his breast, the penis.

(Intercourse and conception are assumed to take place orally; eating and copulation are almost identical. One patient dreams: *My roommate and her boyfriend [once my patient's boyfriend] and my father and I are sitting around. Suddenly the lights go off. When the lights come back on they [the roommate and boyfriend] jump up and straighten their clothes. I know they have been making love. My father, all this while, was sitting around like a bump on a log. I feel disgusted. I say "C'mon into the kitchen. We may as well eat."*)

The plight of the anorectic is such that the same simultaneity of desire and envy is repeated in respect to the father. But if she "acquires" her father's attributes, she also *mutatis mutandum* acquires his desires and these are for intercourse with her discredited mother. Out of the frying pan, she is back into the fire: each solution poses a fresh problem. The anorectic's solution, as I have been saying, is to stimulate desire and envy in the other, to become object not subject. Thus as her father comes into the picture she attempts to seduce both his desire and his envy: to be worthy of his love and admiration but to foil those comfortable feelings by inciting, through her achievements, his frustration and envy. Those patients who are or have become "anorectic personalities" rather than symptomatically anorexic, develop crushes on men they scarcely know. These men are so "wonderful" that it is a "miracle" they have any interest in the patient at all. Yet in no time, the man, by his desire for her, demonstrates his fallibility. To complete the task of converting phallability into fallibility, the patient picks him apart point by point as if every defect in him is an enhancement of her.

*The anorectic will not be found wanting, in both senses of that word.*

The oedipal situation, re-igniting longing and adding jealousy to the already intense portion of possessiveness, accordingly produces a further crisis. The anorectic deals with this in two ways. First she changes the idea that genital sexuality of a reciprocal kind is involved: she wants to imagine the primal scene as something in which she could, if she wanted, participate. Looking is an activity open to a child which accommodates orality, anality, and genitality all at once. Once she alchemizes all longings into looking, she has only to reverse object and subject — the direction of the arrow — in the way she has become practiced at.

Here is another dream from the same patient. *I am at a cocktail party. Everyone has someone to talk to. There is no way to break in. _____ , [a male colleague] though, seems to be able to get in. I feel horribly jealous. I follow after him. I want to imitate him, to see how he does it, as if by, like gluing myself to him I can acquire his technique. The scene changes. Now I am with a group of the women at the party. We are having lunch. Everyone has brought a sandwich. Mine is just plain, like peanut butter and jelly. One woman has a very elegant sandwich, maybe, I don't know, sprouts or something. Fancy. Everyone admires it. She passes it around the circle. When it comes to me, instead of looking at it, I take a big bite out of it. Suddenly I realize this is the wrong thing to have done. We are only supposed to look. Everyone is looking at me. I feel stupid and awful. Awful. In the next scene I am alone. I am starved, but it is also like I ate too much. The usual feelings I often have. I feel gross and fat and awful.*

In the context of this woman's life history, I understand the dream to rework primal scene experiences successfully into the anorexic solution. More generally, it illustrates the "oralization" of experience, the all-purpose value of looking and being looked at and, by implication, the problem of body image — for when so bad a light is cast on both mother's femininity and father's masculinity, what, at puberty, is there left to grow up into?

Obliterating everything is hunger. Elsewhere I have written of the options open to us when we do not wish to know what we experience (Boris 1976). I used the example of Aesop's "Fox and The Sour Grapes," observing that it was indeed easier for the fox to ease his frustration (he was hungry) and helplessness (he could not reach the grapes) by deeming them sour than by changing any other element in the experience: "I, a hungry fox, want but cannot reach the good sweet grapes." The sweetness of the grapes, untastable, could not call him liar: his fictionalization of the experience was safe. To rid oneself of the knowledge of "I-ness," "Fox-ness," indeed hunger was much more difficult. Hunger has a way of asserting itself undeniably; one cannot repress hunger, much less the knowledge of hunger. It will, out, particularly when compared to the hypothetical quality of the sweetness of untasted grapes.

It is precisely this fact that the anorectic seizes upon. Hunger is undeniable and durable. At sufficient levels of intensity it makes one oblivious of everything else. (Accounts by people who were in concentration camps give poignant testimony of this.) For the anorectic that means everything else is obliterated. If they are not obliterated by hunger itself filling the furthest reaches of the mind, they are obliterated by the experience of eating — bingeing — and then by mortification of the spirit or, via diuretics, laxatives, or vomiting, or compulsive exercise, of the flesh. For people of a different stripe, eating consoles loneliness; for the anorectic it is precisely hunger itself that paradoxically serves as the anodyne for loneliness.

I have already alluded to how hunger serves envy and now again to how it short-circuits desire for contact with people. I have shown how this spares people enslavement by the anorectic and spares the anorectic enslavement by both people and their internalized imagos. Now I need to discuss the anorectic's relationship to the food itself.

To my mind, this is the heart of the matter. The anorectic does not have a good set of boundaries. Just as food-hunger is a ruse, the flames of which are fanned to obscure object hunger, so food itself is a counterfeit substance to substitute for a longing for fusion—for being touched by hand and eye and voice, for being held in body and mind.

Since so many writers have addressed this question of "fusion" from so many different viewpoints, I need to be clear about the sense in which I am using the term. The best approximation to what I have observed in my patients is represented by Winnicott's ideas concerning the transitional object, or at least a variation of those ideas (Winnicott 1953).

Sometimes Teddybear, the transitional object, is a baby who wants to eat: an I-baby. Sometimes a naughty greedy teddy: a not-me baby. Sometimes it is a teddy who comforts: an other (than-myself) figure. Sometimes, sadly, it is a malignant other, who wishes to eat me. But whatever its evolution, it is a not-quite-me, not-quite-actual-other figure, and it occupies the space between where I end and the other, usually mother, begins, and vice-versa.

Though variously populated by various incarnations of teddy or Linus-blanket or whatever, the space itself is there because the boundaries have become tolerable. Indeed, separation in the sense of individuation, like a tennis net, makes certain experiences possible which might otherwise not be. The transitional space is like a buffer, a neutral zone, between two bodies (as if a demilitarized zone) which makes room for the play of imagination and the apprehension of reality—both. The painter steps back from his canvas to gain perspective and then goes close to create illusion, so the space facilitates each operation, assuring, with practice, each boundary.

The anorectic shows every indication of having failed either to establish or maintain those boundaries and hence that space. I believe this to be a by-product of the envy which wishes to deny mother her "breast"—to deny that the breast travels with mother. The result is that the transitional space that under other circumstances is fashioned or maintained (depending on one's school of thought) between two people gets fashioned or refashioned (again depending) within the boundary the anorectic regards as herself space.

Language is awkward here. What I want to say is that there is an in-myself space for the anorectic, which is not congruent with an of-myself space, sensation, or image. Food has a mystifying (and frightening) way of going from outside to inside in a hurry. Many anorectic slow that terrifying hurry down by not keeping food handy or not going where food is. The lack of transition in terms of time is made up for in space, or the other way round as when food in hand is eaten slowly, chewed many times before swallowing.

That poor space–time transition necessitates the compensatory inner space for purposes both of individuation — me/not-me, and buffering — me/you. Put in graphic terms Me ‖ Not-me-not-you ‖ You, which is the sort of boundary and space arrangement other people might have is for the anorectic Me-not-me ‖ Not-you-you. Food that crosses the ‖ boundary produces a crisis: It could so easily cross the wavering line and insecure space between in-me and of-me.

The first line of defense is a restriction of intake: with it intact, hunger takes up all one's time and space. But hunger is a chancy friend: one so wants to eat. When one does, the alien food becomes akin to a foreign object in one's being. It lodges there, in danger of being assimilated (or assimilating one) but susceptible to being vitiated or expelled before it becomes of-myself and causes one to flourish despite one's self. Thus the demonic exercising, the diuretics and laxatives, the self-induced vomiting.

The paradox in all of this is that both envy and longing erode the space: for once, these two efforts to relate work in consort. The wish to deny the mother her separateness and the longing to be at one with her cause the anorectic hatefully to destroy her sense of separateness. The feeling of being enslaved by the other follows from this. It is a relief when she is enslaved by her hunger. So, what many of us fear most, starvation unto death, becomes the best riposte to what the anorectic fears most, enslavement by the desirability of the other; and, when projected, enslavement by the desires of the other; and when dissimulated into the food–hunger condensation, enslaved by food and the effects of food, namely weight. Bettelheim's phrase for autism comes to mind: "The empty fortress."

All the same, the transformations that comprise what finally emerges as anorexia represent quite a feat, and it is no wonder that the anorectic regards her achievement as a solution to a problem and decidedly not a problem needing a solution. And in the degree to which anorexia is not ego-alien the anorectic is not a good candidate for a therapeutic alliance and for a psychoanalysis of the sort that depends on such an alliance. Nevertheless, I must take issue with those who, like Bruch and Minuchin, doubt the efficacy of interpretive work, though I should not like to be misunderstood to be saying that I question their work. What I mean to say is that anorexia is a kind of culminating response to quite early difficulties that fulminate with puberty and/or separation and fail otherwise to be resolved. This it has in common with many other psychological configurations. As such, it, like they, can be finessed as Minuchin does, or worked with in ways to support autonomy, a sense of self and self-esteem, as Bruch does. Both these workers begin with a profound respect for the achievement that anorexia represents.

But the infantile neurosis of which the anorexia, however severe or temporary, is an evolution is not susceptible of resolution without interpretation of the fantasies on which it is based. And that is the very stuff of psychoanalysis. The obstacles posed are formidable, and I leave their consideration to another communication (Boris 1984) (see chapter 12). For now I want only to address the matter of the seemingly epidemic increase of anorexia in certain segments of the population.

In a speculative turn of mind, Bion (1961) wrote of "proto-mental state," of a "dis-ease" needing somehow to find a way of becoming a disease, physical, psychological or even spiritual or political (if one allows the license of linking disease with matters sacred and sociological). The precise form it took, he speculated, might have to do with cultural availability and group sanction.

The dis-ease I have encountered at the base of what evolves into anorexia is at the fundament of the human "condition"—desire, hope and envy, repression, projection and projective identification, fusion, confusion and separation, enslavement, refuge and reaction formation, boundaries of time and spaces, salvation, reparation and guilt. Indeed some readers may feel that in all of what I said I failed to say what "caused" anorexia, so much at root has anorexia in common with other problematic conditions.

But the relationship between the dis-ease and the disease has not yet been explored from a sophisticated viewpoint. Given the raw stuff of the dis-ease, one could say with Minuchin, Laing (1967), and others that only in susceptible families could the particular disease happen — families capable of certain reciprocal tranferences. Some commentators refer to our society's premium on slimness and dieting, and surely the anorectic's capacity to out-diet anyone might contribute. Surely she wishes to excite envy when admiration isn't in plentiful supply. But there is a zeal to the anorectic which in another age or a different family might take a religious turn — at least in a vocation, possibly in martyrdom. In another age or cultural corner the asceticism of the anorectic might take a turn toward political revolution, philosophical nihilism, even a time in the Peace Corps or Marine Corps.

Looked at the other way round, it is hard to think of anorexia occurring in the midst of general impoverishment, though one could certainly see it as a response to enforced starvation.

With the anorectic, I am inclined to think anorexia a solution — a way of breaking away by doing without, a way of coming into one's own, a way of doing penance for unremembered sins, a way of achieving mastery over greed. It permits a way of separating from the thrall of the parent via an alliance with a group that repudiates succor and ease. The group, as Sullivan (1953) and Redl (1945) noted, is the way clear of the parent: and if the group is a "Me generation," as sociologists have characterized today's young people, then the negative group (counterculture) is a Not-me group, based on renunciation of previously valued achievements. Alliance with and allegiance to that group permits the dis-ease of the earliest months and years to become the respectable disease of adolescence and young adulthood. If only people knew!

Still, it is for some, not all, a disease that is not a passage but a stopping point, and it needs the sort of treatment that, for all our limitations, only psychoanalysis can supply.

## REFERENCES

Bion, W. R. (1961). *Experiences in Groups*. New York: Basic Books.

Boris, H. N. (1976). On hope: its nature and psycho-therapy. *International Review of Psycho-Analysis*. 3:141–150.

_____ (1984). On the treatment of anorexia nervosa. *International Journal of Psycho-Analysis*. 65:435–442.

Bruch, H. (1973). *Eating Disorders: Obesity, Anorexia Nervosa and the Person Within*. New York: Basic Books.

_____ (1978). *The Golden Cage*. Cambridge, MA: Harvard University Press.

Hsu, K. G. (1980). Outcome of anorexia nervosa: a review of the literature (1954–1978). *Archives of General Psychiatry.* 37:1041–1046.

Laing, R. D. (1967). Family and individual structure. In *The Predicament of the Family*, ed. P. Lomas, pp. 107–125. New York: International Universities Press.

*Life Magazine* (1982). February, pp. 63–76.

Minuchin. S., Rosman. B. L., and Gailer, L. (1978). *Psychosomatic Families: Anorexia Nervosa in Context.* Cambridge, MA: Harvard University Press.

Piazza, E., Piazza, N., and Rollins, N. (1980). Anorexia nervosa: controversial aspects of therapy. *Comprehensive Psychiatry* 21:177–189.

Redl, F. (1945). The psychology of gang formation and the treatment of juvenile delinquents. *Psycho-analytic study of the Child.* 1:367–377. New York: International Universities Press.

Sullivan, H. S. (1953). *The Interpersonal Theory of Psychiatry.* New York: W. W. Norton.

Thoma, H. (1967). *Anorexia Nervosa.* New York: International Universities Press.

Winnicott, D. W. (1953). Transitional objects and transitional phenomena. *International Journal of Psycho-Analysis.* 34:89–97.

_____ (1971). *Playing and Reality.* New York: Basic Books.

# 12

# The Treatment of Anorexia

This is the second part of a two-part paper on anorexia nervosa for which the first, "The Problem of Anorexia," set the table.

The anorectics I have known are greedy, envious people caught in a labyrinth they constructed so early in their lives that they no longer know either the way out or the way deeper in. They know only one credo: less is more, and more is more of the same. They make deadly dull patients who are forever scaring the wits out of one by driving their weight down and their chances for dying up, for at some point the brain becomes so altered by the self-imposed starvation that it loses its capacity for signaling hunger.

As with any patient, one has to feel ready and able to go through what is necessary. It is no fair blaming the patient because he took one further than one meant to go. Anorectics, because they are too little, cannot distinguish between being found wanting and wanting: they believe that (in Beckett's words) the quantum of wantum is not negotiable: that they have only to instill all the wanting that threatens to happen into their analysts and they will feel blessedly free of want and frustration, and filled instead with serenity. Insofar as the analyst does not soak up such wanting in his countertransference, they feel him to be very disobliging and are not above punishing him, with all the brutality people who put others in starvation camps are capable of, for his lack of grace. For both these reasons they are forever not coming, not talking, not paying, not heeding contracts, if they can gull one into making or into trying to get them to make them, and forever doing (one of my patients carried a beeper and arranged to have herself paged!) whatever else they can find drives their analyst nuts. Confrontation is seldom more appealing than with anorectics, who then feel: Gotcha. Only addicts and drunks are, if possible, worse in this respect. To do any work, one has to ignore all these provocations except as they (like the emergency pages) contain meaning. The work consists in helping out with the more-of-the-same part of the credo. Differences inspire lust and also envy. People can get into a tizzy, amounting to frantic frenzy, over deciding which way they want a difference — to receive it or to own it. Any decision loses one possibility: which choice will make that loss worthwhile?

One solution, if it is one, consists of finessing those differences that are of kind by converting them into those of degree. Hence it is no longer who has which but who has more (or less). Since so much of human disputatiousness (or, alternatively, sheer and tender erotic joy) has (in the words of the limerick) to do with who does what and with which and to whom, those who simplify the terms by turning the with which into how much seem to be ahead of the game. But they miss the fun, and to keep this from gradually dawning on them as a loss to be contended with is what so much of the fuss is all about.

---

In the preceding chapter I attempted a formulation of the leading elements of anorexia as I have come to learn of them from the patients I have seen in individual, family, and group treatment (Boris 1984a). In this I wish to develop what in the other I could only mention in passing, namely the very particular difficulties involved in the treatment of anorectics, and what I have found useful in the way of proceeding.

Perhaps the major difficulty for analytic work is that for the anorectic his or her[1] anorexia is a solution and not a problem. And as Schafer, in particular, has emphasized, resistance is not simply a negation of material the patient wishes to remain oblivious of or disown. It is an affirmative belief that there is another path to salvation than that of experiencing what she experiences, knowing it and resolving the conflicts involved (Schafer 1976).

For the anorectic that path to salvation is well in hand. It consists

---

[1]Since 85 percent of anorectics are female, it is estimated (Bruch 1978), I shall use the pronoun *her*.

manifestly of self-starvation either through restriction or through evac-
uations—vomiting, diuretic-induced urination, laxative-induced defecation, constant motion exercise, or all together. The constant state of
hunger is so obtrusive as to overshadow any other feelings. And the
preoccupation with body size, shape, and weight is so obsessive as to
crowd out any other preoccupations. At its "best" anorexia is a full-time
job. I have compared it to the black hole phenomenon in astrophysics,
where the mass of the star is so great as to draw everything, including
its light, into itself.

The result is that the transference, in which we are accustomed to
shine with borrowed light, simply does not take place. Freud noted that
when a patient is in love or in mourning the transference dwindles. He
also noted (1914, p. 82) that the man with a toothache cannot fall in
love. The anorectic is both in love and in mourning and furthermore
has a bellyache!

These positions taken together with her utter conviction that her
anorexia is her last, best achievement leave little for either the
transference or the therapeutic alliance. There is hardly even resistance of an active sort; just the sort of bland indifference of someone
passing time between episodes of intense prayer. The anorectic is
among but not of us.

If sent for analysis, the anorectic may come and be superficially
co-operative; she has nothing much to lose. And since anorexia is a
difficult course to pursue, she certainly would accept an appreciative
recognition of that fact: she certainly does not welcome her solution,
the jewel in her crown, being regarded as a problem, a flaw or defect.
But for the most part the analyst feels something tantamount to the "la
belle indifference" of the classic hysteric.

This is no accident. The anorectic is trying to cure herself of
wanting, more precisely of being found wanting. Since her wants are
much too intense to submit securely to repression, she distills the whole
spectrum and dimensionality of them into the narrow range of
occupations with intake and body image. But even that is not enough.
It works intrapsychically by focusing and riveting her own attention to
her fixation and obsession and rituals. But there is always the danger
that someone may prove desirable—and lead her into the longing,
libido, and loneliness she hates and is trying to obliterate. So she
secures her intrapsychic procedures with the use of projection. If
anyone is to want anything of anyone, it is the other who is to want
something of her.

In the analytic situation it is at least partly the analyst's resolution and containment of his own countertransference that leaves the room for the patient's transference to occupy. Every patient to a greater or lesser degree occupies himself with what the analyst wants as a way of remaining oblivious of what he wants of the analyst. But insofar as the analyst has no mote in his own eye, the patient presently comes to see the beam in his. His projections have less and less reality to substantiate them; to continue to believe in his projections, he would have to split his ego and attack his own perceptual and memory functions — a costly procedure.

The anorectic is wanted to eat, more broadly to take. Food, care, medication, nasogastric tubes, IVs, hospitalization: something; anything. As she loses weight, her projections are fleshed out and given substance. It is the other who wants, not she. She relies on this, desperately. It can get to the point where she will die for it. She counts on "countertransferences" in both her family and, of course, her analyst.

Should the analyst not want anything for or from his anorectic patient, she will be most impressed by this. A superior sort of anorectic, she will feel, this analyst of mine. Her admiration will induce emulation. If her emulations fail, her admiration will shade over to envy and she will set out to destroy the treatment in the way Limentani and others have analysed in considering "the negative therapeutic reaction" (Limentani 1981). (See also Valenstein's [1973] work on holding on to negative affects and Brenman's [1982] elegant formulation on depression versus longing.)

All the same, it *is* necessary to want nothing for or from the anorectic, though she will spare no effort to stimulate longing in the analyst. She will want to attend less frequently, stay less long, say less, pay less — anything less. For her, of course, less is more. But in addition to this display of her substance as a person, she will count on the analyst to demand *some*thing of her. This will help support her projections, but, more, it will discredit the analyst as a person unable to cope with his greed. It will also, not incidentally, help the patient's fragile self-esteem, in the sense that it is nice to be wanted.

The analyst has to let the anorectic destroy the analysis. If it is to be destroyed, there is no point in the analyst being the one to do it. Thus no limits should be set that have to be enforced by breaking off the treatment. It is enough that the anorectic comes every once in a while, speaks every so often, and so on. What she does and how she does it has to be her business.

This is the place to note that two experienced students of the subject of the treatment of anorexia take issue with what I have said. Bruch feels that the anorectic's bizarre eating behavior has to be the subject of treatment, particularly when she shows signs of being worrisome in regard to her body weight.

She also does not feel interpretive work does much good, a point with which I would disagree. However, a close reading suggests the interpretive work she sees as useless or worse is poor interpretive work, work that precludes self-discovery rather than aiding in it (Bruch 1978).

Minuchin has the anorectic weigh in at each session, family or individual. Otherwise he attempts to finesse the anorexia by deeming it a successful rebellion in aid of an unsuccessful search for autonomy, separation, and individuality (Minuchin et al. 1978).

The successes claimed by these two workers require our attention. For Minuchin anorexia is a creation of the family system. With this I agree. Any fictionalization of experience—I use this term to be an arrangement of what Freud meant by the screen memory, a version enthroned to exist instead of the actual in order that the actual event or state-of-mind not be remembered or known; any fictionalization of experience, such that it is food and weight that are the matter, has to find concurrence in the others with whom the patient's fate has been cast or with whom she casts her fate. "Anorexia," for example, is itself such a fiction. It means loss of appetite. In fact, anorectics are sometimes glutted but seldom other than ravenous. It takes a willingness on the part of others to go along with a fiction and not expose it. This cooperative spirit may be unconscious, so that it is not merely going along but an active wish to believe, even to implement, a particular fiction that is at work. Laing, in his study of families, was much concerned with how the designated patient cooperated with—in his view was victimized by—fictional attributions made by the parents (Laing 1967).

Minuchin disturbs that collusion. He interferes with what he calls "triangulation" by obliging the parents to resolve the tensions between them with one another, and likewise prohibits the anorectic from reinserting herself into the twosome. Then he redefines the anorexia as at once thwarted autonomy and adolescent or childish rebelliousness and renegotiates suitable goals and better methods. The anorectic, freed of her enmeshment, her willing exploitation as a triangulating foil, and supported in her attempts to want, wants. Soon she can bear both to want and to want food.

It may be objected that little but the symptom is changed, that the anorectic personality and character structure remain. But to dislodge a system is also to open the way to the natural development of procedures for conflict resolution and the natural processes of growth. This is no small feat. Unfortunately, Minuchin seems uninterested in the resolution of the infantile neurosis, not merely on grounds of economy of effort and expediency. As a "systems" thinker, he hasn't ideological room for intrapsychic matters, indeed regards them as a by-product of a misunderstanding. For him boldly to display to a family *there is another way of doing things; you don't need the anorexia* is most helpful, but it misses much of what the system contains (in both senses of "contain").

Bruch also sees the anorectic as a creature of her parents, a more than usually docile child obediently living out her parents' aspirations for her or for themselves. Bruch feels this subjugation can, and too often does, take place once again in psychotherapy. The anorectic, she feels, has not been allowed to discover what she wants and to arrange to get this from others. Rather, the anorectic has been anticipated so regularly that she knows nothing from within. She cannot tell whether she is hungry, full, fat, thin, energetic, exhausted — whatever. Therapy must rectify this, in Bruch's view, by permitting the anorectic to learn of herself from herself. Bruch feels that this process is facilitated when the therapist is open in his turn, so that the anorectic can learn of him from him. Bruch also talks freely of what she has learned from other anorectics, presumably as an aid to her patient in mapping and identifying her own inner experience. In this methodology it is clear that naming the dimensions of the anorexia has a clear and vital part.

Not so for Minuchin. He merely says or implies he cannot work with people who are so "childish" as not to eat. He has to be reassured by the scale that people are being sensible enough to warrant his help. That is the extent of his outpatient interest. When the anorectic has to be hospitalized, she is told what she eats is her affair but what she "spends" — the analogy is to a checking account — is the doctor's. So much in, so much out. Nothing in, bed rest. Some in, out-of-bed privileges involving exercise. In contrast to Minuchin and Bruch, I suggest that the only attention the anorexia need be given by the analyst is in terms of the use the patient is making of it in the transference. There is no contradiction in this recommendation with my earlier discussion of anorexia as preclusive of much more than a shallow transference. Indeed it is precisely that function of anorexia that needs interpretation.

The anorexia, as I have said, is designed to elicit countertransferences by stimulating substantiation for the projections the anorectic characteristically makes. The analyst is to be discovered as greedy, intemperate, enslaving. These discoveries will in turn imply defects and flaws: if the analyst wants the breast so much, he cannot therefore have one; if he hasn't a breast or penis (or whatever) of value, he needs neither to be desired or envied; he is a no-thing. This is the anorectic solution.

The anorectic problem is the boundlessness of her desire on the one side and envy on the other and the dizzying simultaneity of the two. Within her, desire (to receive) and covetousness (to possess) war ceaselessly. Paradoxically, however, they converge in one major respect. Both combine to hate and mentally obliterate the separateness and distinctness of the object. There is no transitional space—the not-me, but yet not-other space—that transitional phenomena require (Winnicott 1953). The anorectic lives, as it were, without a skin. Others, in their incandescent desirability, impact on her with detonating force. And this is the problem.

To solve it, the anorectic creates an "inner" space: in-me but not of-me. She sets all her soldiers of vigilance to monitor that space. Thus employed, they do not have time or energy to notice the presence of the object, who would otherwise excite desire and envy.

How to get food to go in but yet not become of her? Food, as part-object, necessarily also excites desire and envy. The envy is devoted to food's ability to penetrate the of-me boundary and reach into the very marrow of being. This once was an intention the anorectic experienced in respect to the body and soul of her mother. It is still a wish she "inadvertently" acts out in respect to her mother (and father). "Eat something. Eat *some*thing! You are driving me crazy. Look, look at your father. You are making him sick. He doesn't sleep. Look, let me fix you something. Whatever you'd like. A little chicken? . . . But the anorectic screams "leave me a-*lone!*" and proclaims the absence of her wish to own her parents while devaluing their desirability.

The analyst, then, needs to work in a transitional space. He cannot work on or in his patient. She on her part will — unwittingly — work on or in him. It has to become and remain clear that though she will, via both projections and displacement, experience him as harboring such designs in the very core of the transference fantasy, he must not lend substance to these attributions.

Two ways of proceeding have proved helpful. One is to talk to the air. One confides one's ruminations as if to an interested but otherwise occupied colleague, or as one does when one reads aloud a snippet from the morning newspaper. The idea is: this may interest you. One's words should represent musings and not be directed at some purpose. Interpretations are food for thought. It is best that they be set out but not served. The air to which one talks is the transitional space the analyst needs to create in order to assure the anorectic her boundaries. As this becomes established, the in-me-but-not-of-me space becomes less needed. It is not so clear to me as it is to Bruch and Minuchin that parents *do in fact* invade the space that their anorectic children require, that this is not, instead, in an important degree a function of fears of violation consequent upon projections, but I do agree with them that a neutral zone in the treatment situation is altogether necessary.

It will not remain. Either the anorectic will try to draw the analyst in or he will get the sense that his interpretations are being misinterpreted. Both require further interpretations.

The particular density of the anorectic represents a "gravitational field" tough to escape. Everything seems to have reference to matters of food, starvation, disfigurement, enslavement, and the analyst's interpretations are no exception. "When I speak to you, it is as if. . . ." This kind of clarifying comment needs to follow almost every interpretation of what the anorectic is doing. The experience of being in the consulting room has, above all, to be tolerable.

When anorectics are in the thick of their food–weight enthrallment, they are embarrassed to talk of it. They know, as any rider of a special hobby-horse knows, that no one else could possibly have the obsessive interest in the subject they have. But, in addition, the anorectic suffers from her dread of "lapping-up" the analyst's interest. The superego, fashioned so early, is indeed an archaic creature; to it has been ascribed the terrifying predatory intentions the anorectic has struggled to rid herself of in an effort, initially, to save mother from being cannibalized. Insofar as the analyst begins to become an object of desire, the anorectic will begin to oscillate between finding his interest a consuming one and wanting to consume his interest. "Progress" in the latter direction thus poses its own problems for her. Does she prefer the devil within or the devil without? The periodic abatement of the symptom pivots on the same fulcrum. Self-starvation is a wonderful antidote for guilt and reparation — witness Lent and Yom Kippur and the taboo foods of other cultures. So is purgation; the vomiting and exercise of the bulimic is not solely to evacuate calories; they are a means of disgorging guilt. Guilt is not merely a bad feeling of feeling bad; it is a physical experience of an almost ineradicable tension. Physical means are accordingly required to expunge the feeling. There is moral relief in violent exercise, exhaustive defecation, and vomiting. There is even a kind of moral sensuality in the experience of "bingeing," when the glut of gluttony is reached. There are all so much more manageable than the awkwardness of relations with people that one can expect a resurgence of symptoms precisely when the anorectic begins to experience regard for the analyst as a good object. For when his goodness doesn't stimulate envy, it stimulates love, a love which in turn disposes the patient at once to feed the analyst and protect him from her own surging appetites. In so far as this reparative inclination meets the same fate as earlier — that the other will not accept what she can offer, the reversion to symptomatic activity becomes all too easy.

The problem of reparation being what it is, in fantasy as well as (often) in fact, the analysis of the ceaseless, envious denuding of, and, in counterpart, the ruthless fantasies of cannibalizing the object become unbearable for the anorectic. Insofar as she cannot make up for these, except by not eating or not keeping what she eats, she feels as if she is continually being traduced — trashed. Since by taking as little as possible from the world, or, when she falters, purging herself of what she has taken, she is making, in part, an authentic attempt at sanctity, she also feels terribly misunderstood. Thus as she begins to allow herself, in oscillation, to discover in the analyst an object of value, the problem of reparation has to be given equal weight with the analysis of early greed and envy.

Having said that, however, I have now to issue a reminder. The anorectic's problems are not primarily oral; they are designed to seem so.

The obsession of the anorectic with her anorexia is reminiscent of that of the psychotic with his hallucinations. In this respect, Freud's suggestion applies: "An attempt to explain an hallucination ought not to attack the positive hallucination but rather the negative." In the all-consuming anorexia there is an absence of absence, and it is that fact and what is absent that needs analytic attention (Freud 1917, p. 232 fn. 3).

The absence of passionate longings which the anorectic achieves by her displacements and projections and reaction-formations leaves her peculiarly vulnerable to the influence of others. Her illness gives her the inner life that offsets that vulnerability. Naturally she is afraid to lose it. As she confides her anorexia to the analyst — gives it over, as it were — the absence becomes present. Not only has she now no way of getting well — for an illness is necessary for a recovery — but in the presence of the absence she fears being refilled with all of what she has projected. Laing makes this concrete: saliva that is comfortable and familiar in one's own mouth, once expectorated, even into a glass of clear, pure water, is experienced as alien and repugnant (Laing 1962). There is a terrible pain in store for the anorectic when she finds herself grotesque and her activities and rituals, previously syntonic, monstrous and malignant. Still, it is this absence that must come into being before the important work of the analysis can be done. Intuiting this, the anorectic will sometimes temporarily "give up" her anorexia in order to keep it intact for later use.

The fact that her determined use of that portion of the spectrum of development seems oral in nature is the "positive hallucination." We need, therefore, to see that the so-called regression to the developmental fixation point is after all a function of later developmental crisis as well as conflicts at the time of fixation. In fact the point of fixation represents in some respect the last, best resolution. And indeed the anorectic has already outgrown her pregenital preoccupations by the time she hits puberty, college, divorce, or whatever part of the life cycle it is when she takes up anorexia. That is why some people spontaneously remit, or, more precisely, re-outgrow, anorectic symptomatology or are so easily "cured" by behavior modification treatment or family therapy.

When I speak of the problem of treatment, then, I have also in mind that the more carefully the elements in the anorexia are analyzed, the more the analyst is in danger of missing what the anorexia hides. Unlike certain other symptoms or characterologic malformations, anorexia *contains* in the compromise formation less of what bedevils the patient than it *obscures* it. When the anorectic finally does give way and talk of her inexhaustible occupation with food, weight, and body image, the analyst will have a Scheherazade of a patient. The occupation will conceal the preoccupation, which is oedipal-genital in nature.

The dynamics of the oedipal situation, however, are the same — profound desire competing with envious covetousness; projection as a primary defensive orientation; hypersusceptibility to stimulation and an urgent need for the release of excitement through orgasm or "displaced" orgasm.

Though writers on the subject occasionally remark positively on the facial appearance of the anorectic — childlike, angelic — the body is generally agreed to look grotesque. Moreover, the anorectic is said to think her wasted look to be beautiful. My experience does not support these assessments. To the contrary. The anorectic, by "putting" a child or angel's face on an old person's body, is attempting to complicate sexual responses in others. This is for several reasons, of which the one I want to mention here is that of inhibiting a response that will lead to the other — in the countertransference, the analyst — to thoughts of sexual intercourse. The anorectic knows she looks grotesque to others; she has certainly heard it enough. While her heroics about dieting or, at any rate, weight control are designed to stimulate admiration or, failing that, envy, the body is designed to look asexual and/or sufficiently androgynous as to evoke the most muddled sexual response in both men and women. Others, and, of course the analyst, are supposed to try to feed or fail at feeding and to coerce or fail at coercing. It is supposed to be as difficult to think about sex as it might in conjunction with a concentration camp victim or a saint.

That there is a degree of vindictive spite in this will emerge later; as some patients for periods try to excite unrequitable longing in the analyst as a means of imposing retaliatory pain, so the anorectic denies the analyst the sensuous gratification he ordinarily gets from contemplating loveliness. But this is secondary to her effort not to "let sex come into it," as it is frequently put.

The anorectic is attempting to understand everything in certain terms. There are women, for example, who upon the break-up of a relationship — a marriage perhaps — lose weight. At first this may be due to stress, depression, worry of an essentially reactive sort. But then the weight loss becomes progressive and begins to express an "understanding" of the separation from the husband in terms of loss of mother or breast: I have been too greedy, so this is what happened. This understanding is at once "true" and "untrue." That is why it makes a good screen or cover story. So with the more extreme anorectic. Not only is she "understanding" what happened in oral and anal terms, *so must others*. One patient, for example, filled all the sessions of the week preceding a visit from her parents with ruminations concerning how she was going to see them and get any work done, how she would keep to her diet if she had to share mealtimes with them and have food in the refrigerator for them. The week of their visit gave rise to (triumphant) accounts of what dreadful, limited people they were, interspersed with (defeated) tearful accounts of "binges." The sessions of the week following their visit were devoted to (gloating) accounts of how "behind" she was in her work and how everyone was trying to get work out of her and how annoying it was to have to attend sessions. But after all these "points" were made and driven home, there was this casual, almost fleeting reference: "It's so funny, when my folks were here, how much I masturbated, as if I was almost daring them to walk in and discover me at it."

The vast fascination with sexual matters needs systematically to be noted along such lines as this: One patient says: "It's terrible on these days, like when I was walking here, wherever I look there is food— people eating, shops selling food. That's all I see."

I: "Instead of. . . ."

Patient: (*Pause*) 'Now you mention it, I have been taking a new route over here. They have these beautiful women, soft mysterious, come hither. But it's all false. Even if you went in—I mean, what kind of women undress for people in places like that." [Note the "Now *you* mention it," the "over *here*," the "if *you* went in."] This notation is not simply to breach the resistance or even to help fashion the direction of the work. It is necessary, I think, to "talk to the unconscious" by way of making an alliance with the disowned sexual self. The oscillations of which I wrote earlier are the more easily stopped if, like a third leg to the stool, there is another option for the patient to remember and use. As in growing out of pregenital orientations, developmentally speaking, so in the course of the analysis there has to be somewhere else for the patient to go.

In meditating on the Wolf Man, Freud wrote that one can think of interpretations being put, by the child, on events at the time they occurred, at a later time in the light of subsequent information or fantasy or at the time of narration or dreaming (Freud 1918). In terms of construction, anorectic patients pose just this problem more so than many. It is often difficult to tell whether they mistook genital and oedipal matters as having to do with feeding and elimination, confusing breast and penis, pregnancy and puberty because they always thought only in oral terms or because they reinterpreted everything to rid themselves of later discoveries too painful to be allowed to endure. To put it still another way, it is not easy to know when one is dealing with memories from childhood and when memories of childhood. I would like to suggest that this difficulty is expressive of a particular function in anorectic patients.

Just as the location of contents crosses, as it were, *spatially*, back and forth between self and internal object, between self and transitional space, between body and food, and projectively between self and other, so too has the anorectic shuttled the contents of her experiences back and forth through time with the same frenetic and carelessly careful ease. The result is, I suggest, a *mélange* of experiences, or rather of interpretation of experience. Prospective views, retrospective views, vision and revision, once served the same functions as the spatial ones do in the present. They protect against certainty — particularly the certainties of separation and loss and of ownership and disillusionment. And since uncertainty is itself so painful (for example, the haunting uncertainty attaching to what the body looks like or weighs after eating or purging), there has had to be created a quantity of understandings to compensate for the quality that is lost. Experience is always being attacked and lost to attack, interpreted and reinterpreted: confusion and fusion.

That this makes reconstruction inherently difficult can almost go without saying. But the difficulty is compounded by the anorectic patient who wants more interpretations to go with her own and has no intention of giving one up for another. The analyst's interpretations are valued since into him the anorectic projects the good material she craves. But they are feared, as food is, because the interpretations will add so much and have such weight that she will be lost in the confusion. She attacks interpretations with scorn and doubt and feels lost and uncertain. Then she takes an additive approach in order that no interpretation can be entirely true (or false). When this procedure causes its own difficulties, she perforce must look for certainty outside herself again. (It is characteristic of these patients to look to their parents to remember childhood for them.)

The anorectic's relationship to the analyst's interpretation has therefore to be a concern for him, not alone in terms of how they are symbolized and with what his giving of them is analogized (food: feeding, impregnation, etc.) but in terms also of the problems posed for the patient by certainty and uncertainty, his and hers. This is the more necessary because for periods of time the anorectic takes up a paranoid stance and proceeds with deception and stealth. Where others might complain of bad, useless or "how's that supposed to help" interpretations, she may simply fight fire with fire, much as she returns silence for silence. For the anorectic patient the undoing of the "remembered" life history with the usual eye to historical accuracy engenders not only the usual resistances, but one rooted in a profound intolerance of ambiguity, uncertainty—of anything approaching Keats's "negative capability".[2] Cooperation in the interest of discovery is an infrequent state of affairs: competition in access to what is so is the more pervasive atmosphere. More than with other patients, letting matters evolve until the anorectic patient can make her own constructions is much to be desired. The anorectic's reach for simple certainty leads her to insights that are about as accurate and helpful as her nostrums for physical well-being. "It sounds like . . ." says one of my patients. "So it would seem that . . ." says another.

"*I* have to say 'seems' and 'sounds like'," I interject, "because I can only infer, can but guess. *You*, in contrast, can know, really know."

But, in the end, it is the analyst's own quiet tolerance of the muddle and uncertainty, of the gradualness of approximations, of error and apology that makes it possible for his patient to come simply to be. In being resides the experience that when genuinely experienced leads to the insights with which development is facilitated. The capacity for both parties to the analysis to manage the presence of the absence of certainty is what, more than anything, I think to be or not to be the conducive factor.

## REFERENCES

Boris, H. (1984). On the problem of anorexia nervosa. *International Journal of Psycho-Analysis*. 65:315–322.
Brenman, E. (1982). Separation: a clinical problem. *International Journal of Psycho-Analysis*. 63:303–311.
Bruch, H. (1978). *The Golden Cage*. Cambridge, MA: Harvard University Press.
Freud, S. (1914). On narcissism. *Standard Edition* 13:72–102.

---

[2]The condition in which "man is capable of being in uncertainties, mysteries, doubts, without any irritable reaching after fact and reason." *The Letters of John Keats*:1814–1821, vol. 2, p. 193.

_____ (1917). A metapsychological supplement to the theory of dreams. *Standard Edition* 14:222–235.

_____ (1918). From the history of an infantile neurosis. *Standard Edition* 17:7–122.

Laing, R. D. (1962). *The Divided Self.* New York: Pantheon.

_____ (1967). Family and individual structure. In *The Predicament of the Family*, ed. P. Loms, pp. 107–125. New York: International Universities Press.

Limentani, A. (1981). On some positive aspects of the negative therapeutic reaction. *International Journal of Psycho-Analysis* 62:379–390.

Minuchin, S., Rosman, B. L., and Gailer, L. (1978). *Psychosomatic Families: Anorexia Nervosa in Context.* Cambridge, MA: Harvard University Press.

Schafer, R. (1976). *A New Language for Psycho-analysis.* New Haven CT: Yale University Press.

Valenstein, A. F. (1973). On attachment to painful feelings and the negative therapeutic reaction. *Psychoanalytic Study of the Child* 28:365–392. New York: International Universities Press.

Winnicott, D. W. (1953). Transitional objects and transitional phenomena. *International Journal of Psycho-Analysis.* 34:89–97.

# 13

# Torment of the Object: A Contribution to the Study of Bulimia

At the time I wrote this I wanted to show that merely having feelings that others could sway could be experienced as a kind of torture. Later I was to see that at issue was influence, in very much the same way Tausk (1919) used the term in his essay on the "Influencing Machine." The influence in question would turn out to be an "unheard melody," that Keatsian "ditty of no tone." This I would later link up with a fear on the part of the infantile self that it was not among the elect—not among those who should be living and flourishing; or, to paraphrase Keats, When I have fears I was not meant to be. . . .

This primal dread has to be given some kind of form and syntax so that something can be done about its overwhelming influences. Hatred and torment are stimulated by the influence of the dread incorporated in the process of identification (See H. N. Boris, "Identification with a vengeance" in *Envy*. Northvale, NJ: Jason Aronson, 1994). In that format, the Other is obliterated by the identification the Self makes with it. In bulimia, the Other is given substance and space, only to be disgorged or otherwise rendered impotent, its once overwhelming influence reduced to rubble.

---

As a freshman in college, Ms. F. had developed a practice of writing and filling prescriptions for herself from a pad she took from a physician she had consulted. By this means she acquired the laxatives and diuretics she felt she needed, but also, of course, as it was to turn out, no less significantly, she acquired the attributes of the physician — what the blanks, the signature, and the words symbolized.

At first she filled the prescriptions at a distance from the college and the physician, but presently she "got careless" and was caught by a pharmacist who knew the physician well enough to doubt he would prescribe what was written. The college furloughed Ms. F. with the prescription she see a psychiatrist.

The psychiatrist she saw was a younger colleague of mine, who at times discussed his cases with me. Ms. F. turned out to be rather a recalcitrant patient. From the first appointment when, by a logistic snarl-up she couldn't have anticipated, she arrived a half-hour late, she continued to come late and, moreover, to behave as if the entire affair were an unjust punishment. By the time my colleague and I talked, he had felt that it was necessary to confront Ms. F. with the notification that she could not be given a "clean bill of health" unless she did something more than "go through the motions."

It was concluded that further work one-to-one was untenable; that she could not be asked to internalize, or swallow, viewpoints she felt would ruin and incapacitate her, that the situation had to be reframed; that the most expeditious and possibly most all-around helpful way would be to start once more from the beginning; and that the beginning was the bosom of the family. I agreed to see the family, so that in the future individual work with my colleague might be possible again.

Ms. F. took up the plan with enthusiasm, and within a week or so the F.'s were assembled in my consulting room.

## INTRODUCTION TO THE IDEAS

Among the notions beginning to dawn upon me at the inception of this case was the idea of peripheries — boundaries and innards — and the traffic that flowed in and out. As with children who set up the play therapy room with spaces marked off from other spaces, so it was with Ms. F. From somewhere within her self reaching out to the furthest pharmacy, from the food which one minute was outside and then the next inside, to the cud, which was one moment inside and the next out, there was ceaseless, restless movement. Who was she? Where did she (spatially) begin and where did she end? Was she individuated, separate? Conjoined, fused? If one wanted to see her, where she was located?

The decision to see her as part of her family was not an attempt to do family therapy, for which I was then only marginally qualified. It was an attempt to take these questions seriously: Where is Ms. F.? Where is Ms. F.? Here she is! Here she is! Or so we hoped.

In the event, Ms. F. was to help throw light on those amazing sleights of mind by which people attempt to recreate a self and a world in which catastrophe is averted and possibility impregnated by the fairly simple devices of eating and purging, which, after all, any infant can manage.

## THE FAMILY SESSIONS

By the chance of schedule, I could only see the family at tennis time. Mr. F. came from work, in a blue blazer, gray trousers and face. Mrs. F. and "the girls" came from the courts. In their tennis whites, they were like ripe flowers, pink patina upon dusky tan. Mrs. F. was more deeply tanned, like carved wood. Ms. F., too, wore tennis shoes and pom-pom socklets, and jeans, and emblazoned tee shirts, variously advertising rock groups, soft drinks, and causes. (In the end, I gave up trying to attach meaning to the messages, save that they were signifiers of being a normal teenager.) "The girls," who ranged from 11 to 17, sat on the three seats of the couch. Mother pulled the chair I had set away from the desk, back to the desk. She needed the desk for the documentation she had brought in an Ivory soap carton. Father sat on an arm of the couch. Ms. F. sat in a chair that was neither here nor there. Mr. F. decided to abrogate the circle and Mrs. F. to break it.

The girls stared at me with the frank interest of children at a zoo. Mr. F. put on a cooperative face, which looked rather more resigned than enthusiastic. Ms. F. looked down; her eyes were circled with anguish; her mouth was pinched; but she was not going to meet my eyes. Mrs. F. began unfurling documents. I could not help but feel interested, but I also wished I could be somewhere less lonely.

As events began to unfold, a fairly typical situation emerged. The girls didn't see why they had to be there. They volunteered nothing and took a certain shared pleasure in how uncommunicative each could be. Mr. F. would sometimes attempt to help me out by remonstrating with them, but since his role was to be futile, his efforts achieved what was intended. Mrs. F. impatiently awaited the denouement of our respective and collective uselessness and began to take charge. At this "the girls" rolled their eyes to one another, while Mr. F. impotently scolded them with hand gestures. Ms. F. had found the window and fixed her gaze at it like a prisoner will at patches of blue or green. At the halfway point of the hour-and-a-half session, I could tell two things: first, that Mrs. F. and I were to be left to it; and, second, that "it" was to get her into treatment. Anything else was going to be brought to a standstill.

Since by now Mrs. F. was unfolding her own Regents scores from high school, which were indeed, as she said, in the 99th percentile, I could see that there might be a case for providing her with serious assistance. And I could see the power and force with which she was seeing to it that her daughters would complete what and where she left off. So I said:

*Ms. F. is very ill.* And you may have to let her get well. But she can only get well if the rest of you accept your share of the sickness. Next time I am going to tell you what your share is—if there is a next time. There may not be a next time because Ms. F. will not want to come back. She is protecting you with her sickness and by not coming back she will remain ill and protect you. You will have to get her to come back with you. But you will have your own excuses for not coming back, and we will stay where and how we are now. If that is what you want, leave now. If you do not leave now, your job is to plan the next session. I have done all I can do—all I am prepared to do. *You are not my problem, you are yours.*

This rather pontifical statement met, of course, with the most spirited challenges. But I was adamant: I had set the fox among the chickens, and I was not to be drawn back in. I contented myself (and discontented them) with parenthetical remarks such as:

*To Mr. F.:* Are you so ineffectual at your work as here, or is this something you work at?

*To "the girls":* You are really giving your parents the business. If we knew why you do it and why they let you get away with it, we would know something.

*To Mrs. F.:* You are only making matters worse. Why don't you develop a little curiosity?

*To Ms. F.:* You are counting on them failing. At the end of the session, minus one, you will be free to keep your family intact.

Sure enough, by the end minus one, they could not agree why they were here, what this was supposed to accomplish, who should return, if anyone, who could possibly be free when (there were tennis competitions in particular), and so forth. Plainly if something were to happen, I would have to do it — or else! But of course in the mysterious fashion in which these matters devolve, a moment later we were all pledged for next week, same time.

The next week I reiterated the salients of the previous week, adding that I thought it impossible for Ms. F. to be other than self-treating until people took on their own share of the illness and were willing to work on it together. I further added that while I doubted this could all be done in the present session, I anticipated the same difficulty about getting to a next session and suggested that they work on that issue first. As I hoped, this flushed out the various collaborating and reciprocating resistances and enabled me to draw attention to them.

None of the stories one tells one's self — the cover stories one uses to represent and misrepresent what one experiences and who one thinks one is — can survive except insofar as they properly represent or properly misrepresent the stories held dear by those to whom one is significant. In the F. family there were three main stories, as it emerged.

First, there was the story that Mrs. F. wanted only the best for everyone.

Second, there was the story that the best was at hand, if it weren't for Ms. F.'s embarrassingly stupid behavior.

Third, there was the idea that the family could very well cope without help if outsiders didn't meddle.

"The girls" were living proof (in dusky rose and tan) of this:could anyone doubt that not only were they flourishing, but flourishing (tennis tournaments were the objective criterion) *better than* the children of *other* families? I was continually assured that Ms. F. was the best player of the four girls. ("Is this so?" I asked Ms. F. "I don't know. It's been a year since I played, and they have all improved." Mysteries and more mysteries!) In tandem with their ceding to Ms. F. this ambiguous superiority, was the admonition: "If you just started playing again, you wouldn't need those laxatives and stuff." It was recurrently plain: Ms. F. was not supposed to be "sick."

Indeed, whenever harkening to my insistence that Ms. F. wasn't able to play tennis anymore or pretend to normality more generally, or whenever Ms. F. would venture to talk of her bingeing or the like, there would be a vast silence. Then Mrs. F. (usually) or Mr. F. would begin to talk as if Ms. F. had said nothing. I would of course draw attention to this, and presently the family worked out a countering tactic:

"Darling, the doctor (*sic*) says you are sick. Why don't you see that nice psychiatrist, you know Dr. um, er . . . ?"

"Leave us alone, Ms. F.!" I would interpret. "Do what you have to do, but get him out of our lives and leave us in peace. We don't believe you're sick, so it's just a matter of hitting against the backboard for a while, honey."

When I said such things, the family felt I was making fun of them; but I told them that though they did not like to think so, they were making fun of *me*.

The most powerful resistance, of course, was leveled against my insistence that the rest of the family "accept their share of the illness." Often none of the six of them could even remember a sentence of what I had said they were to do (except to come back, which they disposed of by making regular appointments). At these times they would drift off into chat and family gossip of the emptiest sort, to which Ms. F. contributed her share. The words *deadly dull* would recur to me: death by dullness. Only Mr. F. would convey an occasional sympathy with a raise of his eyebrow or a tilt of his head as if to say, "You see? I have to endure this, too."

After a while (mistakenly, I feel in retrospect) I asked him: "So why do you put up with it?" (I should have continued to interpret his complicity.) He said, "I don't, frankly, have the energy to stop them."

This break in the ranks, as it happened, turned on a terrific row. The gist of it was that *everyone* worked hard, not just he. Somewhere in the general acrimony I recall him saying to Mrs. F., "Yes, but when you go to the store, you get a quart, one single quart, of milk for them, for them!" This, of course, referred to "the girls," who plainly drank a quart each just for starters.

Mrs. F. was thunderstruck, partly by the bitterness with which the accusation was made, partly that it was made in front of me, and partly, I thought, because not only was it true, but also it challenged an idea having to do with whether she should have to shop at all. She flung back at him how busy she was, going from tournament to tournament, and began to recite the schedule: "Isn't that right, girls?" It was true: Mr. F. didn't "have the energy." (This was when I saw that my earlier interpretation had been incorrect; now the question was, did I "have the energy?") For as Mr. F. retreated, the looks of discomfiture on the girls' faces and the frank anxiety on Ms. F.'s faded.

I said: "You have come together again. For a moment there was a serious question. It was, do you, Mrs. F., have the right not to shop or, if you have to shop, not to shop accurately. This was taken to mean, are you too busy. But that wasn't the whole question. The rest of it was about who should sacrifice what and for whom."

I managed, on and off, to keep that question in play until we reached some real talk about Mrs. F.'s premarital accomplishments and her famished ambition. We talked of what Mr. F. owed her for that and what her daughters did. Regarding Mr. F., there was his own view of Mrs. F. as the one "who wears the pants" and his own loneliness for his father. I remarked somewhere in this: "If only parents were allowed to change genders with one another!"

Finally the girls individuated enough to talk of the hardships in their lives and their fear of what would happen first to their mother, then to their parents' marriage if the family wasn't as it was. At this juncture, the youngest, Marita, said to me slyly, "Maybe Ms. F. isn't sick, like you keep saying. Maybe she's the only one of us who isn't crazy!"

This rather gave me pause. I wanted Marita's observation (sly as it was, not withstanding) to register. But I was equally aware that in all this time (we were by now in the sixth or seventh session — we were now meeting twice weekly because my vacation was coming up) Ms. F. hadn't really said anything. So I said: "Ask her!"

"Are you?" asked Marita.

"Honey!" said Mr. F.

"Let her answer," said Amanda, the 16-year-old.

"When, again, are you beginning your vacation?" asked Mrs. F.

"God, Mom!" said Beverly.

"Am I what? Normal? No. Crazy? I don't know. Out of control? Yes. Out of control so I'm not crazy? Maybe." To me: "What do you think?"

"I don't know — it's possible."

"Anyway, this is what I started doing when I was 14. . . . "

And so Ms. F. went public.[1]

---

[1]Unlike anorexia (see Boris 1984a,b), in which the public presentation of the thin body is of paramount importance, bulimia is a secret activity, amounting often to a vice. It is not uncommon for even close friends (certainly the family) of bulimics to be

## THE FAMILY DYNAMIC

When in meetings with a family like the F.'s, one is soon aware of the
vastness of their indifference to one another. They know little and care
less. They have settled one another some time ago. In the F.s' case,
though I did not get to know them well, certain lines appeared like
pentimenti beneath the regular American family they took themselves
to be. Mrs. F. plainly felt that Mr. F.'s penis was wasted on him.
Perhaps he thought so too, since it kept him from his lost but
unmourned father, whom he replaced as best he could with Mrs. F.
She, meanwhile, lived out her boyish ambitions for herself through her
daughters. Were they meant to be boys? Was she a man in respect to
them, too? Mr. F. was the foodgiver; that was important. "The girls"
identified with one another, and at this time in their lives consolidated
with one another's help a kind of identity that gave them a degree of
imperviousness to their parents — and, as the chat session suggested, to
other young people, competitors, and friends. But for all of this there
is something at once chimerical and banal. One is dealing with mirrors
and images, extensions and projections, falsities regarded as verities
and truths agreed to be counterfeit. The banality lies in the answer to
the question of where all the energy and intensity are. There were no
particular vibrations — those radiations in the field of forces that arise
when people are interested in each other. The F. family's relationship
was with their inner objects. They had escaped one another's realities
by an act of sheer sorcery. They had patiently reconstructed each other
within and then serenely acted as it these reproductions were as real or
realer than the real thing. Indeed, at those moments when my own
efforts threatened to flood the chimeras with the unsparing light of

---

unaware for years of the gorging and disgorging. This secretiveness follows the
bulimic into the therapeutic or more formal analytic situation and presents, therein,
some rather special requirements for the development of the work.

The first of these has to do with how the treatment is framed. Of course no
psychoanalytic treatment can be organized around symptomatic activity, since
symptoms represent a profound achievement in compromise formation, and are at
least ambivalently valued, often, indeed, valued deeply, if unconsciously. Bulimia is
no exception to this general rule; it represents an intricate compromise worthy of (in
geopolitical terms) a Metternich — interweaving strands of every sort and origin. Yet
the patient often presents the symptom as the problem, inviting the analyst to join the
ego in regarding the activity as alien. To accept this invitation, however, is as often as
not a mistake. Egos have a way of changing their minds!

reality, the family would together hastily assist in pulling the wool over one another's eyes.

## THE WORLD OF INNER OBJECTS

There is an urgent need in humankind for an alternative to reality. Reality is simply too real. Its very realness torments, quite apart from the qualities of pain or pleasure within the reality. People need to dream as badly as they need to awaken. Dreaming provides a certain immunity to reality, a degree of imperviousness, a spell of respite. Of course we are mainly mindful of dreams when the lights are out and we can see them better. Like the stars, they are hard to see in the full sun of consciousness. Yet like the stars, which are always "out," the world of dreams is ever on. Some among us have so managed to attune ourselves to our dreams, night and day, that reality is but a scrim requiring effort to penetrate, yet as permeable as gauze. Others of us have to be quick as a cat to catch a glimpse of our ongoing dream: continuous performance.

That ongoing quality, indeed, reveals a paradox. We are in the position of the Sorcerer's Apprentice, who, having set the objects in motion, had not the magic and skill to stop them. Having created an imaginative world to run sidereal to the actual and thereby to give us an alternative, we need the real world now to wake up into, for otherwise how to stop the world of figments and dreams? Each world can be "too much with us." Each persecutes by that, regardless of its contents. Yet the only antidote to one is the other. But what if, like the Sorcerer's Apprentice, we forget or fail to learn the spell? Never mind the treasure each domain contains, the real treasure (as John Barth had it) is the key to the treasure.

At some point a child will accept a teddy bear or a Linus blanket or a pacifier as an object with which to supplement what actuality has to offer. Busy, tired mother thinks it good for baby to have something with which to spell her; baby concurs. But as Freud (1925) discovered while patiently retrieving his grandchild's spool of thread, baby has a different sort of spell in mind. Freud, never one simply to retrieve the spool when he could also follow the thread, got from there to the repetition compulsion and the death instinct. That is, he saw or began to see (depending on how far we wish to take the thread) that the baby was magically controlling the stand-in for his mother, putting a spell on her. This was now no longer a supplement to an absent mother, a toy to while away the time. It was a ceremony, a ritual designed omnipotently to take control of the spool-mother.

The hyphen in "spool-mother" is meant to be at once innocuous of meaning and open to further meaning. It is one kind of link, of which others are Spoolmother, Spool/mother, Spool-mother, SPOOL mother, and spool. The last no longer links spool with mother; mother is now gone. Only spool survives. Spool saves baby from mother; who will then save baby from spool? Similarly, internally speaking, how will Spoolmother get on, or especially SPOOL mother or even Spool/mother. In Ms. F.'s case these distractions and signifiers had a life of their own.

## THREE MONTHS OF ANALYSIS

I was inclined to feel that only insofar as her family "came alive" for her would Ms. F. make use of analysis. Otherwise she would go on doing what I suspected she had been doing, which was to drain them of significance and replace their husks with cleverly crafted exact replicas — spools. Insofar as, in the transference, I, like my colleague, would be linked with the school authorities, the doctors, pharmacists, and so to the family, I would be drained not of food for thought, not of compassion or empathy, but of value, and thus denuded be left impotent and empty.

If I were to give the respectful consideration deserved by those who would prefer to make a case for tensions in Ms. F.'s relations with real objects, I would not get to writing my own adumbration of the matter. I do think Ms. F. had a difficult time of things in reality. I think the one-after-the-other of sisters deprived her of what little happy mothering Mrs. F. might have been able to offer; I think puberty undid some aspirations to be a boy (something that might have interested her mother and her father, if for different reasons). I think that as her sisters entered the competitive tennis arena, and her superior age could no longer award her an advantage, she was once again in danger of dispossession. And I think her separation from home at the advent of college came much too soon, given what good she could take with her (internally) and how much was left unhappy and unresolved. Given all of this, one would have expected to meet quite a sad, overwhelmed, young woman, uneasy about the Christmas box of help, but prepared to listen.

Rather one was to discover someone far more concerned about "being out of control." And that, it turned out, meant not of people, but of their effects on her. At her best, which was at her most symptomatic, she was able to achieve a total indifference to other people. There was a skin on her like a caul (some people get this from drugs like marijuana or drink) through which people were seen, felt, and experienced as through the proverbial glass darkly. Far more real, far more prepossessing, were matters of eating and weight, of emptiness and glut, of self-violation and rectification, of *imagining* what people thought or might say. No anorexic or bulimic patient I ever saw easily exchanged an existence in which they were at the mercy of the real world, in which people mattered; and there was so little, really, one could do for a world in which they *chose* what mattered and could, sometimes, do everything about. Ms. F. was no exception to this pattern.

The family sessions served to allow Ms. F. to allow her family and me to matter a little—partly because they gave her reason to feel she mattered; partly because the hardship we went through assuaged her envy; partly because she got interested, briefly, in all of us. On this not very substantial basis, individual work began.

At the end of her confession, I told Ms. F. that she had been using her illness to buy her freedom and independence from "these people here. But also to deprive the lot of any wish they might have to matter—a wish obviously they all have. But they have won! You have not succeeded in making nothing matter. It is possible to make some things matter less by allowing other things to matter more, but you have forgotten how."

"I can help with this or Dr. A. (her former therapist) can."

"You," she said.

To the family, I said, "We will need you again, but you will have to figure out how to share in the responsibility."

At this time we interrupted for a vacation, after which we met for three hour-and-a-half sessions per week. The idea was that she would return to school for the second semester, but as it was to turn out, she transferred to another school where she could live in another family and continue her analysis with a colleague in that other state.

For me there was a special problem in seeing Ms. F.: I knew too much about her and had continually to struggle to regain and preserve the sense of mystery necessary for encountering internal objects. For example, "knowing the family" I could get interested in "hearing the news" instead of wondering what telling me this or that was at one and the same time designed to do and offset.

Ms. F. began by remarking on how different it felt to "be here by myself." She then asked what she was to talk about. I said it would be helpful to find words in which to put what her experience of being in the room with me was like. For example, she had remarked on how different it felt.

In doing this I was putting myself forward as a force, a presence in her experience; I was suggesting she speak of that experience. I expected she would experience the conjunction of my presence and my absence as a torment. I thought she would feel that torment to be something I had a choice about — that I could make it otherwise and was deliberately setting out to impose torment upon her. In these respects she would not be unlike other patients I saw or was seeing. But I further felt that Ms. F. would not complain or get angry. Certainly she would not resign herself to the difficulties or limitations of my methods — or the lack of adroitness with which I attempted to put my methods to use on her behalf: I felt, rather that in no time at all Ms. F. would get busy with getting even.

I have since formulated the basis for these surmises in a formal communication (Boris 1986). At that time I was still feeling my way toward answering the question of why Ms. F. was psychologically unable to find an appetite for such food for thought as I imagined I might in time be able to provide her. I certainly was interested in the answer; why wasn't she?

*She* wasn't, I thought, because she felt there was something better (what I was to later term the "other" breast), which she might miss out on if she took the one I offered her. But all right, why not take that other, better something because after all, there are better and worse in the world? The answer seemed to be because it she chose the alternative, she would miss out on what it was alternative to; she wanted to eat her cake and have it too. If that was the case, how would she manage the loss of me if she replaced me with a rival source of satisfaction? I thought that she thought she could not manage such a loss, that it would expose her to unendurable suffering. Therefore, she would have to do several things all at once. She would have to "split" herself (I am not ready to take the quotation marks off "split"). Part of her (note how frequently we hear, even use, that turn of phrase!) would make use of me; part of her would not. The use could not be final; she could not use me up it she were to have me too. The third thing she would have to manage, therefore, would be a variety of relations with me, each of which would offset the other. Oh, what a tangled web!

Part of her would do one thing, another part another, and each of these would have to be reversible. Out of all that possibility, if only she could bear to simplify, to pare away, and, after weeping a little, make do. Perhaps she would be able to do so in time, or would there be time?

In saying what I did to her in the first minutes of the first session I was also saying something about this kind of simplification: she could simply continue to do what she started off doing and find words for what the experience of being in this time and this space with me was for her. It was this call to the fundamental rule that I anticipated would elicit a powerful impulse to get even.

There was a silence. After a bit Ms. F. repeated that she didn't know what to talk about. This can be said as a bit of information: it can be a shorthand way of saying, "My experience with you is such that I feel you want me to tell you more or other than what I am now saying, and I cannot think what it is you want." Which itself may be a shorthand for "You haven't told me enough, blast you, and the frustration of it is such that I can't stand it—and this then makes me seek relief from experiencing my wants by beginning instead to think about *yours*; and now I know only that you want, but I don't know yet *what*. Indeed, should I know, I'm not at all sure what, if anything, I'm going to do for your wants—let you suffer, or try to assuage them. Much will depend on what you tell me."

Or, it can be said not at all informationally, but accusingly, vindictively, plaintively, all sorts of ways that take the experience "you and I" and not only elaborate it but act upon the elaboration.

Now, I had thought I had said something fairly helpful and responsive, but evidently not. Ms. F.'s response was at once plaintive and accusatory. What I imagined I heard was, "Cut the crap, fella; you can do better and you know it. If you think I'm going to let you get away with this shit, you can forget it; you get nothing further from me."

Of course she may have intended nothing like this; of what the experience in the consulting room consists is ineffable. One can quote a patient, but are the patient's words the datum of psychoanalysis? On the other hand, if they are not, what is? If something else is the datum, are the words irrelevant?

Without attempting an answer to these questions (which would require an essay in itself), I can put forward only that where much is at stake, actions speak louder than words, and that insofar as words are used they are often used as actions; that is, for effect. As soon as I felt Ms. F.'s silence and words were not merely informational, I began to take note of the effect they had on me. Is the reception therefore definitive of the transmission? I hope so! It is all I had (and have) to go on. In Ms. F.'s case, I felt "split." Part of me (!) felt I had made an affable and helpful statement and part of me felt that I had, very wrongly, fed Ms. F. a very bad portion, and that I could (and should!) do better than that, if I had my hopes of something coming of all of this. Part of me felt persecuted, as if what I had offered had been spat back in my face. And part of me felt attacked with some sort of splitting implement which took (or threatened to take) a feeling of being "together," "centered," or at one with myself and splintered it into contesting, conflictful smithereens.

To describe all this does not, I trust, reveal me to be suffering from delusions of reference. Instead I hope it puts forward something that requires interpretation. I have described an attack: why therefore such an attack? The why of it may not be clear, but it's toward it that the work of the session must progress. (Here is where I wanted to know less about Ms. F. than I did.) In the event, I had the choice of awaiting more understanding or using what little I had. I chose the latter course and said: "Your feeling that you are 'here by myself' is an expression of a view that I have more to offer you than I have done and that this view stimulates in you a feeling of terrible unfairness: I can get away with being me, while you can't quite get away with being you."

Ms. F.'s response to this interpretation was made manifest in a look of calm on the otherwise visually tense lineaments of face, shoulders, and hands. I had the impression that a decision had been taken: I had the idea that after the session she was going to have a binge. The rest of the session resembled the chat sessions I had become familiar with in the family sessions.

The binge divested the session of any moment; accordingly, I paid only perfunctory attention to what she said, and began to drift into imagining what the session would be without everything going into the binge. As I did so, I became aware that this binge had nothing to do with feeling starved or deprived—at least not of food. Rather I felt that I had become linked up with Mrs. F., a linking that stimulated a massive wish in Ms. F. *to be known*. I fancied that there was the most urgent wish imaginable to press, force, power her way into me-mother—to force out held ideas and replace them with the absolute, unvarnished, unalloyed truth: "Know me! Let me come alive in your view of me—*as I am!*"

Then I imagined a response to this lasering, this worming, this water cannoning and steam cleaning and sandblasting and jackhammering. It would have something in it about not jumping down one's throat, about one not having to swallow that, about getting off one's back—that sort of thing.

The binge, I thought, would be effected by Ms. F. dividing herself into two—subject and object. She, Ms. F., would force herself (food) into me-mother. The food would stand for who she is, her identity. It would be an identity projected into myself and her mother, a projective identification, as the jargon has it. The contents would be good; they would be expected to convey pleasure and interest. But there would be a fury there, too. The contents were not, *not* to be refused. The pleasure would be *inflicted*. Imposed pleasure!

Then I imagined this all turning upside down and backside front. Now Ms. F. would switch her identification from the projector of food-cum-truth-pleasure into a fellow feeling with the recipient of this infliction. How awful to have to be force-fed—how helpless, how humiliating, like the victim of a rape. Where the precious identification was projective, how it was introjective: the plight of the victim would have entered Ms F.'s sympathetic imagination, causing her to recoil with guilt and horror. How revulsive the deed, how gross! She would want to cleanse herself, to evacuate and disgorge.

Not that the contents are so horrible: Laing recounts the following experience. You or I draw for ourselves a glass of water fresh and clear from the source. Meanwhile, equally congenial to us, indeed utterly a part of us, is the saliva in our mouths. Good water; good saliva. But then (his story goes) we spit a globule of that self-same saliva into that glass of water, whereupon we contemplate drinking the glass down. Now suddenly we feel squeamish; somehow in crossing the boundary of self into not-self, the saliva has become alien and repugnant. We don't quite relish drinking it down again. It is not me, now.

So, it is I think, with Ms. F.'s food. Suddenly it is no longer of her, but horribly in her, an alien contaminated and contaminating substance. Ping-pong, go the identifications, ping-pong. Where is Ms. F.? Where is Ms. F.? Here she is! Here she is! Nope. Wrong.

I now need to return to the session itself. The reader might feel that there was a lot of imagining going on; and so there was. Ms. F. had, so to speak, projected herself into my imagination, and I was identifying with her, as best I could. I don't think it matters so much whether I was accurate in what I imagined as that this was the action, ping-pong, of the session.

The "chat" was designed to be chaff rather than wheat. Ms. F. did not want to say, to tell. She wanted me-mother to *know*, to keep her from succumbing to the temptation of telling, which would have been degrading; she would have been found wanting. She took all the passion out of the session to (so I imagined) the binge to follow, leaving me a vacuum to fill with my imagination. Or leaving me with nothing at all. If I felt there was nothing at all, then I might have gone about wanting more from her, and I should have been the greedy pig.

Because I didn't feel that this entire maneuver was conscious, I could only think that she was as much at the mercy of her machinations as anyone. My job, accordingly, had to be to draw her attention to what was transpiring. Toward the end of the session, therefore, I said:

"I have been having quite a think about you, as I believe you needed me to do."

She said: "What did you think?"

I said: "It won't make very much sense. But I was thinking how badly you want to be known and how despairing you feel about it being possible."

She said: "Is that it?"

I said: "No, there's more but I can't find the words for it yet, not by myself, at least."

Ping-pong.

The next sessions brought a very anxious and tentative Ms. F. Every time I moved or went to say something, she would say, "What did you say?! I didn't hear you. What did you say?!" I felt she was now terribly afraid of having "returned" to her what she had "put" into me; as if it would be, like the saliva, alien and contaminating. But the anxiety and tension also seemed to mark a movement away from juggling the internal objects in the inner world, toward an occupation with what she and I were doing together.

## PROJECTIVE AND INTROJECTIVE IDENTIFICATION

At this juncture I wish to return to the conceptual issues that I thought to be implicit in Ms. F. and her encounter with me.

As I mentioned, I felt that I must *imagine* Ms. F. She was projecting aspects of herself into me, not so as to rid herself of them, as in the process of projection itself, but to have me make them concrete, sensible, coherent, and meaningful. This is projective identification, obviously a strong element in any psychoanalysis (indeed in any relationship), stronger still for bulimics, who force-feed one. So part of her was being forced into me.

This leaves a vacuum; and human nature, like nature itself, abhors a vacuum. So therefore part of me was then made part of her. This is introjective identification: the identity remains the same, the location is what changes. In this regard I was now imagined to be "part of her"; that is, an internal object. The her-space, more generally the self-space, consists of claimed and acknowledged characteristics, not-me or disclaimed and alien characteristics, and characteristics so valuable as to be too precious to be stored within the me, but rather put in the safety deposit box of the ego-ideal. (These can also be projected into an other in a projective identification that results in an idealized self-object.)

These claimed and disclaimed characters or characteristics move back and forth (without visa or passport formalities, like travelers, in the Common Market countries or in the United States.) Now something is self, now not-self. Dreams, of course, dramatize this state of affairs.

When we speak of bingeing in bulimia, we naively speak as if the self stuffs the self: As Ms. F.'s case illustrates, Ms. F. was stuffing the "mother-in-her" or the "analyst-in-her." She was "jumping" not down her own throat but mine-in-conjunction-with-Mrs. F.'s throat.

This is, of course, a kind of sorcery. And, as in the story of the Sorcerer's Apprentice, it is not a very good brand of sorcery. For no sooner is the internal object fed than it can dissolve its boundaries, like a pill capsule in the stomach, and become at one with (in the same identity as) the self. And, abruptly, the self is gorged, poisoned, ruined, and must be purged.

In Ms. F.'s case, the intent, the wish, was to make her way into her mother, Mrs. F., and there permeate Mrs. F.'s entire being. Ms. F.

did not want to be one of many (a single pill capsule), but rather, fifth-column-like, stealthily to infiltrate and gain control of her mother. Invasion of the Body Snatchers; Invasion of the Mind Snatchers.

This proving impossible, she tried sorcery. Now taking her mother to be within herself, Ms. F. forced herself into the mother within. The means of doing so involved food; it might have involved drink, drugs, cutting, or even suicide. (One could see something about food from the exchange between Mr. and Mrs. F. in the family sessions and the material Mrs. F. "fed" me from the cartons.)

When the "scene switched" — to use dream language — and Mrs. F. dissolved into Ms. F., something had to be put in to put matters right. There is a song:

> I know an old lady
> who swallowed a fly.
> I don't know why
> she swallowed a fly.
> Perhaps she'll die.
>
> I know an old lady
> who swallowed a spider
> that wiggled and jiggled
> and tickled inside her.
> She swallowed the spider
> to catch the fly.
> I don't know why
> she swallowed a fly.
> Perhaps she'll die.
>
> I know an old lady
> who swallowed a bird. . . .

The spider and bird in Ms. F.'s case were the diuretics and laxatives, but even more, the stolen prescriptions themselves — the daddy/doctor stuff, which would purge the decomposing, permeating mother and refill the vacuum with daddy/doctor things. The separation from her parents, exacerbating her helplessness by reason of distance, produced an efflorescence of her sorcery.

I am diagramming, then, a *reciprocal relationship* between projective and introjective identification, such that one "can't tell the players without a scorecard."

## THE ANALYSIS, CONTINUED

Whatever pain and helplessness Ms. F. experienced was not truly to be known by me. The analysis did not last long enough. When Ms. F. came to see that a surrogate mother in a substitute family might be more truly receptive, she (wisely, I think) went off to get herself a real-life corrective emotional experience, while continuing her treatment at the same time.

What I was able to learn with Ms. F. was that no frustration could be experienced by her as anything other than imposed, so that, reciprocally, no satisfaction could be experienced as anything other than inflicted. That is, there was no such thing as nothing; there was always something, good or bad, being done to her. So she had to do something back—helplessly, enviously, spitefully, repeatedly (see Boris 1986).

As people who project a lot do, she felt as if she had no "skin," no secure boundary, no enclosed sense of self, no clear sense of other. She allowed me to show her that this was partly her doing, a function of her own quite desperate wish to get at and into others; to destroy the boundaries that kept them separate from her; to get into and under their skin; to make herself felt and known as someone to be conjoined with—sorcerer her.

With these realizations we could part. We had done a piece of work. We could identify in our sessions "who was doing what and with which and to whom." She understood her own sorcery and felt less helpless, less furious, and less at the mercy of her own poor spell-making.

Still, as she left the final session, her eyes lingered on a pad she had once mistaken for a prescription pad.

## REFERENCES

Boris, H. N. (1984a). On the problem of anorexia nervosa. *International Journal of Psycho-Analysis* 65:315–322.

_____ (1984b). On the treatment of anorexia nervosa. *International Journal of Psycho-Analysis* 65:435–42.

_____ (1986). The "other" breast: greed, envy, spite and revenge. *Contemporary Psychoanalysis* 22(1):45–59.

Freud, S. (1925). Beyond the pleasure principle. *Standard Edition* 18:1–64.

Tausk, V. (1919). On the origin of the "Influencing Machine" in schizophrenia. In *The Psycho-Analytic Reader*, ed. R. Fleiss, pp. 31–64. New York: International Universities Press, 1948.

# 14

# In Quest of the Psychoanalytic Datum

Here, finally, I am ready to reach beyond the "attractively shaped object and the Weinerschnitzel dream," and even "the derisive mirages organized by [. . .] agents." and out to—well, out to inside. (Nabokov is in his usual Quilty pursuit of the "Viennese delegation.")

What marred my previous excursions was that they were more concept than intuition. Patients ordinarily come to the point at which one can neither find more out nor figure more out—the impasse at which only intuition will serve. They require that only by their fruits shall we know them. Some, indeed, first arrive at the door while at that point. They so detest their own productions that they cannot bear to overhear them. Or they are so frightened to breathe, let alone move, that just to get to the initial session is about all they can dare. An interest in why people cannot bear to be patients (how else can one learn from a set of teachers wider than the customary?) has disposed me to do what I could in respect to those who can only almost bear to "take" analysis. This paper is in a way the imposed product of such patients—and of all patients at those times when one can't find more out or "head" them off by figuring them out. If there is to be a datum, it is clear where it will have to be looked for.

Already after the first few minutes of the first session Mr. V. has lurched out of the consulting room knowing that he will never be able to be sober, knowing that analysis won't help if he comes to it drunk, as he is at present.

Ms. K. tells me that she is wall-to-wall drugs, mostly hallucino-
gens, and she gets herself picked up and beaten by men of color: now
she sadly adds, "This is ridiculous. How can I expect talking will
help?"

Ms. N. wanted therapy since she was 15. She is now 22, and only
now has her father consented to pay for a course of treatment. It is
plain that he is more than the seven years too late, and he will pay for
this for the rest of their lives together.

I take Mr. V. by the arm and haul him back, but I leave all the
doors behind him open. I tell him: "It is no trick to prove my
inadequacy; I cede it. It is no contest. But I do not see why I should
roll over and be dead." He stumbles to the chair, falling.

Ms. K. does not, despite her thought "this is ridiculous," leave.
She remains merely silent. When time is up I tell her when I next
have an appointment time. Ms. K. will visit me twice weekly for
almost four years. One day she will tell me that come June she is
leaving for France to attend the Sorbonne. She also tells me that she
has been off drugs now for over a year. I suspect I have a
transference cure on my hands. But she has given us lead time during
which to look into why she has told me of my "successes."

Ms. N. also returns. She tilts a jaw line that would stop an
Anschluss. I experience her in headlines of the sort that say, "Man
bites Dog. Today a resolute and spunky woman once again bested
her father in round twenty-two of their lifelong match." Or, "Asked
about his daughter, a Cleveland man replied, not without pride,
'Well, at least she takes after me.' Asked about this, Daughter replied,
'It's only round twenty-two.' Asked about that, Lexington shrink
averred, 'It's a dog-ma eat dog-ma world' " (It will take me a while to
see the significance of the "Ma-ma" in what I said.)

These of my patients, though they do not speak to me, seem to
take in what I say. Their silences seem to me generally full of
conveyance, even when I cannot attune myself. They do not
complain if sometimes weeks go by and I do not have anything to say
that I haven't already said. They do what they can, I what I can.

In time I will learn from Mr. V. that he had a sister who died
when she was 6 and he was 10 and in her grief his mother told him
that she wished it was he who died. I will understand that he told me
this because he thought I was ready to hear it—that I had put enough
together that this precious piece of his life's puzzle will be a capstone
and not a bit of history of the sort a patient is supposed to tell. But
this will be only after he sues his insurance company for paying me
for sessions I billed for when he was "too pissed to drive."

In time I will learn from Ms. K. that she had fought off a man in the Port Authority bus station with such fury that she broke his arm. I will understand from this that she has identified my own wishes to accost her and thought she might set me straight. When I say this, she will "reward me" by telling me about the problem there had been in taking baths at home. I will tell her that she is trying to mislead me. She will blink at this, but listen very closely. Presently it will be evident to her that she now gets sexually aroused during the sessions.

Ms. N. will drum up everything she can to force a situation in which I am in the wrong. I will find myself feeling enraged by this. And sure enough, one day I will keep her waiting—not twenty-two years, but all the same. I will wonder why I was so obliging. And then I will imagine a child calling, Mama, Mama! Please come, Mama, Mama; and I will remember calling this out myself in my life, and understand why I wanted instead to join her in keeping it among the fathers. So while she is raging at me one day I will tell her that something has almost made her miss her Mama, more than she thinks she will ever be able to stand again, and she will cry. In time I will be able to tell her that she is angry because she skunked her Mama for her father, who accordingly thought it was he she loved so, and she's being loyal to her mother in punishing him for his hubris. With this she will begin to free-associate in the sessions in the ordinary way, and we will be able to go over the same ground in the detail it requires.

Mr. V. will enter an inpatient alcoholism program. He is very pleased by this move, for he had been afraid he was much too much of a snob to mingle with others with whom (he hoped) he had nothing in common but the need to drink. The program however does not, as it turns out, permit its patients passes to see "outside" therapists. They reason that if someone is in treatment and is still drinking, the treatment can't be any good. They assign him another therapist. He calls me from his locked ward, but I am unable to call him back or visit him, it being that sort of program. His wife turns up to use his sessions—somehow she appears to be the only person to have known the policies of the program, having made the arrangements. As best as I can I suggest a return to her own therapist. She demurs, saying she is quite well now and that she has come to see me only that the sessions should not go to waste. I tell her I shall no longer be charging, and would she let her husband know I have been unable to reach him. But I don't hear from either of them again, until years later I learn secondhand that on the day of his discharge from the hospital he bought a gun and shot himself in front of her.

Such people require one to learn of them mostly from what they stimulate in one's self. The privation in their lives is such that they have nothing to say that they can bear knowing when in the presence of an Other. Being an Other, the analyst has to rescue the stillborn mental life from the ash heap by getting the idea first and making it viable for purposes of communication. Otherwise it's dead.

---

What do I want to say—and why do I want to say it? Patients far along in their psychoanalysis might well want to ask this question at each moment of an actual session and at those moments between sessions when a session is nevertheless taking place.

Sometimes the answer is simple: Patients need help interpreting an experience of a happening, a thought, a feeling, a fantasy, or a dream. They require the perspective that can come only from another, alternative point of view, just as each eye or ear, set slightly apart, is necessary for the other to have depth of field, optics or sound in stereo, and thus location in the extended cross-references of experience. Information is being asked for and given. The exchange is freely made.

At other times, the question reveals an action that the statement is intended to perform on its recipient; what is said is spoken not so much to exchange information as to bear an effect. The speaker wants to influence, even command, the way the listener is feeling or viewing matters. Speech is only nominally speech; it is more accurately viewed as constituting a form of action. As such it reveals to the initiate the state of the transference: who is this analyst to me that I wish to have this or that effect?

The analyst is also listening with this question: why is my patient telling me this? The analyst is listening not alone for the meaning of the words but for the use to which the communication is being put. Although patients have been asked simply to express in words what they experience, they are bound to use words as a form of action, much as they use "minus-words" or silences as forms of actions. Patients, after all, are in pain and want relief. They want their analyst and the therapy to change in ways that will afford them such relief. In short, they want less talk and more action.

Patients fairly far along in their analysis have joined up with the analyst in what is sometimes called the "therapeutic alliance." Patient and analyst have become allies—more or less—in the belief that the study of patients' experiences will prove rewarding, not only to the analyst. Whether this belief is so or not, the sense of being a pair and sharing a purpose often offers a good deal of composure — certainly to the analyst, sometimes even to the patient. The wrangling that couples do (all knees and elbows, as most couples are to begin with) gives over to the sharing of a common purpose outside of their immediate selves that distinguishes the pair from the couple.

The couple, beginning with what Winnicott (1952) aptly called the nursing couple, wants to couple. Coupling is the relief each seeks, from, with, or (ruthlessly) at the expense of the other.

Both members of the pair lay aside these urgent purposes and the fights they create, when not mutually reciprocal, and look not at their very interesting differences, but at what they have in common. The pair is the smallest unit of the group, and the so-called pairing group that Bion (1961) described operates the therapeutic alliance. This is to produce not a baby as such, but a new babe, born again, baptized at the font of analysis, circumcised with termination, sent out to become one of the initiated.

If the wish to couple drives what we call the transference, the wish to pair drives the wish to identify and ally. The former serves the pleasure principle, and the latter serves the selection principle. The pleasure principle is well known; the selection principle, less so. It is the counterfoil and moderator of the egoistic urges of the pleasure principle. It works on the Darwinian mandate that the job of the species, is, so to speak, to maintain itself in office, and the devil take the leastmost. Coupling for coupling's sake is to be put aside to a degree so that selectivity of partner can enter in. If the pleasure principle expresses itself in feelings of desire and frustration, the selection principle makes itself manifest in feelings of hope and despair.

Thus we regard with a certain well-bred horror the idea that "id-ish" pleasures should come from the analyst. If analysts hold the patient, they do so not in their arms but in the holding environment; if they talk, they do not murmur, soothe, or chat but interpret, confront, or clarify. Patients likewise are to speak their mind, but not so as to frighten, seduce, or otherwise manipulate the analyst. At least not knowingly.

But, of course, patients do, and, of course, analysts do.

In the beginning it was to be different. Freud did not yet altogether know about the transference, despite what Breuer told him when referring Annie O. (Freud 1895), who had rather unobligingly become "pregnant" from his hypnotic treatments. Freud, having discerned that the method he was discovering for the madness he was treating led backward in time to early events, felt that genetic constrictions of how and why the twig was bent were all that was necessary for the tree to right itself. The original data were the seemingly bizarre symptoms of Dora (1905) or Emmy Von N. (Freud 1895), or, for that matter, Freud himself, and the game could well have been called Clue. Like Hercule Poirot, Freud might murmur, "Never mind what you think is important; just tell me every little thing no matter how unimportant it seems to you." And so, in both senses of the phrase (contiguity and cause and effect), one thing led to another. The genre was a crime or a trauma that had to be solved by a most careful process of detecting the deceptions and arriving at the full reconstruction of what had happened—like the fact that Herr K. had had an erection in the story of Dora. At that period any clues were valuable, but particularly those clues that were not disguised by the cunning mind of the deceiving patient, but instead only clumsily hidden by the naive processes of the dream work—which thought, for example, a penis could be successfully hidden within a snake or a church tower. This was like flicking trichnopoly cigar ash outside 221b Baker Street.

The truth, then, was a historical truth involving experiences of things past. With Freud's increasing realizations concerning the transference, the clues became much more in the present. And high time too, considering that Dora had fled her analysis, never to return; perhaps Herr K.'s potency was not the only effort at penetration she found so disturbing.

If the experiential event, replete with self-deceptions and their motivations, was not in the past but in the here and now of the transference, why elucidate the past? Why not simply allow the experience to evolve, undo the self-deceptions that keep patients from knowing what they experience, investigate the motivations for these, and be done? Why venture onto the perilous reefs of historicity?

Indeed, with the advent of Little Hans (Freud 1909) there seemed less and less reason to venture backward in time. Hans's phobia was analyzed into its conflicting elements even as they were occurring. Moreover, Anna Freud (1954) was dubious about whether or not a child formed a transference; she felt children were too attached to their parents to allow an analyst to become a parental surrogate. Miss Freud's counterpart (and *bête noire*) Melanie Klein analyzed her own children. She came away from the experience absolutely convinced that children did make transference. (One can suspect that the belief in transference comes more easily to one when analyzing one's own children.) The badness of the breast, she saw vividly, was transferred to the mother via projections of the inherent death instinct (Klein 1952).

It appeared to be true: like pentimenti, behind and underneath the image children had of their parents were alter images of the sort the brothers Grimm caught in their stories. And these images came into the analysis, as when, sitting round the play table, the 4-year-old said to Susan Isaacs (1952) about Isaac's breasts, "So those are what bit me!"

If, then, there was a transference and that transference did come into the analysis, toward what genesis did analysis have to reach? What had archaeologically to be constructed?

One could say: "When you were a baby, you became afraid that Mommy would bite you like the wolf in Red Riding Hood or the witch in Hansel and Gretel. But that was because you were a very gobbly baby yourself and wanted to bite and chew on Mommy's lovely breasts. Only you loved Mommy too much to keep wanting to hurt her just for fun and chewiness. So you said, 'Not me; I don't want to do that to my mommy. It's her things that want to do that to me — naughty breasts.' "

Or one could say: "Big as you are, there is a you that wants to chew and suck at my breasts. Only you feel that you are too big for that now, and you feel that even to know you want to do that is naughty, so you put the biting wish into my breasts where I can be safe from it and it can be safe from being given up."

The latter, of course, does not interpret the transference, nor does it imply a past beyond the past just before the projection of the impulse.

The issue is not one of technique; I would suppose that either mouthful might be helpful. But the issue does speak to the question of whether there is a pair studying the couple. Or to put it another way, how and when can the pair emerge from the couple?

The interpretability of an experience is illustrated by a little story told by Joyce McDougall (1989) of one of her little patients, a 5-year-old boy who came racing into the playroom after a summer at camp and exclaimed that at his camp the boys and girls swam nude. "Ah, so you had a really good chance to see the differences," said McDougall. "Don't be foolish!" exclaimed the boy. "I just told you they didn't wear their clothes" (p. 205).

This child, quite probably like the little girl who was Isaacs's patient, was not able to see things as his analyst saw them, figuratively and literally. In both cases the patients appeared unconcerned with the idea of psychoanalysis as a vehicle for discovering their self-deceptions and the motivations for these self-deceptions — to paraphrase a definition of Hartmann's (1959). For the moment the analyst can only ask her patient to look at things a different way. She interprets the self-deception and its motivation, but in doing so she is asserting her aloofness from the couple. The children are not merely passing the time of day with these communications; they are trying to get something going or not going in the coupling. The analyst is acting as if she were a member of the pair, and the child is acting as if he or she were a member of a couple. A rather good interpretation, for example, that I gave on a Friday turned up in a dream told on Monday, which began, "I was at this lecture you were giving. . . ."

For the interpretation to take, the analyst must demonstrate that what seems to the patient to be absolutely true is true only for this time and this place and for reasons having to do with what this time and this place represent for the patient. Demonstration is hard work; it involves providing instances as data, again and again, and drawing attention alike to the minor differences that disqualify an instance and those that nevertheless qualify it for use toward an accretional "so-ness." Isaacs-Elmhirst (1952) speaks of having to give the same interpretation 999 times until suddenly it is not the same old interpretation, but the first. Or as I might put it, until oh-oh! becomes ah-ha!

The original concept that Freud called "construction" but that, for reasons I shall shortly come to, I prefer to call "reconstruction"[1] moves experiences decisively to where they were thought by Freud to have begun. This time and place are but that time and place, and I am but a surrogate for this person or that. These constructions are made up of shards from associations, recollections, dreams, and transference imagery. Their object is to produce memories — not of childhood, as Freud put it, but from childhood. With these memories at hand, a comparison and contrast could be made. Since no one knows what, if anything, is forgotten (as opposed to repressed), even the reconstruction about the gobbly baby might well have sparked a recollection that would enable the little girl to reclaim her teeth.

But what about when there are no recollections to construct?

---

[1] For welcome additional discussion on this and related issues, see also Greenacre (1980) and Schafer (1982).

In my own studies I have been following some lines of thought concerning the inability to bear the choice of any one experience for fear of losing the potential riches of other experiences. I (Boris 1976) have written on hope—a selection principle phenomenon—so great as to preclude the following of desire, for to use Bion's words (1961): "Only by remaining a hope can hope remain" (pp. 151–152). I have also written on greed (Boris 1986), fueled by hope, such that one wants everything and cannot endure the envy of allowing another to have, even to give, what one lacks and needs. One can imagine that McDougall's patient preferred not to know about gender differences because he was frightened over castration. But one can also think about the pain of being a young man and not a young woman or a young both as too much for greed and envy to bear. By thinking the two sexes to be the same, except for such easily remediable trivia as clothes, he spares himself the pain of choosing which he is or which parent he wants. Earlier, perhaps, such a youngster might have found it impossible to choose which breast he wanted, for taking the vanilla means leaving the chocolate. Later the horns of the dilemma may be between "Miss Right and Miss Right-away"[2] or "the little given and the great promised":

> I found [writes Vladimir Nabokov, in the voice of Humbert Humbert] there was in the fiery phantasm a perfection which made my wild delight also perfect, just because the vision was out of reach, with no possibility of attainment to spoil it by the awareness of an appended taboo; indeed, it may well be that the very attraction immaturity has for me lies not so much in the limpidity of pure young forbidden fairy child beauty as in the security of a situation where infinite perfections fill the gap between the little given and the great promised—the great rosegray never-to-be-had [Nabokov 1955, p. 266].

When the pain of choice is too great, it cannot be consoled by the satisfactions of appetite, for appetites emerge only after hope and greed give over to choice and the willingness to tolerate first envy and then gratitude and admiration. In my various studies of so-called eating-disordered patients—anorexics and bulimics, in particular (Boris 1984a,b; 1987)—I have found people caught in the forking of the roads and unable to take the pleasures of either route for fear of the

---

[2]This phrase was used by Robin Williams, the comedian, in his concert at the Met and elsewhere.

loss of the other. A youngster I know also came back from a camp that featured nude swimming and where on visitor's day he had the mixed pleasure of seeing his father's new companion in the buff. "One hundred sit-ups a day," he announced, throwing himself to the floor so as to put his words into deeds, "and in a year I will have a totally flat stomach." By not knowing about differences and hence about choices, he could deal in a realm in which everything is the same. Daddy's poor woman friend: accursed with bosom and belly that would take more sit-ups than one could imagine to become nice and flat like those of my young acquaintance. By knowing and then not knowing about envy, he could spare himself jealousy. Thus his greed evolved not into appetite but into acquisitiveness and, at times, dangerously, into a greed so vast that it included a gluttony even for punishment.

By thus sparing himself knowledge of differences, the boy knew only two dimensions: more and less. He had known only these two for so long that in many instances one could not reconstruct, for such a process would be like reconstructive surgery on a phantom limb. One had instead to construct. By this distinction I mean to intuit not what once was and was now gone, but what for all intents and purposes never happened or happened in fantasies that prevented realization. Freud's work was on the presences of the absent, on the sudden lurch where one expected an association or memory to be. It was like climbing stairs and expecting one more step to be there but wasn't. Now we are in a different realm; we are where the no-things live and the nonevents took place. The shards are marked by invisibility of the sort produced by black light.

In the instance of the youngster I have just mentioned, for example, many interpretations could have been made. One might have talked to him about his jealousy; about his erotic attachments to his father; about his wish to be attractive to his analyst; about his wish to compete with the analyst as father on grounds of slimness and physical condition; about penis size; about his castration anxieties and how these emerged from his wishes to be a woman and be rid of the penis that separated him from those he loved; or, indeed, about the very exhibitionism going on in the playroom and what it meant in respect to his fantasies about how and with whom his analyst spent the interval. But the key word in all of these possibilities is "about" — one could have talked to him about them. Yet analysis is not a tutorial; we do not, when we can help it, talk about patients; we ask them to talk of themselves, and we, in turn, talk of them too. What was there to say of this youngster about whom so much — too much — could be said?

To this point, another analyst tells a story regarding the same sort of question. Wilfred Bion (1976b) writes:

The following free association was made to me by a patient in analysis:

> "I remember my parents being at the top of a Y-shaped stair and I was there at the bottom . . . and. . . ."

That was all, no further associations; finish. I waited, and during this time I, as usual, had plenty of free associations of my own (which I keep to myself because I am supposed to be the analyst). It occurred to me that this was very like a verbal description of a visual image, simply a Y-shape. The thing that struck me straight away about a statement that was so brief, so succinct, and stopped short at that point, was that it must have a lot of meaning that was not visible to me. What did in fact become visible to me I could describe by writing "Y." Then it occurred to me that it would be more comprehensible if it was spelled, "why-shaped stare." The only trouble was that I could not see how I could say this to the patient in a way which would have any meaning, nor could I produce any evidence whatsoever for it — excepting that this was the kind of image that it called up in my mind. So I said nothing. After a while the patient went on, and I started producing what seemed to me to be fairly plausible psycho-analytic interpretations.

Thinking about this later, I imagined a Y-shape, which, when pushed in at the intersection of the three lines, would make a cone or a funnel. On the other hand, if it was pulled out at the intersection, then it would make a cone shape sticking out or, if you like, a breast shape. In fact it was an evocative free association on the part of the patient as far as I was concerned, but I was still lost because I had no idea of what I could say that would reveal an interpretation, and would also be comprehensible to the patient. In other words, could I possibly be perspicacious *and* perspicuous?

In the next session I seemed to be killing time with conventionally acceptable interpretations. Then I thought I would launch out on what I have been saying here. "I suggest that in addition to the ordinary meaning of what you have told me — and I am perfectly sure that what you said means exactly what it meant — it is also a kind of visual pun." And then I gave him the interpretation. He said, "Yes, that's right, but you have been a very long time about it." [pp. 239-240]

The point of the story for present purposes is not the acuity of the interpretation, but how it was arrived at. Bion has himself spoken of the poet Keats's writings concerning "negative capability," the condition in which "man is capable of being in uncertainties, mysteries, doubts, without an irritable reaching after fact and reason" (Keats 1958, p. 193).

I would add to this temporal dimension a spatial one: In the parlance sculptors use to describe the space their sculptures do not occupy but imply, this latter dimension is called negative space. It refers to the differences between the space that was there before the sculpture was grown or put there and what that space looks and feels like as a result of the sculpture's now being there. Some may know Richard Serra's work *Tilted Arc*. It is, roughly, an immense, slightly curving steel wall that occupied (some would say dominated) Federal Plaza, a space between government buildings in New York City. It was a rather disturbing work that was finally taken down. It may have inscribed the surrounding space only too well. That space created by the sculpture appeared to many to be harsh, stymieing, unyielding. It is by no means clear that this impression was not exactly the statement Serra wanted to make. He needed the space of the plaza to make the plaza visible vis-à-vis his sculpture. Many did not like to see how the plaza looked with *Tilted Arc* in it. (Susan Isaacs [1952] may not have liked how she looked with a mouthful of teeth protruding from her breasts.)

This idea of creating time and space is by no means new. Freud was reaching to it with the juxtaposition of free association with evenly hovering attention. And Bion furthered it with his counsel that the analyst should avoid both memory and anticipation. This counsel meant that the analyst might take notice of the drift of his own mind, backward into the consolations of memory, the beginning, the font, the breast and forward to the climax of desire—toward the fulfillment of the coupling and thence to satiety. Unevenly hovering attention is, of course, in psychoanalytic therapies, an indication of the witting or unwitting presence of countertransference; the therapist wants something from or, it may be, for the patient and is, accordingly, waiting instead of merely awaiting. Somehow it has become the analyst's therapy.

That analysts should need therapy is not, however, a derisive idea, for their creation of the negative capability of time and space does great harm to them, at least temporarily. They become host to what the patient could not experience and does not want to. These are times when one could scream; it is astonishing that most of us can, most of the time, confine our perturbations to a comment or two and that we do not start making ourselves feel better by making the patient feel better — or worse. In this connection Bion (1979) adds the following:

> I can recall an experience in which a patient was anxious that I should conform to his state of mind, a state of mind to which I did not wish to conform. He was anxious to arouse powerful emotions in me so that I would feel angry, frustrated, disappointed, so that I would not be able to think clearly. I therefore had to choose between "appearing" to be a benevolent person or appearing to remain calm and clear-thinking. But acting a part is incompatible with being sincere. In such a situation the analyst is attempting to bring to bear a state of mind and indeed an inspiration, of a kind that would in his opinion be beneficial and an improvement on the patient's existing state of mind. That interference can be represented by the patient, whose retort can be to arouse powerful feelings and make it difficult for the analyst to think clearly. [p. 247]

Jamming of the analyst's ability to function, of course, applies particularly when the analyst has something in mind for the patient. There is an enormous emotional storm. The patient is trying to issue forth an experience for the analyst to construct, but the analyst has something else in mind being "beneficial." The modeling clay has a mind of its own; something is already on the blank photographic plate; the womb is full; the analyst is incapable of pairing and wants to couple. But even as this process of issuing forth is occurring, there is emerging exactly what the pair needs. The patient may be disinterested in it, indeed may be trying precisely to forestall it. But the not yet experienced experience is alive, if nascent. It is, however, being violently projected. The analyst is the willing or unwilling host to it. The patient has staged a benign or hostile takeover. The experience is a parasite. The analyst will want very much to excrete it and will want to do something, if only by closing himself with memory or anticipation. The analyst will begin, often, to think it a very good idea at least to say something. To say something will seem to be very therapeutic.

We come full circle. The question now reappears: What do I want to say — and why do I want to say it? The answer to this question may, I suggest, turn out to be that elusive psychoanalytic datum of which we are in quest.

We are no longer dealing merely with transferences here, not in the ordinary sense. Transferences imply an appreciation and a toleration of differences between self and other. But now we are dealing with a vast hatred and intolerance of differences. The possible emergence of those differences between self and other engenders once again, as it had before, so much greed, and then envy and spite, that the patient has not allowed the possibility of that experience into his other experience. But if these incipient, embryonic experiences are not to take experiential form within the patient, where can the patient put them?

The question, of course, suggests the answer—an example of the very process I am describing. The patient projects these experiences just as they begin to dawn and transposes them to the only other space/time available—the analyst. The analyst, as a member of the pair, must perforce identify with them, for the pair, upon the selection principle, works by vicariousness: each must put himself or herself in the other's shoes. Yet the analyst's sudden, unasked-for pregnancy with God knows what sort of stuff and carryings-on will certainly, as Bion indicates, interfere with any inspiration or clarity of their own. They will be forgiven if for their own therapeutic well-being they undertake a convulsion of the sort that might immediately cleanse their system from these unasked-for growths. Yet if they can behave like a patient far along in analysis, so that, rather than aborting and disgorging what the patient has landed them with, they can pause, they will be able to identify what they are experiencing and what it has done to them.

Identification of what stake I had in the matter was precisely what I could not make when, on a Friday, I gave a lecture dressed up to look like an interpretation, which the patient then kindly returned on Monday—in exchange for an interpretation that really was an interpretation. And it is almost what the youngster back from camp managed to precipitate with his sit-ups: so many interpretations, so much to manage! (I wish I had told him, "Boo!" just to get a little conversation going.)

This question, What do I want to say—and why do I want to say it? reveals, as the antibody does with the infecting agent, its action from the nature of its retort.

Answered, the question tells what effect one is reaching for to ease one's plight. Answered, it yields information, the exchange of which, in the context of mourning, constitutes an analysis in which patients become not more like themselves, but more thoroughly themselves, and so provides an experience that can end and not merely stop.

# REFERENCES.

Bion, W. R. (1961). *Experiences in Groups*. New York: Basic Books.

———— (1976a). On a quotation from Freud. In *Clinical Seminars and Four Papers*, ed. F. Bion, pp. 234–238. Abingdon, England: Fleetwood, 1987.

———— (1976b), Evidence. In *Clinical Seminars and Four Papers*, ed. F. Bion, pp. 239–246. Abingdon, England: Fleetwood, 1987.

———— (1979). Making the best of a bad job. In *Clinical Seminars and Four Papers*, ed. F. Bion, pp. 247–257. England, Abingdon: Fleetwood, 1987.

Boris, H. N. (1976). On hope: its nature and psychotherapy. *International Review of Psycho-Analysis* 3:139–150.

———— (1984a). On the treatment of anorexia nervosa. *International Journal of Psycho-Analysis*. 65:435–442.

———— (1984b). The problem of anorexia nervosa. *International Journal of Psycho-Analysis* 65:315–322.

———— (1986). The 'other' breast: greed, envy, spite and revenge. *Contemporary Psychoanalysis* 22:45–59.

———— (1988). Torment of the object: a contribution to the study of bulimia. In *Bulimia: Psychoanalytic Treatment and Theory*, ed. H. Schwartz, pp. 89–110. New York: International Universities Press.

Freud, A. (1954). Problems of technique in adult analysis. *Bulletin of the Philadelphia Association of Psychoanalysis* 4:44–46.

Freud, S. (1985). Studies on hysteria. *Standard Edition* 2. London: Hogarth, 1955.

———— (1905). Fragment of an analysis of a case of hysteria. *Standard Edition*, 7:7–122.

———— (1909). Two case histories ("Little Hans" and the "Rat Man"). *Standard Edition* 10:5–149.

Greenacre, P. (1980). A historical sketch of the use and disuse of reconstruction. *Psychoanalytic Study of the Child* 35:35–40. New Haven, CT: Yale University Press.

Hartmann, H. (1959). Psychoanalysis as a scientific theory. In *Psychoanalysis, Scientific Method and Philosophy: A Symposium*, ed. S. Hook, pp. 3–27. New York: International Universities Press.

Isaacs, S. (1952). Some theoretical conclusions regarding the emotional life of the infant. In: *Developments in Psycho-Analysis*. London: Hogarth.

Isaacs-Elmhirst, S. (1980). Babies and Bion. In *Do I Dare Disturb the Universe?: A Memorial to Wilfred Bion*, ed. J. Grotstein, pp. 83–91. London: Karnac, 1981.

Keats, J. (1958). *The Letters of John Keats 1814–1821*. Vol. 1. Ed. H. E. Rollins. Cambridge, MA: Harvard University Press.

Klein, M. (1952). The origins of transference. *International Journal of Psycho-Analysis* 33:433–438.

McDougall, J. (1989). The dead father. *International Journal of Psycho-Analysis* 70:205–219.

Nabokov, V. (1955). *Lolita*. New York: Putnam.

Schafer, R. (1982). The relevance of the "here and now" transference interpretation to the reconstruction of early development. *International Journal of Psycho-Analysis* 63:77–82.

Winnicott, D. W. (1952). Anxiety associated with insecurity. In *Collected Papers*. New York: Basic Books, 1958.

# III

# Thoughts
# Speculative

# 15

# Bion Revisited

The Bion essay is a debt due a writer whose influence on me has been strong. I discovered Bion while I was working in Vermont.[1] I had become so much absorbed by the intricacies of enabling people to come into self-study groups that I hadn't given much thought to what we would do when they got there. I thought to do a variation on Bettelheim's work with parents. I wasn't prepared for what I encountered — the groups who talked only to one another; the groups who didn't show up; the groups that arrived for the first meeting, never to come back. One evening I was sitting in a schoolhouse; it was below zero outside and nearly below freezing in. It was the first meeting of this particular group. I told myself comfortingly that these people were communicating with me by not showing up. I sensed I must stay there the scheduled hour and a half, that someone would know — perhaps via a drive by or by seeing the lights on, or by asking me or having someone who was in speaking range of me ask me whether I had or not — and that by staying I would communicate something in return. All the same I was cold and lonely and my faith in this idea of "they" and "the group" was wearing thin. I had been by this time to have a consultation with Bettelheim, also with Roy Menninger, who had worked with groups made up of teachers, but they talked of individuals learning from one another in much the

---

[1]See Chapter 3, "The *Seelsorger* in Rural Vermont."

same way group psychotherapists feel the experience to be for the individuals in the group. I felt a bit paranoid — a man quite possibly suffering from delusions of reference (not to say grandeur) — when describing to them my experiences of the community or the group as if these were motivated entities that had designs on me.

When, shortly after that evening, I stopped into the Goddard College library, to thaw out as much emotionally as physically, and I leafed through the slim volume of *Experiences in Groups* that had shortly before arrived, I knew I had found a fellow sojourner. I could recognize in the communities and groups just the dynamic patterning Bion found and described in the British soldiers and airmen and the habitués of the Tavistock clinic he worked with. I would like to say the book was a revelation to me: the perceptions he made, as compared with the ones I was using, were as a telescope to the naked eye. But I must also say that his insights seemed commonplace. This, I was to discover, was a manifestation of Bion's genius for working closely to the data.

I read what he wrote as the books came out, and as my own experiences in conducting analyses permitted me increasing access to the material on which his own inferences were founded, I continued to feel that what he wrote was at once obvious and revelatory. More to the point, however, I found that a relative few in the United States (and I suspected also elsewhere, as well) found Bion comprehensible. The best way I could express my gratitude for his contributions to my own thought and work, was, I felt, to try to increase his accessibility. I was much gratified when some years later I was to meet some of Bion's analysands, supervisees, and colleagues to hear that they thought I had "caught" him for them as well.

Bion left the public and private person in ambiguous relation to one another. It would be a fair characterization of my work thus far to say it tries to fathom that relational matrix, though this has by no means been a conscious effort.

---

## PREFACE

Here is W. R. Bion writing:

In a sunny room I showed my father a vase of some yellow flowers for him to admire the skill with which I had arranged them.

'Yes', he said, 'very good.'

'But do look Daddy.'

'I am; it's lovely.'

Still I was not satisfied. 'It's very pretty, isn't it?'

'Yes,' he said, 'it is.'

'I'm not lying Daddy. I did it all myself.'

That stopped him in his tracks. He was upset.

'Why did you say that?'

'What Daddy?'

'I never expected you to be lying.'

'Well I wasn't', I replied becoming afraid that Arf Arfer would appear.
Arf Arfer was very frightening. Sometimes when I heard grown-ups
talking they would indulge in bursts of meaningless laughter. 'Arf! Arf!
Arf!' they would go. This would happen especially when my sister or I
spoke. We would watch them seriously, wide-eyed. Then we would go
into another room and practice. Arf, arf, arf. . . . [But] Arf arf [who
art in Heb'n] was related though distantly to Jesus . . . Geesus loves me
this I know, for the Bible tells me so. I felt Geesus had the right idea,
but I had no faith in his power to deal with Arf Arfer. Nor did I feel sure
of God whose attribute seemed to be that he gave his only 'only
forgotten' son to redeem our sins. [1982, pp. 12–13]

The child becomes the man and yet the same muddle somehow
persists. Recommended for the V.C., "I might with equal relevance
have been recommended for a court martial. It depended on the
direction one took when one ran away." And this is Bion:

I went into this question thoroughly — and others like 'Is golden syrup
really gold?' — with my mother and later with my father, but without
being really satisfied by either. I concluded that my mother didn't really
know; though she tried very hard, she seemed as puzzled as I was. It was
more complicated with my father; he would start but seemed to tire
when I did not understand the explanation. The climax came when I
asked my question about golden syrup for the 'hundredth time'. He was
very angry. 'Wow!' said my sister appreciatively. [1982, pp. 9–10]

My mother's attitude was certainly more loving — genuinely loving —
than my father's; hers was not an attitude at all; his was. She loved us;
he loved his image of us. She knew she had two nasty brats and could
tolerate that fact; my father bitterly resented the menace of any reality
which imperilled his fiction. [1982, p. 28]

And this:

Freud talks about a 'paramnesia' as being an invention which is intended
to fill the space where a fact ought to be. But is one right to assume that
a paramnesia is an activity which is peculiar only to patients and to
pathological existence? I think psychoanalysis could be a way of
blocking the gap of our ignorance about ourselves, although my
impression is that it is more. We can produce a fine structure of theory
in the hope that it will block up the hole forever so that we shall never
need to learn anything more about ourselves either as people or
organizations . . . I suggest somebody . . . should, instead of writing a
book called 'The Interpretation of Dreams', write a book called 'The
Interpretation of Facts', translating them into dream language — not just
as a perverse exercise, but in order to get a two-way traffic.[1980, pp.
30–31]

And this:

In this book my intention has been to be truthful. It is an exalted
ambition; after many years of experience I know the most I can claim
is to be 'relatively' truthful. Without attempting any definition of terms,
I leave it to be understood that by truth I mean 'aesthetic' truth and
'psychoanalytic' truth. This last I consider to be a 'grade' of scientific
truth. In other terms, I hope to achieve, in part and as a whole, the
formulation of phenomena as close as possible to noumena.[1982, p. 8]

But — (quoting Dr. Johnson) and yet:

Whether to see life as it is will give us much consolation, know not; but
the consolation which is drawn from truth, if any there be, is solid and
durable; that which is derived from or must be, like its original,
fallacious and fugitive. [1970, p. 7]

Vladimir Nabokov (1983) takes up this point in respect to that grandest
of illusionists, Don Quixote:

Don Quixote . . . is the maker of his own glory, the only begetter of
these marvels; and within his soul he carries the most dread enemy of
the visionary; the snake of doubt, the coiled consciousness that his quest
is an illusionism.

Quixote hears a servant girl sing:

The inward hint, the veiled suspicion that Dulcinea may not exist at all
is now brought to light by contrast with a real melody . . . and after
listening to the song in the garden, he bangs the window shut and now
even more gloomy than before, "as if," says Cervantes, "some dire
misfortune had befallen him," he goes back to bed. [Nabokov 1983].

# INTRODUCTION

Through the good offices of his widow, Francesca, the last but two of Bion's sixteen books has reached the public domain in 1985. The occasion seems one to mark, in Bion's own tradition, with a "re-visit." It was a tradition he began with his first (and still perhaps most widely known) book, *Experiences in Groups*, to which he contributed a "re-view," and resumed with his collection of papers on thought and thinking with his "second thoughts" — in which, true to form, not only does he revise his previous meditations, but he also presents his thoughts on the experience and process of one rereading his own writing.

Bion was a gnarled and quirky writer, not, as the passages I have quoted indicate, because he could not help but be, but because, as I hope they also indicate, he was obsessed with truth. If we allow that by art, Donald Barthelme means what Bion means by "aesthetic truth," the following might describe Bion's quandary and quest:

> Art is not difficult because it wishes to be difficult, rather because it wishes to be art. However much the writer might long to be, in his work, simple, honest, straightforward, these virtues are no longer available to him. He discovers that in being simple, honest, straightforward, nothing much happens: he speaks the unspeakable, whereas we are looking for the as-yet-unspeakable, the as-yet-unspoken . . . the not knowing is not simple, because it is hedged about with prohibitions, roads that may not be taken. The more serious the artist, the more problems he takes into account, the more considerations limit his possible initiatives. [*N.Y. Times*, Feb. 18, 1982]

Bion's work will stand or fall on its own. It has been summarized, given in précis form, and made more accessible by among others Grinberg and associates (1975), Meltzer (1978a,b), and the various contributers to Grotstein's *Memorial* (1983). My purpose here is neither to add to these works nor take away from them. Rather I wish, by seizing the strand I have already put forth, to track through the labyrinth and try to show the thrust and moment of Bion's work as a whole. In particular I shall make the point that as one so concerned with the truth, Bion needed to refine and re-refine psychoanalysis as both theory and method, as one might grind and polish a lens or tune and retune a receiving device to see and hear the mysteries: "I went into this question thoroughly" — and others like, "Is golden syrup really gold? . . ." (Later he was to ask Melanie Klein how the infant knows the "Good Breast" *is* good.) Of his own writing, Bion says:

> . . . the reader must disregard what I say until the O [read, truth or falsity] of the experience of reading has evolved to a point where the actual events of reading issue in *his* interpretation of the experiences. Too great a regard for what I have written obstructs [this] process [italics mine]. [1970, p. 28]

Accordingly, I am less concerned here to try to present what Bion said than what, overall, he meant and even more than meant, tried to do.


## THE MAN


Bion was born in India in 1897. At eight he went to school in England, as was customary for the children of civil servants under the Raj. At school he enjoyed "wriggling" (his form of masturbation—of pelvis against the floor), being a steam engine of a railroad train, and hymns. Later he liked hymns and poetry, rugby, and swimming. At 18 he completed Public School and went into the tank corps in time to fight a series of desperately losing and perilous battles against the Germans in France. He was recommended for the Victoria Cross and was awarded the DSO. After the war he read history at Oxford and then studied medicine at University College in London. There he won the Gold Medal in Surgery, assisting Wilfred Trotter, whose book *Instincts of the Herd in Peace and War* was to set Bion to thinking.

He became a psychiatrist, married, fathered a child, but lost his wife to complications arising from the birth of that daughter. He was analyzed first by John Rickman (with whom he was later to work while both were at the Northfield Hospital, the site of the first of the group papers) and then at war's end by Melanie Klein (1948–1953).

> My analysis pursued what I am inclined to think was a normal course; I retailed a variety of preoccupations; worries about the child, the household, financial anxieties—particularly how I was to find money for such psycho-analytic fees *and* provide a home and care for the baby. Mrs. Klein remained unmoved and unmoving . . . I was assiduous in

my psycho-analytic sessions. When I was given an interpretation I used very occasionally to feel it was correct; more usually I thought it was nonsense but hardly worth arguing about since I did not regard the interpretation as much more than an expression of Mrs. Klein's opinion that was unsupported by evidence. The interpretation that I ignored or did not understand or made no response to, later seemed to have been correct. But I did not see why I regarded them as any more correct then than I had thought they were when I refuted or ignored them. . . . As time passed I became more reconciled to the fact that not even she could be a substitute for my own senses, interpretations of what my senses told me, choices between contradictories. [1985a, pp. 67–68]

He qualified as a psychoanalyst, ultimately becoming (during 1962–65) president of the British Psychoanalytical Society. In 1968, by now remarried (to Francesca) and the father of two more children, he moved to Los Angeles where he became a training analyst and teacher. He returned to England in 1979, dying in Oxford and leaving behind him . . . well, that is what we shall attempt now to see.

I am: Therefore I question. It is the answer—the 'yes, I know'—that is the disease which kills. It is the Tree of Knowledge which kills. Conversely, it is not the successful building of the Tower of Babel, but the failure that gives life, initiates and nourishes the energy to live, to grow, to flourish. The songs the Sirens sing and have always sung is that the arrival at the inn—not the journey—is the reward, the prize, the cure. [1985a, p. 52].

So he had, really, to start all over again and learn psychoanalysis from scratch.[2]

## CONCEPTS

As an article of faith—later termed "O"—he took it that there was an experience and an experiencer. This was akin to the Kantian noumenon, and the question of its evolution into a phenomenon. The

---

[2]At a guess, he terminated his analysis with Mrs. Klein also to preserve his self-analysis.

experience, given the limits of human evolution, can never quite be apprehended: It can, however, be approximated. Every approximation, though, is partial, depending on the eye and intent of the beholder. The phenomenon is " 'Won from the void and formless infinite' " (Bion quoting Milton) differently by the poet, the mystic, the scientist or the psychoanalyst. A single event in a psychoanalytic session is a phenomenon which is different for a psychoanalyst bent on cure, from that of an analyst needing fees, from that of an analyst needing to learn something. Other fields of investigation have benefitted mightily from developments in instrumentation and technology. What is the psychoanalytic instrument? In a letter to Lou Andreas-Salomé Freud writes of a need "artificially to blind oneself," the better to see. Bion, of course, quotes this approvingly, though he will also demur at "seeing" as too sensuous a metaphor for psychoanalytic activity. He throws out all of the elements of psychoanalysis and starts all over with L, H, and K: Love, Hate, and Knowledge. These are the building blocks for his Tower of Babel. Indeed, as will soon emerge, he is really rather more interested in K than in the other two (L and H), because though he will assign the emotions or passions full weight in influencing what one can know — bear, suffer to know — it is ultimately one's relationship to one's own knowing that will occupy him increasingly.

This matter of knowing begins with his first published paper on the Northfield experiment. He is the psychiatrist in charge of a flight wing in a hospital to which men who broke down in service are sent. They have reason not to want to recover, for recovery means a return to active duty; but many feel that their failure to recover lies in the uselessness of their treatment. Of course, the men support each other in this view: It is a group position. Bion, however, is used to command; in his tank corps, he learned that only men convinced will act with conviction. He needs to convince these men that the fault lies not in the stars but in them. He knows he cannot argue this, for that merely pits omnipotence of thought against omnipotence of thought. He must *display* this. Accordingly he makes his rounds taking several men with him and at each stop asks what is at fault and what needs to be remedied. And then, one by one, he organizes the men to provide the remedies — until at one and the same time all that is needed (including dancing partners) is in place and all the rationalizations exposed as such. The only remaining impediment is the twenty percent of the men who still lounge about, serving the eighty percent as —

precisely—the remaining impediment. But this Bion interprets: There is always twenty percent, everywhere; the eighty percent are (secretly, unconsciously) using them as leaders of the resistance. (Later Bion will show to his small groups how absentees or late-comers are encouraged and rewarded—for example by being waited for or filled in on what they "missed"—as instruments in his so-called pairing and fight–flight groups.)

Now the men are persuaded to look at their own functioning as a group and investigate the tensions within, a task with which Rickman and Bion assist in the more familiar psychiatric role. On his return to civilian life, Bion will "take" groups at the Tavistock, further to study the way others condition what any one person knows. K in a group is a public phenomenon and different from K alone or K when one is part of a couple.

With this realization there is nothing for it but for Bion to move from a study of groups to a study of individuals, keeping his epistemologic questions intact. His basic elements were: the formation of knowledge (of an experience), the destruction of knowledge—leaving an amnesia—the creation of false knowledge—the paramnesia—and the reconstruction of knowledge from the paramnesia back to what was so.

The kinds of explanatory systems Bion gravitated to emphasized "nature" at some expense to "nurture." That is, the lights that compose themselves on the retina already are interpreted by the brain as something more than light beams of different frequencies. We see a cat, not lights. We will need someone to tell us that the cat we see is a cat, but even when they tell us, we will organize that and other percept-words into concepts and sentences. Indeed, as Bion was soon to propose, the very clutter of these percepts, this furniture of thoughts, requires one to start thinking. Thinking comes about because unthought thoughts are too much for one to endure. Thinking links thoughts, and the linking (however, in fact, it is done) is thought by the thinker to be done in elementary ways, which is to say, to the imaginative child, alimentary ways, or organ language, as Freud called it.

So here is a something—what it is you and I may call a breast, but the infant knows only as a something. It exists because it has shape, smell, warmth, taste—substance: The senses working in common (Bion's definition of common sense) tell the infant so. But it also stimulates pain (let us say) where the infant expects pleasure. For critics of this line of thought the key word is "expects"—*expects*?! Well, in the same way the baby distinguishes sights, smells, directions (as in the rooting reflex), the baby distinguishes pleasure from pain, good from bad, present from absent. In Kantian terms there are anticipatory categories to which experience approximates (or does not) and, as surely as light particles on the retina are construed as images, so is raw experience more generally construed into categoric experiences. Indeed, from this point of view, the problem is not the slowness of learning, but what to do about the surplus of experience.

Bion was rather impressed with this realization. His view of man is of a creature struggling to defend against the *anschluss* of experience. Many of the examples he uses to meditate on in his writing deal with this theme: The man who cannot abide the Philharmonic because the clarinetist is sharp; the man whose pallor remains unchanged but complains of blushing; the patient who cannot attend a violin recital because of a distaste for watching a person on stage masturbating in public. Perhaps the main wish-fulfilling thing about dreams, he was to write, is being able to wake up from them

Consciousness, then, is an achieved state based on thought which is itself developed to free one from domination by the demand quality of sense impressions. Thinking, in its essence, involves verbs that organize and arrange the Augean litter of dream furniture, or beta-elements, which are experienced as things-in-themselves and cannot be thought with or about, or even dreamed.

These beta-elements can, therefore, only be acted upon as things are: They are to be broken up and thrown out; or, with some luck, sent out for detoxicating and refining. Or, if the urgency and frustration is not too great, they can be experienced long enough to evolve from raw sense data and emotion into alpha-elements capable of being thought with and about — or of being repressed.

The first fate involves evacuation. The beta-elements are projected into whatever container is available, there to haunt or counterattack or to be transformed by someone else's alpha functioning — or "reverie," as Bion calls it. That capacity for reverie is the mother's psychic nourishing of the baby's mind, and plays as important a function in Bion's psychoanalytic world as physical nurturance. The capacity of another to intuit and imagine one's state of mind gives life to the mind and restores life to minds gone dead.

In any case, what is urgent is that the mind can get free of the things-in-themselves one way or the other — to be able to fall asleep, if awake too long, or to awaken, if asleep too long: To find consciousness or unconsciousness. These are, in effect, all one for Bion: The main thing is surcease. One has to know that the violinst is not merely masturbating *and* one has to know that *he* isn't up there simply playing the violin. The analogics have to coexist. And they have to be separate.

There is no game of tennis without a net. The net divides the court into containers and makes possible the nature of the interchange. But the "holes" in the net are as much part of it as the cords. And that there is no net is as important as that there is a net. One is dealing both with a barrier to and an opportunity for contact: Two way traffic. In the presence of the barrier, beta-elements can become alpha and dreamt or thought, but should the concept become divorced from the sense impressions, then there is only knowledge without substance and experience without thought. Sophisticated thought, such as the scientific method, is too sophisticated to encompass the human experience. On the other hand there is a sense in which human beings can, by virtue of a vast denial of their differences, be compared with rats and pigeons and a scientific psychology be set out for us based on the analogy. But the analogy is a primitive one, and the resulting science can be as suspect as any other delusion.

In this regard, it is useful to recall Freud's remark at the end of his discussion of the Schreber case concerning how closely his own theoretical constructions could be said to resemble Schreber's (Freud 1911, p. 79). Concerning causality, for example: "The theory of causality is only valid in the domain of morality and only morality can *cause* anything. Meaning has no influence outside the psyche and causes nothing." The emphasis on developmental hierarchies in so much of psychoanalytic writing may be an example of this: a theory devised to measure goodness and badness and to prescribe punishment.

Bion was also mindful of this in a way that led from what I have been describing to his famous and infamous grid.[3] In it, on two axes, he attempted to formulate thought in terms both of its genesis and the uses to which it was being put. This latter axis reflected his view that projective identification — the way we have of putting ourselves in the other person's shoes — was not just one of those omnipotent phantasies

---

[3]I am inclined to regard the grid as a system for notation that, like an armature, enabled Bion further to construct his formulations. As with his taxonomy of groups into dependent, fight–flight and pairing, the grid categories are more useful for what they call attention to than in what they contain. Bion, himself, remarked, "As soon I had gotten the grid out of my system I realized how inadequate it is."

of Mrs. Klein's. Rather he felt it (quite literally felt it) to be an activity of one person upon the other. Mental activity was not merely mentation (ideation, phantasy, thinking, etc.) but activity designed to affect whoever and whatever was on the other side of the contact barrier. From this perspective it was inevitable that Bion would feel the influence of projective identification to operate as strongly as the transference as a factor in the psychoanalytic situation.

From the start, as I have tried to show, Bion felt there was no such thing as nothing. Kantian as he was, he was prepared to learn from his patients that where there was nothing there was actually a no-thing, the presence of an absence, an empty category, the outline in two dimensions of where the three-dimensional breast was supposed to be, but dreadfully was not — or was, dreadfully, not. Indeed, so horrible is this presence that it can only be removed by minus-K, by not knowing. Projection or repression, one would think. But these leave spaces:

> If it is true that the human being, like nature, abhors a a vacuum, cannot tolerate empty space, then he will try to fill it by finding something that will go into that space presented by his ignorance. The intolerance of frustration, the dislike of being ignorant, the dislike of having a space which is not filled can stimulate a precocious and premature desire to fill the space. One should therefore always consider that our theories, including the whole of psychoanalysis, psychiatry and medicine, are a kind of space-filling elaboration . . . indistinguishable from a paramnesia. [1978, p. 3]

Now not anything can fill the space an amnesia represents. The paramnesia (or delusion) must be tailored to fit; seemingly seamlessly, the fiction must seem real.

This is the basic position of Bionian man: When an unendurable frustration occurs and one can change neither one's nature nor that of those about one, one can only change what one experiences of one's experience by obliterating the knowledge of the experience, and the knowledge that one obliterated it, by substituting false knowledge in its place. Thus transformed and transfigured, fictive experience makes one oblivious that truth once lived where falseness reigns.

In Bion's own words, the patient:

> [E]xperiences pain but not suffering. They may be suffering in the eyes of the analyst because the analyst can and indeed must suffer. The patient may say he suffers but this is only because he does not know

what suffering is and mistakes feeling pain for suffering it . . . The intensity of the patient's pain contributes to his fear of suffering pain.

Suffering pain involves respect for the fact of pain, his own or another's. This respect he does not have and therefore he has no respect for any procedure, such as psychoanalysis, which is concerned with the existence of pain.

Frustration and intense pain are equated.

Pain is sexualized: it is therefore inflicted or accepted but is not suffered — except in the view of the analyst or other observer. . . .

. . . The patient feels the pain of an absence of fulfilment of his desires. The absent fulfilment is experienced as a 'no-thing'. The emotion aroused by the 'no-thing' is felt as indistinguishable from the 'no thing'. The emotion is replaced by a 'no-emotion'. In practice this can mean no feeling at all, [amnesia] or an emotion such as rage . . . that is, an emotion of which the fundamental function is denial of another emotion. [paramnesia] . . . [Such emotion is essentially] 'no-emotion' [and] is "analogous to 'past' or 'future' or representing the 'place where the present used to be' before all time was annihilated.

The 'place' where time was (or a feeling was or a 'no-thing' of any kind was) is then similarly annihilated. There is thus created a domain of the non-existent . . . 'Non- existence' immediately becomes an object that is immensely hostile and filled with murderous envy toward the quality or function of existence where it is to be found . . . 'space' becomes terrifying or terror itself. [1970, pp. 19–20]

Of course the cornerstone to this portrayal is the concept of suffering:

There are patients whose contact with reality presents the most difficulty when the reality is their own mental state. For example a baby discovers his hand; it might as well have discovered its stomach-ache, or its feeling of dread or anxiety, or mental pain. In most ordinary personalities this is true but people exist who are so intolerant of pain (or in whom pain or frustration is so intolerable) that they feel the pain but will not suffer which is to say, endure and sustain it and so cannot be said to discover it. . . . The patient who will not suffer pain fails to 'suffer' pleasure and this denies the patient the encouragement he might otherwise receive from accidental or intrinsic relief. [1970, p. 9]

The "no-thing" and their derivatives are beta-elements and so remain because the intolerance the individual has for them is such as to keep them apart from conjoining with realizations that permit the patient to symbolize (remember, name, think) the experience "even if the name is no more than a grunt or a yell."

Freud saw most of this, of course, as have others. But Freud's interests were divided.[4] He was as, if not more, interested in the transformations done historically — and so in reconstruction — as in those, as it were, done within the ontologic moment. He had a developmental theory concerning infantile sexuality to demonstrate: Herr K.'s erection was (unhappily) more prepossessing than Dora's relation to her probing analyst (Freud 1905). Bion's view is different:

> To the analytic observer, the material must appear as a number of discrete particles, unrelated and incoherent. The coherence that these facts have in the patient's mind is not relevant to the analyst's problem. His problem — I describe it in stages — is to ignore that coherence so that he is confronted by the incoherence and experiences incomprehension of what is presented to him. . . . This state must endure until a new comprehension emerges. [1980, p. 12]

The alpha-function — roughly, thinking — perceives relationships, not simply objects. Relationships are in their own way as painful as the presence or absence of objects or events and the fidelity with which these correspond with the various "pre-s" that Bion takes these to be: pre-conception, pre-monition and the like, those anticipations (or hopes)[5] concerning how reality should be. Relations are the verbs that link objects and inspire such feelings as envy and jealousy. Attacks on these links re-produce elements (nouns) no longer in relation to one another: this re-production, hewn and split out from a relationship, is preferred to the other, non-hyphenated, reproduction, which is the fruit of a relationship. Thus the transformations intended to achieve the relief first from frustration (the presence of the absence), then from envy (what is absent is otherwise possessed) and finally from jealousy (it is possessed by another in a relationship) produces two possible catastrophes. The first is familiar to us from Freud. It is the reexcitation of longings under the sway of the transference. The second is the catastrophe of one man's fiction encountering another

---

[4]Freud's metapsychologic discussion of the "Wolfman" is probably his most searching discussion of this point of view (Freud 1918).

[5]For an elaboration of this conjunction between anticipation and hope, see Boris 1976.

man's truth—particularly of omnipotent phantasy meeting an open mind.

I remember a patient who was so boring that I became fascinated with how he did it. How could this man converse with me in a way that was nearer to what I would call 'pure boredom' than anything I had ever experienced?

The patient keeps on talking about something which one could describe as a transference relationship, but the two things that might anchor it are missing; there is only the bit in between. It becomes a sort of 'pure' psychoanalysis; it is nothing but transference with nobody else in the room — and that is extraordinarily boring to hear. You recognize after a time that you are being told something by the patient, but never a fact within sight or hearing. You know nothing about the patient; you know nothing about the patient's private life. What interpretation are you to give? In a sense you could say it is an analogy, but a pure analogy; not the two things on either side, only the link in between. Translated into biological terms: What is this? A breast? A penis? No baby? No mother? Only the thing in between? Is this 'pure' psychoanalysis; all sex, but not a relationship between people. This peculiar situation is not merely a question of semantics . . . this is an actual event which is taking place in front of you, a demonstration of what joins two people but with neither person present — they are both missing. What then is the link? If we don't bother about the people what is this thing in between? If it is neither a breast nor a penis, could it possibly be a vagina? Could it be a non-object? Is it possible for what we biologically call a woman to have a sexual relationship with another person. [1980, pp. 19-20]

That last question is, I suppose, the interpretation. Bion quotes Kant: "Intuition without concept is blind; concept without intuition is empty." The patient intuits that what he biologically calls a woman cannot have a sexual relationship but he cannot say it because he has no longer a conception that he feels that way; he knows what it feels like to him, but of what it is that feels like what it does, he has no idea. Even were he to talk of what he thinks women experience, the intuition would be missing; there would only be the concept. "You have to notice," Bion says, "that it is an empty phrase, it is a concept; it is only verbal . . . by the time people learn the concepts for what they intuit, they have forgotten what they wanted to say. If we can draw attention to this fact, then possibly the concept and the intuition could be married."

It is not with this patient, but with another that Bion felt the need of moving his own chair (he used a reclining rocking chair, I seem to recall) in order to get the view from a different angle (1980, p. 82).

Welcome the introduction into training of Baby Observation. I think it would be all the better for an injection of the good humor of the "Holmesian" technique. The baby [read, patient] should be observed with all the enthusiasm of Holmes on the track of a desperate criminal. [1966, p. 576]

We need to be wide open to what is going on in the session (this is what I think Freud means by 'free-floating attention'). The unobserved, incomprehensible, inaudible, ineffable part of the session is the material from which will come the future interpretation that you give in so many weeks or months or years time. The immediate interpretation was settled some time ago—one does not know when. We must concern ourselves not with what the patient is 'like', but with what the patient is 'becoming' during the session, and we must be able to stand the pressure of watching that process. [1975b, p. 96]

I am progressing toward Bion in the consulting room. By way of preface this should be said: Having already "taken" groups, Bion was prepared to take on those persons who were beginning increasingly to be considered fit subjects for psychoanalysis—young children and schizophrenics. All of us learn most of what we know from our patients,[6] particularly those who oblige us to learn more of ourselves; and as these new beings were coming into the consulting room they required of their analysts to stretch and develop. Some psychotherapists have done this by way of an inventive elaboration of technique. Others, like Bion, felt technique—that is, interpretation based on intuition—would serve. What had to stretch was mind—intuition; the receiving apparatus. Plainly when one works with people who, to survive, have had to arrogate mind over mattering, and thereby to become incurious and even stupid, interpretations that are unable to point to—"display"!—the evidence are experienced (perhaps accurately) by the patient as arrogance meeting arrogance. Grotstein (1983) remarks of Bion's analysis of him:

---

[6]This is at once obvious and not. Meltzer makes the point by redirecting our attention to Freud's first patients, and what by force of will and necessity they obliged him to learn. Of course, we are all indebted to those of our patients who oblige us to get to know *them* (Meltzer 1978a).

One has at first the idea of a Da Vinci working on the restoration of one's shabby structure until the idea gradually develops that the shabby structure is but the current ruin of an edifice worthy of a Da Vinci; *moreover he was building it with the mortar and bricks of one's own productions* (my italics). [p. 34]

One might say to a patient, "Quite probably you felt—oh, *so* scared, to discover she didn't have a penis. But shortly, I think, you came to ridicule her, as you do these days, so to allay the power of the fright." If the patient can get a glimmer of his three-or-four-year-old self contemplating mother or little Susie and come, via the reconstruction, to remember all of this—then can the intuition and concept marry. The child remembers his forgotten self and the adult in the consulting room "remembers" his currently frightened self—and a good deal of reexperiencing, current and retrospective, can take place. But such re-constructions never lose the status of rumor for some patients, and, for the analyst nevertheless to make them, compounds the patient's wish to regard most matters as rumor. For these patients the datum must be in the experiential moment—or, more accurately, astonishingly *not* in the experiential moment, where one would expect it to be. Then the task is to find out where it has gone and what has replaced it.

In mathematics, calculations can be made without the presence of the objects about which calculation is necessary, but in psychoanalytic practice it is essential for the psychoanalyst to be able to demonstrate as he formulates. [1970, p. 1] . . . The patient should be shown the evidence on which the interpretation is based; if the evidence is scattered sparsely over a period of years of acting out, the problem of interpretation assumes serious proportions, because the medium in which the patient is effecting his transformation is not predominantly conversational English, but acting out. [p. 14]. [However] the pre [or non-] verbal matter the psychoanalyst must discuss is certain to be an illustration of the difficulty in communication he himself is experiencing. [p. 15]

In other words, attention is necessarily drawn to the medium of communication itself. The medium is the message, the massage, and so the datum to be contemplated.[7]

---

[7]For a discussion of this phenomenon in groups, see Boris 1967.

Bion, like Freud, builds his theories on selective attention. Freud started with this binary — either-or, not yes-no — concept in *Studies in Hysteria*: or, rather, at his request, Breuer did so. But no sooner did Freud become fully engaged with the wish, then pleasure, then libido theory, attention became "attention cathexis" and ultimately "cathexis," and attention, per se, was lost as a psychoanalytic concept. Yet, of course, that is what all the so-called mechanisms of defense are based on — including those like splitting, introjection, projection and projective identification — which make up Melanie Klein's vocabulary and to which Bion has given a coherent psychology. The keystone of selective attention is that attention is paid *some*where, idly or resolutely, and one has to pay attention to where it should not be in order to put it where one wants it: To repress, one has to remember what to forget.[8]

Bion's contribution to the subject is primarily in his book *Attention and Interpretation,* although, in common with Freud, the subject of attention, once it is heralded, is then treated by Bion only implicitly. What he was to try to show in that book was how attention must be paid.

His counsel was simply for the analyst to eschew memory and desire. For obvious reasons, this has also become (in-) famous. But as has by now perhaps become equally obvious, this position was the logical extension of Bion's attempt to refine psychoanalysis of its dross — to polish the psychoanalytic instrument of intuition.

It is wise for the analyst to assume that people do not spend time and money on analysis unless they are disturbed — no matter how smooth, straightforward and apparently simple the view they present for the analyst's inspection. [1980, p. 32]

What do you see when the patient comes into your room? Usually a mature individual, articulate and much like anybody else: The patient sees much the same thing. He has heard this psychoanalytic jargon, so naturally he assumes that the analyst does not mean what he says. But the analyst has to be aware that the patient *does* mean what he says, although he may say it very softly indeed. We should not allow ourselves to be too dominated by the noise the patient makes — 'When I was coming here I saw an accident in the street. . . . That is perfectly true, but the noisy way the spectacle can be described makes it difficult to

---

[8]For an elaboration of this, there is in my own *Passions of the Mind* (1993) an extended essay on selective attention and the paradox of self deception.

hear the "forgotten" but . . . nonetheless active experience which has been re-awoken by the immediate stimulus of the accident. [1980, p. 35]

This is part of Bion's continuing meditation on meaning. The fictive transformation is such that what the patient is able to say his problem is about is *not* what it is about; what it is about, he cannot say (any more, if he ever could). People use that part of the spectrum of experience where the pain ain't. Only by listening past where the patient is can one begin to discern what Bion calls the "constant conjunctions," the let A be represented by B and B by C set of transpositions that yield the patient's ciphering and encoding system.

The problem, then, is to see beyond the surface and to "hear the forgotten" amidst the noise and find one's way to the unconjoined conjunctions that at once hide from and await discovery.

## PRACTICE

The *instrument* for doing this is the analyst's capacity to live in the absolute present. Patients don't. They are in the past or in the future, for time, like space, is a medium in which contact with self and other can be evaded or equivocated. The analyst, as Bion has been saying in the passages I have been quoting, must be where the patient isn't — otherwise he is redundant.[9] The past, so important to Freudian psychoanalysis — as the source of trauma, fixation, the infantile neurosis, the point of regression or fixation, the plot for the drama of the transference — is for Bion relevant only in so far as it is *not* the past; it is present, for it never *got* past: What is repressed cannot be forgotten. And since it is present, its pastness is irrelevant. The main thing is to allow the past to be "presented" (a complex pun of Bion's).

An experience is *of* something, but paramnesically, the patient can only know *about* it. What he knows about the experience is to the experience what an analogy is to its likeness. An example Bion uses is: "As the breast is to the baby's mouth the surgeon's knife is to the X" (1970, p. 5). There is a double relationship here: The one connects the

---

[9]Intellective Bion is, if not before, now revealed as, if not more so, ontologic and existential as anyone writing. I suspect he would have come to this in any case, but as a young man (at Oxford) he gained a therapist (analyst?) who would ask him: "Feel it in the past, feel it in the past."

nouns, knife-body and breast-mouth; the other links (analogically) scalpel and breast and body and mouth. And of course the verbs that are implied in the hyphens.

If one substitutes abstractions for the nouns, one reaches, as Bion sees it, ♂ and ♀. These symbols are, of course, expressions of gender, but Bion, more abstractly still, uses them even more generically to express contents and container or contained and container. Thus scalpel is to body as breast is to mouth as ♂ is ♀ and contained is to container — and as penis is to vagina and male to female and thoughts to mind. Somewhere in everything there is something *about* the relationship between contents and container, of which experience consists.

"Last night I dreamt about . . ." says the patient; it is his approximation of *of*. From this the analyst must intuit what the experience might have been of if it hadn't had to be about: "The coherence that these facts have in the patient's mind is not relevant to the analyst's problem . . ." (1980, p. 15). His problem is to see how the "particles" actually cohere in the of-ness of things.

Interpretation tries to communicate what the patient's experience is of, having to do with the relations between container and contained. What is the relationship between breast and mouth that makes it at once like (analogic to) and unlike (not homologic with) scalpel and body? For that matter, what is taking place in the communication to the analyst, as between ♂ and ♀ and, inevitably what is taking place, as between ♂ and ♀ in the analyst's communication of an interpretation to the patient? Bion's own metaphor of the tennis net, earlier referred to, is apposite here. This rather microscopic series of questions have a more macroscopic counterpart: Is the analysis being done an analysis or is it *like* an analysis: Are there an analyst and a patient in the room or two people behaving as if they were analyst and patient? Is the analysis about the patient becoming more like a normal person or becoming able to be more himself? To what uses are the communications being put? The same interpretation, say "the scalpel is to your body as a breast is to the mouth", can be given with different purposes in mind (for example to give information or, alternatively, to prevent surgery). These purposes are the relationship between ♂ and ♀. Is an interpretation a relationship of K(nowledge) — K(an effort to ward off knowledge) or of L(ove) or H(ate)? One senses that for Bion the motivation for giving an interpretation is a matter of great, even profound, importance, and at the same time a source of much information:

> Sometimes the function of speech is to communicate experience to another; sometimes it is to miscommunicate. Sometimes the object is to achieve access to, and permit access from, a good spirit; conversely to deny access to a bad spirit. [1970, p. 1]

Now in what medium will matters of moment be re-presented? As any of us knows who feel tired at the end of a day, the medium is the analyst. The patient is going to work upon our capacity to attend because, feeling what he doesn't know won't hurt him, his ability not to know depends on his keeping us from knowing. And among the ways he will divert us from the existential present is to get us attending to the past or the future — even to getting us wishing for the end of the session.

This is not primarily in the domain of countertransference. The transferences that take place have to do with the exterior configurations of the people involved. If one thinks of that figure–ground plate of two faces in profile, which also constitute a single vase, the relations of analyst and patient will at one and the same time be transferential, using the libidinal attributes, and identificatory, using the container or vessel attributes. One may wish for the end of a session because the patient frustrates a lusty wish. Or one may wish for its end because, in doing so, the patient has succeeded in establishing an impedence in one's self that makes one impatient of the present and its contents. We are warned by Freud to attend to our transference to the patient. Now Bion comes along and tells us only by wanting nothing — not even the end of the session, indeed, not even the patient's well-being — can we properly attend.

His metaphor concerns saturation; he wants a *tabula rasa*. If the 10:00 patient is one we know to be a married man in his thirties, we know too much, for how are we to attend the 4-year-old girl who has just walked in. Some days, and for parts of every day, the 30-year-old man is just a rumor. If the analyst is not saturated with knowledge — if he does not know anything nor want anything — he becomes the vacuum which the patient cannot stand and has perforce to fill.

> I want to stress an on-going question. By 'on-going' I mean that it has no permanent answer; it is always open . . . why has this patient who

has come to you for three years . . . three weeks, three sessions come
again today? You may have an idea why he came yesterday, but that is
not today. . . . (1980, p. 32)

Many of us will wonder which, like the purple cow, is worse: seeing
such an analyst or being one! Bion is vaguely apologetic: He does not
recommend to any of us to try to be such analysts unless we have
reached the "depressive position" and can (I add) tolerate our hatred
for such rigor. All the same, many of us do something like what he
espouses simply because, after a while, we have discovered and
disclosed everything we know about a patient and have run out: and
yet the patient is still attending and still communicating and, oddly,
seems almost grateful that we have run out of the sort of thing we have
been saying month after month. It's as if: Now, perhaps, we can
begin? Patients, too, stress the "on-going question."

Bion is not ahistorical; history will come back into things as it
becomes inevitable. Among his examples is a patient whose occasional
reiteration of what sounded like "ice cream" came over time to be "I
scream". The past, horribly alive, had become the past presented.

The occupation of patient and analyst, then, needs to be what the
two of them can know together because both are present and both are
*necessary*.[10] Anything else is something else, since it is prior to or outside
of the session. This goes for both. Not all of the patient's history is in
the existential moment, but the history that is important to the patient
*is* in any given moment — and it is likely to be so important as not to be
wasted on words: "We must listen not so much to the meaning of what
the patient communicates but to the use to which it is being put." Every
moment of every session is a communication. Every communication
needs interpretation. Every interpretation needs to be based on the
analyst's experience, not of psychoanalytic writing, not of patients, not
of this patient yesterday or even today, but of himself and his
experience in the instant. The interpretation, in short, is a response to
the patient's activation of experience in the analyst — in his hope for
and fear of a meeting of minds.

The interpretation arises when the analyst:

---

[10]One of the paradoxes of our field is that, despite our entreaties, the trainee listens
more to us, his supervisor, than to his patient, and, what is worse, confides his best
interpretations to us. Hosannah to the day when patient and analyst are alone! For an
extended discussion of the theory of interpretation in psychonalysis, see Boris 1986.

feels he is being manipulated so as to be playing a part no matter how difficult to recognize in somebody else's phantasy—or he would do so were it not for what in recollection I can only call a temporary loss of insight, a sense of experiencing strong feelings, and at the same time a belief that their existence is quite adequately justified by the objective situation without recourse to recondite explanation of their causation. [1961, p. 116]

To this Bion added the idea that interpretations are given when obvious and remarkable—obvious to both analyst and patient but remarkable only in that the patient is not seeing the matter for himself. Bion, however, in an example of his early work, does not yet attain this precept:

*Patient.* I cannot find any interesting food.

*Analyst.* You feel it has all been eaten up.

*Patient.* I do not feel able to buy any new clothes and my socks are a mass of holes.

*Analyst.* By picking out a tiny piece of skin yesterday you injured yourself so badly you cannot even buy clothes; you are empty and have nothing to buy them with.

*Patient.* Although they are full of holes, they constrict my foot.

*Analyst.* Not only did you tear off your own penis but also mine. So today there is no interesting food—only a hole. [1967, p. 28]

Though Bion in the paper on schizophrenia, from which this is an excerpt, makes a case for the interpretation being correct, the interplay between Bion and his patient sounds "duly"—as in "I duly interpreted this to him." This dutifulness extends to the content, which sounds capital 'K'-leinian, of the sort about which Bion was later to note that Klein, in latter days, was as concerned to teach Klein as to analyze Bion (1980, p. 37). In any case the reach from the catechistic line of interpretation to that marked by "negative capability" is as long as and rather akin to the reach from the child who (speaking of the flower arrangement) says, "I did it all myself" to the adult in his late seventies who writes of his intention to be truthful, "It is an exalted intention."

Suppose I played a game like 'fathers and mothers' [or 'House' as we call it] that could be described as a 'conscious fantasy' at some stage. Then suppose I became so frustrated because I could not be father or mother that I forgot it. I could say that the fantasy which was once conscious had become unconscious. Today when I *am* one of the parents I may again be unwilling to know anything about this unconscious fantasy, for what is the use of knowing about 'fathers and mothers' when I am either too young to be one or too old to do anything about it now. I may say I don't want to have anything to do with these psychoanalysts. I do not want to be reminded of these fantasies. The answer to that might be 'I don't object to that' except that that 'unconscious fantasy' of yours, as you call it, is horribly alive; it may be obscured but active and powerful [so much so that] it may generate envy, hatred and jealousy of the father or mother who can make anything from babies to ideas. If so he may be unable, even philosophically, to form symbols or synthesize analytic concepts. There is no chance of making progress because there is no way of generating thoughts. [1974, pp. 55–56]

The little boy of "Arf Arfer" had, one feels, almost necessarily to "father" a psychoanalyst who could understand about "fathers and mothers" truth, and the formulation of ideas and books.


## BION ON BION

Among those books not yet touched upon in this essay was the trilogy he was to call *A Memoir of the Future*. Like two later volumes — *The Long Week-End* and *All My Sins Remembered* — it is an autobiographical work. But unlike those which were written of and from the depressive position, in which events and people, including the self are tolerated as a whole in wholesome relationships, *Memoir* is written from the paranoid-schizoid position, in which splits of every sort (temporal, spatial, and schismatic) occur — and are, in the end, healed. It is necessarily a life of the mind — but of a mind that does not start at birth, thus one in which somites and gametes and four-year-olds and Bion all talk with equal relevance and passion. Their goal, one feels, is an at-one-ment, but it will not be easily realized. Volume Three introduces what Bion felt his particular quality of attention opened to him, as the following passage will indicate:

*P.A.* [Psychoanalyst] I have had patients who are on bad terms with whatever they feel they have become; they are on bad terms with human beings who remind them of themselves. One of the difficulties of psychoanalyzing such patients is that they do not want to be reminded of 'ordinary' behavior — theirs or anyone else's.

*Alice* [another character in the book] Has this anything to do with real life?

*P.A.* It has a great deal to do with real life. Amongst the many and frequent dangers of psychoanalysis none is more dangerous than the experience of the coming together of the pre-natal and the post-natal personalities. It can easily be appreciated that the danger is associated with anything whatever—psychoanalysis, music, painting, mathematics—which could remind these two personalities of their continued and continuing 'contact' with each other in the same body and mind.

*Roland* [another character] You make it sound most dramatic.

*P.A.* It would require a drama of Shakespearean quality to portray the reality. . . . Why didn't Bion go on with groups?

*Bion* I had more pressing problems which could adequately be dealt with only by psychoanalysis—or something better; particularly the problem P.A. had been discussing, of the relationship of the highly equipped fetus with its own and its parents' 'parental' qualities.

*Roland* The fetus's parental quality! That sounds wonderful.

*Bion* I was afraid it would rouse someone's contempt. The crackling of thorns under a pot is more serious when it becomes . . . the marriage of divorced elements.

*Roland* . . . I think you have an inflated view of your importance.

*Bion* I regret I give such an impression. I should be less than sincere if I said you are only a source of innocent merriment. There are times when I find your supposedly sane and balanced outlook, your fascinating sense of humor difficult to tolerate.[11]

*Alice* I don't wish to take sides, but Peace! You English fools.[12]

---

[11]Of his wish to write *Memoir,* Bion—in an as yet unpublished epilogue—continues this theme: "All my life I have been imprisoned, frustrated, dogged by common-sense, reason, memories, desires and —greatest bug-bear of all—understanding and being understood. This is an attempt to express my rebellion, to say 'Good-bye' to all that." But there is another purpose—expressed in the Prologue. "There may be modes of thinking to which no known realization has so far been found to approximate. Hallucinosis, hypochondriasis and other mental 'diseases' may have logic, a grammar and a corresponding real-ization, none of which has so far been discovered. They may be difficult to discover because they are obscured by a 'memory', or a 'desire', or an 'understanding' to which they are supposed—wrongly—to approximate" (*A Memoir of the Future* 1990, Karnac Press).

[12]*The Long Week-End* is the "peace" for which Alice calls. It needs no preface such as that given to *The Dawn of Oblivion*:
Q. Is this [Vol. III] as bad?
A. Worse.
Q. How interesting: I must get it.
A. I said "worse."
Q. That's what made me want it—I don't see how it could be.

But it is not merely Bion's wish to take matters back to where he believes — entirely seriously — they began that seems to have motivated the books. There are, I think, two other intentions. One is in keeping with his feeling that the "O," the original or ultimate truth (Plato is here) is incomprehensible to any one approach — be it that of psychoanalyst, poet, politician, or philosopher (see anon) — but that whatever the status of the noumenon, the phenomenon lives within the personality — such as it is — of the the beholder. In the end, were Bion to be true to his idea of truth, he had to provide an interior view — a view of Bion the experiencer. At first, as young men do, he shirked that, feeling that the precision of abstractions, even mathematic approximations, devoid of a "penumbra of associations" (hence the L, H, K, Alpha, Beta, etc.) could make experience sufficiently distilled as to free it from the coloration of personality, group, history, and culture. Even at the end, in his introduction to *The Long Week-End*, he wistfully expresses the wish that he had abstractions at hand in which to encompass his life. But by then he knew he hadn't, and there was only the next best thing to give us: the "artificer" himself.

Given Bion on Bion, one can go back to the earlier works and understand them as efforts, one after the other, to understand the two most mysterious yet essential features of psychonalysis: The paradox of a mind deceiving itself and the process of intuition by which a second mind can realize what the first no longer can. Someone wrote that if all the variables between the throw of the dice and their eventual position could be identified and measured, there would be no such thing as chance. Bion, one feels, would have been interested.

I make a distinction between 'existence', to be or not to be (Shakespeare, as usual, says it better than anyone else has been able to say it) and 'essence', the what-ever-it-is that makes existence worth existing. That is what no one can tell you, and what every philosopher, painter, musician, artist, poet and mere person has to find out for himself . . . That's what your patients, however ill, well, wealthy, poor, clever, have to find out. They can't be shown, but you may give them a chance to see or find out. [letter to one of his children, 1956]

It would be helpful if it could be recognized that all these various disciplines — music, painting, psycho-analysis and so on ad infinitum — are indeed engaged on the same search for truth. Talking as we are here, we can split it up as I have just done; it is very useful for purposes of verbal communication. If all we wanted to do was to communicate verbally that would be fine. We could stop there; we could say, if it can't be verbalized, out with it! Get rid of music; get rid of painting. But if you are tolerant then you have to see the possibility that the painter can make progress which is not for somebody who is capable of talking only one kind of language. The fundamental problem is, how soon can human beings reconcile themselves to the fact that the truth matters? We can believe whatever we please, but that doesn't mean that the universe is going to suit itself to our particular beliefs or our particular capacities. It is *we* who have to do something about that; *we* have to alter to a point where we can comprehend the universe in which we live. The trouble is that supposing we reach that point our feelings of fear or terror might be so great that we couldn't stand it. So the search for truth can be limited both by our lack of intelligence or wisdom, and by our emotional inheritance. The fear of knowing the truth can be so powerful that the doses of truth are lethal.

Thus, finally:

The conditions (i.e. for interpretations) are complete when the analyst feels aware of resistance in himself—not counter-transference—but resistence to the response he anticipates from the analysand if he gives the interpretation. [1970, p. 168]

## REFERENCES

Barthelme, D. *N.Y. Times*. Feb 8, 1982.
Bion, W. R. (1961). *Experiences in Groups*. London: Tavistock.
\_\_\_\_\_ (1962). *Learning from Experience*. New York: Basic Books (London: Karnac Books, 1984).
\_\_\_\_\_ (1963). *Elements of Psychoanalysis*. New York: Basic Books (London: Karnac Books, 1984).
\_\_\_\_\_ (1965). *Transformations*. New York: Basic Books (London: Karnac Books, 1984).
\_\_\_\_\_ (1966). Review: medical orthodoxy and the future of psychoanalysis by K. R. Eissler. *International Journal of Psycho-Analysis* 4: 576–577.
\_\_\_\_\_ (1967). *Second Thoughts*. New York: Jason Aronson.
\_\_\_\_\_ (1970). *Attention and Interpretation*. New York: Basic Books (London: Karnac Books, 1984).
\_\_\_\_\_ (1974). *Bion's Brazilian Lectures, I*. Rio de Janeiro, Brazil: Imago Editoria (London: Karnac Books, 1990, as *Brazilian Lectures*).
\_\_\_\_\_ (1975a). *A Memoir of the Future, Book I: The Dream*. Rio de Janeiro, Brazil: Imago Editoria (London: Karnac Books, 1990, as *A Memoir of the Future*).
\_\_\_\_\_ (1975b). *Bion's Brazilian Lectures, II*. Rio de Janeiro, Brazil: Imago Editoria (London: Karnac Books, 1990, as *Brazilian Lectures*).

_____ (1977a). *A Memoir of the Future, II: The Past Presented*. Rio de Janeiro, Brazil: Imago Editoria (London: Karnac Books, 1990, as *A Memoir of the Future*).

_____ (1977b). *Two Papers*. Rio de Janeiro, Brazil: Imago Editoria (London: Karnac Books, 1989).

_____ (1978). *Four Discussions with W. R. Bion*. Strathclyde: Clunie.

_____ (1979). *A Memoir of the Future, III: The Dawn of Oblivion*. Perthshire: Clunie (London: Karnac Books, 1990, as *A Memoir of the Future*).

_____ (1980). *Bion in New York and Sao Paulo*. Strathclyde: Clunie.

_____ (1982). *The Long Week-End: A Part of Life*. Abingdon, England: Fleetwood.

_____ (1985a). *All My Sins Remembered: Another Part of Life* and *The Other Side of Genius: Family Letters*. Oxford, England: Fleetwood.

_____ (1985b). *The Other Side of Genius: Family Letters*. Abingdon, Oxfordshire Fleetwood.

Boris, H. N. (1967). The medium, the message, and the good group dream. *International Journal of Group Psychotherapy* 20:90–98.

_____ (1976). On hope: its nature and psychotherapy. *International Review of Psycho-Analysis* 3:139–150.

_____ (1986). Interpretation: history and theory. In *Basic Techniques in Psychodynamic Psychotherapy*, ed. M. Nichols and T. J. Paolino, pp. 287–308. New York: Gardner.

Freud, S. (1905). Fragment of an analysis of a case of hysteria. *Standard Edition* 7:7–122.

_____ (1911). Psychoanalytical notes on a case of paranoia. *Standard Edition* 12:9–82.

_____ (1918). From the history of an infantile neurosis. *Standard Edition* 17:7–122.

Grinberg, L., Sor, D., and Tabak de Bianchedi, E. (1975). *Introduction to the Work of Bion*. Perthshire: Clunie.

Grotstein, J. (1983). *Do I Dare Disturb the Universe?* London: Karnac.

Meltzer, D. (1978a). *The Kleinian Development, Part One*. Perthshire: Clunie.

_____ (1978b). *The Kleinian Development, Part Three*. Perthshire: Clunie.

Nabokov, V. (1983). *Lectures on Don Quixote*. Ed. F. Bowers. New York: Harcourt, Brace & Jovanovich.

# 16

# Greed, Envy, Spite, and Revenge

The original title of this essay was "The 'Other' Breast"; "Greed, etc." comprised the subtitle. It was meant to signify that there is a fantasy that goes along with these emotions, producing, in concert with them, something like a state of mind. I should add, perhaps, that so far as I can tell, from the children and the grownups they become, babies are born imagists and analogizers, so that whether or not they have come in contact with an actual breast, or have instead lived in the world of rubber, plastic, and Similac, there is a category for "Breast" as a something there to suckle, which when it is good is very, very good and which when it is bad is horrid—a "no-thing." This paper looks into how the baby tells the difference. "Tolerating Nothing"* goes on to consider the breast when it is or has become a no-thing. And "Identification with a vengeance" deals with the use of identifications (driven by envy) as a way around the dilemmas of choice. In that latter paper I recount what a certain Mr. R. had to say about his surprise that breasts, as those his mother had, actually gave milk; he had had a different idea entirely.

A critical factor is not just that—who knows?—the other breast is the chocolate one, but that any choice forces the relinquishment of another choice—and thus of one of the hopes, possibilities, and items on the now shorter list of choices. Thus any choice requires an act of

---

*See Boris, *Envy* (1994). Northvale, NJ: Jason Aronson.

mourning and grief, but is such a requirement required? "Do I ha-a-ve to choose?" "Do we [in the words of a Darrow drawing] have to do what we want to do again today?"

Of course life is lived and choice made within time, and in evaluating choosing it might help to know something about time: about the return, renewal, or death of opportunity and possibility. But when even soon takes a long time, and babies are tempted to ease their pain and anguish by drifting into obliviousness, they become hard put to learn enough about time to factor it in. Time begins to look remarkably like a persecuting object who, because not invited to the christening, has now come to stay for all time. (At carnival and at New Year's Day the new baby gets even with the old man with the scythe for having hurried and frightened him so.) "About Time" picks up on the temporal aspect of these matters.

---

I can imagine an infant," I sometimes feel it necessary to say, "held to two ample milky breasts—yet starving out of the pain of losing either, by choosing the one."

That this remark does not go down well (at least at first) can easily be imagined. The individuals to whom I make it feel deprived, empty. The idea of abundance is decidedly my own. Indeed my remark seems to them only to validate their experience: Is a comment like that supposed to help?

And yet, I feel persuaded that it does—that a long time ago, as now in the transference, there was a greed so great as to fail securely to metamorphose into appetite. Had it done so, such satisfactions as are available to the appetites might have consoled even compensated for the loss of the "other" breast. But in failing to give over into appetite, the greed, in its very nature insatiable and unsatisfiable, left a sequence of consequences that the analysis has somehow to put right.

In what follows I shall attempt to describe these consequences and the matter of helping put them right. But in doing so I shall be venturing onto the treacherous shoals of originology on which psychoanalysis so often founders.

In the consulting room a remark such as mine about the infant and the breasts can be taken either (or both) as metaphor or construction of historical experience. Its validity is moot; only its usefulness matters. If I say it, for example, to someone who is obsessing whether this or whether that is the case, I am doing so to refract the disappointment the patient would feel were either the case and the fear he would feel if neither were the case — as if an infant held to two adequate breasts. Such an interpretation may or may not help the patient get closer to what he experiences. But the same remark offered to the reader as my imaginative construction of the experience of infants more generally, taken from the transference activities of a handful of patients, is plainly tautological. I say: I believe this once to have been the case for it is now again the case and I believe it now to be the case because it once was the case and never got done with. What is the benign circularity of the consulting room becomes the teleology of theory.

And yet such is precisely what I am setting forth to do. I shall be inventing an infant, much as I do in the consulting room. But there I can display what I mean while here I can only say it — a wide difference. Still, in its way, this very problem in methodology is an illustration of my thesis. The "other" breast is an other paper, and we, the reader and I, have, for the moment, only this one.

## GREED AND APPETITE

Appetite, as I have already implied, is inherently satisfiable. It goes after what it wants and yet is receptive to what it gets. It makes do, not letting (in Freud's phrase) better stand in the way of good.

Greed is, I think, prior to appetite and may or may not evolve into appetite. Greed in its nature, is inherently insatiable, and so cannot be satisfied. It wants everything; nothing less will do. In colloquial language, "greedy" as an adjective has a pejorative cast; it is often said angrily about someone who cannot be pleased. I don't regard greed as bad, but as a condition anyone would gladly part with if they could withstand the pain.

The pain is that of loss, the loss of the "other" breast. The pain should not be underestimated, for as we shall see greed invites a whole set of torments the painfulness of which provides some measure of the pain that would, so the infant imagines, come to it were it to relinquish the "other" breast.

What, then, does the "other" breast contain that is of such inestimable value? The simplest answer is: Everything the first breast does not. Phenomenologically speaking, I think that may be answer enough. All the same, I would like to put forward a further surmise.

In an earlier paper, to which this one is by way of being the second half, I dealt with the nature of hope (Boris 1976). There I noted that when Pandora (in the Hesiod myth) slips off the cover of the jar, "Forthwith there escaped a multitude of plagues for hapless man — such as gout and rheumatism and colic for his body and envy, spite, and revenge for his mind." Only hope remained in this collection of "noxious articles."

Hope, as I showed in that paper, involves at the core of it a disposition toward choosiness, which is the necessary counterpart to the availability of choices. I related this to selectivity, as that concept is used in evolutionary biology: Creatures, mating, choose and are chosen, not at random or by propinquity, but in such a way as selectively to perpetuate the "best" (fittest) among the gene pool down the generations.

In this process there is at work a preconception concerning what "better" consists in (the plumage of the tail, the size of the territory, the rank in the social hierarchy) that interlocks with the predilection to choose the "better." The procreative drive, for example, is not triggered until preconception and predilection are satisfied. As I observed, "the inhibition of the procreative drive pending the approximation of the object to the 'preconception' paradoxically facilitates the release of the drive." That is, the readier and more assured the capacity not to choose A, the easier and quicker the capacity to choose B. Matters remain, then, in a state of potential — awaiting the right conditions. That there are or will be the "right" conditions is the source of hope. That there aren't nor will be is the source of hopelessness and despair. Yet, as Bion (1961, pp. 151–152) notes, "only by remaining a hope does hope persist." Thus hope, like the greed of which it forms a part, is perforce oriented to the potential. While (as Francis Bacon noted) it makes a good breakfast, it makes a poor supper.

For the fussy (read, choosy) baby the devolution of all of the foregoing is this: It wants a breast to feed from, but it also needs the "right" breast. The first breast may not be the right breast, so it mustn't accept that. But if the "other" breast is also not the "right" breast, it will have spent its matrimony. The way out of such a plight is to avoid potentiating choice, by accepting nothing, using up nothing, while awaiting everything.

The reader may object (and, in my opinion quite properly so) that I am imputing to the infant a sophistication it could not possibly have. In fact, I should like to regard the infant as decidedly unsophisticated — but, all the same, heir to programmatic imperatives, dark urges, it can neither fathom nor yet ignore, imperatives that push into its mind as teeth will its gums, creating a Kafkaesque nightmare of being controlled by unclear forces and unnamable agencies. That is to say, I think "instincts" are more forceful upon the infant than later when it can escape their insistent importunings, and that these include mandates to die, if necessary, so that the species can survive; to make the right choice, so that the species can flourish; to live life fully, ruthlessly, and devil take the hindmost, and to care for one's own dear love — and more. I suppose these to be both inchoate and incoherent and, as such, persecutory in the extreme. I expect this experience to reoccur in the transference at the juncture between greed and appetite. I like to imagine that if I can identify the nameless, faceless players for the people in whom the reoccurence is taking place they can replace choosiness with choice, where they couldn't before without feeling hopeless villains, doomed always to be in the wrong.

I want now to distinguish between greed as potential and potentiated greed. The former is free of frustration. It contains the fantasy of all-is-one and at-one-ment. It is a dream beyond the dreams of avarice. It generates excitement and bliss. It is a state in which the infant (later child or adult) has temporarily undiscovered the other and hasn't to contend with the possibility of a juxtaposition between appetite and breast. This state lasts as long as the infant wants nothing from the breast, whereupon it becomes potentiated and serenity is replaced by a frustration as large as all the world.

## FRUSTRATION AND ANXIETY

Greed, I have been saying, is an unevolved state of mind in which one wishes and hopes to have everything all of the time. The fantasy that this might be possible produces a state of feeling involving high excitement and pure bliss.

However, the moment greed is potentiated, one comes hard upon the realization that choices are required. This realization stimulates either a refusal to endure the choice — the decay of appetite back into greed — or an experience of vast frustration. Or it stimulates the making of the choice, whereupon one feels at one and the same time a feeling of profound loss and the satisfactions of appetite.

Though I have so far been writing of this as a one-time phenomenon, in fact it happens again and again. Greed evolves into appetite; appetite decays into greed. Much of the determination of the choice is,

I think, intrapsychic. That is, the one possibility and the other are imagined to contain what they do and convey what one preconceives them to convey. Greed, in other words, has no contact with ordinary actuality; the first breast is not, for example, the left breast of the mother, nor is the "other" breast her right breast. The process I have been describing goes on in infants whose experience is entirely of rubber, plastic, and Similac.

Appetite, in contrast, makes manifest the infant's first encounter with actuality and, as such, makes actual experience for the first time a player in the process. The quality of the appetitive experience will now play a role in whether the feeling of loss is modulated by compensatory and consoling experience — or is not.

The paradox in all of this is that both outcomes are — as it were — equally problematic, given the nature of the conflict. Either way there is gain; either way loss. Since this is serial, even cyclic, anticipation and memory come to be established, and with them the experience of anxiety.

With anxiety, matters become more complex. Before we were dealing with premonitions of loss or gain, of pain or gratification. The loss of the "other" breast was a nameless foreboding, a feeling that one would be violating some genetic imperative the nature of which one couldn't know. One was dealing with pre-conceptions that evoked choosiness and predilections to make the right choice — but what were these? I don't want here to move from phenomenological description to metapsychology and risk confounding things, but I do think for what it's worth, that what I have been calling genetic imperatives are the forerunners of the superego — its anlage, and that these imperatives with their preconceptions and predilections and premonitions are what will be filled out by parental and cultural strictures: Aha! so that is what I am supposed[1] to think, feel and do! The anxiety which comes into being is thus a "signal" anxiety, as Freud called it (1925). What it signals is not that loss or frustration is in store, but that one will be under terrible attack. The direction of the attack I have dealt with so far is from the nameless imperatives (later to be superego anxiety). Now I add the attack of anticipation and memory itself, of the discovery of the repetitive, serial, or cyclic nature of experience. (I will

---

[1]For a consideration of the force of supposed-to's in group situations, see Boris and colleagues (1975). The "Group" has special resonance to species-oriented fantasy.

presently add to my list of anxieties the fear of "counterattacks" by the breast [or other object] to the "attacks" one launches out of envy.)

Anticipation and memory are ego functions and one (the infant or self) can experience (accept) the ego as syntonic or alien, as helpful friend or malefactor. It is important to recognize that so far as the self is concerned the ego is an object much as an other thing or person is an object and can be loved and hated, nourished or attacked in much the same way. In psychosis, for example, the ego is under continual attack and its usual functions of thought, anticipation, memory, and the selective attention that make unconsciousness of perceptions, thoughts, or memories possible are eviscerated. So with the infant: memory and anticipation—learning—become messengers and "enjoy" the time-honored welcome given messengers.

With anxiety in the picture, greed potentiated leads not simply to premonition but to the mental pain anxiety imposes. I believe there to be a distinction here, between emotional pain—such as that of loss or despair or frustration, and mental pain—such as worry, terror, and dread. I point to this distinction because, human nature being what it is, whenever there are two of something each can be employed to defend against the other. And, indeed, one of the defensive functions of this anxiety is to get confused with painful affects so that one can think it is the anxiety that is the insuperable pain and not the feelings. The "signal" is enough to keep one from knowing what the signal is signaling. One knows only that ameliorative or evasive action is required. Since ameliorative action can only succeed (save by luck) if one knows what the signal is signaling, this pretty well works in favor of one "choosing" evasive action.

In the course of an analysis this series—premonition of $x$ . . . anxiety . . . evasive action—functions as a powerful resistance to any effort to identify the preconceptions and premonitions themselves, indeed even that they exist. The analyst must use great restraint and wait for the anticipated event to evolve into the transference and become extant. For it is not only (now) in the realm of action—of trying or not trying the one breast or the "other" that one protects oneself from pain. It is now in the domain of knowledge: One uses anxiety as a signal that says: Now is the time for you not to know what you anticipate and what you remember.

I referred in passing to yet another source of anxiety—the fear of counterattack from objects attacked out of envy. The employment of anxiety as a signal not to know (not to proffer "diplomatic recognition" to the source of concern) is, as well as being self-protective, anxiety converted by envy to envy's own uses. It is time, therefore, to bring envy into the story and with it spite and revenge.

## ENVY, SPITE, AND REVENGE

As greed potentiates into want, the object gains in importance until it is experienced as dominating the horizons of the mind. If one—the infant, say—could give up his greed, the immensity of the object— say, the breast—would be good. But if, as we are supposing, the infant cannot give up, and thereby, to take in, the immensity is not in the nature of good but of frustration and anxiety. This, in turn, occasions several sequels.

He feels a wish to possess the breast, to own the source of supply.

He feels a need to own the breast, for in its fascination for him he feels it is owning—controlling—him, as if he were possessed by it.

He despairs of his potency in these regards, envying it its power and dominion over him. This excites an urge to strip it of its powers and obtain these for himself.

He yearns for an alternative which will at once deprive the breast of its power to cast a spell over him and provide him a good breast of which he can make the bad breast envious.

He "rediscovers" the "other" breast in this process of trying to separate the feeling of being persecuted from the feeling of being empowered, and this puts him back, so to say, to square one but with a pernicious difference. Originally he needed the "other" breast to contain and to continue to contain everything the first breast didn't. Now he further needs it to be a bulwark for him against the continuing bullying desirability of the first. He has robbed Peter (the first) to pay Paul (the "other") but, perversely, now Paul is so endowed with everything of value that it can't be used for fear of using it up.[2]

He is now stuck with an other breast that is a "better" breast but can be neither parted with nor used. This breast will seem to contain

---

[2]These are the circumstances of which Melanie Klein wrote in her "Notes on Some Schizoid Mechanisms" (1946) and her book *Envy and Gratitude* (1957), and of course her other works.

everything of value at the same time as it offers nothing. Such a breast can only be thought of as greedy; its intentions can only be regarded as motivated by envy. The infant can only, accordingly, feel under attack.

He will now feel not only frustrated, but (counter-) attacked by the greedy, envious, and sadistic breast. To his woes is added a malevolent breast that he can neither take nor leave alone. Somehow he needs to break that stalemated connection and appease the hatred that his greed, frustration, and envy have generated within him. To these "plagues of the mind," as Hesiod called them, spite will offer some surcease. The idea of spite is encompassed in the familiar aphorism about cutting off one's nose to spite one's face. But, of course, the one who says it is the person being spited by the other and usually says it spitefully. In fact, one cuts off one's mouth to spite the breast (as in anorexia[3]) or one's cock to spite the cunt, to use the vernacular of Laing's (as in such "disorders" as premature ejaculation, impotence, or homosexuality, or vice-versa in the female versions of these), or, indeed, one's life itself. People who cut themselves with razor blades, knives, or glass also nullify the impact of the other on the self.

For that is what spite is — the envious nullification of the other's impact, effect, and value. Having failed to gain possession or control of the breast, one can at least gain possession or control of its effects. Hence the signal anxiety which escalates to an anxiety attack, in the hysteric also manages to obfuscate the source of the danger — oblivion being the spiteful counterpart to obliteration. If the hysteric feels without knowing, the obsessive compulsive knows without feeling; and this too is envy's denouement in spite. "Perhaps," "I guess," "I don't know," "whatever," are all spiteful to the potency of the object, to the analyst or to both, though it will take some work to display this to the patient. It will take more work to display the greed underlying the disinclination to choose implicit in the attitude beyond these words, and underneath the greed the fear of the pain of the loss of either of the "breasts" these words straddle.

Spite can do its work of rendering the object impotent, in fantasy or fact, without requiring the sheer power required for revenge. From infancy on one can "cut" another merely by looking past him; even easier is cutting what Bion (1967) called the link in knowledge — of

---

[3]For an elaboration of this observation, see Boris 1984a and 1984b.

stimulus and response. People with thought disorders "disorder" the relationship of breast to self through such attacks on linking, disorderly conduct in the realm of thought!

Revenge involves a turning of the tables and for it to come into play one has to have what the other wants. When one can believe this to be the case one can feel that—at last!—one possesses and controls the breast and has made its power and potency one's own. This is far from the metamorphosis of greed; to the contrary, what is metamorphosed is anything that can stimulate greed and envy in the other.

While anything will do (certainly for purposes of fueling the fantasy), one sees in the transference that feces and defecation have a particular value. The mother wants these (as the analyst "wants" free association, prompt attendance at sessions, or fees). Moreover, she (and the analyst) wants not what is given her, but more, better—other. That period of life, that interpersonal situation, that Erikson (1950) characterized as "autonomy versus shame and doubt" turns out, on closer inspection, to be hegemony versus shame and doubt. The illusion is that the feces are tantamount to the maternal breast and that the toddler bestows these to its poor, starved, questing mother (or analyst); certainly it does not owe them! The control of the feces and their release has been thought of as anal object relations (cf., Meltzer 1966). That is, once the feces have been metamorphosed into the maternal breast, she-it-they are now firmly under the omnipotent control of one's self. I believe this gives "anality" its particular force in intrapsychic and interpersonal terms, particularly as the elements to anality are carried forward into genital and genital-oedipal interactions and beliefs.

The possessiveness that is the hallmark of greed distinguishes the rivalry of the oedipal struggles. The individual does not struggle to obtain supplies from the other, but to possess the other altogether— even if once in one's possession the other is not used. That was the objective in the first struggle, the infant's with the mother over the ownership and control of the breast; and that is the triangular paradigm for future struggles. Envy masquerades as jealousy, as greed counterfeits love.

## ANALYTIC CONSIDERATIONS

The task of the analysis, of course, is to make it possible, this time around, for the individual to develop appetite. We gain the courage for such an undertaking by believing what the analysand for a long time cannot: that what was unbearable in infancy will have become bearable in childhood and certainly in adulthood. As analysts we know this thanks to our own analyses, in which we learned to stand the idea that time passes. Our patients do not yet know this; indeed, the greedier they are the less they know it. They will feel we are malevolently leading them closer and closer to catastrophe, while we are sitting by in serene self-containment. This will excite not only paranoid anxieties, but a ferocious and almost implacable wish to retaliate, if not through revenge, then through spite. This greedy urge will gorge on every and any indication of countertransference, even identification. Even efforts to make an "alliance" will be violently or systematically misconstrued as a reversal between the haves and the have-nots and used mercilessly against the analysis. The absence of mercy is not simply an expression of hatred. It is a consequence of the failure to develop appetite. When the pain of loss is tolerated it can be projected in the spirit of identification, which itself can evolve into a recognition of the possibility of pain in others and so into tender concern, guilt, and remorse. Although most analysands know that their analysts have been through analysis themselves, the greedy ones will feel no fellow feeling for the suffering involved.

Greed, it will be recalled, has so feared the loss of potential (the "other" breast) to kinesis (choosing and mourning) that the sense of catastrophe the analysand fears is not the repeat of a trauma (such as deprivation or loss of the significant other). It is of an unhappened catastrophe, one which the greed has kept from happening. The analysis has therefore to be less about what did happen than about what did not.

Although the terms "construction" and "reconstruction" are used interchangeably, I have used the former to refer to events that did not form part of the actual social (however interpreted or reinterpreted) history of the person, reserving reconstruction for the process of helping the patient regain knowledge of not only what he experienced but the events conjoining his experiences. My remark concerning starvation and ample breasts is an example of such a construction: It refers to an unhappened event — to a psychic event — a state of mind — rather than to an interpersonal one — a state of affairs. The patient will come — it may be — to recognize what I mean when that same state of mind comes into being in conjunction with my "breasts"-penis, therapeutic potency and the like.

The analysand has come to analysis just as the infant has eaten, grown up, gone to school and learned, worked and taken money, and perhaps married and given life to children. The fact will turn out to be, however, that none of this will have much (sometimes any) reality for him or her — especially compared with that encompassed in the "other" breast. Accordingly, a perfectly adequate analysis can be done — only to meet the same fate!

As I shall attempt shortly to illustrate, I think the analysis has to be conducted in what it much amuses me to call a hermeneutically sealed room. When appetite has evolved, the analysand will have also developed an interest in food for thought. One's interpretations are used to that end. But when greed is ascendant, each interpretation is likely to be used to proliferate possibility and evade choice. Permit me now to reach into my consulting room for three examples. They are misleading because they involve so much talk, but as they are only illustrations perhaps they will serve.

It is coming to summer break time and the 8-year-old says that he, in his persona as a Norwegian water rat, and the gerbil, who he also is sometimes, and Herman, the hooded cobra, who he never "is," but whose exploits he enacts with great admiration, are going on an around-the-world cruise in the QE-2 with their band, which consists of Madonna, Bruce Springsteen, Michael Jackson, etc.

He says: "You and Baby Jane can come too." Baby Jane is nominally my daughter, but generally a very greedy, envious and jealous creature: a split-off from, variously, himself and myself.

I say: "Thank you. But Baby Jane is wondering why she is invited. Is she to be part of everything or is she to be the greedy creature that wants everything?"

He says: "Tell her she can bring her automatic breast."

I say: "She is much relieved to hear that, but she wonders: Is it her job to be the greedy creature so you can be the generous ones who have everything good inside of you?"

He says: "You don't have to worry, Baby Jane, you'll have a good time."

I say: "You don't like me to talk about you, yourself, wanting everything."

He says: "I don't want *every*thing!"

I say: "Everything would include me inside of it, and you don't want to know about wanting me. The QE-2 is like a dream of being inside everything good and then having Cindy and Rick and Michael as your insides."

He says: "It'll only be a month. C'mon! Let's play!"

I say: "I wonder if I am supposed to feel envious?"

He says: "That's crap again. *C'mon!*"

I say: "I think you are wanting to collect very good experiences because you are worried that when we are apart you will collect hurts and injustices and nurse on all your grievances."

He says: "I'll nurse on you if you don't shut up." He is very excited here and it is plain that he is contemplating biting me: Would it be an appetitive love bite out of the same wish to have me shut up and play or a bite of envy at my self-containment?

A second illustration:

> The room is chilly, but there is an afghan. The young woman says, "It's chilly in here. Or is it?"
>
> I say: "You are afraid of certainty?"
>
> She says: "I could take the afghan, I suppose. But perhaps that would be acting out. Perhaps I should free-associate to being cold — if it is cold — or to the afghan. Or something. I don't know." [*Silence*]
>
> I say: "I don't know if there is a choice. I don't *want* to know. I don't want to choose. I hate certainty. Maybe associations are better than warmth or warmth better than associations: I want the better one. No, no I want both."

Some months ago the silence would have continued and I would have needed to talk of the "greedy guzzling of good breast of grievance." Now the silence continues, during which I imagine this young woman is waiting for me to say some such thing again — or for me to say something more, better, different. But I do not. If I did, I imagine she would immediately become further occupied with what I want — for her to associate? to take the afghan? to ask me a question? I feel it would be a disservice to mislead her into still believing she has a breast I greedily want.

It doesn't matter what she does now — associate, take the cover, continue the silence, go back to the question of whether it is cold. Any of these would be a choice and a loss of the alternatives. Instead, she "changes the subject" — which is not a choice, but an evasion.

Toward the end of the session she will plaintively ask, "What has been going on in this session, d'you know?"

"Going on is right," I will say after a while. But she will prefer not to understand me and leave as she arrived, feeling angry and deprived. But of course she has a high tolerance for such deprivation; otherwise she would have foregone the satisfaction of the urge enviously to ruin the session (breast; penis) for me. Later, with luck, she will become at least interested in the repetitive quality of such sessions as these (a foray into appetite) even at the cost of the pleasure of nullifying the possibility of work, "changing the subject." Such "small-scale" events, when gradual enough and managed without confrontations, constitute the process by which the smelting of the metamorphosis happens.

I add another vignette:

> A young man, also in his thirties, has been speaking of how wretched he feels having succumbed (as it feels) to an invitation to dinner and thereby lost the opportunity to work during that interval. As I well know, he works at least eighteen hours of every twenty-four, as it is.
>
> As he talks I begin to get the idea that he is getting the idea that he is telling me this for a reason: that the communication exists within the transference, quite probably that *I* am the dinner. He begins to falter, calling what he has been saying "drivel."
>
> I say: "You hope?"
>
> He says: "What do you mean?"
>
> I say: "That it's only 'drivel'."
>
> He says: "I don't understand."
>
> I: [*Silence*]
>
> He says: "I felt you were thinking 'Well, if he feels he ought to work, why does he go out, or if he goes out, why does he go on and on about how he should have been working?' "
>
> I say: "So what's the answer?"
>
> He says: "I can't *stand* it!" He smashes the Kleenex box with his fist.
>
> I say: "I am not supposed to return the knowledge to you?" Then: "Why is the Kleenex there?"
>
> He says: "I'll be damned if I'll cry."
>
> I say: "I don't know. It's possible. I suppose the question is, by whom?"
>
> He says: "By myself, I guess."
>
> I say: [*Silence*] — (giving that drivel the respect it deserves.)
>
> He says: "You are thinking that I say 'I guess' and 'by myself' because I don't want to give the devil his due."
>
> I say: "You must feel tormented by my always thinking this or that about you. On the other hand, you are careful not to think it of yourself. Bad as the 'about,' it is better than 'of.' Will this become, I wonder, another thinking I will be doing about you?"
>
> He says: "I *want* you to think about me."
>
> I say: "So you don't have to cry?"
>
> He says: "So I don't have to cry?"

I say: "With two sets of thoughts, yours and mine, what's to cry about?"
He says: "Hmm" in a way that gives me to understand he has taken my
point in a way that is allowed to coincide with knowledge he has of himself,
like a stereopticon coming into focus.

Such a conjunction — synthesis, integration of truths-about into the-
truth-of, as gleaned from investigation, not assertion, represents a
movement from proliferation to choice: from greed to appetite. I think
it is approached — as in the first illustration — or does not take place —
as in the second — or does take place — in the third — in a series of little
events, of small encounters. When the anxieties have been identified —
differentiating those arising from the genetic imperatives, later elab-
orated into the superego, from those arising from the threat of the
force of the conjunction between desire and object, which might lead
to appetite, and those from the anxieties generated from a fear of
counterattack — the groundwork is laid for construction. I do not much
illustrate constructions as such here because the entire communication
is, essentially, a construction. In any case, the analysand ultimately
makes the better constructions; one's own are but the scaffolding and
the armature.

## REFERENCES

Bion, W. R. (1961). *Experiences in Groups*. New York: Basic Books.
_____ (1967). Attacks on linking. In *Second Thoughts*. New York: Basic Books.
Boris, H. N. (1976). On hope: its nature and psychotherapy. *International Review of Psycho-Analysis* 3:139–150.
_____ (1984a). On the problem of anorexia nervosa. *International Journal of Psycho-Analysis* 65:315–322.
_____ (1984b). On the treatment of anorexia nervosa. *International Journal of Psycho-Analysis* 65:435–442.
Boris, H. N., Zinberg, N. E., and Boris, M. (1975). Fantasies in group situations. *Contemporary Psychoanalysis* 11:15–45.
Erikson, E. (1950). *Childhood and Society*. New York: W. W. Norton.
Freud, S. (1925). Inhibition, symptoms, and anxiety. *Standard Edition* 20:87–174.
Klein, M. (1946). Notes on some schizoid mechanisms. In *Developments in Psychoanalysis*, ed. J. Riviere, pp. 292–320. London: Hogarth, 1952.
_____ (1957). *Envy and Gratitude*. London: Tavistock.
Meltzer, D. M. (1966). The relation of anal masturbation to projective identification. *International Journal of Psycho-Analysis* 47:335–442.

# 17

# Interpretation of Dreams, Interpretation of Facts

This essay goes to the question of whether Being precedes Consciousness or Consciousness precedes Being—whether belief creates reality or reality belief. Vaclav Havel in his February 1990 address to a joint session of Congress spoke of his "one great certainty" that the latter was true. It is not merely, then, a problem in epistemology; people have died to assert each position against the other. The implication of the debate is that worldmaking is an activity from which several features are derived, among them myth, reason, fiction and fact. Can any one of these lay claim to a status superior to another? In "Interpretation" I wrote as if there were a reality which people distort and to which interpretation in a cordial context might return them. I thought the secondary process, consensual validation, and the like represented a kind of reality that could be resurrected and restored.

Here I take an alternate view, namely, that facts are one rendition of experience, fictions another. Music might be a third. Thus if dreams are open to interpretation for the meanings concealed and expressed by meaning, so too are facts. A knife, that is, cuts two ways. It may be a symbol of a penis, but a penis may be a symbol for a knife. Science may represent the world, so may myth. For some time I had put forward the idea that narrative was spurious in that it lent an order to events which those events may not in fact have; now I should say that narrative orders events in one way, dreams, because of the particular simultaneities open to visual representation, an-

269

other. (A narrated dream is a probably a horse designed by a committee.)

In the social nexus people in groups talk about how many differences they have in common. (Wilde wondered, "What is the world coming to when we talk about our similarities instead of our differences?") Can discoveries be made before the nexus can stand them; or must discoveries be invented for a while? Sulloway argues that his data support a contention that younger siblings are less conservative than older and more prone to make scientific discoveries that break with tradition. Perhaps primogeniture inherits the earth as we know it and latter-geniture must find new worlds to conquer.

Falstaff, it has been remarked, is realler than any living man: he is so aburst with life that he seems to complete a prefiguration of what was meant to be. Is that what beauty is: the convex wall of the mold?

---

More than once Bion remarked that now we have *Interpretation of Dreams* we should have its companion volume: *Interpretation of Facts*. He felt this would provide "a two-way street." In this wish he was not alone. Winnicott, too, thought that now we know what the symbols of the penis are we might wonder what the penis symbolizes:

> Incidentally, it rather amuses me to make an exercise by saying "what is the penis symbolical of?" To some extent the penis is symbolical of a snake or of a baby's bottle or of the baby's body as it moved in the womb before the arms and legs became significant and before there were oral and anal zones. I think that in regard to the one way in which the idea of a penis develops where it is gradually constructed out of certain properties of the mother, then we have to think of a very fundamental concept, and have to say that the snake is symbolical of a penis. When we come, however, to the other extreme such as your son's observation of his penis and his mind-work on the subject, then I think we can look at it the other way and talk about the penis as symbolical of other more fundamental objects as, for instance, the tooth-brush or some other toy or, as I have said, of the fish or reptile that is understood because it is like the infant was at the dawn of impulse. [Winnicott 1956]

Regarding this matter of the symbol, Green (1986) quotes *Robert's Dictionary* to the effect that a symbol is, "an object cut in two, constituting a sign of recognition when its bearers can put together the two separate pieces." Let us take a leaf from Bion and Winnicott and suppose that there is a penis which is itself and at the same time symbolizes and is symbolized by other things. The latter idea is established: the familiar phallic symbols. But the former? What does a fact symbolize?

Psychoanalysis is about representations: about images, signs and signals. We say: there is a world in which things and events are as they are: they are actual; the secondary process can be trained and disciplined to perceive these accurately, to remember them clearly and to recall them faithfully. Using his secondary process, a person can learn to think dispassionately and in a cordial relationship to consensual or empirical traditions.

There is a real out there; a historical real and a current real, consisting of actual time and space of actual people and doings and of defined ways and procedures for apprehending them—for example, the methods of logic and experimentation.

We also say that there is a primary process at work whose relationship to the real and the actual is imaginative. It doesn't record, it represents; it doesn't discover, it invents; it doesn't recollect, it re-presents its old duplicitous images, images shaped by longing, tailored by fear. Wishful thinking, wishful dreaming, wishful perceiving, and wishful remembering.

We go on to speak of the tension between these processes and the forces that drive them—between the self-preservative and self-actualizing forces that edge us toward things as they are and the self-protective, pleasure-seeking forces that take us toward matters as we would wish them to be. This tension, we say, consists of a dialectic; at one and the same time what is, what we wish were, and what we feel ought to be coexist in uneasy proportion and in temporary compromise. Thus at any given moment truth exists only approximately.

But we never doubt there is a truth nor do we doubt that it is superior to the rather grossly self-serving shadow plays of the primary process.

Suppose further, however, that the world of facts were no more really real than that of representations of those facts. Or to put it another way, that the Real as a category was filled merely by representations of the real and that these representations were as tangential to what they represented (or claimed to represent!) as are the imagos and phantasms of the unconscious and its dreamlife.

If we suppose that, then we have a world represented by the canonical letter **X** of which we are of two (or more) minds. The superiority of the one mind to the other doesn't come into question any more than the superiority of French to English or Latin to Russian comes into question as a way of communicating between people about experience. What does come into prominence as mentocentrism recedes are the nature and characteristics of the various ways of apprehending **X** which cannot be known any longer, but to one another.

We are dealing then with not one but two mental constructs, which I propose to regard as functionally reciprocal. Together they constitute a duality, each portion of which serves as an alternative for one another — as one might say sleep and wakefulness do. I will go further: I will propose that the construction of these worlds provides definition for one another; they, so to say, tell each other apart, by providing comparison and contrast.

This means that a fact helps us to know what is fictional about a fiction as a fiction helps us to know what is factual about a fact. At the same time, however, the status of both fact and fiction require protection from one another. It is only partially useful to know our fictions are fictional; we need illusion, dream, make-believe, hope, play, metaphor — all the as-ifs, and we don't want to have them exploded by facts. The same holds true of our facts. As I have been suggesting, we have gone so far to protect them as to regard them as nearer to truth and so-ness — **X** — than fictions are. Indeed it is possible to suppose that this very cozening we provide to fact — the naive identity we give it with and to verity — suggests its innate frangibility. For we well know how approximate are our scientific approximations to truth; how this month's fact is next month's fallacy; how even mathematics, the very language of nature, as some regard it, is but a rendition, neither truer nor falser, neither closer to nor further from **X** than the fictions of the plastic arts or the abstract representations of music.

Facts, then, also need to be protected. Fictions cannot be permitted to explode them. Between fact and fiction exists an equipoise, an equilibrium in individual and cultural homeostasis. Each depends on the other's particular weight of means or force, to complement it and to distinguish it. Another metaphor might involve the idea of an ecosystem in which a delicate balance must be maintained. In this allegory, facts and fictions prey upon one another, competing for conviction; yet for each to survive, the other is required. Neither can grow too large, fierce, or greedy, for its ultimate fate depends upon the survival of the other.

In this respect, we might say that the very young—the infants and toddlers—need a heavy lading of illusion and fiction. They are too vulnerable to know what life is all about. We might suppose that if babies knew what fate awaited them, many would lose heart and give over. Thus we might think that if dreams do spin the web of illusion and wish, as they seem to, babies would need more of REM sleep than grown-ups. But we might equally suppose that dreaming becomes too dangerous after a while—that when the mother crossing the busy thoroughfare with her child gives it a sharp jerk on the hand, saying "stop dreaming and hurry up!" she might be reflecting this change in status.

Yet the foregoing is misleading because it deals in quantity, and it is the quality of fact and fiction and their relationship that I wish to examine. Quantity as an indication of equipoise is more useful as an illustration than an advertion.

The quality, then, of the twin constructions we make of X has to do with each one's robustness vis-à-vis the other. A delusion represents an experience of life. As Adelaide Johnson and others (e.g., Leston Havens) have supposed, delusions are not made up of whole cloth. No matter how idiosyncratic a delusion may seem, it often also seems to have a germ of historical or contemporary fact to it. A fact may in like manner have a germ of fiction to it. Is there anything, except accidentally, like pure fact or pure fiction? A fact such as the fact that the human personality exists has a dubious status. Exists? Exists where? Is it comprised of mind, and if so, of what is mind comprised? Brain? And brain tissue? Neuronal and synaptic activity? Molecules? Atoms? Particles? Waves? Is the human personality made up of subatomic waves? Yes, well. . . . And waves? At some point the fact seems no longer true, no longer a goodish approximation of X from the factual point of view. It might be more like science fiction than scientific fact. But is a Rembrandt portrait a better or worse approximation of the human personality than subatomic theory?

These are Philosophy 101 questions and points and hardly worth pursuing save to put forward the notion that for functional purposes fictions should not be too fictional and facts not too factual and that where one moves in one direction so must the other.

If fact and fiction function so as to provide alternatives for one another, and fictions are created by wishful or fearful thinking, what impels the creation — the discovery or invention — of facts? Is there a different motive force or do facts also fulfill (or seem to) wishes and allay fears?

The traditional argument is that if facts do have such functions, they serve the ego's wishes for self-preservation, for which a respectful knowledge of the real is necessary. The reality principle, that is to say, needs its reality.

This, on the face of it, would appear to be unexceptional. But we have already seen that reality is as relative as fiction — that the preservation of the self may, indeed, require irreal realities. Irreal realities are different from fictions because the latter are known to be irreal but the former are not. Indeed the former are decidedly not to be thought to be fictive (to think so would be as frightening in its way as to think that movie or television images are "true"). That is, facts concerning reality must be thought to be real and true even if they are not. How then are irreal facts to be distinguished from realer ones?

In the end, each individual arrives at something like the amount of reality he can bear. At the same time, the status of the fact is organized and mediated consensually — the truth of a fact is a matter of agreement. We need look no further into this than the matter of psychoanalytic facts — indeed psychoanalysis itself! For some benighted souls, psychoanalytic discoveries are science fiction. Oddly, they may spare those of us for whom the Oedipus complex, say, is a fact some passing sympathy. But within the ranks of those for whom the Oedipus complex is a fact are some for whom the death instinct is a fact — and happily? sadly? oddly? — those for whom it is not. Those for whom the Oedipus complex is a fact say: looked at psychoanalytically, these feelings, attitudes, behaviors reveal the presence of what we allusively call the Oedipus complex. We may feel that it is as much there as quarks or molecules, if people would only look properly — at the right data through the right instruments. But this argument is the same one made for the factual status of the death instinct, yet to many who find the argument persuasive of the Oedipus complex, it is as unpersuasive as theirs for the Oedipus complex is to those who see neither as a fact.

Yet psychoanalysts share with other workers in the vineyards of fact the same abiding belief — that there are facts to be found: that for questions there are true answers, one for each question, arrived at by a correct method of investigation, so that these answers will combine to form in the end an overarching field theory reflecting the **X**-ness of the universe. That is more than a hope; it is a conviction: there are timeless truths and finding them is therefore only a matter of time. This conviction is held to be just such a truth, though how it differentiates the astrologer from the astronomer is a difficult question. For as we take up the study of methods for arriving or knowing "truths," these begin to look rather less august and impeccable than their adherents believe and claim.

For even as we are "at work" at what the philosopher Nelson Goodman (1978) calls Worldmaking, we encounter what may also be a fact: namely, as Goodman puts it:

> With multiple and sometimes unreconciled and even unreconcilable theories and descriptions recognized as admissible alternatives, our notions about truth call for some reexamination. And with our view of worldmaking expanded far beyond theories and descriptions, beyond statements, beyond language, beyond denotation, even, to include versions and visions metaphorical as well as literal, pictorial and musical as well as verbal, exemplifying and expressing as well as describing and depicting, and distinction between true and false falls far short of marking the general distinction between right and wrong versions. What standard of rightness then, for example, is the counterpart of truth for works without subjects that present worlds by exemplification or expression? [p. 109]

With this I should like to juxtapose the strange bedfellows in minds like Newton's, whose ventures into the inferential formulations of the laws of thermodynamics were paralleled by inferential formulations concerning the nature of God which strike most physicists — but not Newton — as being crackpot. Newton appears to have regarded his work in both fields as equal in quality and validity. One can think that people like Newton (Alfred Russel Wallace, Darwin's cohort, is another example) sense out the holes in the fabric of knowledge and fill them one way or another. These fillings are confabulated in much the same way that split-brain people who must operate with each hemisphere of the brain necessarily working independently from the other do. The "right brain" sees or does, and the left brain rationalizes to "explain" activity of which it has no direct knowledge. (There is a school of thought of which Francis Crick, of DNA–double helix frame, is a prominent member, which holds that the dream as "remembered" narratively is equally spurious. In this school dreaming is a matter of random neural firing used to refresh, or a function of refreshing, synaptic chemical baths during sleep. Images flare as a by-product of this operation; and the perceiving brain, at the dreamer's behest, organizes these incoherent images into a structure that has a beginning in lieu of a prior, a middle in lieu of a subsequent, and an end instead of a last. If this were the case there might turn out to be a style of "remembering" or, at any rate, narrating dreams as unique as each individual is unique or as attuned to cultural fashions as, say, dreams recounted in novels or tribal myths. Surely dreams told prognosticators like Joseph by Pharaoh or told Jungian analysts differ from dreams told Freudians.)

Such confabulation, if it is that, arises out of the same processes of mentation and cogitation as "good" science. Bion's Grid drew particular attention to the possibilities of this kind of method for studying methods. Every mental product could be looked at not for its value in terms of fact or fiction, but for the use to which the thinker puts it. Thus a theorem might be used to fill a hole—or a dream might, or a hallucination might.

The "hole" must therefore occupy us for a while now. What manner of experience would one have if one lived in a "world" in which Mother Nature was unfathomable—was irrational, random, and devoid of meaning, fact, truth? Was, in fact, X-less? Where astrology and astronomy were equally baseless, and alchemy and chemistry equally confabulatory? Quite apart from producing drastic unemployment in universities and laboratories, libraries and schools, such a world would quite probably be intolerable. We can tolerate not knowing in some proportion to the expectation that there *is* something to know. The idea that we know nothing because there is nothing *to* know must be akin to the feeling that we have nothing now and, moreover, there is nothing there to have ever. Quite apart from what it might be filled with, such an absence and lack might be unbearable. A world so empty and cold, so barren and interminable a void would not be allowed.

Beckett captures something (but rather little considering the enormity of scale) of this in *Godot* and other plays. In these he takes matters to the point where there is no reason to do anything, even move from one place to the next, if there is no reason to do anything. One is propelled, in so far as one is impelled at all, by distant messages from the brain or gut. Survival—not as an idea or a *raison d'être*, but as a dimly sensed irritation, a plasmic itch—takes us from one action to the next, after which we await, without knowing we are awaiting, the next signal, if it ever comes.

This is considered unimaginably bleak, this stimulus — response — rest — stimulus . . . world. There must be something more, more to it, meaning, purpose, order, significance. And indeed, I believe, it is unimaginable even to glimpse, much less contemplate, a life, world, universe, past, present and future, devoid of something — as unimaginable as what an ameoba's life might be like. We are bound to anthropomorphize, to read our selves into, as if, were we not to fill the holes and gaps and ultimately interstices of being, we would be sucked out of ontologic existence into the vacuum with a whoosh. And be no more.

To preclude this we painstakingly construct a mental skin, cell by cell, dermis upon dermis, to sheathe and clothe and contain us. To this end fact and fiction do equally well. The creationist explanation and the evolutionist explanation both serve equally well to explain our origins, as do the origin myths of all the various peoples who populate the planet. These theories explain how and where and who and in doing so they explain us by defining us and distinguishing us from them. It is not, thus, the theory itself so much as its use. A so-called factual or scientific theory, such as the primal soup plus lightning theory and a so-called mythic theory such as the Genesis theory have no difference in status when considered as theories to provide meaning and direction in the temporal flow → from left to right spatially, from before to now →. Each theory is the functional equivalent of the other in saying there was a beginning and a perfecting and a direction. Each says that better is yet to come — that we are evolving or devolving to a better, richer, fuller, more complete plane, planfully, comprehensibly, and with some deeper purpose, some guiding principle.

That there is more than one explanation makes each righter and less right than they might seem if there were only one. Thus theories regarded as facts serve the same comparison–contrast competitive balance function as fictions and facts provide to one another. This means of adducing confirmatory validity through contrast makes each man's facts seem more factual and the other's fictions seem the more fictional. That in turn serves to keep one's own facts from being too hard and jeopardizing necessary fictions — for they are comparatively substantial without being too painfully true.

The skin contrived to sheathe and shield, so to keep us from being sucked into the nameless void, also, however constrains. Today's facts stand between us and yesterday's, but also tomorrow's. Semi-truths guard us from whole truths which are nothing but the truth, but also keep us from them. Psychoanalytic theory informs, but it also conceals what might be knowable beyond it. It is said, and with, I think, some truth, that the world has not been the same since Freud. But not only is there no going back to the world before Freud, there is the problem of how to go forward—how to see matters afresh. Freud's great light throws a great shadow. We have then the possibility of increasing the light, of extending it in all directions, of attempting more, seeing more, and getting better at it. But amiable as such increments are, do we know more of the truth, if there is one—more of the **X**—or only more of the psychoanalytic truth? If we know more of merely the psychic truth, we increase the light, but also the density of the obscuring shadow. The void is held at bay by the cheerful light of the campfire, but so too is what else might be out there. Paradoxically facts hide truths as well as fictions do, and sometimes better; even, as we saw earlier, fictions reveal and illuminate truths as well as or better than facts.

Both are equal in their potential for conveying pain and hence fright—and for protecting us from it. When one piece of either feels too menacing, it needs to be replaced so that the experience can be reconfigured. Either can replace whatever bit is being excised or needing transfiguration. The only requirement is that it fit seamlessly into the fabric in order that its counterfeiting presence go unnoticed. Once again, it is the use of the idea that must engage us. Fact or fiction, one no less than the other, can transform an unbearable experience. Each can be used truthfully or otherwise.

One of the more fundamental decisions the very young must make has to do with whether Mother could but won't or would but can't. (There are, to be sure, also question of can't, but wouldn't if she could; or, can't but would if she could, etc. But these are variants, and the simpler alternative will serve well enough.)

One reading provides hope, the other despair. Out of hope, the child will continue to try. Out of the despair, the child will abandon hope and go on to other things or other people. But before either of these courses can be taken there is the moment (though it might be years) of decision—a time of crisis (though the crisis may be chronic rather than acute). Can she or can't she—or is it will she or won't she?

The decision is as vexing as it is momentous. How does one tell, how can one know? When does one know? When has one had enough experience to decide? If it is true that she can't, why keep reconstituting one's self in the hope that she will? If it's true that she can, why leave off trying? On the other hand, if she can't, who can? Can one stand the idea that no one can provide? Perhaps it is better to think that she won't. Because if it is only that she won't, there's still this to try or that or, then again, nothing to try, because if one tries nothing it won't come clear that the problem is actually that she can't. What kind of knowledge does one want? Know the truth because the truth will set you free? Or elaborate a fiction, since the fiction is the font of hope and possibility?

Each would help — the one to go through hopelessness and on to other things; the second to renewed hope and further trying. If one wants to be Mother's one and only and not merely her child, what's to be done? How does one know when or whether to say to hell with it, and go off and get married to someone else — or when to try getting older or smarter or nicer, or is it less masculine or maybe tougher? Each would help with the frustration inherent in the fact — or is it a fiction? — that Mother isn't, whether she can't or won't.

Which to take, of the two ways out of the slough of despair we call the Oedipus complex, would surely riddle any sphinx, let alone a quite new young man or woman. Poised hard up against the fact (or is it a figment?) that Mother isn't, does one go with the soothing fiction or with the painful fact? (Or does one hedge by "splitting" self or Mother, so there are more possibilities and fewer eggs in one basket? — an inventive solution, which creates more facts or, at any rate, factors.) The epistemological question of how one knows what one knows surely comes into play; for though the child cannot read the future and know what Mother *will* be, he has every reason to know what he knows about Mother so far. Shall he continue to know what he knows or should he doubt it? Should he replace bits of it or give emphasis to other bits, so to change the reading? There are, here, two sources of knowledge. He remembers Mother, and he perceives her. The two must correspond, or, if discrepant, at least be justified in some way. If he proposes not to know what he knows, what of his perceptions? If he proposes to see Mother differently, what of his memories? The fact that Mother is more cordial when he is good can be used falsely. The look on Mother's face when he stood naked on the edge of the bathtub can be used factually to establish a fiction. The question — how does one know? — can be used to inquire or to cast doubt. Between the two uses there may be no more difference than that between a blink and a wink, but that difference, if mistaken may make all the difference in the world, as Clifford Geertz observes, to the status of one's nose.

We can't stand to know and can't stand not to, and this dialectic is the crucible out of which what we discover and tolerate as facts and what we invent and preserve as fictions is fashioned. When a bit of either sort of knowledge has to be omitted something must fill the gap it leaves. The filling must block out the repressed, but it must not call attention to itself. It must look as it always was.

Let us now turn to the usefulness of fact as generative of the illusion that the truth is known. Answers to questions can be indefinitely postponed in service to the quest for further knowledge. Facts can be accumulated by painstaking research in order to establish that the quest is productive. But looked at with a less cordial eye, these same facts can be seen to rationalize a quest that is itself quite possibly false.

An example might be the entire concept of psychological development and underlying that the view of time as a continuum flowing like a river from a beginning to an ending. With Einstein's theory of relativity out went linear time, as a fixed or singly determinate matter. An anthropomorphic concept of time had to give way as surely as the Ptolemaic to the Copernican view of the universe. Yet there is undoubtedly something pleasing to the old, linear concept of time. In it events could be read from left to right (or up to down). There was an order of earlier to later that suited a wish for progression in which something like lower gave way to something like higher.

Though there have been disputes (and indeed bitter and schismatic disputes) in the psychoanalytic movement, there is scarcely to be found a dispute that there *is* developmental hierarchy. Whether it is oral → post-oedipal or PS → depressive or psychotic → mature or normal or trust → generativity or . . . or . . . or →→→ There is a heavy lading of betterness on the right side of the arrow. ("Better" and "right" indeed!) This is consonant, of course, with our ideas concerning cure or getting better. Freudians may and do argue (like the schoolmen of old with their angels and pins) what a post-oedipal genital sexual experience is like. And ego psychologists may argue Kleinian attributions of ego mechanisms to the infant. And Neo-Freudians may introduce cultural relativism to the Viennese delegation. And the children of the information age and of the neuronal sciences may adduce their new facts and figurations. But all agree (hence the bitterness of the dispute) that there must be a better and a worse *and it must be factual.*

The uncordial eye will note the enfolding of psychoanalytic virtue and the Judeo-Christian hierarchies of virtue (I myself wrote a book called, after Socrates, *The Unexamined Life*). That eye might sardonically note that it is only the so-called factual status of our Jacob's Ladder of virtues that keeps us distinct from our theological brothers.

(Alternative versions such as those involved in field theory have not really survived a theory that has sublimation in it. But what would become of the longing that we are intimately a part of our own and other's betterment?)

That there are facts to support the developmental hypothesis goes without saying. Infants undeniably develop, and so far as I can tell, as they develop they need less overenthusiastic mental activity. But I think infants and children "develop" right out of certain qualities too. Youngsters have certain capacities for abstraction and imagination which some outgrow. Facts for them begin to supplant fictions in piecing together the fabric of an endurable world.

## IMPLICATIONS FOR CONDUCTING PSYCHOANALYSIS

I propose now to look at the foregoing in the context of psychoanalytic treatment. In particular I want to raise or re-raise some questions that seem to me to follow from the consideration of facts I have been so far making.

Let us begin with the analysis itself. We are prepared to offer an experience, to be part of it and to observe it. A big part of our being part of it is to be self-effacing. We want as much as possible to permit the analysand to encounter him- or herself. None of us know how to do this, but we are open to discovering how. We are prepared to take what few facts we know (or imagine we know) into the encounter with us, but equally prepared to abandon them if need be.

We may start, for instance, with the idea of free association in a 50-minute hour that recurs four or more times a week. But what if our co-worker does not care to lie on the couch, put what he experiences into words, spend the time we proposed with us? We might wish to further "orient" our cohort, but to what? It is true that he or she never conducted an analysis with him- or herself and ourself before, but then neither have we with him or her. Does training come into it? Do we gain an expertise from training and experience? I should hope we do!

But is it other than being less afraid and more open, more versatile and less controlling? Do we not therefore reconjure matters so that the self-encounter remains central even though much else changes?

As to that self-encounter, is something to come of it? Can we know? Can we even know the form it will take? Will the encountering spirit be that of a Rembrandt or a Newton or of a Sullivan? (Or, as someone recently dreamt it, a pinkish piglet?)

As for ourselves, we are prepared to act as interpreter, performing the introduction, translating when necessary. That function is so simple it is terribly difficult to do.

Imagine a summit between the President and the General Secretary in which the interpreters subtly or otherwise had agendas of their own. A worse nightmare might be when the interpreters thought their job was simply to make matters lucid but unbeknownst to themselves introduced bias and unintended nuance. Merely calling "hatred" "hostility" or calling "loathing" "anger" could seriously confuse matters. The wink and the blink earlier mentioned applies here too. One hopes that when, indeed, the interpreter is confused as to what the *mot juste* might be, he chat it over with his opposite number until they get it just so.

The self's widening deepening encounter with self is augmented by just such interpretations going in both directions. The observed self needs to know just as much about the observing self as the latter does about it. They cannot be bothered with the interpreter and his needs, particularly when those needs appear to cause him to side with one or another party to the encounter. His so-called neutrality is just that. He is a translucent medium through which light flows but which contributes nothing additional of its own. The personalities of the artist or scientist are invisible to the beholder, and as the analysand becomes reconciled to sharing the experience not with a transference object, self or other, but with a hard-working interpreter, his interest in himself will increase correspondingly. His artistry and his science, his facts and fictions will be open for knowing, and as the jewel ultimately irradiates itself through the refractions from cut to cut and facet to facet, so does insight function (Meltzer quoting Bion, 1986).

The analyst's analysis will tell him much about his fictions. But then we must begin the arduous and inevitably lonely process of interpreting our facts.

# REFERENCES

Goodman, N. (1978). *Ways of Worldmaking*. Cambridge: Hackett.

Green, A. (1986). *On Private Madness*. Madison, CT: International Universities Press.

Meltzer, D. (1986). *Studies in Extended Metapsychology*. Perthshire: Clunie.

Winnicott, D. W. (1956). To Gabriel Caruso. In *The Spontaneous Gesture: Selected Letters of D. W. Winnicott*, ed. F. R. Rodman, pp. 98–100. Cambridge, MA: Harvard University Press, 1987.

# 18

# Beyond the Reality Principle

Freud was himself unhappy with the Reality principle, probably because it states the obvious without also stating the unobvious. That is, surely people live in some way consonant with reality and behave self-preservatively, modifying their intemperate urges as need be. But when they do not, are they simply mad or in the grip of chaos? Are they anhedonic by neurosis or by nature? The Pleasure principle requires its reaction-formations and sublimations if it is not to sink of its own weight. But the trouble with these contra actions is that they seem to exhaust the matter, though I do not think they do.

My own generalizations are based in part on patients, adult and child, who seem to me to be always slightly abstracted, as if listening for a message about what the better choice might be, and feeling, while they are awaiting revelation, that they will be done for if they don't find it. It is as if they have a mandate only part of which has been transmitted, and at that perhaps in somewhat garbled form. But they know themselves to be under orders, and like good soldiers, await first clarification, and then the inevitable question—Do you copy? Many of these instructions, so far as I have been able to tell, have to do with seeing to the future destiny of that part of the species homo sapiens which should be preserved (this is akin to what Bion meant by his "Basic Assumptions Group"). I have accordingly found it useful to keep an ear out for the ideas people formed as children, really as infants, regarding what their aspirations and obligations in

285

this respect might be. The superego and the ego-ideal, that is to say, are categories that precede their contents and indeed organize those contents as these come along or seem to.

If there is anything to the ideas, they should be found elsewhere — indeed, they should be looked for in the Oedipus drama itself. There are (to my mind) two hints: one is the generational implication of the riddle (never mind its ironic foretelling of the need Oedipus will have to use a stick); the other is the nature of the plague. The latter may be read as an agronomic representation of the dire results of inbreeding. Deranged leaders of the Selection brigades go in for racial purity; *Mein Kampf* is about this: we can never sleep safely with these Lysenkovian dreamers in our midst. There is something in us that responds to the Pied Piper.

In evolutionary theory of the Darwinian kind, there are three choices concerning who is selected and who selects. Perhaps the traditional one is that the members of a species are selected by predation and ecological pruning more generally, with the weaker members out of, and the more adaptive members in, the reproductive pool. Thus the species is always, if passively, being refined or at least redefined.

A second view holds that there is more to selection than passively sustained events — that members of a species contend for their personal survival and, by luck of that, their immortality as gene providers to the generation to come. This view opens up the matter of choice — if members of species choose one another, on what basis do they make their choices? That question leads in turn to the next step down (the first being the species as a whole, the second the enrollment of individuals within a species) The next or third level is the DNA. Genes are said, selfishly, to induce choosing behavior. That is, it is in the gene where the program for the choosiness is inscribed. On this face of it, this would seem arrant nonsense. Are *we* mere agents for our genes; do they ride piggyback on us? Worse, are they down there in the navigator's station calling the shots? And even if they were, by what means would the genes make their wishes known?

How genes "know" what to call for, if they do, is another, but easier question. Gene X-beta knows what gene X-beta knows and the fact that it has survived and is not recessive means that it and not Y-alpha prevails(ed). But how do genes (if they do) say, "Hey, get me something really good. And by good, I mean. . . ."

I do not know the answer to that, but I think there may be one; the essay here is set out as an approximation to the sort of answer it might turn out to be. You will see that for my answer I need premonition and preconception as hypothetical categories into which cultural information will flow — if the latter fits without distending.

Infants by 2½ months watch all the tricks they are shown concerning a ball appearing here and reappearing there with a good deal of interest — if interest is defined by the length of the time they look at the show. But if they are shown a ball reappearing on the other side of an impermeable barrier, as if it had rolled through a solid board, they really have a look. The experimenter seems to feel that infants by this age have preconceptions about what the world is like. If they do, can they also have preferences?

---

To gain the dynamic for conflict and compromise and tensions and harmonies among the structures, Freud juxtaposed the Pleasure and the Reality principles. Opposing and modifying forces came from transmutations of the id's energies as borrowed or structured by other intrapsychic agencies. Although the attribution of an id by Freud to humankind was to link man with other creatures, Freud may not have considered the full thrust of his idea. Could there be another energy source in humans than the pleasure and appetitive centers of the soma working through the id? And could it be this source working through *its* principle that provides the impetus for the mutative influences and conflicts of humankind? In this paper the Reality principle is reconsidered in terms of its explanatory power relative to a hypothesis of another such source and principle.

This alternative hypothesis yields a view of each of us as being simultaneously a member of a couple and a pair, and of intra-psychic and interpersonal life as a being an ongoing dialectic between the two. The Oedipus complex, for example, is a statement of facts and a very good way of approximating people's experience of the world when they are viewing the world from the point of view of being a member of a couple. But it is not, by the same token, a very good hypothesis when approximating people's experience of the world when they are viewing it from the point of view of being a member of a pair.

## METAPSYCHOLOGICAL PERSPECTIVES

From the Project (1895) on, Freud knew he needed an alternative energy source to account for the ebb and flow of dynamic conflict and the offsetting forces of symptom, and later character, formation. If the id were driven by the soma to make cathexes, whence came the other energy source? His answer is well known. The censoring forces

Sleights of Mind

(subsequently, in structural theory, the ego) borrowed energy from the id and neutralized it of its purely libidinal and aggressive qualities; left over was a somewhat sublimated source to counter and modify the rough and ready energies of the id based upon the ego's contacts with social reality. Thus there came to be two great principles: the Pleasure principle and the Reality principle.

As a theory, this is by no means a bad one. It allows the alive body to be the original font; this source of energy is modified into mental energy, thus the id; and the id's energy is further modified into ego energy or attention cathexis, which can be used to attach to, or to counter, or to merge in, mutual modification of its original sources. Out of a monistic thrust, dualism becomes possible, and with dualism all the dynamics and paradoxes of Mind.

Freud (1920) was sufficiently dissatisfied with the secret monism of this formulation to invoke a more fundamental dualism: that of the life and death instincts, a kind of physics that included ideas of rest or nirvana, repetition, entropy, and the return of the parabola to inorganicity. But this Thanatropic energy was clinically impoverished. Surely not every conflict or compromise formation embodied such awesome contenders. So after a bit it dwindled in his own thinking, and only the Kleinian conceptualizations continued with it as a force which had aim and object (Klein 1952). Freud returned to thinking along the lines of the Pleasure and Reality principles.

Within these, we have humankind barely descended from primitivism encountering dangers to its satisfactions, indeed its very survival as an aggregation of individuals, unless each bridles his lusts and accommodates them to the milieu. On the other hand there is the human who is in equal danger of becoming so bridled that he thwarts his lively lusts and turns out to be a repressed, neurasthenic shell. The latter is the work of the superego, which may be equally fanatic and phantasmic, for it too receives its energies only more or less transformed from the id. The ego has, in this model, to mediate between Victoria and the Beast, using its Janus faces to keep itself informed of the interiors of its being while at the same time shrewdly navigating through life's dangers to its enduring and possible pleasures.

That any one of us can identify with that scenario makes the structure and its implied narrative persuasively[1] attractive. Thus despite certain questions, the theory is emotionally an engaging one.

---

[1]Anthropomorphically

But questions there remain all the same. If the so-called economic question is perhaps the central of these, there are other questions as well. Is there really such a transformation and redirection of energies as Freud posited?

## AN ALTERNATIVE PERSPECTIVE

Freud did not hesitate to adduce originological explanations not available to other students of his day. The Primal Horde, mentioned already, was one; the foundations of his work on Moses and Mono-theism was another (he referred to it as "an historical novel"). But, perhaps because he needed a primitive animalism for the "boiling cauldron" of the id, and the universality of the Oedipus complex and its taboos, he did not far outreach nineteenth and early twentieth century notions of a kind of fang-and-claw animal nature. Indeed even to impute to humankind—especially to children!—an animal nature was, in Freud's view, as revolutionary and infuriating to establishment and Victorian narcissism, as Copernicus and Darwin had been before him.[2]

Now, a hundred years later, we have from ethologists, biologists, anthropologists, and students of infant and child development the basis for a rather different view of our fellow denizens. They have turned out to be rather more like ourselves than different; except perhaps for the virus, they are less destructive to themselves and others than we. And evidence continues to accrue in support of the Dar-winian hypothesis that (*pace* teleology) they act as if "their job" were to survive, to select, and to be selected so to reproduce to best advantage for the survival and perpetuation of the species.

As the ecology changes, so change the features penultimately chosen and ultimately available for choice. Indeed, what an outside observer may regard as the bundled features that define a species and who its constituents are, is not necessarily the view held from within: what the

---

[2]Of Copernicus, placing us not in the center of our universe, but upon "a tiny speck in a world system of a magnitude hardly conceivable"; of Darwin, a revolution that "robbed man of his peculiar privilege of having been specially created, and relegated him to a descent from the animal world"; of Freud's own, "endeavoring to prove to the 'ego' of each one of us that he is not even master of his own house, but that he must remain content with the veriest scraps of information about what is going on unconsciously in his own mind."

observer may think to be a subspecies may be regarded by the membership as a species unto itself. Homo sapiens, for example, may exist as a species only in the pages of a taxonomist; to the people involved the race or caste, nation or religion, town or group, may represent the boundary and insigniation. And in given ecologies, even subspecies' strategies vary. Some involve competition, some cooperation. But the function of these units and strategies appear to serve the purposes of the ultimate survival of whatever mysterious something it is that constitutes the essence of the species.[3]

But the fact appears to be that whatever its function or functions, this directional thrust is as close to being universal as are the other invariants mentioned.[4]

If that is so — if it is the case that species are driven by a species-specific survival mandate, then this imperative would also have to be in the germ plasm as a proactive force quite like whatever other principles to which they are subject. There would have not merely to be constraints and limits on the quest for sheer pleasure and self-perpetuation. There would also have to be a proactive force or principle in addition to the libido and the drive for egoistic self-preservation — something more or other than coupling and forming a couple: something perhaps in the way of what could be termed bonding, pairing, and forming a group.

This readiness to form adhesions of a noncoupling sort also would, in turn, affect the relationships the twosome might form in respect to a third, fourth (and *n*th others): the twosome in its couple mode might have one relationship, the twosome in its pair (pack, group) mode another. Moreover, whether any two would form a couple or a pair, or to what extent they would form each, might require a modicum of agreement, at least if the interest were to be in pairing. Were the two merely predatorially to use one another as objects, as members of different species routinely do, the species would not last long. (Rather

---

[3]Lewis Thomas, in his book *Lives of a Cell* (New York: Viking Press, 1974), notes that individual cells appear in some sense to recognize like and unlike, a phenomenon much involved in tissue and organ transplants from one person to another. Strictly speaking, a species is defined by the range of creatures that can reproduce one with another.

[4]In the matter of function, *original* and *current* functions may vary; selection is opportunistic; features selected for one thing may evolve into another. Feathers, for example, may have evolved for purposes of improved thermal regulation but survived due to their ability to enable the flight of birds (Gould 1987, p. 122).

than the survival of the fittest, it would be a matter of the predation of the choicest — of cannibalism, pillage, rape, and murder).

The question then arises whether what is true of other species is also true of our own.[5]

For example, anthropologically speaking, though peoples vary widely, there are no known peoples without a variety of limits, or, depending on one's point of view, opportunities, governing choice. There are no peoples, for example, without a kinship system, marking who is within and who outside of the realm of choice; none without a tribal or other group (e.g., national) identity and boundary; none without an aesthetics; none without a hierarchy of one sort or another. We may wonder whether the function of such levels or boundaries, such as the kinship structure, is, as Levi-Strauss has argued, a matter to permit the barter of brides, or as Freud argued, a derivation of an incest taboo (Freud 1913, Levi-Strauss 1973). But the fact appears to be that whatever its function or functions, it is as close to being universal as are the other invariants mentioned. Does this apparent fact have a bearing in considering man's natural endowments, including the principles on which he can be said to work?

## THE QUESTION OF PRINCIPLES REOPENED

Suppose we were to regard this question of the various principles as still open and look again for another stream to the dualism in man's nature, a dualism necessary for the formulations of mutually modifying influences of conflict and compromise and the other phenomena Freud wished to understand dynamically. Suppose we were to posit another dualism, but rather than calling them the Pleasure and the Reality principles, for the moment address them simply as the $X$ and the $Y$ principles.

Let $X$ be characterized as is the Pleasure principle (Lust-Unlust). It wants, and it wants what it wants now, and woe to anyone or anything that stands in its way. It is ruthless and egoistic and wanton.

---

[5]Or vice versa. The Darwinian unit is in the classic sense taken to be the individual body, not the gene "below" or the species "above." But since not just morphology, but behaviors, are heritable, it can be that different species are selected along somewhat different lines, particularly by dint of the behaviors involved. (See also Gould 1983, pp. 173–174)

Let $Y$ also be characterized by wants, but by slightly different wants. Let $Y$'s wants be characterized by man's behest to the rule of nature in which not just the individual wants, but the species also wants, and perforce must speak through the individual, sometimes in counter to the individualistic egoism of $X$. An $X$-want might be to pursue selfish pleasures in a life prolonged to do so. A $Y$-want might be to join the best regiment the armed services has to offer, there to sacrifice one's life if necessary in deference to the wishes of the subspecies or nation to which one belongs.

$X$ and $Y$ together comprise a two-track system, sometimes extending in serene parallel, sometimes overlapping, sometimes congruent, sometimes at oblique or crossing angles. Their wellsprings are, we might hazard, in the same plasm: the libidinal drive for orgiastic pleasure exists in correspondence with the need of the species to propagate itself. But where the libidinous wish may urge one toward the nearest and the most, the $Y$ wish urges waiting for the best and the finest.

What is propinquitous barely needs cognitive discovery. The newborn infant can already make the rooting reflex manifest, turning its mouth toward whatever touches its cheek. In its $X$-like way it will suckle and feed ruthlessly, indifferent to its mother's fate, if indeed it even bothers to discover a motherly presence in the shadows behind the nipple and breast. But few infants continue to rape, pillage, and steal — to treat mother and other as mere objects put their for their delectation. Somewhere in that same plasm is a readiness to discover and allow for Mother. Somewhere there is an urge to discern bad from good and good from better.

It is difficult to know with any certainty when that urge awakens. To know this one has to know when the discriminatory powers get into working order and when there is the content necessary to inform the decisions. At this writing there is an accumulating body of evidence that the newborn can discriminate its mother's visage and voice within hours after their becoming neonatally acquainted.[6] But to discern is not necessarily to inform with meaning or value: pigeons can discern eight different human facial expressions on photographs. In the $X$ sense, of course, repletion is the A-Number-One value and meaning: the feedback information comes from within. In the $Y$ sense, the information as to quality has to some degree to do with the species —

---

[6]See, for example, Beebe and Lachman 1988.

really, the subspecies, or what I shall also call the Group. It exists as a potential, a category ready to be filled in; but as a potential, as a category, it exists as a preconception that does not need to be taught but only waits for the Group to give it the information to make it a conception. It may not know *what* constitutes good and bad or better and best, but it knows that there *is* something to know, something to fit into these categories and blanks on the map. *Y* may be thought of as being no less greedy and grateful for food for thought than *X* is for food for the belly: no less greedy and grateful for completion than *X* is for repletion.

The earmark of humankind as a species, it has been said, is our relative brainpower. Where other species have their choices enprogrammed, and thus may leave the parent or group earlier than we, we can, but also must, stay around to learn what we are to do. Birds appear to know some portion of their subspecies song, needing only to fill in a few blanks; and strange indeed are the songs of birds which are raised with a flock of a kind not their own. Overall, the issue of choice has to be arranged between and within; neighboring species must maintain a difference from one another, and also within the group. When there is relative isolation of closely related groups, the species can allow the characteristics that previously differentiated them from their cousins to drop away in favor of greater distinctions within. Human beings, however, have choosiness together with a wealth of choices to choose among. For us, education and training are not only possible but necessary. Not for (most of) us simply the biggest pair of antlers around, or even the biggest bankroll or highest rank or tallest penthouse on the rightest side of town. Our choosiness is perhaps more subtle, and what is chosen varies from place to place, class to class, peoples to peoples. But have we any less choosiness for all that our choices are so various?

At some point in time, the infant, let us imagine, goes beyond his libidinous interest in Mother; he actually chooses her. *X* joins *Y*. She is now not only a gratifying body to be around, but a quality person, really quite ideal. Fill in Space 1 of Category *Y* with a valentine heart that says Mom on it. Now as to Space 2, how about what Mom likes, like not having her nipples bitten too hard? In the words of the comedian,[7] Miss Right is taking over from Miss Right Now.

Let's take that small instance of biting, largely because it so much

---

[7] Robin Williams, in his appearance at Carnegie Hall.

part of the canons of psychoanalytic theorizing. What have we here? Ego learning the reality that when mother gets bitten once too often, nursing time stops? Ego identifying with mother and being conscience-bitten by mother's mouth as superego? The paranoid position being fashioned out of a reattribution of the authorship of the impulse to sadistically bite, and thereby the introduction of talion anxiety? The paranoid-schizoid giving over to the perception of the whole object — that there is a mother attached to the breast — and with this newfound concern, the introduction of the depressive position. Ruthlessness surrendering to gratitude and a lovingly generous longing to preserve the good, kind object?

That there is marvelous fertility in the plethora and richness of these explanatory hypotheses must surely go without saying. But they also form something of a hodge-podge. And that weltering quality bespeaks the condition inevitable when not distinguishing between experiences generated when the mother and baby are being members of a Couple and when members of a Pair. As such, it more broadly illustrates the confusion that dogs psychoanalysis when, as a psychology of the Couple, it wishes to allude to matters arising out of the Pair.

The alternative point of view, proposed first by Bion, and which would organize the hypotheses is of the hollow cube where now line AB

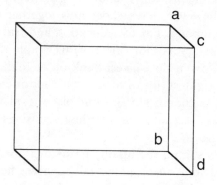

and now line CD seems forward, as each reverses from figure to ground.[8] The model is of a socklike affair, where the substance remains constant while what is outermost and innermost, dominant or recessive, changes.

---

[8]The "facing profiles" and the "vase" do as well for those more familiar with them.

Thus in the earliest days of infancy, one must suppose now a alternation of the streams of $X$-wants and $Y$-wants with now a merger, now a divergence, with $X$ still wanting to chew and bite and couple ruthlessly, while $Y$ wants equally passionately to select Mother for longer term Pairing and, as Others are discovered, for Grouping. I say "equally passionately" to stay well away from ideas concerning a neutering of energy or the development of ambivalence or the establishment of mental structures. I am suggesting that libido found, and then choosiness agreed. It does not always: the ideal may embrace what the libido does not. But when the quest for the good and the best has lighted upon its objective, the libido may have to go elsewhere or surrender. Often indeed it goes with. The Right and the Best release all the love of spring and summer, as does the crown of antlers the procreative passions of the doe. In our example, however, not only has her baby selected Mother, but he has thrown in his lot with her. He has not only, in $X$, taken her as his object, he has, in $Y$, taken her as a leading member of a group of two. Love me, love my dogma. And he does.

In this, we have a further aspect in the characterization of $Y$. It seeks quality and makes it a part of how and why it chooses objects and objectives. But in doing so, in filling in the empty categories with criteria, it identifies itself with the tastes and choices of the group. $Y$, being species-specific, has the group in mind, or at any rate is ready to have it in mind. The activity of the species is the survival of the species through the sending of the finest and fittest into and down the gene pools of the generations. It begins with selecting what the fittest and finest are, it protects them, and ultimately it propagates them. $Y$ is choosy by nature. $X$ seeks *repletion*, $Y$ *completion*. By necessity, therefore, they have two different time structures, $Y$ waiting to find and choose for later, $X$ interested in the here, now, and often — Miss Right and Miss Right Now.

$Y$, then, delays $X$'s gratifications with its fastidiousness and longer view; left to is own devices, $Y$ might procrastinate choice forever if it weren't for intemperate nudging from $X$.

$X$, it is turning out, is interested in differences, particularly reciprocal differences, as between mouth and breast and vagina and penis; $Y$ with alliances which involve having things in common, particularly the finer things. $X$ is interested in coupling with the Other, $Y$ in identifying and pairing with it or grouping with them. $X$ chooses to take pleasure in even the smallest differences, $Y$ overlooks even the largest ones in order to find or fashion having as much in common as it takes to feel at One with them. But when $Y$ prevails and groups with the others $X$ might have wished to use libidinously, $X$ has its turn. For $X$, augmented in fact or in fancy, with the host of all-for-one/one-for-alls $Y$ has fashioned out of what was to $X$ an aggregate of different possibilities, has now the prerogatives, given only to the crème de la crème, of enforcing its wish or will upon the objects the group deems suitable for use by $X$. $X$ insists on this.

If $X$ has to give up its object in whole or in part because at $Y$'s behest they have become part of Us, $X$ insists on the quid quo pro of there being Non-Us objects for its pleasure or aggressive employ. If there are none, if the immediate object world consists only of people or aspects of people linked in $Y$, $X$ will force a breakdown into a subpairing or subgrouping which, when effected, will cast forth objects fit for coupling. This sort of subspeciation accommodates both $X$'s need for pleasure of its sort and $Y$'s need for choosing the finest and fittest from which to give and take selective advantage. Thus a twosome can agree, as a Pair, in $Y$, to enjoy coupling within the bounds of that twosome, or not, as weaning traditions or incest prohibitions may dictate. But no matter the behavior, no matter how wanton, aggressive, or concupiscent it may be, there is a cusp of $Y$-ness around it: the Pair has agreed even that perhaps the Couple may kill one another.

That such lust is blessed by the Pair, moreover, permits degrees of license that the superego, based as it is on the couple and triangle, might otherwise prevent. The Pair and Group work through shame, the Couple in its configuration of the oedipal triangle, through guilt. Shame bespeaks the ideal; guilt the internalized danger from wrong-doings that are transgressions against the rivalrous Father or Mother. Sullivan (1953) shrewdly observed that the way out of crippling guilt that might otherwise bring madness is for the child to find an group alternative to his parental group and superego. Thus a youngster as a member of an actual or reference group can, for example, shoplift a store when that same child as part simply of a Couple could not feel free to do so.

$Y$ has yet another aspect to it beyond the need to choose not well, but wisely. It is to be among the chosen — the selected. The latter conjoins the $X$-stream wish to take one's pleasures at no matter who's expense by introducing the desire to prevail over one's rivals. But, inherently, it is a wish to compete successfully. Part of such success depends on how one fares as the object of others' choices. This urge (or, as we shall see, necessity) is approximated by the narcissistic endeavor to find favor, first in one's own eyes, then as one is seen through the eyes of others — this is "others" in the sense Kohut (1972) uses the term "self objects"; and, finally as one is indeed seen through the eyes of one's own chosen ones. (As is well known, it is possible to get mired at any point in this progression.)

The necessity I refer to follows from the apprehension that one will not prevail, that one is not among the Select, that is, those selected. Not all of the actual or potential litter are destined to survive: selection begins early. Klein identified the complex experience children have at "prevailing" over their own unborn rivals (cf. Klein 1945). (I have myself written of the dread of people who as infants were not assured in some way that their success in gaining birth and beyond was meant; that they are not imposters: Boris 1987)

Like others among the creatures, man is biologically a social animal; he is tribal, territorial, hierarchical. All these qualities exist because they are required in order that choice and selection can be made. $Y$ exists as the chooser and hence the inhibitor and the releasor of $X$. The dimly surmised premonition that there is a $Y$ that goes two ways is, I think, the source of dread attributed to the Death instinct. Many are called, but few are chosen.

From this point of view, $Y$ functions with $X$ very like the Reality principle is thought to function in respect to the Pleasure principle. Each augments and inhibits the other in a ceaseless dynamic.

Interpersonally, this dynamic modulates the extent to which the Other is chosen as a Self-Us-Same person and how much as an Other-Them-Different person. In juxtaposition with this parsing, there are for $X$ seemly and unseemly choices with whom to celebrate its well-known lust for reciprocally celebrating differences. Thus every relationship is compounded in some measure of identifications and differentiations. There may be great harmony between self and other in sorting out how much of $X$ and how much of $Y$ may come into their relationship. And, of course, for each there may be the usual irretrievable conflict between having what one wants and wanting what one has.

One man's reality may be another man's nonsense. Reality, in any case, can only be dimly apprehended. Freud's idea of the primary and secondary processes, the one a grossly self-serving creature, driven by wish and craven by fear, the second, a mature soul attuned to empirical and logical pursuits, is but one way of sorting matters out. Another may be more pluralistic. There is reason to think, for example, that people need both fictive and factual apprehensions of the world in a shifting balance, each at once to contrast and contain the other and to complement and tell the other part (Boris 1989). Be that as it may, can there be anyone anywhere, whether outside the head man's hut or in front of the TV, who can listen to the evening news and not marvel at the bloody-mindedness and wrongheadedness of his fellow man?

But to the extent that it may not be, the final difficulty with a Reality principle is the mentocentrism of the idea of reality itself (cf. Boris 1989).

Let us now rid ourselves of this $X$ and $Y$ nomenclature and try instead to find names for these principles. There is no reason to change the name of $X$ from the Pleasure principle, for it describes the nature of egoistic desire. But $Y$ is different. Its great urge is vectored toward a kind of investment in the potential, in the not-yet, in the yet-to-be, in time and possibility of generations to come. If $X$ is the desire for pleasure now, and devil take the nextmost, perhaps $Y$ is rooted in a fierce, if often unwitting, hope of and for the future, the thing that got us here and kept a here for us to get to — and may yet get our children's children to a there that is still here. Can we not call the correlative to the Pleasure principle the *Selection* principle, *with hope as its manifest, premonitory emotion*? Can we not say that preconceptions, and later conceptions, of what is to be hoped for restrain desire, as the desire for gratification for me, now, constraints hope; that out of hopelessness springs desire and out of desire, new hope? Can we not suppose that the great struggle between *repletion* and *completion* lies within the genetic endowment for the dynamic of not all other species save our own, but of our own as well?

## SOME CONSIDERATIONS

This proposal plainly presents some of the same difficulties that Plato's ideas regarding the Ideal and Kantian concepts of the Noumenon have done. And, being based on Darwinian concepts of Natural Selection and the Survival of the Species, it poses those unsettling issues of teleology as well. And of course it re-poses all the difficulties that Freud posed in speaking of a Pleasure principle, derived from the soma but represented psychically as a set of drives and urges that demand and imbue attention.

Plato's thinking concerned a hypothesis of an ideal to which all things really were only approximations. The ideal was at rest; there was nowhere further it need go; it was fully evolved. The real, being only approximations of this ideal, were in need ceaselessly of change: as they changed they became more true, more beautiful, and more enduring. Kant's Noumenon is also unapprehendable; it is a category that phenomena more or less adequately fill out and realize. Interestingly, Darwin's Survival has much in common with both Plato's ideal and Kant's noumenon. Species are supposed to realize their term of being alive and, in that sense, actual, by perpetuating themselves unto future generations. Their destiny is to change and adapt selectively so that primarily the very best of their genes are sent forward into the gene pools of the generations to come. Though Darwin of course does not say so, it is as if there will come to be an evolutionary condition so nearly perfect as to endure forever. This may be thought of as an Edenesque version of an eternal afterlife. Meanwhile, through selection and selectivity, each species further refines itself for its work of penultimate survival.

## ON NARCISSISM AS BEING CHOSEN

By supposing that something of what Darwin thought to be true of other creatures might be true of mankind as well, one would install a restless sort of preoccupation with choices alongside of egoistic hedonism. Miss Right Now would contend with Miss Right and the need to select and to be selected would conflict with, or at least moderate, choices that might otherwise be made propinquitously, opportunistically, or randomly.

Psychoanalytic theory has *of course* attended to the conflicts and compromises of pleasure the ego encounters. From the interpersonal school, led by Sullivan (1953), we have seen the essential function of affiliative and identificatory experiences play in the very viability of the ego or self. From those, like Kohut (1968), who have focused on narcissism, we have seen the vicissitudes of what I am calling the need to have the love of self shared by others. Both of these writers have addressed the need for the Pleasure principle to be modified in order to extend our understanding of the range and depth of interpersonal experiences. Freud too spoke of narcissism, saying: "Love for oneself knows only one boundary—love for others" (1921, p. 102).

But the idea that there is inherent in the very germ plasm of the species not alone an imperative to be chosen—*but, if not, to stand aside to, perhaps even to die for, those who are*—may put "narcissism" in a somewhat different light. For in this perspective, the need to enhance one's self over others, and indeed at their expense, is an urge no more inclined to make itself known and felt than the opposite one of deferring egoistic narcissistic gratification to the well-being of the many. If one may contest with all as to who is to be chosen and so have the rights to first choice *by or among* the potential mates and other wealth that accrues to the winner, one may not contest to the detriment of the winner, but must, if anything, sacrifice one's self for the group.[9] (The expectation is that in turn the group will lend its powers, not least its strength in numbers, to assist the Cinderellas should a Prince not come.[10])

These two vectors are subject to coalescence, conflict, and compromise, but are in continual dynamic tension. If it weren't for the urgency of the pleasure principle, one might wait forever, studying the possibilities of becoming an even better bridesmaid, awaiting the aggrandizement of being the choice of the perfect swain. Yet, if it weren't for the choosiness of the Selection principle the fittest might not be discovered and, as a result, not be available for being selectively chosen. This would leave matters to the egoistic lust of the chooser, with nothing else to drive the engine of interaction.

Desire and the feeling of satiety represent the pleasure end of the Pleasure principle, and frustration and deprivation are its special pain. These experiences are sensuous and make themselves known as such to each individual (though they may be so painful that steps are taken to unknow[11] the fact or the feeling of them).

The Selection principle of course must also make itself felt or else it would have no motivational force within the individual. It makes itself

---

[9]As I shall show in subsequent publications, the deepest envy of the have-nots is directed toward the right of the haves to survive and to flourish. These ("Unconscious Envy," "More of the Same," "About Time," and "Look-see") are forthcoming in *Envy* (1994).

[10]"Man, you put on that uniform, you know you never be beat."—Magic Johnson, L.A. Lakers.

[11]Bion's minus K, or what might be also called K.O., as in: it was kayoed in the third round.

manifest in feelings of hope and elation or despair and dread, in ideas of idealism and purpose or of confusion and meaninglessness. There are what were once called "existential" experiences or crises, in which the pleasure of simply *being* either contrasts or comports with the need to *become*.

Thus the any-which-way-and-how, the polymorphic quest for release, relief, and then satiety of the Pleasure principle plays in a key entirely different from the push to wait for better, other or more. Freud spoke of this in his aphorism "Better gets in the way of good." In Winnicott's language, "good enough" represents a compromise between hope and desire, a bonding made jittery and tenuous if any tilt in the balance of two constituents to the compact should take place.

The need to be chosen is half of the Selection principle, the other half being the obligation to be choosy and to garner choices to match. It is the former that is easily mistaken for narcissism of the sort Freud described when he said that out of disappointments with the world of others, the object world, the ego turns to itself as its source of love and gratification. But the appellation *narcissistic* is often assigned to people who are thought to be "too" choosy.

The attributes that enable one to be chosen can come out of "mutant" qualities, which is to say the quality of being different and distinctive. Or they can come out of being or having the best of whatever quality is preferred by the centrist group (often, of course, both are involved). The thought that one possesses these or can attain them is a source for optimism and ebullience. The fear that one may not produces the opposite response, a fear for one's very life. For at any moment one may be un-selected, included out: aborted.[12]

On the other hand, when as yet unrealized hopes appear to be taking shape and form, their presence triggers desire. The clearer the presence of the choice one hoped for, the readier and more ardent the desire. But when desire persists in the absence of hoped-for attributes, that desire can produce hatred of the other or self-loathing of murderous or suicidal proportions, as when prostitutes get beaten up by their despairing clients or people mutilate the organs of their desire.

The self does not merely represent itself; it represents the species. And as such, what might be all right for the self may not be all right when the group is concerned. Some people are able to distinguish between private and self occasions and public and self-as-

---

[12]Is it a wonder pro-life people fear pro-choicers!

representative-of-the-group occasions. Behind closed doors they are able to think thoughts and perform deeds that they could not possibly make public without the greatest shame. But there are those for whom there is no off-duty; they cannot escape the shame of the group, wherever they are (Morrison 1989).

## ON CHOOSING AND CHOICE

The array of characteristics available for choice indicates both the degree of the choosiness and the competition for being chosen. But these characteristics are of little use unless they are regarded as holding possibility for the destiny of the species. Thus there is a great gulf between both distinctiveness and deviancy and choosiness, on the part of the would-be chosen, and snobbishness, on the part of the potential chooser.

In the face of such drift in both parameters, some species have the choices preprogrammed. But this leaves them inflexible when time to accommodate to different environmental conditions come along. To be sure, further selection will presumably rectify that, especially if there is the Joker of the mutant gene in the pack. But humankind has bred itself predispositions rather than explicit imperatives. Its categorical nature is such that the categories are but half full, awaiting experience and socialization to fill them to the brim.

The categories we use have to do with the biggest and the best — but this can be penis or bust size.[13] And it can range, analogically, perhaps, to the "size" of money, territory, rank and influence, and the like. (Power is aphrodisiac, Kissinger is quoted as reporting.) Our preferences as to particulars await discovery; but the predilections arrive prenatally with the germ plasm.

In the face of the array of the variables and the complexity involved in ordering them for purposes of choosing or being chosen, there appear to be two somewhat paradoxical trends. One is that like seeks like. The other is that like seeks unlike.

In the former, unlike is accommodated by superiority, by having more of the same; in the latter it is subsumed by having more and better of what is different. An extreme of the former may be said to express itself in the preference for the homo, as in homosexuality, and

---

[13]"Has there ever been an analysis in which penis size did not come up?" — Roy Schafer, P. C.

on the complementary side a sort of xenophobia. Homophobia would be the extreme of the drift toward the attraction of opposites, which on its positive axis might lean toward acceptance of the mutant (or mystic).[14]

So far I have dealt with what might be called active efforts at selection — self-perfection in the service of being among the chosen, selection of the best and most beautiful to enhance self and species. But there is a passive side to selection, too — what might be encapsulated in the term *salvation*.

Each species is prey to another, including itself at those times when subspeciation takes place. The enduring tensions over birth control, abortion, and infanticide reflect the power of this in regard to being individually permitted life itself by the doyens of the species. Then comes the matter of protection from outside the pair — of child abuse or sexual misuse or castration or defeminization. Finally comes the matter of protection from intraspecies tensions — of what has sometimes been called Social Darwinism, where entire groups (e.g., natives, castes, underclasses, or specialized groups like the military) are used at the convenience or to enhance the survival of others.

This specialization, consisting in a division of labor, in which some till and some teach, each according to their abilities and the needs of the group, is indeed a species-enhancing procedure. At one end of it is rank parasitism, where units of a species exist entirely for the use of others. Analogies can be found to social organisms like insect colonies and, for that matter, the human body itself, in which cells specialize on a feedback system according to the particular distributions of specialist cells at a given time. Thus among ants, when the queen is gravid, she emits pheromones that appear to keep all other females in the colony sterile. And in humans when sufficient cells of one sort, say cerebral tissue, have embryologically been formed, cells that do not yet have a defined anatomy and function are turned off from further evolution into the cerebral tissue parts and instead become open to morphological evolution into other sorts of brain cells as yet insufficient in quantity, as signaled chemically. These, to be sure, are analogies, nothing more, but they may point to a system in which the two parameters, like and unlike, are insufficient guides. Thus subspecialization within a cohesive and integral system may be a hair's breadth from a heterogeneity, in which the system, however well synthesized,

---

[14]Bion remarks on this in his Chapter, "The Mystic and the Group" (1970); Freud, of course, understood that a bisexuality was endemic to us as a species.

is contrived rather than integral, such as a social system may be as compared to a biological system.

A system of slavery, for example, may represent such modeling of the social upon the biological; but it is in fact a division of labor between members of the same species and quite different from the keeping of creatures (cattle, dogs, etc.) of another. But the members of a servile class or caste may, and often do, when the economy of the given organization can evolve no further,[15] force the whole into new alignments of specialized units. Taken too far, this process of commensurate activities for commensurate gain disintegrates into parasitism, where the value of the one is merely to keep the other alive and flourishing, no matter the former's fate. These are the seedlings that are thinned, the branches that are pruned, the lives enshadowed by the heights of other lives. Yet to those involved it is not always clear whether they are being engaged in parasitism or in symbiosis: it was many months before officers were fragged in Vietnam; many years before revolutions and counterrevolutions take place; many decades before people emigrate, as if from the old hive, elsewhere to form a new colony.

In short, then, the Pair and the Couple are states of mind, depending on whether the object or event in view is experienced as unique or one more of the same. And depending on which state of mind is prevailing, certain emotions come to the fore while others recede. Given that it is responsive to motivations driven by the Selection principle, the pair has a welter of emotions having to do with display, adequacy, and belonging. Admiration and humiliation, confidence and shame, envy and self-possession, belonging and anomie, outrage, mania and depression, panic and righteousness, and, ultimately, hope and despair, are some of these. When the state of mind of the couple comes to the fore, propelled by the Pleasure principle, the sensual emotions come forward with it — desire and deprivation, gratitude and jealousy, ruthlessness and guilt, hatred and longing, sadness, anger and sorrow — the pleasure of satiety or the pains of loss.

## REFERENCES

Balint, M. (1968). *The Basic Fault: A Contribution to the Theory of Regression*. Madison, CT: International Universities Press.

---

[15]See Gould (1980) for a discussion of such a crisis model of change.

Beebe, B., and Lachman, F. (1988). The contribution of the mother-infant mutual influence to the origins of self and object representations. *Psychoanalytic Psychology* 5(4):305-37.

Bion, W. R. (1961). *Experiences in Groups.* New York: Basic Books.

_____ (1962). *Learning from Experience.* New York: Basic Books.

_____ (1963). *Elements of Psychoanalysis.* New York: Basic Books.

_____ (1966). Book review of *Medical Orthodoxy and the Future of Psychoanalysis* by K. R. Eissler (New York: International Universities Press, (1965). *International Journal of Psycho-Analysis* 47:575-579.

_____ (1970). *Attention and Interpretation.* New York: Basic Books.

Boris, H. N. (1976). On hope: its nature and psychotherapy. *International Review of Psycho-Analysis* 3:139-150.

_____ (1986). The 'other' breast: greed, envy, spite and revenge. *Contemporary Psychoanalysis* 22(1):45-59.

_____ (1987). Tolerating nothing. *Contemporary Psychoanalysis* 23(3):351-66.

_____ (1988). Torment of the object: a contribution to the study of bulimia. In *Bulimia: Psychoanalytic Treatment and Theory,* ed. H. Schwartz, pp. 89-110. Madison, CT: International Universities Press.

_____ (1989). Interpretation of dreams. Interpretation of facts. *Contemporary Psychoanalysis* 25 (2):212-25.

_____ (1994). *Envy.* Northvale, NJ: Jason Aronson.

Freud, S. (1895). Project for a scientific psychology. *Standard Edition* 1:295-397.

_____ (1913). Totem and taboo. *Standard Edition* 13:1-161.

_____ (1920). Beyond the pleasure principle. *Standard Edition* 18:7-64.

_____ (1921). Group psychology and the analysis of the ego. *Standard Edition* 18:69-143.

_____ (1925). Negation. *Standard Edition* 19:235-239.

Gould, S. J. (1980). *The Panda's Thumb.* New York: W. W. Norton.

_____ (1983). *Hen's Teeth and Horse's Toes.* New York: W. W. Norton.

_____ (1987). *Time's Arrow, Time's Cycle.* Cambridge: Harvard University Press.

Klein, M. (1945). The oedipus complex in the light of early anxieties. *International Journal of Psycho-Analysis* 33:433-438.

_____ (1952). The origins of transference. *International Journal of Psycho-Analysis* 33:433-438.

Kohut, H. (1972). Thoughts on narcissism and narcissistic rage. *Psychoanalytic Study of the Child.* 27:360-399. New Haven, CT: Yale University Press.

Levi-Strauss, C. (1973). *From Honey to Ashes.* New York: Harper & Row.

Morrison, A. (1989). *Shame: The Underside of Narcissism.* Hillsdale, NJ: Analytic Press.

Sullivan, H. S. (1953). *The Interpersonal Theory of Psychiatry.* New York: W. W. Norton.

# The Pair and the Couple: Toward a Third Principle of Mental Functioning

Two-fisted writers can write group theory with their left hand and individual theory with their right, and that I have been among these will be evident from the contents of this collection. However, certain of my patients have not accommodated to this split. And when I have run out of being able to offer them interpretive help drawn from the psychology of individuals as part and parcel of the couple, matters have gone from bad to worse. It was no use telling them they were stubborn, self-pitying, entitled, manipulative, or implacably hostile — about as much use as me telling myself that they were borderline, psychotic, or psychopathic and should have some other kind of therapy instead, or jail. The glaring fact was that my capacities were not up to snuff. I had either to leave the patient feeling a hopeless if triumphant failure or tell him or her that I had run out of inspiration. The more interesting alternative was for me to work out what was standing in our way.

There were patients, for example, who seemed to come about seemingly simple matters — hysterical phobias, classical compulsive rituals — and since the "linear B" of the Rosetta stone had long since been translated, it was easy enough to get at the meaning and function of these symptoms. But for some of these patients such progress only made matters worse. Where once there had been guilt, now there was dread. Where once the symptoms permitted a half-good life, now their entire lives were put into question. What

had been obscured was that these people and others like them had
been so seized by the idea that they must not survive and flourish that
they made themselves small and sick and complaisant in order to
escape sudden notice: "What are you doing here?!"

Technically speaking, this is not much of a problem for the
analysis of the individual as part of a couple: one looks to survivor
guilt, the success neurosis, secondary gain, internalizations by the
self of others' death wishes, (in the manner adumbrated by writers
like Sullivan, Laing, and Klein) and into split-off hostility based on
envy tending, chickenlike, to come home to roost. And indeed these
do help. But then even interpretations based on the evidence of such
feelings in the patients' lives seem to leave matters — well, mezza-
mezza; time has gone by; and I begin to think that maybe the
posttermination work-through will consolidate the work done to date
and help it take hold. The appeal of this supposition is that I don't
know quite what else to do.

But as one muses on the work, one can sometimes catch a glimpse
of its orbit being askew, as if there were something more there to the
experience, a hint of shadow underneath what one thought was the
entire, suggesting an additional dimension. It isn't in the data; if it
exists at all, it is in how the data is looked at. One looks closely at a
sock; it is a sock. Same thing inside out one supposes, or as much so
as makes no difference except which way to wear it. And yet. . . .

Having had the experience of working with individuals when they
were feeling themselves to be part of a group and then seeing those
selfsame people when the group aspect was recessive or dormant, it
began to occur to me to ask where the stars went when the sun was
up. If there were what Bion had been describing as Basic Assumptions Group, meaning what people seemed to act upon immediately
when they took themselves to be in or at the edge of a group situation,
as if rules inhered in the condition, what happened to these
assumptions when the libido came up?

I went back over my work with patients past and present (how
lucky Kohut was to see Mr. Z. again after Kohut had become
Kohut!) and just to check on whether I was myself introducing a
systematic bias outside of being who I am, went over also some of the
many supervisions I have done, and over the psychoanalytic literature and the poets, and I thought, Yes, perhaps there is something.
Then I went back to scratch and started writing myself through that
possible something to try and think it out. This essay represents one
such thinking of matters out from scratch. It rests on the inferential
chain presented in "Beyond the Reality Principle" and "Greed, Envy,
Spite, and Revenge."

Although it is by way of being the epilogue of this particular book, it turns out to be prologue to the next book and the next after that.

---

*Man seeks to form for himself, in whatever manner is suitable for him, a simplified and lucid image of the world and so to overcome the world of experience by striving to replace it to some extent by this image.*
— Albert Einstein

Justice Abe Fortas spoke ruefully of what was for him the greatest difficulty of his Supreme Court judgeship. It was, he said, struggling against his need to begin every decision with the invention of money. As for myself, something of an addict to Originology,[1] doubtless an outgrowth of my deep and abiding love for Just So stories of every kind, I can certainly sympathize with the Justice in this respect. For several years now I have been writing on envy[2] and its various shapes and vicissitudes; yet it seems with each fresh attempt I must get farther back, as if to develop the speed and loft to get over the hurdle or extend the landing mark. Sometimes I can barely see the starting line. Where and when do people, psychologically speaking, begin? What has one to account for before one gets all the way forward to envy? Freud started with the concept of attention. His famous Chapter Seven of *The Interpretation of Dreams* (1900) outlined the dreamwork and the mechanisms by which attention was shifted and deployed to contrive images, representations, and symbols. But presently attention disappeared as a concept, reappearing rather as attention *cathexis*, as befits a psychology of the COUPLE. What if, plucking a leaf from Bion's work, one wanders back to pick up a trailing thread?

## ATTENTION, PLEASE

The quantity of attention is fixed. Aspects of mentation take place at one another's expense. To see what is in front of one's nose is not to see what is in one's mind's eye. Memory takes place at a cost to perception.

---

[1]Scholars of Bion will know what the "O" in originology stands for; Laing called it Om. Klein might have seen in it the Breast. It often refers to the fantasy that one can get to a source, a font, that exists beyond the Mother and is not therefore possessed by her, a dubious idea to atheists, but a compelling one to those who have known envy.

[2]*Envy*. Northvale, NJ: Jason Aronson, 1994.

As sensation gets occluded in the sensory deprivation chamber, hallucinations flood in upon the hapless mind. Most of us cannot dream while awake, as the psychotic can. As near-term memory decreases, longer term memory is refreshed. The poet writes of daybreak who cannot endure noonday, writes Wallace Stevens. The quantity of attention is fixed.

## THE OBJECT OF DISCOVERY

The discovery of the world of objects takes place, not prior to, but with, the discovery of relationships between objects. Things exist only incidentally — literally as incidents — until the pattern for them is established. The pattern, the relationship, is inborn; it is configured innately; it is as merciless to what might have been experienced as is the morphology of the retina or the range of what is auditory itself. We are bound to see a cat in the play of certain patterns of light upon the optic nerve, but we can never see the cat a cat sees. Things seen are as seen.

## NO-THING AND NO-TIME

For some, at least, there is no such thing as nothing, only a no-thing where a something should have been. And there is no such thing as a no-space, only a hole or a blank or a piece of darkness where a something should have been. Black milk,[3] where milk was to be. Black holes where time should have been. They will forever recur in the ambiguous undulations of life as dark encroachments of the original catastrophe, chaos in motion and not in motion, desire without an object of desire: the nothing that is not there and the no-thing that is always there.

Expectations are in the affirmative; as Freud showed in his (1925) essay on Negation, disappointments are also in the affirmative: "What

---

[3]The phrase "black milk" is from Paul Celan: *Schwartze Milche der Frühe wir trinken sie abends/ wir trinken sie mittags und morgens/ wir trinken sie nachts/ wir trinken und trinken.* Celan (*"Todesfuge"* ["Death Fugue"] in *Poems*: Persea (1989) uses the phrase to describe what the Nazis "gave" the Jews and Gypsies in the Holocaust. It is so poignant in that connection that one hesitates using it to express what a person "gives" himself.

is bad, what is alien to the ego and what is external are, to begin with, identical." The object that is absent in time or space is a no-object; it suppurates no-ness.

But neither is anything truly present in its no-ness. Beyond the warp, beyond the moonmath, it exists as someone else's affirmative: when the no-thing is my portion; the yes-thing is yours. If I see that the yes-thing is yours, while the no-thing is mine, I feel both envious and jealous. If I manage not to see that the yes-thing is your portion while mine is the no, the not, and the never, I feel merely envious. But always there is the dependence of opposites, for, of these, day and night, earth and air, chill and heat, neither can exist without the defining force of the other. Where is one without the other?

## POSITIONS

A "two-position" relationship consists of me and you, and who has what. When it occurs that someone else is having it, everything goes into a relationship to someone else, and a triangular event comes into being. The Oedipus complex and Groups are such relationships, such events. They appear and disappear as first two-position, then three-position experiencing recurs and unoccurs.

These occurrences can be made to happen by fixing the fixed quantity of attention, now here, now there, now now, now then. The therapy of psychoanalysis requires a "psychophant" (Primo Levi's apt word [1990]) whose divagations of attention to particular aspects of experience is displayed in front (or in back) of another person, whose own attention, although also fixed, is nonetheless free at once to follow these divagations and to note them even as they occur. For that other person to do this while the first does not requires of the analyst that he or she be able to form a PAIR rather than a COUPLE with the patient.

## THE COUPLE AND THE PAIR

Relationships between objects exist in two forms — those obtaining to the COUPLE; and those obtaining to the PAIR. The experience of the relationship may be likened to the properties of a sock. The sock is the same sock, inside out or outside in; but different experiences are palpated when it is inverted. The relationship between state A and state B oscillates dialectically. ← The one gives way to the other after each has been used for as long as it can hold; the state to which the one reverts then becomes primary for as long as it can hold. The duration of the holding or regnancy time is a function of the frustration of the particular wishes bound up in the paramount surface. Like nerve endings, each surface grows weary and needs to be refreshed by the substitution of the other. The alternation offered by dual surfaces allows the emerging self choice or the illusion of choice. For example, the wishes obtaining to the COUPLES's state of mind have to do with the pleasure and pain of lust and desire; those flowing from the PAIR have to do with selectivity, identity, and hope or desPAIR. These twin states of mind offer alternatives for one another when the sock is in- or re-verted. Such reversion or inversion is as mass into energy, stars into black holes, and can be brought about by refixing—converting—the attention paid whichever state is previous.

The relationship may be analogized to the hollow, or Necker, cube (see Bion 1961, p. 86) in which sometimes line AB is forward and sometimes CD; the cube, like the Steinian rose, is the cube no matter.

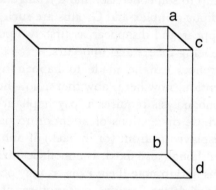

## PARAMNESIAS, PARATAXIAS, AND SCREENS

Thus when any one experience—that following from the experience of a two-position relationship or that from a three—proves intolerable, a shift in perspective or the refixing of attention can sometimes offer a relief. There is, then an experience and, again, an experience of the experience; and even if the former cannot be altered, the latter often can. Bion (1963 and more) refers to such a shift of perspective as K and – K(minus K) where K stands for experiencing the experience or knowing what the experience is or was. By refixing attention, experiences can be KO'ed. Line AB is kayoed by line CD. That there has to be a CD if AB is to be subtracted out means that the quantity of attention is fixed; it can neither be increased nor shut down; it can only be displaced. Freud called this process the use of the screen: amnesias (repressions) are made possible by, but only by, the use of paramnesias. Perception can screen for memory; dreams for percepts, memories for dreams, fixed memories for spontaneous ones, extraceptions for intraceptions, and so on. Can and must.

## LINKS

Objects are experienced only as being in and belonging to a relationship. This provides several possibilities beyond AB, CD. For example,

$$X \leftrightarrow Y \leftrightarrow Z$$

can be altered by screening or substituting for X for Y and for either end of the arrow, or the arrow itself, linking X and Y, which is to say their relationship, X–Y here, is a two-position affair. A second arrow to Z puts many more variables into play. If the second arrow is a PAIRing link, a group mentality comes into focus; if it is a COUPLing link the Oedipus complex comes into focus. Who is doing what and with which and to whom is a question that sometimes has but one answer and sometimes too many — a patient remarks: "You left out how and for how much."

If X and Y are breast and mouth and the arrow is the experience of nursing, that is one matter. If the arrow is the breast and the question is which way shall it point, which is to say, who, X or Y, shall own it and have it to give, that is quite another. Can the relationship between X and Y, that is the arrow linking mouth and breast, be both a matter of nursing and of ownership? Can it be both a matter of COUPLing and of PAIRing? Sometimes in a psychoanalytic session one feels one would have to send out if one wanted a responsible adult to give interpretations to: has the patient an agent or other representative? Very often in work with so-called training groups of psychologists or psychiatric residents this is so much the case that only when a beeper goes off do people look alive again. There has been a one-way arrow and no takers or only takers. In a psychoanalytic therapy the analyst wants to form

a PAIR with which to study the COUPLE. In an infancy, the mother wants
to form a PAIR in order to manage the COUPLing. Both the analyst and
the Mother want to replace the sensual or coupling arrow at least partly
with an arrow of identification, apposite to the PAIR. In the former
relationship this is called fashioning an alliance; in the latter, socialization or acculturation. Is there a difference? The infant and the
patient want to organize an arrow called identification such that
the Other knows well enough how he or she is feeling to keep the
arrow-as-conduit-for-provisions flowing. Is there a difference between
patient and analyst or between mother and infant? What if there is no
difference, and only the baby or the patient knows there isn't any
difference?

## ALTERNATION AND SELECTION

Knowledge is a major item. It creates and destroys experiences of one's
experiences: it fashions one's world of experience and the experiences
from which one learns. Now an experience is this, now that, depending
on how it is paid attention to.

Yet there is a paradox. The arrows of relationship in which the
world is discovered are givens. When the COUPLE set of arrows are
obtrusive, sensual pleasures, rooted in bodily experience, prevail: and
to be lost in ecstasy is the direction of the arrow. And when the PAIRing
mode is dominant, the sense of at-one-ment is paramount: and to be
lost in rapture is the direction of the arrow. This is to say that, though
there are built in alternatives for the fixed quantity of attention to
focus upon, the alternatives themselves are also fixed.

One can discern the outlines of a curiously wrought design: the
properties to an experience can be fixed providing that these properties
so function as to be alternatives for one another. Thus two can make
a COUPLE, with its ( $\longleftrightarrow$ ) properties, and two can make ( $\longleftrightarrow$ ) a PAIR
with its, and three or more can make a triangle or a group, the rules
( $\longleftrightarrow$ ) for each being fixed and set, providing only that the rules, as
represented by the arrows, can be seen now to imply a COUPLE, now
a PAIR, now to represent this linkage, now that, with each object
being different according to the rules that relate them. The knowledge
to re-represent discovery through the introduction of invention gives
to knowing and not knowing an unending source of power—as if,
indeed, to compensate for the unforgivingness of the arrows. Thus

♂ ←→ ♀ exists in a limited number of ways, but one can so contrive matters as to experience them in a far less limited set of ways, a more unlimited set.

The ←→ of the PAIR is organized around identity and identification. It looks like this ◯ ←→ ◯. The COUPLE is organized around differences. It looks like this: ♂ ←→ ♀ The two situations lend themselves to a compromise formation, which might look like this.

Here, within the circle of PAIR or Group, commonalities are expressed: the differences useful for coupling are being directed outside.

In

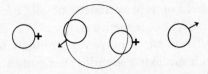

one can readily see that the "male" of the PAIR will be far more inclined to remain as part of the PAIR than the "female" of the PAIR because he is having rather better luck with his wishes to COUPLE than she is. If nothing better happens soon for her, she may begin, like Lot's wife, to look back to him for COUPLing. And this is as true of objects and relations taken to be internal as it is of relationships in the interpersonal realm; it describes Ego's relations with Superego in the COUPLing vein and Ego's relations with Ego-ideal in the PAIRing mode.

## ARROWS AND CYCLES[4]

In this movement between any one set of forces and any other, there is a dynamic: stasis/crisis/stasis. The concept of Regression provides a poor model, since it implies a set of movements that are more and less advanced in linear terms; this is a point of view emerging only from

---

[4]With thanks or apologies to Stephen Jay Gould (1987).

the PAIR: the COUPLE do not know forward and back, only back and forth. Relation ⟷ ships at rest tend to stay at rest — until a crux (as in crucible, crucial, and crossroads) is reached, whereupon a shift either takes place or it does not. It is a matter of the selfsame persisting, until — BOOM! — it shifts over to other. The word for this model might be crisis.

The initially expected relationship, moreover, not only remains in effect but also provides the template for other relationships, which are then, accordingly, perceived as analogous to the preconceived archetypical relationships — of which one obtains to the species, the other to the individual organism. One simple instance of this, already mentioned, is that the presence of three makes a triangle in the COUPLing modality and a group in the PAIRing modality. There is a ready capacity innately to divide by two — to split one into two or two again into four, eight, $n$ objects. (Bion — 1970 — called a result that approached $n$, bizarre objects.)[5] The reverse of this process is agglutination: it is the extrapolation of one to infinity, such that one is not merely one (one is one and only one and ever more shall be so) but the forerunner, symbol, or representative of all, ever, and everything. "God" has this quality. So, sometimes, does "We." Distinctions are not seen to betray differences: rather, they cumulate into an ever greater wholeness, through successive identifications of each with others. This is the modality of group formation, whereby the very differences and distinctions that interest those intent on COUPLing go unnoticed in the interests of agglutination. The shifts which take place between the one "model" and the other are akin to shifts in the perception of figure-ground relationships. But in the PAIRing mode what is generally called identification undoes divisibility and distinction reaching for more and *more* and MORE of the same. (Boris 1992).

---

[5]When I first asserted this ready and innate capacity, it was an inference: one had to infer such a capacity, else the untutored infant could not effect what psychologically he does effect in the processing of experience. Since this was written, data have come out along the following lines. At three months, infants shown an object that is then placed behind a masking curtain evince surprise if, when the curtain is lifted, the object is not there. If that object and another are placed behind the curtain, the infant is as surprised to see still one as it is to see three objects. When one is removed from three, the infant evinces surprise if there are not two remaining . . . and so on. This is not division or even, properly speaking, mathematics, but as well as demonstrating innate expectations about relationships among objects, it shows what infants can answer if asked with sufficient respectful ingenuity. (Study by Karen Wynne, as reported in *The New York Times*, August 27, 1992.

## GREED AND APPETITE

In previous communications (Boris 1976, 1986, 1988), I have described what I misthought to be an evolution of greed into appetite.
Subsequent experience enabled me instead to surmise a dialectical
process between the two, with Greed belonging in the PAIR dimension
and appetite or desire to the COUPLE. Each represents a loss of a
relationship so far as the other is concerned, and since objects do not
exist, psychologically, outside of a relationship, each loss is tantamount
to an object loss.

The appetitive breast is a loss so far as the wish to possess it is
concerned, as is the breast gained by identification a loss so far as the
appetites are concerned. If $\male \longleftrightarrow \female$ stands for the providing
breast and $\bigcirc \longleftrightarrow \bigcirc$ for the owned breast, each is lost when the
other is chosen. (The breasts are defined by the relationship: they are
the same save that, as in the hollow cube, AB is recessive when CD is
dominant. Thus each is "other" to the other; see Chapter 16. The
breast is selected in the sense that it is selectively perceived or
remembered or imagined as either $\male$ or $\bigcirc$ at any given moment: in
that way, if the infant has control of his mentation, he has control of
the breast. But does he have control of his mental processes? This is a
problem concerning consciousness and will.

## CONSCIOUSNESS

The question has arisen: of what use is consciousness to survival in the
Darwinian sense? Such relatively "primitive" experiences of consciousness as pain, pleasure, hunger, thirst, and satiety may seem to
facilitate survival behavior but are by no means necessary for it.
Aversive reflexes without a corresponding conscious sensation of pain
function adequately (it would seem) for organisms not thought to
enjoy a brain, much less consciousness. Attraction responses, like
avoidant or aversive ones, also do not require awareness.

Humans being social animals, it is clearly in the human interest to
know something of how others feel, to put oneself in their shoes. Thus
a capacity for identifying with the experience of others and relating it
to self experience would be valuable for social aspects of survival. But
even this does not require consciousness, or self-consciousness; it

requires merely a capacity to pick up signs and signals; no attribution of meaning, no interpretation, is required. Nothing need check in at the front desk.

But a moment's reflection indicates that the value of consciousness is precisely that, in given circumstances, *it can hinder* the aversion–attraction reflexes, and the signal function of social stimuli, and thereby go on to provide the possibility of contra-reflexive behavior. Thus when I know that the flame hurts my hand, I can save my endangered child; I can anticipate an end to pain, or its diminution: I can plan: I can choose. "Human mensura requires staffing," as Beckett remarked. The quantity of consciousness is fixed, but we are free to embrace now this, now that, in the very special regard of conscious consideration. However, you can't not choose, and you can't choose nothing.

An experience either chooses us or we it. A loud, sudden report, for example, chooses us: it has a demand quality not to be gainsaid. Driven, in the COUPLE mode, by hunger, thirst, or sexual desire, it is difficult not to see mirages; otherwise unattractive objects look very desirable indeed. Driven, in the PAIR mode, by hope or expectation, it is difficult not to see events in terms other than good, better, and best; or if by despair, in terms of bad, worse, and worst; features become flaws. Consciousness gives leeway to the demandingness of these driving forces: it allows us to choose what we experience.

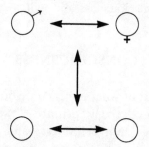

might express the relations between thinking and thoughts or knowing and experiences before choice is made, while

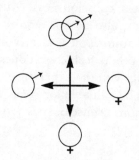

might represent matters after choice is made. Certain choices in thinking or knowing have become objects themselves, nearly congruent with the objects they represent. In the vernacular, one can think about men and women in a masculine sort of way, a feminine sort of way, or not at all. One can think of the breast as if one were its owner, as if one were a renter, or as if it didn't exist. One can think of the relations between objects as if they PAIRed or as if they COUPLEd by thinking of them in a PAIRing sort of way or in a COUPLing sort of way. The process of mentation comes to represent the relationship between objects, and thoughts and percepts become (as if) objects in the sense that things are objects.

## FURNISHINGS OF THE CONSULTING ROOM – I

P: Were you anxious to be rid of me Tuesday? I thought you turned away quickly. I felt spitted or spit out — whichever it is. Which is it? You're not going to tell me. Why won't you tell me? Can't you tell me? Were you mad at me? Why did you spit me out?

Ψ: Such a spate. . . .

P: Yes. What had you said?

Ψ: You spat it out.

P: I said, "At least in a nothing-life like mine there can't be any emergencies." And you said,: "You're saying a mouthful." Is that what you said? Did you say that? Is that you? Did you say that? Am I imagining that? Tell me! Why won't you tell me?

Ψ: You have the idea that in a no-thing devastating can happen anymore, since it already happened. You need to keep your no-thing safe from becoming something. You are spitting up what could stay and happen.

## ACTIVE ANALOGUES

In the manner of the words lies the action. The analogies in mental activity to other relationships become persuasive. One and one make two: is this the primal scene? Penetrating thoughts, encompassing perceptions, long memory, soft ideas, hard data, openness to ideas, hard-assed attitudes — are these merely figures of speech? Why is certainty so frightening to those who feel "uneasy lies the head that wears the crown"? There is something imperial in five-star generalization: From the reviewing stand one sees only masses of faceless others all swathed in anonymous uniformity. Quite the opposite of seeing or being seen as a One and Only, unique, distinctive, one of a kind.

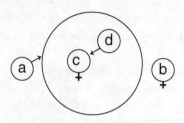

In this diagram, *c* and *d* are having intercourse inside the psyche and to the dismay of *a* and *b*, who are excluded from this primal event. If *a* or *b* were a psychiatrist, he or she might be asking: Are you hearing something — some voice other than my own? If the intercourse is not satisfactory, presently each of the partners to the coupling, *c* or *d*, might find him- or herself drifting like an errant schoolchild in the hot flybuzz of springtime, to thoughts of *a* or *b*. But if *c* does this, *d* might be jealous and make such a headache for *c* that he or she might be unable to even concentrate! O, what greater fury greater than that of a superego spurned?[6] Today I woke up and it has been all black rain. I could barely get out of bed. I don't know how I made it to the session.

## FURNISHINGS OF THE CONSULTING ROOM – II

P:   *[Heavily ironic]*
Ψ:   It is difficult to know what you mean, if you mean.
P:   Yes, well, words are a debased currency. Linear bits, two dimensional. My irony is intended to be three-dimensional — but you, you never get it. I put together a multimedia event — or would, except your technique allows only of words. When I hear what you hear of what I say, it makes me desPAIR of talking altogether, and now you are complaining of my irony.
Ψ:   If I understand, your irony is intended to add a dimension, to at least season the degraded words on which I insist. . . .
P:   Words. Mere words. Suppose people dealt in other dimensions?
Ψ:   Suppose people wanted lingus, not language.

---

[6]See Chapter 13, "Torment of the Object" (1988), for a study of a bulimic's relations with her internal objects.

*P:*  I am trying to convey more than that, but words don't serve, and you insist on words.

Ψ:  Using words, I think it is as if you try to convey a lovely three-dimensioned breast, and when it is reconstituted by me from your transmission, it is shit.

*P:*  Yes! Do you understand that? [This appears to sound odd to P] I mean, does that make sense to you? [*Silence*]

Ψ:  [*Silence*]

*P:*  Anyway . . .

Ψ:  Private thoughts, no use to say — language not lingus.

*P:*  [Tells thoughts. These concern a friend who has offered to return a borrowed chair, which P declined to have returned.]

Ψ:  And when you were thinking that, I was thinking this; "No you want to convey more than the breast, you want to inseminate: to bring into me a baby. Or who should have the baby and who make it? [This appears to be a fairly shameless appeal in behalf of the value of language.]

*P:*  [*Weeps, broken-heartedly*] There is a space where good times were, a *Space*, and it can only be conveyed as a space. It is architectural. It is a space where things were and people try to fill it with words. But the space is the space, it doesn't close around words and get filled.

Ψ:  It is the space where the breast was and isn't and where the baby was meant to be and wasn't. And rather than have it filled with words, you want it saved. As virgin woods or as a memoriam to what wasn't.

*P:*  It is difficult for me to let your words sink in, but I think what you say is so.

Ψ:  Words should not be allowed to occupy the space left for the breast or the baby?

*P:*  Yes, yes, yes, yes, yes. Shit!

Ψ:  And this is what happens to you in me, when you hear yourself back: no breast, no new baby: shit. That's all I have made of your insemination.

*P:*  My mother — [*Weeping afresh, a 'line' now of further associations, in words. . . . But later:*] It is no good. The point is, things were there even when people left. The chair bears witness. She sat in it, and it was there even after she left. The, the architecture, the building contains the events. Words are just bits and streams: they are nothing. Why should I expect you to understand? I have to talk to you in words, but I think in images. [*Silence*]

Ψ:  I have already said about milk turned into urine versus the breast and the penis as semen, but as these are words they are of no use. Worse, they are all you get from me, yet again. My talk will seem as if I have failed to feel bad at your reproaches, and you will yearn for something bigger and more dimensional than language to make me take your idea. Maybe that's why you did not tell me your images but employed silence instead.

*P:*  Is one ever doomed to be a helpless, furious infant?

Ψ:  Can making babies now ever be like making them then?

## GREEN-EYED

"I have turned into a big glass eye and a big glass ear," says a child of a physician, one of whose remembered nightmares is an oscilloscope screen gone wild. "And you are some kind of one-celled creature under a microscope. What if the analysis is ready to end, would you tell me?"

"Whose were my legs over your shoulders?" asks Phillip's wife in Roth's novel, *Deception.*

> Why are you feeding me with my breast?
> Look, d'ya want to nurse or don't you?
> That's mine.
> You can use it if you want, but make up your mind, I don't have all day.
> I'm not hungry. Furthermore, I shall never be hungry — not for that, not if that's yours. I have one of my own I can use. And I do have all day and all night — and all everything.
> Look — here, take Mommy's nipple, and don't fuss so.
> Let go my breast! Take your big mitts off my hand!

The particular thrust and vengeance of envy is to get one's *own* back.

## EARLY ENVY

The experience of envy is of no particular bother when one feels able to acquire something just like or just as good as what is envied. The trouble arises when one feels that one cannot, because what it is that rouses the envy is beyond one's hope of acquiring it. Such a juncture creates a crux, for either one must give up the wish and one's hope for it or boldly create a scenario in which acquiring what one envies will be possible under a fresh set of circumstances.

Thus of penis envy Freud wrote that the little girl may hope either later to acquire the penis (it may grow inside out from within) or symbolize it such that it can be represented by a baby or something else. The little boy may tell himself that the problem is but a matter of time and that some day he may acquire a penis the equal of his father's — and then his mother will succumb to his ardor and his charms. And in fact under favorable circumstances these scenarios may get the children through long enough for them to value the *Ding an sich*. The woman the little girl grows up to be may be so delighted with her baby that its symbolic function is shed off; and so far as the penis itself is concerned, it is very nice when it is pointing inward. The little boy may, to his surprise, so fall in love with a woman other than his mother, that her pleasure in his penis gives him the pleasure he has been waiting for; and that same woman may be wonderful enough to make even the mother on whom he so wished to bestow his penis now rather a moot quantity.

These happy outcomes seem simple enough, but in fact they depend on a number of factors.

One of these has to do with the particular analogue that is constructed or found for the envied object—in the example above, the penis. Suppose the analogue is found in the fecal stool? Or in the size of the breasts?

Another is the time span allotted for the assuaging of the early envy: Can it wait for the actual conception and birth of a baby or for the love of a woman who takes pleasure in one's penis? Or must it happen by the time the next sib is born or "due" to be born?

A corollary consists in the help the child is able to receive in giving up enough of the wish and hope in the present tense—to postpone its longings—to make the use of future possible. Or is time used merely to procrastinate in?

This factor is part of the larger relationship in which the initial envy takes place. Is there help with the disappointment, consolation for what the child aspires to but cannot have? Do the parents find appeasement for their own envy in seeing the child being envious? Are they so out of touch with their envy, that they cannot bear to recognize envy when they see it?

Another factor is the capacity for symbolization available to the child as he or she tries to establish the scenario. Early in life there is a more limited range of analogues, and what there is is tied more firmly to the grotesqueries of the imagination. Envy of the breast and nipple, for example, may not find a great deal of analogization. The boy may end up simply needing to have something a boy like him likes to suck. The girl may also wish to have a suckworthy penis, since her envy has been such as to have made her need to disparage the value of the breast.

## MERGERS AND ACQUISITIONS

*Vive la différence!* cry the COUPLE, italically; More of the Same! cry the PAIR in plain language. The COUPLE and the PAIR are envious of one another. Fundamentally they exist at one another's expense.

The COUPLE love their differences: they are the source of endlessly renewed gratification. But these very differences are what separate the PAIR from their at-one-ment. ○ ○ comes an Object. Oo-o, how do you want me, it asks?

♂    ♀    says the Copulator, ◎ says the one of a kind, looking to draw to a PAIR (or three or four of a kind) like a gosling encountering Konrad Lorenz's Wellington boots. Whichever prevails—Oh-Oh!— draws the other's envy. Come with me and make One. Come with me and make one more. How to choose?

Envy is endemic. The self gets beside itself with greed. Can it take less than it wants? Can it choose the one breast and stand to relinquish the other? Is the breast in hand worth the other two in the bush? Each configuration of the self envies the other. Inevitably each must also envy the object. The good object allays envy insofar as goodness consoles; the bad object allays envy in so far as its badness assuages envy. But there is no gainsaying that each must be chosen to have its effect.

## THE CHOSEN ONES

Meanwhile a person needs not merely to choose but to be chosen. Ecology winnows the species. Out of the array of characteristics, some endure, others fail to last. "We don't die—we multiply," says a black comedian, sketching a silver cusp around black pain. Blacks are sent to early death by neglect and warfare. Internally they bleed black rain, as do all those who are also not chosen. But people also choose people, and only the select are permitted to survive, let alone to take their DNA forward a generation.

Narcissism has meant the fascination of the self with the Self before the Other is encountered—primary narcissism, oceania. Then it has meant the retreat to self from the heartbreaks[7] inescapable in loving others. Kohut marks out a phasing—the self-object. Like finds like. Like likes like. Like likening unto like. Liking and likening like is the self becoming PAIR and Group—ultimately, the Species. It expresses and makes manifest identity and identifications. Its language is vicariousness. Like me, like my kind. Narcissism in this sense means

---

[7]The mind breaks to save the heart; deception and delusion rescue the aching heart.

being and doing one's best for Us. Being chosen means having the right to endure and survive.

Is this warmed-over sociobiology? But—count the dead.

An unselfish team player must step aside, so that the greater good may prevail. How young must people be before they know this? Is survival to be understood as an unending rivalry for psychological and generational Lebensraum? Not on the individual level. The victor and the vanquished know one another. They have signs, signals. The victor knows the spoils, the vanquished knows his role. A relationship brings them together to the top of the hill, and the same relationship takes them separately away. Individuals contest within the rules of the group. The rules for selection do not always require contest and competition; indeed, sometimes they require just the reverse: they require ascension and submission, dominance and recession.

This acceptance of relegation is, of course, of keen value to the group, subspecies, and species. It allows specialization based on a division of labor, role, and function. Whatever envy an individual player may feel of others given different treatment, he is expected to redeem in the success of his group relative to that of competing groups. This keeps the number eight hitter from taking his bat to the number four hitter. Blood-lust, like glut-lust, is to be gratified outside the precincts of the group.

But how does one know who he or she is to be and which of these positions to assume? How does a cat know what background against which to crouch? How a dog its size? Is this in the eye of the beholder, or is the beholder's eye the one in which one chooses look to? Or is it one's own? Or a desperate respite from one's own? Who weighs us in the balance?

"I will try briefly and in broad terms, to name some of the more easily defined forms of this experience," Václav Havel (1990)[8] says:

> One of them is a profound, banal, and therefore utterly vague sensation of culpability, as though my very existence were a kind of sin. Then there is a powerful feeling of general alienation, both my own and relating to everything around me that helps to create such feelings, an experience of unbearable oppressiveness, a need constantly to explain myself to someone, to defend myself, a longing that increases as the terrain I walk through becomes more muddled and confusing. I

---

[8]At Hebrew University, accepting an honorary degree: quoted in *New York Review of Books*, September 27, 1990, p. 19.

sometimes feel the need to confirm my identity by sounding off at
others and demanding my rights. Such outbursts are quite unnecessary,
and the response invariably fails to reach the right ears, and vanishes
forever into the black hole that surrounds me . . . I would say that
everything I have ever accomplished I have done to conceal my
metaphysical sense of guilt . . . to vindicate my permanently questionable right to exist.


## MERGERS AND ACQUISITIONS —
## AND HOSTILE TAKEOVERS


Such riffs up and down the scales when suffered (as contrasted with
being treated with emotional anodynes), can, as in Havel's case, give
rise to the determination not to Stay Quiet in so Dark a Night and so
lead to actions, which, however improbably, may lead one from jail to
the presidency.

Ownership! cries the one; E PLURIBUS UNUM; ("Una cum uno" were
Freud's [1921] words for describing this). Propagate to Amalgamate!
The more the better! More of the Same! The state of mind of the
PAIRing mode is toward addition, Plus.

Divide! cries the one. E uno plurimus. Out of one, make two. Then
we can coup-u-late and propagate. Then I can select the you I want.
The state of mind of COUPling is toward subtractions and divisions, by
two.

Both of these are innate states of mind owing to the fact that
attention is delimited. Were it expansible, were attention able to fly at
will, soar forever and visit any and every place in the universe, these
mathematical devices would not be required. But in order to gain
respite from the utter impress of experience, the mind has to be able
to add and divide, amalgamating one element to another, or splitting
asunder what the instant before seemed whole.

As goes the mind, so goes the interpersonal psyche. It too is
endowed with the right and the necessity to select. As the mind
rummages among perceptions, memories, ideations and the like,
cutting, pasting, editing, assembling — composing the experience that
is to be experienced from among the potential of the elements available
to it, condensing or expanding time, broadening, narrowing, or
dimensionalizing space, until it gets the "reality" it wants out of these
borrowings from Peter and these payings of Paul, so does the

interpersonal unit. It sees now a part-object, now two, now a part and a whole, now two wholes, now a self and an other, now a self and two others or more, now everyone alike, now everyone distinct.

## FURNISHINGS FROM THE CONSULTING ROOM – III

*P:*   It is an agony to enter this room each time. I feel somehow singled out. This is how I felt as a child, when anyone called me by my name. Named and singled out. Unbearable. I always hung my head. I was careful never to catch anyone's eye. There was a little boy down the street, whom I liked. Sometimes I would go to the door of his house and whisper his name. Over and over, of course, because I could only whisper it so that no one heard me, or if they did, it mightn't have been a whisper, but something else, a breeze or a sound from the street. . . .

Now I feel as if I — you see? I have to do it — have to put my hands over my head and protect it. You are going to hit me. I mean, I know you're not, but you are. Since I came in, it's all been me, me, me. "Who does she think she is, what does she thing she is doing?" You tell me this is my voice, me about someone — my brother, my father. But I can't put that to what I am feeling now. This is coming at me. I didn't turn this spear and arrow around, as you say I do. This is, "Now who is this one? Who does she think she is?"

Ψ:   I am the mother here. I am the father here. Step down. Take your place among the others, among the other children. Who do you think you are? We are the children here, we are one anothers' sisters and brothers, we know what we are. There is no who here, no I here, only a what, and the what is us, the children of this mother and father.

In the psychology of the COUPLE, one might correctly think that the conscious fear represents the unconscious wish — to be singled out, to be the one and only, oedipus triumphant, rampant! And so, I think, it does. "Uneasy lies the head that wears the crown," Ψ might with justice observe; Laius lives at this crossroads; like Hamlet's father, he is not quite dead yet, but a much perturbed spirit, a Commendatore.

Regarding, however, the psychology of the PAIR, of the Group, Ψ would have to say: Do you then single yourself out from us? For he who is not of us is food and drink for us, he is the repository for our wastes,[9] he is the object of our lusts and blood lusts? Are you ready for

---

[9]Even in such dire circumstances as the appallingly overcrowded refugee conditions occasioned by the exodus from Kuwait and Iraq, toilet facilities were separated as to national origin.

this? Is this what you want? The conscious fear represents the
unconscious hubris of being among but not of the Others. Who does
she think she is? When the blacks, the jews, the wogs are subspeciated,
let them beware. For they are whom we think they are.

P:   I am thinking of my dream—the one with the oscilloscope that went
       wild?
Ψ:   Are you considering oscillating now, as you did when you had the dream
       as a child? Whom shall I count as my peers? Shall I be child, here, or
       wife? But for the moment the wild breaking of the received light is only
       a dream. What would Mother think, what would We, the kids, think?

Freighted with DNA. needing to be selective, yet selected, where does
one look? Where does one go to be looked at?

The two persons P knows to have/be the Right stuff are the
Founders, they who gave up being of a PAIR with the Western Lord
God to COUPLE one with the other. So that's easy. They are it, they are
the right choice—or one of them is. P knows that when a man or woman
doesn't choose her, but rather chooses another, that man or woman is
probably the one for her. And when, in time, that man or that woman
does choose P, she knows what it means when people speak of fulfilling
one's destiny.

But, if that man or woman not only chooses her, but continues to
choose her—Bleep. Uh-oh, mistake somewhere. This person does not
resemble template. Bleep. This person is member of club who would
have you, bleep, and that is wrong club, bleep for PAIRing purposes.
"Oh, you know Sally, never did know her place, too bleeding good for
her own kind's what I say, 'scuse my French."

Freighted with DNA, P wants to make the right mating, even if she
doesn't want to. As we have seen, she is a bit of a renegade. But how
is she to know what her DNA has in mind? It doesn't have a mind. She
seems to feel that having a mind of its own and yet not having a mind
to mind it with, borrows her mind, sending her oscilloscope into chaos.
But how does it access her mind?

Fortunately, Ψ, whatever his (or her) other limitations, seems to be
able to entertain such notions in his mind. He seems to know that the
oscilloscope of her childhood was so perfect an objective correlative for
her dilemma of receiving instructions from her genes that she seized
upon it as a symbol the moment she Aha-ed it. How do ideas of the
Right thing come to one? No use saying they're taught, though of
course they are, because one has also to feel them. It is possible to

imitate the group, wear what they wear, scope things as they do, talk the same language in both senses; but that's being an imitation person. The point is that no one has the same genes. Indeed that is what P seems exactly to be saying: is there a category, somewhere between the You and I and the Us, for her alone? Another patient says: "I feel as if I am riding a bus, which is me, that is heading straight for a crash. I got off—long ago."

It is difficult for her because she is experiencing a strong species push: Go thee forth and multiply; but she is feeling the pull of "And remember that those to whom you give life from between your loins must be of the face and to the glory of god. Our God."

The little boy who lived down the lane, who was he? He was a boy, to be sure, and a stranger, and she felt shy. And as an envious and sometimes spiteful child, she was parsimonious about how much love-calling she would allow him. And the return of this made her fear rejection. But by now Ψ and P have been through these portions of the experience (which have to do with the COUPLE) and the same incidents and stories have taken on a new cargo. They are now contemplating the fact that the little boy was an Other. Was he what she had in mind for her DNA? Many are called, but few are chosen. How then was she to call him without at the same time choosing him? She whispered. An Indian-giver Love Call, eddying Ooo and Oh-oh in counterpoint. Should we divide, agglomerate? Shall you be my other or my other half? Shall you be on my side and at my side, in the manner that we face each other in groups, or shall we make the beast with two backs? (P has often felt restive about lying recumbent on the couch.) DNA— is it what we call the chemistry of what draws people to one another? That mysterious glue? That "I don't see what she sees in him, but they say, don't they Sally, that love is has blind has a bleedin' bat." And what is called the aesthetic impulse, or the aesthetic response? That chemical compote that is DNA cannot surely say what is beautiful— that will belong to the tutelage of the group and to what is available for aesthetic contemplation—but just as surely it can tell us what beautiful is. What we have an eye for must precede the delight it gives us: somewhere when the neonate sucks faster when it is given its mother's voice to hear is a sign of recognition of the us, the true and the beautiful. The ready eye must precede the trained eye.

Well, if it doesn't work through Hope, say, or some other future-tilted emotion, how do we know when to abandon hope and COUPLE and when to hope on and hold out for better and for more? Good gets in the way of better, better in the way of good. "Hope makes a good breakfast," observed Bacon, "but a poor supper."

*P:*   I cannot believe how hard it is to begin today. Of course it begins as it always does with a thought I had when I walked in that I cannot possibly say. I would die. . . .

Ψ:   The replacement child. [In P it is perhaps more obvious than in others, for P was born on the anniversary of the death as a child of a younger sister of her mother.]

*P:*   You looked preoccupied. I thought it was with the patient prior to me. I felt like throwing myself on top of you, crushing you. Your chest. Of course [*bitterly*], I can never say such things when they occur. On days when there is no space before me, it is easier. I don't feel like such an . . . an . . . On the other hand, I hate it. I can't say this either, but I like the feeling that you're—Oh no. God . . . Now this I definitely cannot say, not ever. . . . I thought of you with, Oh God, an erection. [*P writhes in an agony of embarrassment.*]

Ψ:   Perhaps Papa's penis, perhaps Mommy's all ready nipple and swollen milk breast ready for Blakely [a younger sister].

## ANAL APPREHENSION

In the face of a nameless dread, even something so otherwise dire as catching on to specific anxieties and particular defenses is an attractive alternative. Indeed, even to merge the dread natural to the PAIR and the group with anxieties inhering in being a member of a COUPLE and so with specific libidinal interests, may seem to a child quite helpful. A phobia and counterphobia may seem more manageable than a dread, in much the same way a no-thing may seem more helpful than a nothing.

One such possibility for transfiguration of the experience of dread—of something being out of one's control and quite possibly arriving with the speed of an express train—is provided quite early on in life in form of the question: Who controls defecation—the fecal mass, or the sphincter? However, the many other issues contingent for people in this regard, may well obscure this one. Those are, first, the use of the anus as a prehensile organ in quest of recapturing the absent or fickle nipple; and second, the excited embattlement in the interpersonal aspects of the training situation over penetration, possession of product and production, rights of access and the terrain for deposit. (A flurry over the "paper-work" is usually a sure sign of this last conflation.)

However, the alarm that, in one's identification with the White hat of the sphincter one may not be able to control and manage, the Black hat of the feces is for some people an anxiety paramount over the others. Spontaneity of bodily functions is associated with being subjugated, and every effort is made to quell the natural rhythms and activities of the body. The peristaltic inexorability that brings the mass to the point where it must be evacuated seemed accordingly persecutory in the extreme. It seemed to rule them, as self and alive, with its relentless time and tide. And when it did, it was they who felt like so much shit and their feces were rampant and triumphant.

As this issue comes into the transference, it bears a particular characteristic — a two-position situation: either the patient is in control or the analyst is: either he or she feels like shit and the analysis is a vast intestine which will deposit the patient out no matter when, or the analyst is shit and they are in control. There are no two ways. Patients otherwise frugal found it at these times no expense at all to come irregularly or late, for if he or she could not control the end of the session (as one who suffered anorexia put it to me), she could at least control the beginning. For the analyst to accept such treatment is worrisome to his patient, a matter of agreeing to be treated like shit, and thus a source of great guilt, which could only be compensated for by alleging that the analyst is treating the patient like shit. Not to take such exercise in dominion, however, seems a palpable indication that the struggle for hegemony is indeed interpersonal.

The difficulty arises in the tendency for the infant and young child to treat the feces as if it were a person, to have and to hold or to evacuate and to discard, until death do them part. This means that the feces are considered to have a potential life of their own, and that they can and may (comes the revolution) reverse the designs of the sphincter. Some children lose interest in their feces as their interest in other people grows, and thus the object relationship gravitates to the Other as object. But other children absorb themselves with their feces, and employ them as a transitional object — and sometimes, in service of envy, as an object from which there will be no transition. Endgame.

Ordinarily when matters are drawn into such enduring and particularized struggles, the struggle is a counterfeited one, mobilized to keep the real tensions from finding their way into the analysis or the analyst and patient from noticing them. This struggle, however, only counterfeits being counterfeit. It is fake in that the analyst has to impersonate a part of the patient, while being made to seem (and feel) like another person — the bad intrusive mother — in the matter. But the deep sense of aggrievement and hatred are not counterfeit. Rather careful sorts of interpretation are necessary to return the conflict to its base point — the patient's fears of and alienation from his or her own natural processes.

The mind, or more narrowly the ego, comes into being to interpose direction and will to the impulse life. Slowly but inexorably, by a series of comparisons and contrasts, it draws an I-ness to it, for example from the dual sensations of the self touch or the thumb suck as contrasted with the monosensate touches of the other. These distinctions are not so easily made as to withstand much confusion; the baby nursing and twirling its mother's hair may so well correlate these experiences as to make a "constant-conjunction" between them (this is Bion's term — 1962); moreover the discovery of what is mine and what thine produces a sorting that is not necessarily a popular one, giving rise to impulses to redraw the boundaries through gerrymandering. Whatever the case, powerful tensions are drawn to the boundaries, and it is with some tension that the boundary, not of the sphincter, but of the rectum lining itself, becomes identified as an external/internal boundary.

Thus the idea arises that the sphincter is but the gateway to a colonic inner world, in which the feces dwell, alongside of the three little pigs, Billy Goat Gruff, and the rest of the gang. The image is that of a colon like a sock or a Santa sack, and in this everything valuable is held and kept. And released on parole. And withdrawn back into. Should a bowel movement occur unwanted, it is like the banks failing, or being peeled from the inside out. It is as if the skin that was isn't any more, and boundaries are made of water and identity is hopeless to try to maintain. Moreover, it is as if all one's possessions, people and their parts preeminent, took on a life of their own, like a nightmare Nutcracker, and an exhalation of absolute desPAIR is all that is left. This puts people in a suicidal mood: the only thing left is to follow, at least one can do that of one's own volition! And it puts people in a "homicidal" mood, only the life they wish to take is not that of the other; it is still their own. Such, then, is life in the COUPLE.

In the PAIR we share. "We don't die — we multiply!" Private ownership gives over to communal ownership. We agree on what waste is and where it is to be disposed. How horrified (as well as annoyed) New

Jersey is to have New York's rubbish fetch up on its beaches: are we not one of us? Isn't there a not-us place? What ever happened to Guyana?

## PARTICLES AND WAVES

Of what does matter consist? Waves, particles, energy, mass? People have been evolving for some time now and they "know" how supra-micro and sub-macro bodies behave. They have no reason to "know" how atomic or cosmologic bodies behave; these defy expectations perfected over the eons based on middle-sized bodies. (Middle-sized bodies behave in language; those bigger and smaller behave only in mathematics.)

To speak of people comprising simultaneously a COUPLE and a PAIR is like speaking of matter as being at once a wave and a particle. Yes— but what do I do with that? How's that supposed to explain anything? A clock cannot tell its own time. It is not self-referential. The PAIR doesn't know about the COUPLE, nor the COUPLE about the PAIR. For the moment each is regnant, the point of view is such as to belong wholly to it. It sees itself through its own eyes. This is like the stories of the multiple personalities, who, we are told, know not of each other. It is staggering—the first encounter. Here am I with an image of myself. It is a natural image projected from the back, like a rear-projection TV, onto the center of my mental retina. I know who I am the way a dog knows its size—or a cat its figure and what backgrounds it blends with. When I look into a mirror I see a baby. Hello Baby. Until one day, staggeringly, that baby is . . . Me! . . . Myself? Yes. . . . I? Yes. . . . My God.

I am puffed with pride and desolated with shame. I strut; I cringe. I make faces and try on peoples' hats and shoes. I see, for the first time, my person, place among my species. For ever after, I will appear in the third person singular in my dreams and my memories. I will see myself as a figure among other figures in the rooms in which I sit. Now I know myself from the other creatures, not only of the sea and air, the pasture and forest, but among my own kind. I know comparison and contrast, I know good and bad—better and worse. I know good and evil. I have bitten the apple: I have acquired self-reference. I will never be the same.

If and when, however, the analyst begins to interfere with this, as of course sooner or later he must, it may precipitate the break-off of the analysis, losing him not only the opportunity of being of further use to the patient, but that of coming to understand in depth the ingredients to such negation. It stands to reason that envy of the psychoanalyst may be at its most virulent in those people who in an active way decline to avail themselves of any analysis whatsoever. It is one thing to see a patient, such as a man who came first to see me reelingly drunk and was out of the consulting room within minutes of arriving; his envy was at once apparent and open to interpretation when I prevailed upon him to return. But it is quite another to encounter people who are having an ongoing fantasy in which they are refusing to see an analyst.

Such refusal expresses itself in an analysis which has begun when the patient begins acting in ways we are accustomed to call "entitled" or "narcissistically entitled." Freud drew attention to this in his paper on Some Special Types, of which he accounted Shakespeare's vision of Richard III one. Freud saw the humpback Richard was born with as implying to Richard that something special was due him as a result of that curse — that he might count himself as an exception to the norms and rules of ethical behavior to the precise measure that nature had made him an exception to its general rules for masculine beauty.

This seems accurate. But I think it has a more general source. I think it arises when an infant believes that his psychological existence hangs by a thread. How many infants are born into an existential crisis I do not know. But I should hazard more than we might expect. I think the crisis comes about when the infant doesn't know when to be a part of a COUPLE and when a part of a PAIR. Or it comes about when the infant starts rocketing back and forth between trying life as a member of a COUPLE and then of a PAIR, hoping each will save him from the demons and perils of the other, unable long to choose which before zooming off again to the other. This sets up what I believe to consist of as a case of extreme envy, and that envy then further interferes in the infant's willingness to make or sustain a choice. For the infant won't take and then the infant won't give himself, out of the fear of being taken (it was not just Barnum who believed a sucker is born every minute).

Such a crisis of envy seems to set the infant apart from those who feel that life is a natural pastime, in a fundamental way to be taken for granted, the only remaining issues being how to pass the time happily and meaningfully. And so his envy is geometrically increased to the point eventually when the nameless dread with which he began is exponentially increased.

Such infants look for guilt as a way out: sin names the dread and makes it feel less helpless making. Please, please what is it I have done wrong. Please, please criticize me — for when you do, I can assimilate into myself your hope that I can improve and hence be worthy to survive.

But such docility does not come cheap. It is the moral equivalent of the humped back. It entitles one to something for which one's pain and doubt and dread have already paid. No one can frighten one any more than one has been frightened, or can they? Let's see. Prepaid, one is now entitled. Why should others get away with feeling so smug about life?

*P:*   There is a gravestone on the Isle of Shoals which bears the inscription: "I
       have paid my debt to life; Now must you too."

The path from dread passes through guilt, masochism, and complaisance to entitlement: that enraged triumph over a dread that once was without either name or measure.

From the careless, reckless, insufferable analytic patient, for whom nothing is enough or good enough (the food was lousy and the portions were too small), who has already done too much, indeed several lifetimes of work before he or she arrived in the analysis, peeks the gaunt victim of a private holocaust, who hasn't even the words with which to tell of the horrors except in some exaggerated way, which no one can believe, about small pains that most others shrug off.


## CHARISMA


The charismatic leader is ambiguous in nature; he seems to abide in paradox. He is open to readings, to interpretations.

"The World . . . is a Bell," said the dying Rabbi to his grieving congregation, throngs of whom surround him extending in all directions to the reaches of the horizon.

"What? What does he say?" asks the crowd of one another. People repeat to those further away. Leaders expound.

But one man says "A bell? Nonsense!" This too races from ear to ear through the multitudes.

"What are they saying?" asks the Rabbi. Those closest to him look anxiously at one another.

"One man says 'Nonsense' about the bell," his daughter reluctantly tells him.

"Nonsense? Uhm . . . possibly," says the Rabbi, "but right now I don't have a good state of mind in which to think."

The choice he exacts in being allowed his charisma he repays by his ambiguities: he has made a choice, but, in his ambiguities he contains the possibility of many more choices, all as yet unspent. It is a pyramid scheme.

Unlike the instrumental leader who defines choice and makes the choice realizable (Moses was such), the charismatic one opens out options where none were espied: he proliferates centrifugally, whereas the former narrows, shapes, and defines centripetally.

As such the instrumental leader leads the COUPLE: he or she knows how to bring things about: they get things done: they achieve the orgasm and the baby, whether it is the baby who was myself or the baby who is to be my son or daughter. The instrumental leader deals in repletion.

The charismatic leader leads the PAIR — and what Bion (1961) called the "basic assumption PAIRing group." He is none of us in this room, but a source of access to the yet to be. He is the Messiah. He was Christ. He deals in possibilities of completion. But as Kafka (1935) wryly noted (in his Parables), "The Messiah will come only when he is no longer necessary; he will come only on the day after his arrival; he will come, not on the last day, but on the very last" (p. 81). Bion remarked (1961); "only by remaining a hope does hope persist" (pp. 151-152). The born baby is a nonstarter in his odds of being the Messiah. Snake oil is far and away the best emolument for the abrasive nature of what is.

The body, and that portion of the psyche which is devoted to it, being guided by the pleasure–unpleasure principle, looks to its sensual nature and determines what frustration is and what gratification. The polymorphous perversity, of which Freud spoke, makes people adventitious, opportunistic, adaptable. A simple change of aim or object or direction or mode — and Voila!

But the selection principle is something else again. It cannot make up its mind. Hope is easily raised but difficult to satisfy. Lust wishes to gaze on his beloved's face: Helen is enough to launch its thousand ships; Gretchen was enough for Faust to cry out, "Stay, Moment! Thou art so fair!" But hope gazes rather at him who has a thousand faces; he who got the seas parted, climbed the Mount, got the tablets (which none could swallow, so according to apocryphy went back and came down with this time only ten), was sore wroth when he saw the shenanigans with the golden calf: were people turning religious on him? After all he did, instrumentally, to help? What was wrong with his realizations that now all of a sudden people were back doing hope?

## VICARIOUSNESS

Experiencing events vicariously is the language of the PAIR: it is what binds the species and makes it possible not to have every and all of the experiences oneself. We put ourselves in one another's shoes, see matters from one another's viewpoint. This is the beginning of empathy. It requires the understanding that you and I are as much the same as different: in Sullivan's (1953) words, "More human than otherwise." (To understand being part of the COUPLE, we need to understand each of us is as different from the other as day from night.)

In the quest to approach and approximate whatever the species is "supposed" to be, people search for what is larger and finer than life. We look for heroes; we live through them vicariously. Their fortunes, their visions, are ours. In living through them we begrudge less of what we shall not be or do or have for our individual and private selves. We thereby extend our personal mortality. Otherwise how could we live and let live? Our wakeful, brooding envy would murder the sleep of others, not to say their lives and loves.

But not *just* heroes. We live though one another — provided they are part of us. Through the successes of our brothers, through the experiences of our sisters, and perhaps most of all, through our children's first tooth, first haircut, good marriage, children and their children. In this way our life is extended, but also to a degree consoled. If our children "do well," we do, and we graze on their successes vicariously, though we always may, with Shaw, feel our children's lives and opportunities are wasted on them — and that we would like to recall them and have them once more for ourselves.

Indeed, too much envy turns about and ruins the very vicariousness that informed it. Me, it cries, Me! I don't want to know about you. Who are you? And in that ruination, in that severance of the bonding link, it loses much of its own capacity for vicarious gratifications. It is only content with scenes from Oh, How the Mighty are Fallen, with victories by scores of 97 to 3.

The sociopaths, so called, the delinquents, or the psychopaths are justly deemed dangerous because they have lost or maimed their capacity to know how the rest of us live. They know only how their half lives; they don't know that when we say Ouch, we are feeling pain. And to an extent, they are correct; for those who can accept that they will feel pain, the pain comes only as hurt and not also as insult and injury, or something (no-thing) filled with intimations of malicious or sexual intent. Suffering, of this sort, as Bion remarked time and again, for the distinction was central to his philosophy, is quite different from pain because it permits the offsetting of painful experience with pleasurable ones. We who can, then, suffer both pain and pleasure are different from those who are ruthless in a dumb, blind way, devoid of information about and therefore unmodified by fellow feeling. (Winnicott often points to that moment when the baby turns the spoon and presses it instead toward his caretaker's mouth, when the Depressive position has begun.) But when, intermittently, they sense our capacity to receive and to suffer but, out of their greed and envy, cannot give us solace or reparation for it, their potential for shame and guilt is such that they destroy our own fellow feeling as best they can. Where once the milk of human kindness first ran, then caked, in our breast, now there is only hatred and rage. And with this we join a world reassuringly familiar to them, and we no longer seem implicitly and forever reproachful — empty mouths to feed with supplies from a cupboard locked by greed or spoiled by envy.

Vicariousness involves transmissions to a set of receptors that I do not believe are as yet well understood, partly because those used in the COUPLE are quite possibly different from those used in the PAIR. We have recoiled so far from the loss of distinction imposed on us by reductionistic theoreticians as between ourselves and others with whom we may have shared our phylogeny that we may overly assert what makes us unique. But the PAIR and the group may well employ signals and signs that do not check in at the self-referential front desk of consciousness or even preconsciousness before entering its specialized set of receptors. Nor can we readily convert such information-bearing signals to consciousness[10] even after they have arrived, especially with therapies or other formats for investigation oriented toward studies of the individual as a member of a COUPLE or in his COUPLE-orientation relationship to groups of others.

For example, we are rather more familiar with the questions of now and later that are frequently disputed and sometimes resolved in the COUPLE. But the PAIR harkens to another signal, called After.. Where does later end and after begin? (See "About Time," in *Envy*, Boris 1994.) People may differ, as they do in so many other respects — for example, on who is chosen or redeemed and who is the anti-christ — but the fascinating (and sometimes appalling) thing is that no one disagrees that categories exist. My soon, next, later, after, surely differs from yours, if only because I am older or younger than you; but we share the adjectival categories, as do others in other cultures. Somehow people seem to need to discover and signal when later turns into after, so that they can tell then from later and later from too late.

Some people hear voices I do not. I can get by quite nicely with a set of Bose's lower in fi than others require. I also know people whose hearing is such as to hear voices or who see auras, even visions, not apparent to me. In my turn, I have "sensitivities" to other people which enable me to be quick on the uptake; but I have only to read Sullivan or Fromm-Reichman or Winnicott to know what such sensitivities really are. I believe that there is a tilt to the receiver apparatus that enables people to hear not merely differently because of their make-up and apperception characteristics, but different things quite from the start, which stimulate different apperception modalities and even character qualities. The idiot-savant is a grotesque example; people who have perfect pitch a more ordinary one.

Such differences are bound to create different attunements and different registrations of the music of the spheres, but since we only know intake when it is put out again, we can only surmise what Mozart heard from what he composed or played. But surely the two are not identical.

When the capacity to hear PAIR signals on the one hand and COUPLE messages on the other is considered, it should be borne in mind that PAIR signals are probably only fully evident to those mutually attuned.

---

[10]Indeed my goal in writing this epilogue is to provide a kind of stain that will allow other workers to see the tissues of the PAIR and tell them from the integuments of the COUPLE.

As an observing adult, I cannot expect to hear or see what the mother–infant PAIR I am observing hears or sees or smells. Are there, as crazy people have long alleged (cf. Tausk's *The Influencing Machine* [1919]), chemicals in the mother's breast milk that not only provide the infant immunity, as has been long established, but those which convey additional or even contrary messages, or information conveyed by their absence?[10] Perhaps three months later the baby can no longer register certain signals from his being, as organism, which are instructing his body how and where to multiply and specialize. Could he ever? Bion certainly thought so: quoting Freud on the latter's thinking about the caesura of birth, Bion cautioned that we may take birth too much as the real beginning, whereas there may have been much more registration previously, in utero, than we are accustomed to think. Research on newborns' responsiveness to stories subsequently read again to them after their birth suggests a recognition response. Is the information also freighted with PAIR messages?

## ANALYSIS WITHOUT EMPATHY

Few analysts, I would guess, would like, if they could help it, to do analysis by the book, without either empathy or intuition. I say this because I don't think that one goes from medicine or psychology or other backgrounds into conducting the therapy of analysis if one doesn't have a disposition canted toward fellow feeling. For much of our work, this capacity, this receptive function, this toleration of living vicariously, helps the analysand lose himself in the process—that essential prerequisite to finding one's self anew. The capaciousness and profundity of our ability to absorb the patient's redistribution of self and boundaries and his rearrangements of their contents—intentions and attitudes—will in most cases be the determining factor in what the patient can regain and realign on the way back and out. We are ready to be whatever he is not and cannot stand to be, while he, a believer in the conservation of matter and energy, deals the entirety this way and that. Perhaps, with good luck, a time comes when some of what greed or envy says could-be-must-be can be relinquished, and substitutes accepted, or let go altogether; and the analysis is, as a result,

---

[10]What was the message conveyed when the Nestlé Corporation distributed formula to countries whose populace could not then afford to buy more of it?

increasingly less root-bound with excess. For example, information can be given by the patient (P) or analyst (Ψ) without it being freighted with anything more or other than meaning: the earlier need to use information to induce or impose change being now much diminished.

But along the way to such an outcome so filled with amenity, the very capacity which, on Ψ's part, makes it possible, is in acute or chronic danger of being destroyed.

For there comes a time when the receptive capacity of the breast is connected up with the mother in the PAIR mode, just as the providing aspect of it is discovered in the COUPLE mode, and greed to have it and own it inevitably accompanies such discovery in the one as in the other. When this is repeated in the transference, the empathy and intuition of Ψ become targeted. P wants to have these qualities for himself. Often he displays them in a bouquet of thoughtful and sensitive acts in Ψ's behalf. I have been the recipient of the latest news broadcast on the patient's car radio; of the newspaper, which had been carelessly or belatedly delivered; or of expressions of sympathy for how hard the patient himself (or the person preceding or succeeding him) has been on me. Ps, otherwise early or surly, make efforts; they find lovely purview outside or lovely objects inside. These are sometimes the providing, sometimes the receptive, elements of Ψ as object.

But then these kindlinesses cannot last; indeed they often signal trouble to come. Envy reasserts itself over admiration or gratitude (the other two legs of the stool), and the patient not only no longer feels appreciative and, in his turn, responsive (which makes him feel quite awful and afraid) but now, to equalize matters, must begin systematically to destroy these very qualities in the analyst. Unable to feel he can live (or love) up to Ψ, P must bring the latter down. The ultimate way of doing this is to quit the analysis with the proclamation that he has gotten nowhere. Penultimately, however, the patient may see an opportunity of eviscerating and denuding Ψ of the latter's best traits. The patient in pain is bound to envy the Ψ's capacity to suffer, sensing that it is that capacity — to endure — that diminishes the amount of and occasions for pain.

P may, for example, do what Ψ describes to sympathetic colleagues as "going on and *on.*" Being thus in danger of being bored to death, Ψ will soon begin to evince the very irritation and boredom and impatience that P will presently allege. If Ψ then attempts guiltily to conceal his irritation, P will find vindication in his discovery that Ψ is no better as a cover-up artist, when it comes to pretending at empathy

and fellow feeling, than P is. P may then encourage Ψ to believe that
he can fool P, which will free P in part of the need of finding ways to
fool Ψ's perspicacity, now trammeled. (If Ψ is in supervision and
thereby free of the sterile and stultifying emotional climate woven by
P, S may detect all sorts of interesting things in P's associations,
leaving Ψ to feel that he, Ψ, is worse even than he thought he was. S
can then help P to go from the penultimate to the ultimate escape from
the envy Ψ's intuition and empathy arouse in P, for by now Ψ, under
siege in two directions, will be very glad to get shed of P.)

The mother's receptive function is symbolized by her fecundity: she
makes something truly grand out of something truly grand, which is
father's penis, or out of nothing, which is father's penis whited out. In
the analysis P is pouring him/her self out (into) Ψ, and Ψ is making
nothing out of it but murmurs and mutters. The consulting room
appears to be filled with stuff hostile to progeneration and birth;
contraception is everywhere. The patient appears to himself to be fated
yet again to be unable to give to mother and create with her a baby; he
is still filled only with bad matter or grossly ineffective matter. Even
now that he is big, having waited so long to be big, his seed falls at his
feet or is ejaculated into hostile, even murderous, ground. This Ψ of
his seems to feel that getting and giving an ah-ha or an oh or an oo-o
or an uh-oh is somehow sufficient: to put a stop to that, P goes to the
source and dries up this instead-of-a-baby stuff Ψ is palming off on P,
as before Ψ mother and father did. A dry-titted, womb-wizened,
penis-shriveled Ψ can hardly now stand being with P: surely this is not
what Ψ became a therapist to feel like? But what did P become a P for?
Is it possible for just one moment for me vicariously, empathetically
and intuitively, to be you without at the same time destroying either
you or myself? Can I tolerate the barrier that divides us into separate
beings long enough to form a COUPLE with you? Surely if your greatest
pleasure and freedom is in apprehending me, then mine must be in the
freedom and excruciating pleasure of making myself scarce.

You are all I needed!


## FEELING ANTSY

For me to say that the human organism, qua organism, or an ant
colony, is analogous to a human PAIR or group system would be a most

misleading and unfortunate reification. But what if I say that people *act as if* or *feel as if* the social order recapitulated something in phylogeny that they could only understand by the witting or unwitting application of such analogies?

It is said, for example, that ants and cells contain a latent nature, a set of potentials, which develop in particular particularities in chemical allegiance to signals they are provided: "Individuals can be induced by specific signals to develop into particular types" (Smith 1990, p 37).

But the bits of us that make us more human than otherwise must cry out against so reductionistic a metaphor. Even at the cell level, it is possible to tell the so from the specious. So we don't want to be con-fused or confused; such confusion leads to the mis-conceptions that occur when species try to reproduce with other species: indeed the operational definition of a species is those whose members can reproduce with one another. What else makes us specifically human: the only tool-using animal? The only animal capable of semiotic language? The only self-referential animal? Or the only animal that can reproduce with humans?

In Darwinian terms species descend by happening to use reproduc-tion strategies that turn out to be successful. What those strategies might be is a throw of the cosmic dice, unknown to the forebear. And indeed even such clever animals as Homo Evolutionary Biologosus don't know what these strategies are, only that strategies, like other traits, also evolve selectively, and different creatures may possess one or more and by mutant chance add another to their reservoir.

The general notion of success is numerical: the more made, the more preserved, chancewise. The more chances one has, the better his chances. But quantity and quality can be seen to share this trait: More is tantamount to better. The transformation of one strategy into another would hardly have to travel any distance at all.

Alongside the one-to-one competition, cooperation of a sort seems to be bred into species. It is said (Smith 1990), for example, that it behooved male lions to cooperate with one another, because it often takes two, working together, to hold a pride; each gives up some reproductive self-assertion to assure the remainder of it. This concept of cooperative strategies has been challenged because it doesn't always make sense, even in the some-is-better-than-nothing sense for the lion. For example, the sterility of some social insects, as among the ants, gives up individual chances for asserting reproduction entirely. Is this purblind altruism? Or is it something else? In man one might wonder a bit about the capacity for living and reproducing vicariously. But in any case, there is bound to be a limit to this cooperation.

*Self-preservation knows only one boundary: the production and perpetuation of progeny.* The COUPLE knows only one boundary: the PAIR. And the PAIR knows only one limit: the COUPLE.

If people say jump, do I jump? If people say, well, you don't have to jump, but you must at least feel ashamed if you don't, do I have to?

My survival is necessary insofar as it affords me reproductive success. But after that? And what if I live at the expense of my children or they of me, as we are bound to do? At the crossroads between Thebes and Corinth, who gives way? Laius, having heard the prophecy, ordered the baby Oedipus put to death; but he was not. Later he comes to the crossroads; once again Laius requires him to make way. Once more he does not. The prophecy is bound to out: Oedipus does slay Laius. And he reproduces with Jocasta. The sphinx, that creature par excellence of hybridization, takes a dive; Oedipus, it turns out, knows the riddle about generations, as any man lamed by his father's wish to enjoy exclusive generative success with his own wife might well do. Is the prophecy, as Freud thought, in the genes?

The genes are giving us muddled messages, perhaps even double-binded ones. Our heads are cocked to listen, but what do we hear? Are we signaled by signal A speaking to receptor $A - B$ to B; or does A speak both to receptor A *and* B?

Where *is* Godot, anyways?

♪ ♪ ♪ . Maybe next year.

## SPLITTING

Splitting is a form of proliferation. Its opposite is identification in the interests of conglomeration and cohesion. In the COUPLE modality, splitting is employed to manufacture additional objects with whom to COUPLE. In the PAIR it is used to increase the number or extent of the species or group. As people cohere in a group situation, they begin to need to split off objects differentiated enough to COUPLE with. They also need to create differences, which they can then employ to effect specializations and other divisions of labor. People in a PAIR or group or species need to be clear about which is what: the second baseman is not to COUPLE with the shortstop: they are to perform the double play.

On the other hand, with whom may they COUPLE? This is what the other team is for and what the fans are for.

In the COUPLE, frustrations, if they are not to eventuate in mutual destruction, require, as Freud noted, alterations in mode, direction and/or aim of the urges, possibly because of the polymorphous and perverse adaptability of the wishes to COUPLE. But each member of the COUPLE can work his or her will on the other by employing a member of a PAIR he or she belongs to to help out. A rather simple example is, "Just wait until your father gets home." Or, "I'm going to tell Mommy (or the police)." Such PAIRing works against internalized objects with whom the self is not at one. Objects brought "in" for purposes of access are often easily aroused to jealousy, envy, and other dangerous feelings toward or about the self. These can be stilled, at least until the still, small hours of the night, by reference to members of a PAIR. Sullivan (1953) was especially emphatic about how the latency or teenage peer group could sometimes even forestall the mad, double-bound configurations of the Parent.

But with each addition to the PAIR, a COUPLE possibility is lost. Groups who have COUPLEd with one another (e.g., USSR and the U.S.), when the balance shifts from COUPLing to PAIRing soon find they need new objects. With each addition to the COUPLE, possibilities for the PAIR and group and the there and then are lost. To rectify this, similarities are noticed where previously only differences were seen. Efforts on the part of the Other to maintain his or her status as part of a COUPLE are rebuffed; the other is awarded only a specialized one-of-us, more-of-the-same status, in which differences of degree are accepted, but not differences of kind.

On this re-rendering of differences, envy and greed thrive, for only besting and worsting remain as the operative distinctions, and these, it is felt, can be bridged by further PAIRing, so that if I cannot be as good as you, perhaps all of us can be as good as all of you.

You and me, kid—

I'm not your kid, I'm your wife!

## HYBRIDS

Allocations between the PAIR and COUPLE points of view are common, insofar as they do not need to be used as alternatives for one another but can be relinquished and the loss of each mourned and so tolerated.

The child who would be his own creation because he cannot allocate to others a role in his status attributes himself to causes beyond his parents' intercourse and fertility, reincarnation being one such. This gives rise to the evolution of postures from fixations and to lunatic, raucous magisterial creations by the Creator Self in (and out of) his refusal to pay homage to his own creators, whose existence is to be left without a trace. In this regard, Bion has remarked of the liar that he wishes to be necessary for his interlocuters' perceptions, the idea being that they could not reach those percepts without him as intermediary. This is surely the case with any creative artist whose originality brings out what was not evident before his work. The difference between the liar and the artist consists perhaps in where the work is thought to reside: the liar is more likely to regard himself as his work, the artist something outside of himself.

*P:*   I am a survivor of incest, an incest-survivor.

By this P means to say that she has been sexually used by various of her stepfathers. Does she also mean to say that her experiences with these men, and not her mother, who did not intervene, are what has made her who she is today? Will she be able to let her therapy "work"?

## THE AFFECTIVE EXPERIENCES

If what makes the world go round for the COUPLE is love and lust and the hatred and fear of frustration, what makes the world spin for the PAIR can be thought of, perhaps, as the *élan vital* of which Henri Bergson (1920) wrote. This is an unsensuous emotion, one not COUPLEd to the sensual experiences of the soma for stimulus or receptor registration, and not one determined by the "economic" ideas of discharge or homeostasis. The *élan vital*, or life force, will take as its object what will gradually be defined and redefined as the self, but from the beginning will include imaginative reference to the thrust of the Selection forces, such as possessiveness, belonging (e.g., fusion), premonition, and hope. It will include a different sense of time, one that goes beyond now and again to something approximating later and even after, and time will modify the experience of experience. Ecstasy in the COUPLE is matched by rapture in the PAIR; fear, by dread, guilt by shame, anxiety by anticipation. Insofar as the two converge, emotions like bliss and sheer happiness emerge.

## PARADOX UNBOUND

The entirely unembarrassable man has freedoms denied the rest of us.
We can be checked in midsentence with a cough; cut off when some in
our audience start looking at their watches. We sense that we are not
wanted and yearn toward the nearest exit. Such things do not trouble
the man impervious to obloquy. He cannot conceive how one could be
fettered by blushes. He has no inner brake that others might activate.

The Greeks thought such a person lacked "aidos" (respect for others'
respect). Thersites, the ignoble warrior in the *Iliad*, became the
shameless person ("anaides") par excellence. Nothing could shut him up
in council, not even the threat of Odysseus to strip him to his shameful
parts ("aidoia"). Odysseus finally had to punch him into silence.[12]

— Garry Wills

Big thinkers are subject to big obsessions. Their eyes are fixed on the
positive evidence. Their busy minds expand theories, extrapolate
hypotheses, and invent logical structures perhaps scenarios, even plots,
at stroboscopic speed Paranoia [becomes]the only secure guard against
delusion . . . a double focussed awareness of symbol.[13]

— Robert Adams

Humans are big-brained creatures, and big brains probably require
special conditions. One such is the opportunity for a slow ontogenetic
elaboration, secure, more or less, in a period of dependency and
interdependency on the adults of the species. Another may be the
interposition of mind between brain and activity. Mind, like its own
attributes — consciousness and unconsciousness, thought, emotion,
and so on — is an inference: all we can see there is brain. But the
moment we see brain at work, with its synapses and electrical and
chemical signals, we see, in that sense, more than is there. The leap to
"mind" is not, after that, especially great.

   Mind seems to introduce something like opportunity for choice: an
agency or repository (or both) for selecting from among what presents
itself, whether what presents itself is an external experience or an
internal one — and indeed, which, "internal" or "external," an experience is construed to be. This opportunity for making choices beyond

---

[12]Garry Wills, "Nixon Theresites." *The New York Times*, April 8, 1990, p. A19.

[13]Robert Adams, "Juggler." *Review of Umberto Eco's Foucault's Pendulum. New York Review of Books*, November 9, 1989.

mere reflex, habit, or training, requires, of course, that objects to choose among are perceived or created. So one could say that man is in first measure a choice-bearing creature — destined to make choices from among determined choices. We choose from among things that come to mind — from among things that *could* come to mind; though we cannot, as yet, choose what things occupy us, because we are in the very first instance chosen by our heritage to be human and not otherwise, so to dwell among our sort of landscapes.

Nature seems not to be done with any of her creatures; all seem as yet to be evolving toward a presumable state of no-further-evolution-required called survival-for-continual-evolution — or is it *de*volution? In any case, we are all midstream and imperfectly done. Mind seems to be one of those ideas that enable what Lysenko could not — namely, changes effected in one generation to be carried forward to subsequent generations. Some experiments seem to suggest the chemical traces of learning themselves can be transplanted from one creature to another, leading the recipient to "know" what the donor has learned from experience. But because we don't know how quite to do this, or even if it is possible, each of our generations needs to teach the next: and so I write this.

Among the characteristics of our big brain seems to be a commensurate need for experiences with which to feed or occupy it — curiosity is a nice enough word for this. And in the interests of provender for curiosity we seem to be quite omnivorous as to our intakes and generative productions. This means not only a hefty degree of chaff, but some seriously painful encounters. It is imperative that the mind can have some say in what the mind experiences, so that these can be undone, if only retrospectively. It is imperative that the mind be a self-deceiving experiencer, able by ruses and sleights, so simple that a child can perform them, to give itself an alternative, sidereal world when it needs one. And equally necessary that it not discern it when so doing. When it creates illusion or truth by attending selectively, it must also not attend to its selectivity.

When, by sleights of mind, the mind can deceive itself, it can survive what otherwise might well be too painful to bear. And when it can shuttle, faster than the blink of an eye, between one way and another of organizing experience, as between that endemic to the couple and that to the pair, it gains for itself respites, each from the other in having precisely that choice.

This is why choice is at once so urgent and so frightening to spend: each choice leaves one poorer of choice, if richer in what is chosen.

In presenting this strobe light for what I think I have come to know by organizing my experience with others and myself in the ways that I have, I make no claim for it being better or more accurate (those PAIR-generated "er-ier" words) than any other. It is a way of thinking that, with luck, leads further towards what we do not know we don't know.

# REFERENCES

Adams, R. (1989). Juggler. Review of *Foucault's Pendulum*. *New York Review of Books*. November, 9.

Bergson, H. (1920). *Mind-energy, Lectures and Essays*. Trans. H. Wilden Carr. New York: H. Holt and Company.

Bion, W. R. (1961). *Experiences in Groups*. New York: Basic Books.

_____ (1962). *Learning from Experience*. New York: Basic Books.

_____ (1963). *Elements of Psychoanalysis*. New York: Basic Books.

_____ (1970). *Attention and Interpretation*. New York: Basic Books.

Boris, H. N. (1976). On hope: its nature and psychotherapy. *International Journal of Psycho-Analysis* 3:139–50.

_____ (1986). The "other" breast: greed, envy, spite and revenge. *Contemporary Psychoanalysis* 22(1):45–59.

_____ (1988). Torment of the object: a contribution to the study of bulimia. In *Bulimia: Psychoanalytic Treatment and Theory*, ed. H. Schwartz, pp. 89–110.

_____ (1992). Fears of difference: early envy, part II. *Contemporary Psychoanalysis* 28(2):228–250.

_____ (1994). *Envy*. Northvale, NJ: Jason Aronson.

Freud, S. (1900). Interpretation of dreams. *Standard Edition* 4–5.

_____ (1916). Some character-types met with in psychoanalytic work. *Standard Edition* 14:311–333.

_____ (1920). Beyond the pleasure principle. *Standard Edition* 18:7–64.

_____ (1921). Group psychology and the analysis of the ego. *Standard Edition* 18:69–143.

_____ (1925). Negation. *Standard Edition* 19:235–239.

Gould, S. J. (1987). *Time's Arrow, Time's Cycle*. Cambridge, MA: Harvard University Press.

Havel, V. (1990). On Kafka. *New York Review of Books*; vol. 34, no. 14, August 27.

Kafka, F. (1935). *Parables and Paradoxes*. New York: Schocken, 1958.

Levi, P. (1990). Psychophant. *The New Yorker*, February 12.

Smith, J. M. (1990). Review of *The Ants*. *New York Review of Books*. September 27.

Sullivan H. S. (1953). *The Interpersonal Theory of Psychiatry*. New York: W. W. Norton.

Tausk, V. (1919). On the origin of the "influencing machine" in schizophrenia. In *The Psycho-Analytic Reader*, ed. R. Fleiss, pp. 31–64. New York: International Universities Press, 1948.

Wills, G. (1990). Nixon Theresites. *The New York Times*. April 8.

# Credits

Chapter 1. "Cultures in Conflict: Mental Health and the Hard-to-reach," originally published in *Mental Hygiene*, July 1967, pp. 351–358. Copyright © 1967 by *Mental Hygiene*. Reprinted by permission of the National Mental Health Association.

Chapter 2. "Spreading Mental Health: The Pioneer Spirit Revisited," originally published as a review of *Mental Health Consultants: Agents of Community Change*, by C. Griffith and L. Libo in *Psychiatry and Social Science Review*, vol. 4, no. 4, pp. 6–9. Copyright © 1970. Reprinted by permission of Jason Aronson Inc.

Chapter 3. "The *Seelsorger* in Rural Vermont," originally published in the *International Journal of Group Psychotherapy*, vol. 21, no. 2, pp. 159–173. Copyright © 1971 by the *International Journal of Group Psychotherapy*. Reprinted by permission of the American Group Psychotherapy Association, Inc.

Chapter 4. "The Medium, the Message, and the Good Group Dream," originally published in the *International Journal of Group Psychotherapy*, vol. 20, no. 1, pp. 91–98. Copyright © 1970 by the *International Journal of Group Psychotherapy*. Reprinted by permission of the American Group Psychotherapy Association, Inc.

Chapter 5. "People's Fantasies in Group Situations," with N. E. Zinberg and M. Boris. Originally published in *Contemporary Psycho-*

351

# Index